G000075775

Nation Branding in Modern History

Explorations in Culture and International History Series
General Editor: Jessica C. E. Gienow-Hecht

NATION BRANDING IN MODERN HISTORY

Edited by
Carolin Viktorin, Jessica C. E. Gienow-Hecht,
Annika Estner, Marcel K. Will

berghahn
NEW YORK · OXFORD
www.berghahnbooks.com

First published in 2018 by
Berghahn Books
www.berghahnbooks.com

© 2018 Carolin Viktorin, Jessica C. E. Gienow-Hecht, Annika Estner,
and Marcel K. Will

All rights reserved. Except for the quotation of short passages
for the purposes of criticism and review, no part of this book
may be reproduced in any form or by any means, electronic or
mechanical, including photocopying, recording, or any information
storage and retrieval system now known or to be invented,
without written permission of the publisher.

Library of Congress Cataloging-in-Publication Data
Names: Viktorin, Carolin, editor. | Gienow-Hecht, Jessica C. E., 1964-
editor. | Estner, Annika, editor. | Will, Marcel K., editor
Title: Nation branding in modern history / edited by Carolin Viktorin,
Jessica C.E. Gienow-Hecht, Annika Estner, Marcel K. Will.
Description: New York : Berghahn Books, 2018. | Series: Explorations in
culture and international history series ; Volume 9 | Includes
bibliographical references and index.
Identifiers: LCCN 2018018972 (print) | LCCN 2018030595 (ebook) | ISBN
9781785339240 (ebook) | ISBN 9781785339233 (hardback : alk. paper)
Subjects: LCSH: Cultural diplomacy–History–Case studies. | Place
marketing–Political aspects–Case studies. | National
characteristics–Political aspects–Case studies. | Branding
(Marketing)–Political aspects–Case studies.
Classification: LCC JZ1305 (ebook) | LCC JZ1305 .N339 2018 (print) | DDC
327.2–dc23
LC record available at https://lccn.loc.gov/2018018972

British Library Cataloguing in Publication Data
A catalogue record for this book is available from the British Library

ISBN: 978-1-78533-923-3 hardback
E-ISBN: 978-1-78533-924-0 ebook

CONTENTS

ILLUSTRATIONS

ACKNOWLEDGMENTS

Shortly after the FIFA World Cup in 2006, nation branding became a trendy catchword among top policymakers and the German public. Once the tournament was over, the Federal Foreign Office announced that Germany had successfully used this event to create a positive image of the country abroad, thus overcoming old stereotypes and preconceptions. Simultaneously, the German media labeled the event as a *deutsches Sommermärchen*, a German summer fairy tale. And while politicians, advertising agencies, and marketing experts publicly discussed nation branding, scholars considering the concept's relevance for history encountered intrigued but skeptical looks from professional colleagues. Even while studies on nation branding were already well under way in neighboring disciplines such as media studies, marketing, and political science, historians, in particular, took their time to consider its added value for historical research. Since then, however, an increasing number of historians have jumped on the bandwagon as well; some of them are among the authors of this book.

This volume draws methodological inspiration from history, communication studies, marketing, and political science. As is always the case when experts of different fields and topics in academia band together in a common project, we faced the challenges of overcoming interdisciplinary, methodological, and thematic boundaries as well as geographical distances. This is why we, first and foremost, owe a great debt of gratitude to our authors. They brought individual expertise, challenging arguments, and critical advice to this book. They were patient, tenacious, and ready—more than once—to submit to yet another "one last round of drafts."

Furthermore, we would have never been able to compose and finish this volume without the numerous people behind the scenes who dedicated an enormous amount of time to this project. For this reason, we are profoundly grateful to all assistants and students at the History Department of the John F. Kennedy Institute in Berlin: thank you to Alyn Euritt, Mario Rewers, Valeria Benko, Florian Gabriel, Vincent-Immanuel Herr, Liping Zheng, Rianne Kouwenaar, Catya de Laczkovich, and Tilman Pietz for creating a fruitful and open-minded atmosphere at the JFKI. We also owe a big thank you to Hannah Nelson-Teutsch for her diligence and accuracy in proofreading the manuscript and to Verena Specht for managing the office of the History Department and its particulars so efficiently. A profound *Dankeschön* also and again to Wayne Moquin for compiling the index in good time before our manuscript crossed the finishing line.

Finally, we are most grateful to our publishers at Berghahn Books who took a risk and joined us in jumping into the deep end with this volume. Marion Berghahn and her excellent team of editors—Chris Chappell, Amanda Horn, Melissa Gannon, Caroline Kuhtz, and Ben Parker—gladly offered senior advice when it came to publishing choices. Thank you also to Ilana Brown who diligently copyedited the whole manuscript. Together with the critical, constructive and encouraging voices of the four anonymous reviewers—who gave not only well-thought input but also extensive advice and invaluable ideas for improvement—they helped refine and polish our volume in its final stages. Thank you to all of you for being a perpetual inspiration to us and *ein großes Lob* for your dedication. It was only the collective enthusiasm for our shared field of research that rendered this volume possible!

Berlin, Koblenz, and Munich, March 2018
Carolin Viktorin, Jessica C. E. Gienow-Hecht, Annika Estner,
Marcel K. Will

BEYOND MARKETING AND DIPLOMACY
Exploring the Historical Origins of Nation Branding

Carolin Viktorin, Jessica C. E. Gienow-Hecht, Annika Estner,
Marcel K. Will

This book examines the significance of nation branding for international history. The authors investigate the roots of national branding practices and critically discuss concepts of image production in
international history. They do not aim to promote nation branding
as a current form of national policy; rather, they wish to take stock
of its historical development. In Part I "Branding the Nation and
Selling the State: Case Studies," the contributors consider individual
case studies from the US Civil War to recent Polish image campaigns
in the context of nation-branding concepts, thereby tracing their
genesis and development since the mid-nineteenth century. In Part
II "Promises and Challenges of Nation Branding: Commentaries on
Case Studies," a leading nation-branding scholar and two well-known
historians of different specializations comment on the case studies
while reflecting notions of nation branding. Finally, three authors
present specific sources they uncovered during their research and
explain their analytical potential for historical research in the section
"Annotated Sources."

Nation branding represents a deliberate, collective effort by
multiple constituencies to generate a viable representation of a
geographical-political-economic-social entity. The examples in this
book deal with national-level efforts, but the concept and techniques
apply to subnational regions and places as well. Governmental
and nongovernmental actors contribute to forging an amalgam of

Notes for this section begin on page 21.

practices, policies, values, and aspirations designed to attract internal and external audiences. Successful branding enables people at home and abroad to view a state as legitimate and credible, thereby meriting their allegiance and support. Once thus acknowledged, states can wield influence as legitimate performers on the world stage: administering citizens, collecting taxes, drawing borders, inviting investment, soliciting tourists, attending international conventions, and so on. Since the rise of the nation-state in the nineteenth century, the perception of "the people" constitutes a critical element of this visibility-legitimacy-empowerment nexus. Those who deploy nation-branding techniques seek to control and channel information, to manipulate the resulting imagery, and sometimes, to bring domestic societies more in line with internationally accepted norms. Nation branders create and promote an attractive package for domestic and international consumption.

Nation branding seeks to enhance international credibility, draw foreign investment, create international political influence, charm tourists, intensify nation building, attract and retain talent, and, often, change negative connotations in regard to, for example, environmental or human rights concerns. Inspired by the conviction that there is a link between national characteristics (such as cuisine or music) and a nation's image abroad, governments and marketing experts develop nation-branding strategies. Both have an impact on each other and both can be used to boost each other. Experts in nation branding juxtapose the national interest of international self-representation with market-oriented advertising strategies. They study both foreign images and self-perceptions of individual states and, in particular, the—occasionally stark—incongruity between the two.[1]

The concept of nation branding does not distinguish between "good" cultural diplomacy and "bad" propaganda. Because democratic and authoritarian states likewise pursue nation-branding strategies, this practice is also indifferent to the political ideology of a state and does not analyze or judge the legitimacy of the sender or their initial intention. Those who create effective nation-branding strategies consider all components—true or false—contributing to the image of a nation abroad, including sports, exports, tradition, heritage, and culture. The initiators of branding campaigns cooperate with agents of several institutions and organizations—domestic and/or foreign—who act on behalf of a specific country in a common quest to create what they perceive as a more positive image. These actors can be government officials, members of civil society, or transnational organizations. Their relation to state and society as well as their intention, conviction, and media are secondary. The most important criterion remains the process through which the image of a country changes and improves in the perception of other states and people.[2]

In the last fifteen years, most nations have engaged in nation branding efforts, and as a result, nation brands today have high policy value. They create and relate to images and reputations that are deeply anchored in the minds of consumers and audiences. For example, the United States is commonly seen as a brand of democracy, while Chinese branding stresses the country's ancient culture. These are sensitive issues: once a brand is violated, foreign and domestic protests abound and far exceed global reactions to similar instances in other places. Thus, global protests against US breaches of civil rights far exceed those expressed whenever China disregards such rights. The US brand relates to law and liberty whereas the Chinese brand does not.

The Origin of Brands and Branding as a Practice

The word *brand* originates in the attempt to mark ownership. Originally, a brand was a piece of charred or burning wood, or a mark made with a hot iron, used by farmers to identify their stock.[3] As such, brands and branding are no recent phenomena. Karl Moore and Susan Reid show that in the Early Bronze period the Harappan civilization used animal seals on their trade goods, conveying the identity of the sender and transmitting information for manufacturers, re-sellers, and government authorities.[4] Philip Kotler, Kevin Lane Keller, Mairead Brady, and others perceive medieval guilds as one of the earliest instances of branding: craftspeople put trademarks on their products to "protect themselves and their customers against inferior quality."[5] All these authors agree that brands in premodern times functioned as conveyers of information on the origin as well as on the ownership of goods.

What exactly constitutes a brand in the modern world? According to the American Marketing Association (AMA), a brand is a "[n]ame, term, design, symbol, or any other feature that identifies one seller's good or service as distinct from those of other sellers."[6] This definition stresses distinction as well as the complexity of concrete and intangible elements, both of which characterize a brand. On a more general level, a brand constitutes an idea: it lives in the imagination of the audience and encompasses feelings, perceptions, and mental associations. As such, a brand reflects an emotional relationship between brand owners and prospective customers.[7]

The action of creating a brand—the process of branding—describes practices and tools related to the creation of a brand: it generates a positive image of a product and stimulates a desire to own it by way of consumption. "Branding," writes J. E. Peterson, "is the application of a story to a product ... It is the story that makes one identify or desire a brand, more so than the product ... itself."[8] Jill Avery and Anat Keinan suggest that "building a brand refers to the process of establishing and maintaining a perceptual frame in the minds of consumers, both individually as well as collectively."[9] Hence, branding not only creates distinctiveness, but also involves the audience in the process of branding. A brand can be perceived differently by different people, but it is also part of collective discourse.

In the modern era, branding is first and foremost a business practice. Branded goods—products that vendors promote via advertising tools—have multiplied since the late eighteenth and early nineteenth century.[10] The rise of department stores furthered retail trade on a large scale. At the Great Exhibition in London in 1851, producers showcased consumer goods from all over the world. Unlike bulk goods, producers packaged, promoted, and labeled retail goods with a proper name. Mid-nineteenth century brand names now stood for quality and appealed to consumers' trust. Advertising agencies became mediators between the media, the advertiser, and the consumer. As Stefan Schwarzkopf shows, during the early first half of the twentieth century, advertising practitioners engaged in the creation of brands, often providing them with a unique image and personality—an approach that enhanced prior practices.[11]

In the 1950s and 1960s, the demand for consumer goods exploded and led to intense competition among brands as well as a boom of the advertising industry, first of all in the United States. Marketing experts now sought to differentiate products from one another by giving products distinct identities. Experts also strove to understand consumers by expanding their perspective to consider consumers' motivations and perceptions.[12] Pierre Martineau, one of the protagonists of motivation research in advertising, wondered about how to create an image or personality for products that exceeded mere tangible qualities. In his idea, a brand image consisted of a set of symbols, feelings, and psychological meanings.[13]

At the same time, a number of influential businesses paved the way for today's branding practice: the brand consulting firm Landor, founded in 1941 by Walter and Josephine Landor in San Francisco, set out to create logo designs and marketing consumer orientation. In 1965, advertising executive Wally Olins and designer Michael Wolff founded the business Wolff Olins in London. Olins eventually engaged in nation branding and became one of its most prominent propagators. In 1974, John Murphy founded Interbrand, focusing on brand strategy and design. During the following decade, branding as a tool to provide products with an emotional dimension became a widespread practice in advertising.[14] Scholars of media and cultural studies like Liz Moor, and marketing experts such as the aforementioned Kevin Lane Keller believe that the term "branding" as we understand it today emerged in the early or mid-1990s.[15]

Branding consultancies emanated from different fields, including design, the development of corporate identities, and advertising. Advertising executives then integrated branding into marketing and business strategies, which led to the emergence of professionalized branding consultancies and to the conceptualization of branding in marketing theory. Today, branding has also gained great popularity in public discourse. Branding has been associated with universities, museums, churches, and entire states; religious groups engage in "faith branding," coaches advising professionals recommend "personal branding," and governmental leaders embark on nation-branding campaigns.

Identifying the Nation

Defining the term *nation* has kept scholars busy for quite some time and for good reason. Literally, the word *nation* derives from the Latin expression *natio* and means "the people" or denominates a tribe with a common derivation, language, and customs. In his inaugural lecture "Qu'est-ce qu'une Nation?" at the Sorbonne in 1882, Ernest Renan argued that the nation was a spiritual principle. It resulted from profound connections in the past and was based on "the possession in common of a rich legacy of memories; the other is present-day consent, the desire to live together, the will to perpetuate the value of the heritage that one has received in an undivided form."[16] In other words, the nation yields nationalism. One hundred years later, this approach had changed profoundly. In 1983, Ernest Gellner stressed the importance of the human will and shared culture that finds expression in political units.[17] According to Gellner, nationalism is an integral part of modernity and therefore a result of the transformation to an industrial society: nationalism, Gellner held, creates the nation.

One of the most popular turns in the debate stemmed from political scientist and historian Benedict Anderson. In *Imagined Communities: Reflections on the Origin and Spread of Nationalism*, Anderson outlined an interpretation of the nation as a socially constructed community, imagined by the people who perceive themselves as part of the group.[18] Anderson emphasized the role of the media in creating communities through spreading images. The nation constituted not only a product of nationalism, but also complicated networks of communication along with visions of individual and group desires.

Following Anderson, a younger group of historians, such as Jakob Vogel, Svenja Goltermann, and Sabine Behrenbeck, have elaborated on the specific icons inspiring these "imagined communities," ranging from battlefield heroes to body builders to public holidays.[19] These different approaches all provide hints about the characteristics of a nation and present different, yet interrelated ideas of the nation. For the purpose of this book, following one or another school of definition is less important than understanding that the nation cannot exist without performance and self-representation. It is therefore especially important to grasp not only the imagery but also the actors and mechanisms entailed in this process: how are images crafted, who does the crafting, and what methods are being used?

The Application of Branding to Nations

State authorities and their allies deliberately engaged in building nation brands long before there was such a term as "nation branding," and for at least one hundred years some authors have scratched their heads over this phenomenon. These individuals did not consider themselves scholars of international history or international relations, but they were all concerned with the interplay between countries and products. As early as 1896, journalist Ernest Williams stated in his pamphlet *Made in Germany* that the label of origin, be it a country or a city, had an effect on the customer's buying decision.[20] In 1947, Arthur Lisowsky, a professor at a Swiss commercial college, studied the overlap of nations and the promotion of brand-name products. Lisowsky stressed that principles of *Markenbildung* (branding) could also be applied to tourism advertising.[21] In the 1960s, a number of scholars began to analyze the impact of any given country's image on the perception of a product and its provenience—the so-called "country of origin effect." Here, experts studied how consumers' general perceptions of a country created a collective image that specifically related to the products of that country.

In a gesture to this emergent field, Per Hansen has recently shown how in Denmark export goods, such as furniture, and the country's image are often closely related.[22] The central idea here was to switch causality around: if the sale of products profited from their origins—e.g., "made in Germany"—one could also conclude that these goods likewise coined the image of Germany. Notably the tourism sector traditionally sought to "sell" nations to tourists by associating countries with good feelings, experiences, services, and desirable products.

Nation branding's breakthrough as a term came about in the United Kingdom in the late 1980s and 1990s with a profound reconceptualization of what branding could do for people, products, and policy. During this decade, British marketing experts collaborated with policymakers to rebrand the UK's image. By ushering in Margaret Thatcher's administration, the population of the UK had elected a right-wing neoliberal government. The Iron Lady's program diminished the role of the state and cleared the way for privatization. Her policy influenced the development of branding in two ways: first, neoliberal policy led to new forms of competition; second, Thatcher used public diplomacy to improve strategies of political communication. This very strategy, argues historian Nicholas Cull, paved the way for later branding initiatives.[23]

After the long premiership of Conservative Party politicians Margaret Thatcher and John Major, in the mid-1990s the Labour Party desperately sought to regain British voters' confidence. Tony Blair played a central role in rebranding the party, because he emphasized a new course for Labour that eschewed the socialist credo of state ownership in favor of the free market. Blair thus stood for a third way that contrasted sharply with previous patterns of leftwing or rightwing politics, and he accompanied this new orientation with a comprehensive rebranding campaign. The party now was called *New* Labour, a party that stood for a *New* Britain. To boost the campaign, professional designers developed a logo and changed communication strategies. The incorporation of marketing and public relations had an innovative function in Labour's campaign to win back voters' trust.[24]

When the British electorate chose Blair as prime minister in 1997, the Labour Party continued its rebranding campaign. That year, the think tank Demos published a report considering the tools shaping a new identity for the entire nation. Its author, Mark Leonard, observed that the United Kingdom's image abroad was unfavorable. Most foreigners, Leonard stated, associated the country and its people with backwardness. Worse, British products were perceived as "low tech and bad value,"[25] businesses appeared to be "strike-ridden,"[26] and most British people did not take pride in their country anymore.[27] To overcome this negative reputation, the Blair administration expanded the rebranding process—originally created for the Labour party—to include all of the United Kingdom. The result was the Cool Britannia campaign, aimed at domestic as well as foreign audiences, and designed to project a new sense of pride in British accomplishments in the world of music, media, and the arts.[28]

Cool Britannia does not reflect the first attempt to rebrand a country, but it has been, in recent years, perhaps the most important one. As a result of this experience with rebranding the UK, the British public as well as international observers began to pay attention to the issue of nation branding. The Demos report and Blair's activities spread branding vocabulary far beyond offices of consultancies and led to a conceptualization of nation branding in general, as we shall see below.

US rebranding campaigns after 9/11 marked another important cornerstone in the development of contemporary nation branding consulting as well. Likewise, they enhanced the scholarly debate around nation branding and public diplomacy. After the terrorist attacks by al-Qaeda, the Bush administration wondered why parts of the world had developed such a hatred against the United States. As a consequence, they hired advertising expert Charlotte Beers as Under Secretary for Public Diplomacy and Public Affairs to build a new Brand America.[29] Beers's Shared Values Initiative targeted on Muslims worldwide with a special focus on the Middle East. Although the campaign received negative comments in the news, was abandoned in 2003, and criticized for ethical shortcomings by scholars,[30] it showed the degree to which advertising practices and politics were now interlinked.

Practice and Scholarship: Conceptualizing Nation Branding

Concurrent to the rebranding experiment in the United Kingdom in the 1990s, marketing experts linked the idea of branding to places. In 1993, US marketing luminary Philip Kotler and his colleagues Donald H. Haider and Irving J. Rein postulated that cities, regions, and countries in crisis could learn from brand businesses facing economic downturns and communicate their special qualities to target markets more professionally.[31] Kotler, along with Somkid Jatusripitak and Suvit Maesincee, refined this idea in 1997 in a publication tellingly titled *The Marketing of Nations*.[32] In 1998, independent British marketing and policy adviser Simon Anholt coined the term *nation brand* in an effort to measure and increase a country's reputation by focusing on distinct characteristics.[33] Anholt has published widely on the topic and advised countries all over the world on how to develop a respectable nation brand and competitive identity. Wally Olins likewise contributed to the development of the nation-branding concept. Olins served as a consultant notably to countries that were either unhappy with their (typically negative) images, or tried to put themselves on the map, such as Poland, Northern Ireland, and Lithuania.[34]

Since the year 2000, there has been no shortage of institutions dedicated to promoting nation branding and publications pertaining to the subject; indeed, the recent rise of the concept of nation branding in politics and advertising has initiated a flood of academic research projects. European and US think tanks and academic institutes such as the German research center "Nation Branding" at the Hochschule RheinMain in Wiesbaden, have developed numerous research and consulting projects. They study how states culturally interact with others, and how the efficiency of such a dialogue could be maximized in terms of political credibility, diplomatic cooperation, trade opportunities, and economic investments. Websites and journals, such as *Place Branding and Public Diplomacy* (originally founded by Anholt), explore issues relating to reputation, image management, consultancy, and the interplay of politics and branding.

It is thus not surprising that in the last fifteen years, scholars, too, have begun to investigate nation branding in conjunction with international relations and public diplomacy. A large part of the literature is concerned with political legitimacy and technical measures in the service of promoting national reputation. Some scholars of marketing communications and related fields, such as Jami A. Fullerton and Alice Kendrick, functioned as both scholars on nation branding and academic policy advisors. They "try to step outside the stereotypes and traditional paradigms to understand the milieu in which global citizens form impressions of faraway places."[35] Yet, a number of scholars laboring in the fields of anthropology, cultural studies, and media studies have recently expressed strong reservations regarding this phenomenon. Borrowing from critical theory, these studies often draw a connection between nation branding's imagined discourses and practices on the one hand, and "real" contemporary national identities, culture, and governance, on the other. They argue that nation branding does not merely constitute an instrument of image boosting but, in fact, represents a struggle over what the nation is, to whom, and why, among local, governmental, and nonstate actors and organizations. Scholars like Nadia Kaneva, Melissa Aronczyk, Peter van Ham, and others study the meaning of contemporary nation branding for the collective identity of a nation and its position in the international arena.[36]

The creation of a nation's image has also appealed to scholars of media and communication studies like Michael Kunczik, who dedicated a part of their scholarship to the history of public relations and image making in the international arena.[37] Conceptually international public relations and public diplomacy somewhat overlap, but they do differ in their ultimate goal. As Guy J. Golan and Sung-Un Yang point out, whereas public relations cultivate reciprocal advantageous relationships in the interest of consumerism or philanthropy, public relations underline or enhance goals of foreign affairs.[38]

Nation branding, it is safe to say, serves as an umbrella term for all activities addressed in this literature. It includes nonstate actors along with the ensuing cooperation and conflicts over who is in charge of branding the nation and which image will prevail. Whereas public diplomacy often focuses on political goals, the ambitions of nation branding strategies frequently emphasize economic goals. Therefore, the concept of nation branding stretches concern beyond diplomacy in the sense of state-centered actions. It investigates situations where the state has—quite frequently—a minimal role, where other actors complement or even substitute the state. Actors can be institutions of the state or closely related to it, but they can also be institutionally as well as financially independent from the state. Strategies of nation branding are focused less on mutual understanding and more on image management via positive aspects of the respective nation. Furthermore, this approach helps to explain the domestic processes of setting an agenda for a specific campaign. In doing so, nation branding reflects the process of power distribution within societies "doing the brand" and the impact that these struggles have on relationships with international actors.

In sum, there is a rich literature spanning across communication studies, anthropology, political science, and marketing studies and it is marked by three themes. First, scholars agree that the political context and its impact need to be analyzed in tandem; they also agree that nation branding is a challenging or even dangerous phenomenon. Some argue that contemporary nation branding symbolizes neoliberal understandings of the nation in the context of global markets. In that interpretation, nation branding poses as an instrument to prevent, or at least delay, the demise of the nation-state. By focusing consumers' and citizens' attention on political and economic appeal as well as cultural distinction and economic independence, the government stresses the ongoing significance of the nation. At the same time, nation branding has produced some powerful examples of good practice, including a number of awards, websites, and blogs highlighting the cooperative power branding can bring to national and regional communities. The second unifying theme in this kind of literature is a common conviction that nation branding is a novel phenomenon: either it poses as the (un)wanted child of the love affair between the post-Cold War neoliberal state and twenty-first century corporatism; or, it embodies a new chance to create partnerships with civil society concentrating on values and enterprises within the national community, all of which will presumably lead to more political, diplomatic, environmental, and corporate responsibility. Finally, a third collective issue is that it is almost completely ahistorical, a point which we wish to elaborate on and critically assess below.

Foreign Relations and Imagery in History

Missing from the scholarship to date is a historical investigation of the roots of nation branding beyond regional and temporal confines.[39] Although some experts admitted their interest in history (such as advertising expert Wally Olins), historians themselves have been conspicuously absent from the entire debate outlined above. This is all the more surprising given that nation branding addresses a number of terms familiar to scholars of global and international history, including *stage*, *desire*, and, most notably, *recognition*, *credibility*, and *legitimacy*.

At the same time, historians have grappled with cultural imagery and international history to a significant extent. Readers of the present series *Explorations in Culture and International History* know that for at least the last twenty-five years, cultural and public diplomacy—the informal and formal use of culture in the context of international relations and policy making—has been a powerful parameter in the study of foreign relations, most notably, but not exclusively, in the context of the East-West conflict.[40] Notably after 9/11, the discussion about public diplomacy gained momentum in political science and beyond. Scholars like Jan Melissen enriched the debate on a "new public diplomacy," which included different strategies of official communication toward and relations with foreign publics, be it pursued by a government or by semistate or nonstate actors that have a close relationship with the state.[41] Numerous case studies on cultural or public diplomacy, ranging from transatlantic marriages to public diplomacy in the nonaligned states during the Cold War, have shown the diverse functions of state and nonstate actors in shaping cultural images that, in turn, have had an immediate effect on the conduct of diplomacy and international relations at large.[42]

In addition to the study of cultural and public diplomacy, since the 1990s historians have been fascinated with the genesis of what political scientist Joseph Nye describes as "soft power," that is, a country's "ability to set the political agenda in a way that shapes the preferences of others." Nye believes that public diplomacy can be seen as an instrument to mobilize soft power. Soft power essentially signifies an actor's reputation in the international arena. To Nye, "[t]he ability to establish preferences tends to be associated with intangible power resources such as an attractive culture, ideology, and institutions."[43] Thus, an international actor does not need to use measures of hard power, when soft measures like cultural impact can influence the addressed actor as well. A respectable image can help to accommodate opposing sides at least as much as a nuclear arsenal.

Nation Branding and International History

The present volume seeks to address the gap outlined above while simultaneously tying in the present literature dedicated to culture and international history. Indeed, most of the contributors in this book have, in the past, published widely on public and cultural diplomacy, international cultural relations, as well as soft power and its history. Thus, this volume aims to reflect the emerging debate about the various approaches on nation branding among scholars and practitioners. It focuses on the nexus between cultural marketing, self-representation, and political power by examining current nation branding initiatives as well as historical predecessors. Part I "Branding the Nation and Selling the State: Case Studies" investigates diverse instances of nation branding campaigns in Europe, the United States, Asia, and South America beginning with the US Civil War and ending with the reconsolidation of Eastern European national sovereignties after the fall of the Berlin Wall. The selection is preliminary and not inclusive as this is quite literally a new field in the making.

William McAllister jumpstarts the volume by presenting *The Foreign Relations of the United States* (FRUS) series as a multi-faceted, mid-nineteenth-century form of nation branding. By publishing key official government documents in the Civil War era, and by disseminating them to domestic and foreign audiences, US government agents such as Secretary of State William Seward intended to illustrate the administration's policies and to promote its accountability to Congress and the public. McAllister emphasizes the importance of drawing on unique national characteristics and promoting the essential values of a state at home and abroad. As states will only exist if others recognize their legitimacy—particularly in times of civil war, when the very existence of the nation is challenged—nation branding serves as a means to gain international postwar recognition. Thus, by creating and promoting the image of a credible, democratic "Union brand," the FRUS volumes represented a deliberate effort to brand the United States as a powerful, resolute nation and the constitutional-republican system as its rightful and legitimate expression.

Oliver Kühschelm then links the nation-branding initiatives of Austria and Switzerland by comparing their different traditions in extensive tourist advertising, export promotion, and buy national campaigns, since the early twentieth century. Switzerland appeared as a role model in exercising nation branding since the interwar years when authorities created a Swiss brand based on national characteristics such as neutrality, humanitarian commitment, and high-quality products. Austria later followed in its footsteps when nation branding became a prominent feature of Austrian nation building, which aimed at re-establishing a separate state after having been part of the National Socialist Deutsches Reich after World War II. Kühschelm sees a profound change in strategy, target audience, and approach to nation branding in both countries: those strategies developed from buy national campaigns in the 1920s and 1930s closely linked to moralizing patriotic consumption, into campaigns dedicated to tourism and export promotion in the 1950s and 1960s highlighting the superior quality of national products. They increasingly took account of the importance of foreign audiences to whom the national image or brand was sold.

Ilaria Scaglia sheds light on the cultural interplay of nation branding and internationalism in the interwar period. At the center of her essay is the 1935–36 International Exhibition of Chinese Art, which was the first of its kind to be hosted by both Chinese and British government officials. Scaglia argues that both countries used the exhibition for their own ends in order to brand the national image—China as the rightful and legitimate heir of the glorious Chinese past, the United Kingdom as a center for international cooperation—through a public display of internationalism. More importantly, internationalism itself came to be defined by the nation branding process. The Chinese and British need for nation branding as well as for selling the national image to a foreign audience influenced the way internationalism and internationalist ideas were exercised. Thus, internationalist practices accompanying the exhibition turned to predominantly symbolic forms of international cooperation at the expense of less publicly visible ones to serve the nation branding purposes.

John Gripentrog then turns to the nation branding process in times of crisis and its limits in overcoming negative images abroad. In the wake of the Manchurian crisis, Japanese nation branding initiatives were directed at the US public to prevent imminent political isolation. By establishing the Society for International Cultural Relations (Kokusai Bunka Shinkōkai, or KBS) in 1934 in order to promote the image of Japan's high culture, Japanese officials aimed to restore its political credibility within the international arena, thereby countering the images associated with Japan's military activities in China. Moreover, branding the image of a highly civilized state served Japanese imperialist ambitions by introducing Japan's culture into foreign countries. Gripentrog also points to the limits of Japan's positive nation branding initiatives in the face of Japanese military aggression since 1937, only to re-establish the brand image in the years following 1945.

Carolin Viktorin likewise investigates the nation-branding efforts of dictatorships and their attempt to soften negative images in foreign countries. Viktorin looks at the promotion of mass tourism via international public relations by the Franco government in the United Kingdom as a form of nation branding. Spanish nation branding sought to counterbalance international criticism and to represent authoritarian Spain as a peaceful and welcoming European country. The extensive advertising and PR campaigns evolving in the 1950s and especially the 1960s were established by the Spanish Ministry of Information and Tourism (MIT) and strongly supported by a variety of British professional advertising companies, PR consultants, and journalists. Depoliticizing Spain's image in favor of building a nation brand predicated on culture and scenery was a strategy orchestrated by international public relations experts such as E. D. O'Brien who, in turn, were also deeply involved in the creation and shaping of the official brand itself. As Viktorin shows, the nation branding process—i.e., the promotion of mass tourism—and the ensuing transnational relations were to some extent able to address and overcome international resentments when foreign diplomatic relations remained deadlocked in Spain's political isolation.

Michael Krenn utilizes the concept of nation branding to shed new light on US international art exhibitions during the Cold War. In particular, he discusses the way in which nonstate actors and governmental officials both contribute to the creation of an "official" brand. To Krenn, the nation-branding concept allows scholars to shift focus from the foreign reception of branding campaigns and cultural diplomacy to the domestic arena. The case of the 1946–47 *Advancing American Art* exhibition shows that while the exhibition met with approval in Europe and Asia, it caused profound frictions at home, where many observers felt it represented neither a national identity, nor truly American values. Thus, Krenn demonstrates how a brand may fail if different actors cannot agree on, support, and live the national brand. Krenn explicitly encourages researchers to move beyond traditional studies of cultural diplomacy in an effort to understand the process of image-crafting for foreign and domestic audiences.

Rosemarijn Hoefte introduces us to the importance of nation branding campaigns for postcolonial countries. Hoefte specifically looks at Suriname in the years 1945–2015, and the country's attempt to "put itself on the map." Suriname developed nation-branding strategies such as the 2015 *We Are Suriname* campaign, orchestrated by the Ministry of Foreign Affairs in order to attract international attention and promote foreign investment. The government also directed nation-branding initiatives at domestic audiences in order to address the nation's multicultural and pluralist makeup tinged by a Dutch colonial heritage. Emphasizing the dual purpose of Surinamese nation branding, Hoefte shows how the processes of nation branding and nation building were intertwined to (re)define national identity: nation building in Suriname not only sought to build state capacity but also construct a society. Suriname used nation branding to represent itself as a diverse yet harmonious nation, encouraging citizens to come to terms with their own past and present.

Similarly, Beata Ociepka investigates the efforts of Eastern European states to (re)brand themselves in the transitional period of the postcommunist era. Focusing on Poland and the Baltic States at the beginning of the twenty-first century, the chapter looks at the nation branding campaigns of four countries. Ociepka discusses their different strategies in defining their new, postcommunist, national identity and positioning themselves within Europe. On a domestic level, Poland, Lithuania, Latvia, and Estonia included their long history and traditions in nation branding narratives in order to abandon their communist past and embody a Western (and in some cases Nordic) identity. Drawing on government institutions, professional advisers, and nation-branding experts while staging international cultural events such as festivals, exhibitions, or sports championships, the four countries targeted audiences in the European Union, the United States, and Russia to gain more visibility and attract foreign investment. In the end, Ociepka encourages us to view nation-branding campaigns in tandem with the geopolitical position of a state, given that both contribute to the perception of the state internationally and domestically.

Part II of this volume, "Promises and Challenges of Nation Branding: Commentaries on Case Studies," invites experts of history and communication studies to critically assess the individual findings presented in the preceding section. Justin Hart, an expert in the history of US foreign relations, discusses entanglements and differences between nation branding and public diplomacy within the historical sciences. Communications scholar Melissa Aronczyk emphasizes the origins of nation branding in marketing, while at the same time sharing critical thoughts on the possibility of historicizing the process of branding nations. Finally, Mads Mordhorst provides insights from the perspective of a business historian by considering the contemporary crisis of nation branding in the context of globalization.

In the volume's last section "Annotated Sources," John Gripentrog, Ilaria Scaglia, and Michael Krenn introduce three primary sources and offer analyses through the lens of the nation-branding paradigm. The authors explore different ways in which governmental and non-governmental actors implemented branding strategies; they highlight the instruments used to do so and explain how these shaped the implementation of specific strategies. The sources display a great variety regarding genre and origin, and provide new input for interpretation.

Three particular aspects emerge from the following essays that may help us to grasp the complexity of nation branding:

1. *Agents*. All authors grapple with the question of agency: what kinds of stakeholders can be identified? Who is involved in the creation, development, and execution of a nation's brand? In contrast to propaganda or cultural diplomacy, nation branding relied—and continues to rely—on both state and nonstate actors in order to develop the image of the nation that was being presented abroad. Over time, brand managers became highly professionalized. As the essays by Viktorin, Kühschelm, and Ociepka show, marketing experts and PR consultants were increasingly responsible for official branding campaigns, thereby introducing business practices into the self-representation of states. Finally, nation-branding campaigns were created and executed not only by fellow nationals. On the contrary, alongside professionalization, states tended to assign the development of the national brand to foreign marketing and nation branding experts. Thus, the self-representation of a state and the images constructed were often at least partially in the hands of internationally active professionals.

2. *Audience*. In the analysis of nation branding, all essays of the volume emphasize the importance of distinguishing particular addressees: who is the target audience? How does an individual target audience perceive an individual brand? What is the national population's opinion regarding these images? On the one hand, as Gripentrog and Viktorin show, nation branding generally reflected the state's intrinsic desire to influence foreign audiences—i.e., governments, organizations, or the public—through self-representation in order to gain political, economic, or cultural power. On the other hand, nation branding was directed at domestic audiences as well. Images

of self-representation were controversial more often than not, particularly in pluralistic societies where individual social groups protested against their exclusion from the projected brand. Both Hoefte and Krenn demonstrate that national public support of or antipathy toward the brand image could determine the success or failure of a nation-branding campaign.

3. *Measures.* All authors agree that measures, strategies, and scope of nation branding differed greatly according to their respective social, political, and cultural contexts, as well as the actors involved. In consequence, they all examine the strategies nation branders employed to promote a particular image. Some, such as Spain, Austria, and Suriname used specific national landscape imagery in an effort to promote mass tourism and to entice foreign investors (see chapters by Viktorin, Kühschelm, Hoefte). Others, including Japan, China, and the United States took advantage of their national culture and presented themselves as advanced civilizations by compiling art exhibitions or hosting garden shows, thereby establishing and improving international relations (see Gripentrog, Scaglia, Krenn). A third group, encompassing the United States and Switzerland, drew on specific (and unique) national characteristics such as freedom of expression, neutrality, or humanitarian commitment to advertise national political power and stability (see McAllister and Kühschelm).

In addition to these three specific characteristics in the history of nation branding over time, we can, moreover, distinguish three trends regarding the research of nation branding phenomena in this volume.

1. *Branding and Building the Nation.* There is, in the eyes of a number of authors, an apparent interplay between nation branding and nation building. To Hoefte, nation building in Suriname's pluralistic society functioned as a form of internal marketing of the constructed state and society that closely overlapped with the branding of the nation and the creation and promotion of a national image abroad. Kühschelm, on the other hand, detects in the branding of Austria's national products an effort to promote patriotic consumption as a prominent element of Austria's nation building after World War II. Both Hoefte and Kühschelm show how nation branding

fosters the construction of a national identity at home while promoting a specific national image to a foreign audience. In a curious twist, controversial discussions over the image of a nation (as portrayed by Krenn) are likely to impact understandings of identity, leading to a more detailed debate about national identities.

2. *The Politics of Rebranding.* Some of the authors in this book struggle with the tension between nation branding and propaganda as a tool of government policy. Viktorin shows that authoritarian dictatorships such as the Franco regime used nation branding as an instrument to bypass their own political isolation and to present themselves to European and US publics as major tourist destinations. Gripentrog retraces how, in the case of Japan, nation branding has been utilized to neutralize the political side effects of military campaigns by displaying high culture as a symbol of peacefulness and civilization. Ociepka's chapter likewise demonstrates the ways in which postcommunist states worked to overcome negative past images and integrate themselves into the new European political and economic system. Thus, these authors see nation branding as a handy instrument to access "positive memories" from history and tradition in order to soften the blows of current political negative perceptions abroad originating from a state's authoritarian or fascist political system or military aggression.

3. *Branding Strategies of Legitimization.* A third group of authors sees nation branding as a distinct strategy to gain national and international recognition. As McAllister shows, the "Union brand" earned the republican form of government international recognition and endorsement as legitimate representative of the United States during the Civil War, while at the same time discouraging international powers from recognizing the Confederacy. In a similar vein, Scaglia identifies the ways in which nation branding served as an instrument for Nanjing China to present itself as both the legitimate heir of Chinese art, culture, and history, as well as the legitimate representative of Chinese civilization on the world stage. Krenn's essay on American art likewise shows that there is often great internal disagreement among domestic audiences regarding the legitimacy of the national image that is being produced by nation branding campaigns. In all three cases, nation branding served as state tool both to obtain

international recognition and to legitimate representative power at home.

In conclusion, it is worth noting that historicizing nation branding focuses on investigating the genesis of nation branding. It does not mean to uncritically hail the current nation branding industry. None of the authors in this volume seek to explicitly provide political advice, nor do they assert that nation-branding campaigns effectively "work" (or not). But as historians, we can use diverse sources, case studies, and actions on the part of a broad array of actors—from William Seward to Simon Anholt—as well as sources pertaining to branding activities ranging from antique artifacts to advertising manuals, in order to explore conflicting perspectives regarding the nation and its images. Collectively, the authors in this volume look at historical attempts to market a state to a specific audience by creating unique national selling points. On a conceptual level, they present the opportunities and challenges for scholars of history, sociology, or political science examining nation branding as a marketing technique, thereby adding new perspectives and tools for analysis to the current canon of cultural diplomacy or soft power history. If our selection is geographically illustrative rather than exhaustive, such limitation should be understood as an inspiration and call for further research to future historians working in this new and dynamic interdisciplinary field.

Carolin Viktorin is a doctoral candidate at Freie Universität Berlin. Her research project examines the tourism branding of Spain in Western Europe from the 1950s to the 1970s. She focuses on the interrelations of the travel industry and the professionalization of public relations and advertising. The *Stiftung Bildung und Wissenschaft* as well as the German Historical Institute London supported her current project. Together with Jessica C. E. Gienow-Hecht she recently co-authored a chapter on nation branding in *International History in Theory and Practice*, edited by Barbara Haider-Wilson, William Godsey, and Wolfgang Müller, 695–720 (Vienna: Verlag Österreichische Akademie der Wissenschaften, 2017).

Jessica C. E. Gienow-Hecht is a historian for international and North American history and Chair of the Department of History at the John F. Kennedy Institute for North American Studies, Freie Universität Berlin. Her first book, *Transmission Impossible: American Journalism* *as Cultural Diplomacy in Postwar Germany, 1945–1955* (Baton Rouge: Louisiana State University Press, 1999), was co-awarded the Stuart Bernath Prize and the Myrna Bernath Prize. Her second book, *Sound Diplomacy: Music and Emotions in Transatlantic Relations, 1850–1920* (Chicago: University of Chicago Press, 2009, 2012) has won the Choice Outstanding Academic Title Award. Gienow-Hecht's most recent research focus is on humanitarianism and nation branding; specifically, she seeks to understand the link between humanitarianism, interventionism, gender, and self-representation in US foreign relations.

Annika Estner is head of unit in the German Red Cross Tracing Service, responsible for inquiries and projects regarding World War II. Her research focuses on the history of Eastern European dissidents during the Cold War as well as on the history of German POWs during World War II. In 2014, she coordinated the conference Culture and International History V taking place at the John F. Kennedy Institute in Berlin. The same year, the German Historical Institute in Moscow awarded her a short-term doctoral fellowship for archival research.

Marcel K. Will is project coordinator and lecturer at the University of Applied Science Koblenz. In 2015, he received his Ph.D. in history for a study about US President Jimmy Carter's China and Taiwan policy. Currently, he is working on a concept to introduce gamification in history classes.

Notes

1. Jessica C. E. Gienow-Hecht, "Nation Branding: A Useful Category for the Study of International History," unpublished manuscript, 2016.
2. Gienow-Hecht, "Nation Branding."
3. Wilson Bastos and Sidney J. Levy, "A History of the Concept of Branding: Practice and Theory," *Journal of Historical Research in Marketing* 4, no. 3 (2012): 351.
4. Karl Moore and Susan Reid, "The Birth of Brand: 4000 Years of Branding," *Business History* 50, no. 4 (2008): 422–24.
5. Philip Kotler, Kevin Lane Keller, Mairead Brady, Malcolm Goodman, and Torben Hansen, *Marketing Management* (Harlow, UK: Pearson Education Limited, 2009), 426.
6. American Marketing Association, "Dictionary."
7. Paul Temporal, *Branding for the Public Sector: Creating, Building and Managing Brands People Will Value* (Chichester, UK: Wiley, 2015), 12.
8. J. E. Peterson, "Quatar and the World: Branding for a Micro-State," *The Middle East Journal* 60, no. 4 (2006): 744.

9. Jill Avery and Anat Keinan, "Consuming Brands," in *The Cambridge Handbook of Consumer Psychology*, ed. Michael I. Norton, Derek D. Rucker, and Cait Lamberton (New York: Cambridge University Press, 2015), 209–32, esp. 210.
10. Stefan Schwarzkopf, "Turning Trade Marks into Brands: How Advertising Agencies Practiced and Conceptualized Branding 1890–1930," in *Trademarks, Brands, and Competitiveness*, ed. by Teresa da Silva Lopes and Paul Duguid (New York: Routledge, 2010), 166.
11. Schwarzkopf, "Turning Trade Marks into Brands," 187.
12. Burleigh Gardner and Sidney Levy, "The Product and the Brand," *Harvard Business Review* 33, March–April (1955): 33–39.
13. Pierre Martineau, *Motivation in Advertising: Motives that Make People Buy* (New York: McGraw-Hill, 1957), 146.
14. Liz Moor, *The Rise of Brands* (Oxford: Berg Publishers, 2007), 3.
15. Moor, *The Rise of Brands*, 3; Kevin Lane Keller, "Branding and Brand Equity," in *Handbook of Marketing*, ed. Barton Weitz and Robin Wensley (London: Sage Publication Ltd. 2002), 151.
16. Ernest Renan, *What Is a Nation?*
17. Ernest Gellner, *Nations and Nationalism* (Oxford: Blackwell, 1983), 55.
18. Benedict Anderson, *Imagined Communities: Reflections on the Origin and Spread of Nationalism* (London: Verso, 1983).
19. Svenja Goltermann, *Körper der Nation: Habitusformierung und die Politik des Turnens 1860–1890* (Göttingen: Vandenhoeck & Ruprecht, 1989); Jakob Vogel, "2. September—Der Tag von Sedan," in *Erinnerungstage: Wendepunkte der Geschichte von der Antike bis zur Gegenwart*, ed. Etienne François and Uwe Puschner (Munich: C.H. Beck Verlag, 2010), 201–18; Sabine Behrenbeck, *Der Kult um die toten Helden: Nationalsozialistische Mythen, Riten und Symbole, 1923–1945* (Vierow: SH-Verlag, 1996).
20. See on *Made in Germany*, Ernest Williams, *Made in Germany* (London: Heinemann Haucap, 1896). For further research, see, for example, Justus Wey and Christian Jens F. Barmbold, "Location Choice as a Signal for Product Quality: The Economics of 'Made in Germany,'" *Journal of Institutional and Theoretical Economics* 153, no. 3 (1997): 510–31.
21. Arthur Lisowsky, "Fremdenverkehrswerbung als Markenwerbung," *The Tourist Review* 2, no. 4 (1947): 133–35.
22. Per H. Hansen, "Cobranding Product and Nation: Danish Modern Furniture and Denmark in the United States, 1940–1970," in *Trademarks, Brands, and Competitiveness*, ed. Teresa da Silva Lopes and Paul Duguid (New York: Routledge, 2010), 77–101.
23. Nicholas J. Cull, "The Iron Brand: Margaret Thatcher and Public Diplomacy," *Place Branding and Public Diplomacy* 9 (2013): 67–70.
24. Moor, *The Rise of Brands*, 4.
25. Mark Leonard, *Britain: Renewing our Identity* (London: Demos, 1997), 1.
26. Leonard, *Britain*, 1.
27. Leonard, *Britain*, 2.
28. "Cool Britannia: Nothing Is Sadder than Trying Too Hard to Be Cool," *The Economist* (12 March 1998), retrieved 16 March 2016 from http://www.econo mist.com/node/370877.
29. Jami A. Fullerton and Alice Kendrick, *Advertising's War on Terrorism: The Story of the U.S. State Department's Shared Values Initiative* (Spokane, WA: Marquette Books, 2006).

30. Patrick Lee Plaisance, "The Propaganda War on Terrorism: An Analysis of the United States' 'Shared Values' Public-Diplomacy Campaign after September 11, 2001," *Journal of Mass Media Ethics* 20, no. 4 (2005): 250–68.
31. Philip Kotler, Donald H. Haider, and Irving J. Rein, *Marketing Places: Attracting Investment, Industry, and Tourism to Cities, States, and Nations* (New York: Free Press, 1993).
32. Philip Kotler, Somkid Jatusripitak, and Suvit Maesincee, *The Marketing of Nations: Strategic Approach to Building National Wealth* (New York: Free Press, 1997).
33. Simon Anholt, "Nation-Brands of the Twenty-First Century," *Journal of Brand Management* 5, no. 6 (1998): 395–406.
34. See, for example, Simon Anholt, *Brand New Justice: The Upside of Global Branding,* (Oxford: Butterworth-Heinemann, 2003); Wally Olins, *On Brand* (London: Thames & Hudson, 2003).
35. Jami A. Fullerton, "Introduction," in *Shaping International Public Opinion: A Model for Nation Branding and Public Diplomacy,* ed. Jami A. Fullerton and Alice Kendrick (New York: Peter Lang, 2017): 3.
36. Melissa Aronczyk, *Branding the Nation: The Global Business of National Identity* (Oxford: Oxford University Press, 2013); Nadia Kaneva, ed., *Branding Post-Communist Nations: Marketizing National Identities in the "New" Europe* (New York: Routledge, 2012); Peter van Ham; "The Rise of the Brand State: The Postmodern Politics of Image and Reputation," *Foreign Affairs* 80, no. 5 (2001): 2–6.
37. Michael Kunczik, *Images of Nations and International Public Relations* (Mahwah, NJ: Lawrence Erlbaum Associates, 1997).
38. Guy J. Golan and Sung-Un Yang, "Introduction: The Integrated Public Diplomacy Perspective," in *International Public Relations and Public Diplomacy: Communication and Engagement,* ed. Guy J. Golan, Sung-Un Yang, and Dennis F. Kingsey (New York: Peter Lang Publishing, 2015), 3.
39. For a notable regional exception, see Louis Clerc, Nikolas Glover, and Paul Jordan, *Histories of Public Diplomacy and Nation Branding in the Nordic and Baltic Countries: Representing the Periphery* (Leiden and Boston: Brill/Nijhoff, 2015). See also Gienow-Hecht, "Nation Branding: A Useful Category."
40. See series *Explorations in Culture and International History*, Berghahn Books, since 2003.
41. Jan Melissen, ed. *The New Public Diplomacy: Soft Power in International Relations*, (Basingstoke: Palgrave Macmillan, 2005).
42. Laura A. Belmonte, *Selling the American Way: U.S. Propaganda and the Cold War* (Philadelphia: University of Pennsylvania Press, 2008); Nicholas J. Cull, *The Cold War and the United States Information Agency: American Propaganda and Public Diplomacy, 1945–1989* (Cambridge: Cambridge University Press, 2009); John Fisher and Anthony Best, eds., *On the Fringes of Diplomacy: Influences on British Foreign Policy, 1800–1945* (Oxon, UK: Routledge, 2016); Jason C. Parker, *Hearts, Minds, Voices: U.S. Cold War Public Diplomacy and the Formation of the Third World* (Oxford: Oxford University Press, 2016).
43. Joseph S. Nye Jr., *The Paradox of American Power: Why the World's Only Superpower Can't Go It Alone* (Oxford: Oxford University Press, 2002), 8–9.

Bibliography

American Marketing Association. "Dictionary." Retrieved 10 October 2016 from https://www.ama.org/resources/pages/dictionary. aspx?dLetter=B.

Anderson, Benedict. *Imagined Communities: Reflections on the Origin and Spread of Nationalism*. London: Verso, 1983.

Anholt, Simon. "Nation-Brands of the Twenty-First Century." *Journal of Brand Management* 5, no. 6 (1998): 395–406.

———. *Brand New Justice: The Upside of Global Branding*. Oxford: Butterworth-Heinemann, 2003.

Aronczyk, Melissa. *Branding the Nation: The Global Business of National Identity*. Oxford: Oxford University Press, 2013.

Avery, Jill, and Anat Keinan. "Consuming Brands." In *The Cambridge Handbook of Consumer Psychology*, edited by Michael I. Norton, Derek D. Rucker, and Cait Lamberton, 209–32. New York: Cambridge University Press, 2015.

Bastos, Wilson, and Sidney J. Levy. "A History of the Concept of Branding: Practice and Theory." *Journal of Historical Research in Marketing* 4, no. 3 (2012): 347–68.

Behrenbeck, Sabine. *Der Kult um die toten Helden: Nationalsozialistische Mythen, Riten und Symbole, 1923–1945*. Vierow: SH-Verlag, 1996.

Belmonte, Laura A. *Selling the American Way: U.S. Propaganda and the Cold War*. Philadelphia, PA: University of Pennsylvania Press, 2008.

Clerc, Louis, Nikolas Glover, and Paul Jordan. *Histories of Public Diplomacy and Nation Branding in the Nordic and Baltic Countries: Representing the Periphery*. Leiden and Boston, MA: Brill/Nijhoff, 2015.

Cull, Nicholas J. "The Iron Brand: Margaret Thatcher and Public Diplomacy." *Place Branding and Public Diplomacy* 9, No. 2 (2013): 67–70. Retrieved 8 March 2016 from http://www.palgrave-journals. com/pb/journal/v9/n2/full/pb20139a.html.

———. *The Cold War and the United States Information Agency: American Propaganda and Public Diplomacy, 1945–1989*. Cambridge: Cambridge University Press, 2009.

Fisher, John and Anthony Best, eds. *On the Fringes of Diplomacy: Influences on British Foreign Policy, 1800–1945*. Oxon, UK: Routledge, 2016.

Fullerton, Jami A. "Introduction." In *Shaping International Public Opinion: A Model for Nation Branding and Public Diplomacy*, edited by Jami A. Fullerton and Alice Kendrick, 1–5. New York: Peter Lang, 2017.

Fullerton, Jami A., and Alice Kendrick. *Advertising's War on Terrorism: The Story of the U.S. State Department's Shared Values Initiative*. Spokane, WA: Marquette Books, 2006.

Gardner, Burleigh, and Sidney Levy. "The Product and the Brand." *Harvard Business Review* 33, March–April (1955): 33–39.

Gellner, Ernest. *Nations and Nationalism*. Oxford: Blackwell, 1983.

Gienow-Hecht, Jessica C. E. "Nation Branding: A Useful Category for the Study of International History," unpublished manuscript, 2016.

Golan, Guy J., and Sung-Un Yang. "Introduction: The Integrated Public Diplomacy Perspective." In *International Public Relations and Public Diplomacy Communication and Engagement,* edited by Guy J. Golan, Sung-Un Yang, and Dennis F. Kingsey, 1–12. New York: Peter Lang, 2015.

Goltermann, Svenja. *Körper der Nation: Habitusformierung und die Politik des Turnens 1860–1890*. Göttingen: Vandenhoeck & Ruprecht, 1989.

Ham, Peter van. "The Rise of the Brand State: The Postmodern Politics of Image and Reputation." *Foreign Affairs* 80, no. 5 (2001): 2–6.

Hansen, Per H. "Cobranding Product and Nation: Danish Modern Furniture and Denmark in the United States, 1940–1970." In *Trademarks, Brands, and Competitiveness*, edited by Teresa da Silva Lopes and Paul Duguid, 77–101. New York: Routledge, 2010.

Kaneva, Nadia, ed. *Branding Post-Communist Nations: Marketizing National Identities in the "New" Europe*. New York: Routledge, 2012.

Keller, Kevin Lane. "Branding and Brand Equity." In *Handbook of Marketing*, edited by Barton Weitz and Robin Wensley, 151–78. London: Sage Publication Ltd., 2002.

Kotler, Philip, Donald H. Haider, and Irving J. Rein. *Marketing Places: Attracting Investment, Industry, and Tourism to Cities, States, and Nations*. New York: Free Press, 1993.

Kotler, Philip, Somkid Jatusripitak, and Suvit Maesincee. *The Marketing of Nations: Strategic Approach to Building National Wealth*. New York: Free Press, 1997.

Kotler, Philip, Kevin Lane Keller, Mairead Brady, Malcolm Goodman, and Torben Hansen. *Marketing Management*. Harlow, UK: Pearson Education Limited, 2009.

Kunczik, Michael. *Images of Nations and International Public Relations*. Mahwah, NJ: Lawrence Erlbaum Associates, 1997.

Leonard, Mark. *Britain: Renewing Our Identity*. London: Demos, 1997. Retrieved 15 July 2016 from http://www.demos.co.uk/files/britaintm.pdf.

Lisowsky, Arthur. "Fremdenverkehrswerbung als Markenwerbung." *The Tourist Review* 2, no. 4 (1947): 133–35.

Martineau, Pierre. *Motivation in Advertising: Motives that Make People Buy*. New York: McGraw-Hill, 1957.

Melissen, Jan, ed. *The New Public Diplomacy: Soft Power in International Relations*. Basingstoke: Palgrave Macmillan, 2005.

Moor, Liz. *The Rise of Brands*. Oxford: Berg Publishers, 2007.

Moore, Karl, and Susan Reid. "The Birth of Brand: 4000 Years of Branding." *Business History* 50, no. 4 (2008): 419–32.

Nye, Joseph S., Jr. *The Paradox of American Power: Why the World's Only Superpower Can't Go It Alone*. Oxford: Oxford University Press, 2002.

Olins, Wally. *On Brand*. London: Thames & Hudson, 2003.

Parker, Jason C. *Hearts, Minds, Voices: U.S. Cold War Public Diplomacy and the Formation of the Third World*. Oxford: Oxford University Press, 2016.

Peterson, J. E. "Quatar and the World: Branding for a Micro-State," *The Middle East Journal* 60, no. 4 (2006): 732–748.

Plaisance, Patrick Lee. "The Propaganda War on Terrorism: An Analysis of the United States' 'Shared Values' Public-Diplomacy Campaign after September 11, 2001." *Journal of Mass Media Ethics* 20, no. 4 (2005): 250–68.

Renan, Ernest. *What Is a Nation?*, 1882, Retrieved 18 December 2017 from http://www.nationalismproject.org/what/renan.htm.

Schwarzkopf, Stefan. "Turning Trade Marks into Brands: How Advertising Agencies Practiced and Conceptualized Branding 1890–1930." In *Trademarks, Brands, and Competitiveness*, edited by Teresa da Silva Lopes and Paul Duguid, 165–94. New York: Routledge, 2010.

Temporal, Paul. *Branding for the Public Sector: Creating, Building and Managing Brands People Will Value*. Chichester, UK: Wiley, 2015.

Vogel, Jakob "2. September—Der Tag von Sedan." In *Erinnerungstage: Wendepunkte der Geschichte von der Antike bis zur Gegenwart*, edited by Etienne François and Uwe Puschner, 201–18, Munich: C. H. Beck Verlag, 2010.

Wey, Justus, and Christian Jens F. Barmbold. "Location Choice as a Signal for Product Quality: The Economics of 'Made in Germany.'" *Journal of Institutional and Theoretical Economics* 153, no. 3 (1997): 510–31.

Williams, Ernest. *Made in Germany*. London: Heinemann Haucap, 1896.

Part I
BRANDING THE NATION AND SELLING THE STATE
CASE STUDIES

Chapter 1

NATION BRANDING AMID CIVIL WAR
Publishing US Foreign Policy Documents to Define and Defend the Republic, 1861–66

William B. McAllister

To "brand" democracy, for example, and thus create widespread "purchase" of the democratic "product" in undemocratic countries, would surely be the least harmful, most cost-effective and most benign instrument of foreign policy that human ingenuity could devise.

— Simon Anholt, *Places: Identity, Image, and Reputation*

[M]ake no admissions of weakness in our Constitution, or of apprehension on the part of the government. You will rather prove, as you easily can, by comparing the history of our country with that of other states, that its Constitution and government are really the strongest and surest which have ever been erected for the safety of any people.

— US Secretary of State William Seward, 1861

Nation Branding in Historical Context

The *Foreign Relations of the United States* (*FRUS*) volumes, first produced by the federal government during the US Civil War, demonstrate that mid-nineteenth-century US officials apprehended the principles and employed many of the methods espoused by modern nation branding advocates.[1] Simon Anholt's "Competitive Identity" thesis stresses that managing a nation's internal self-image and

Notes for this section begin on page 46.

external reputation requires a "clear, credible, appealing, distinctive and thoroughly planned vision, identity and strategy."[2] Anholt emphasizes that good policy requires good governance practices, which include voice opportunities and accountability; the government must employ mechanisms to receive citizen input, to account for foreign perceptions, and to report what it has done in the people's name.[3] Nadia Kaneva characterizes "the most ambitious architects of nation-branding" in the twenty-first century as promoting a receptor-sensitive creation/implementation/reconsideration cycle as an integral element of policy formulation and governance because that approach holds the potential to (re)constitute nations "at the levels of *ideology*, and of *praxis*,"[4] and Fiona Gilmore states that the goal of nation branding is to "amplify the existing values of the national culture."[5] For Keith Dinnie, the term denotes a polity that possesses a "sustainable differential advantage" derived from a "unique, multidimensional blend of elements that provide the nation with a culturally grounded . . . relevance for all of its target audiences."[6] These modern definitions echo the understanding of Secretary of State William Seward and his US government colleagues who promoted what one could label today the "Union brand" in its nineteenth century context during the Civil War era.[7]

Federal officials recognized that the validity of the "Union brand" depended on how the diplomatic policies they pursued, as well as their demonstration of accountability to the public concerning those policies, embodied US political values. Union leaders promoted the constitutional-republican system to domestic and foreign audiences as a unique and superior form of government. *FRUS* volumes exemplified how popular sovereignty suffused the process of governance, embodying the principal elements of Anholt's "Competitive Identity" nexus: brand identity (creating shared meaning among citizens and external audiences), brand image (developing a consistent, positive reputation acknowledged at home and abroad), brand equity (recognizing the asset value of reputation), and brand purpose (leveraging the power of goals held in common across domestic and international constituencies).[8] The Lincoln administration, particularly in the iconic figure of Secretary of State William Seward, presented US constitutional government praxis as credible, legitimate, powerful, and replicable; the volumes' producers took it as axiomatic that the Union drew its strength from an informed, engaged electorate and that the extension of representative government to other countries would mutually benefit all the world's inhabitants.

Comparisons with twenty-first-century concepts and practices must necessarily account for the small size and circumscribed mandate of nineteenth-century governments. In 1860, the domestic staff of the Department of State totaled a mere forty-two persons; diplomatic and consular officials abroad totaled only 282 souls.[9] The US archival record contains little of the information necessary to provide a detailed assessment of precisely which role(s) nineteenth-century actors played that could be directly compared to their twenty-first-century counterparts formally tasked with nation branding. Government bureaucracies were so small that officials rarely created records of internal discussions. Although in a few instances a modicum of personal material survives that sheds some indirect light on the inner workings of government, we know little about their daily activities. The scope of government activity also remained limited: officials promoted trade and economic development, but no sophisticated transnational corporate entities or marketing techniques necessary to forge modern public-private partnerships existed. Nor did international tourism comprise a significant phenomenon. The use of iconographic shortcuts to convey meaning was less prevalent—government messaging relied much more on documents—and the format of *FRUS* volumes (text-heavy by modern standards) constituted a standard communications medium of the period.

Conversely, nineteenth-century practitioners faced problems and deployed strategies similar to those of modern nation branders.[10] Civil War-era leaders operated in a "mediatized" environment: the combination of increasingly ubiquitous periodical publications, ever-longer-distance telegraphy, and progressively faster steam transportation facilitated an unprecedented volume and speed of communication. Indeed, the government created a regularly scheduled documentary publication precisely to influence the intercontinental exchange of what contemporaries often labeled "intelligence." Lincoln, Seward, and their colleagues fully understood the need for horizontal alliance building and coordinating vertical integration; near-contemporaneous dissemination of official foreign policy documents to myriad educational, religious, business, media, civic, and diplomatic communities secured support from below and facilitated multilevel policy making, policy implementation, and messaging. *FRUS* operated as an instrumental mechanism that highlighted the agency of the nineteenth-century equivalent of "brand managers" (the foremost example being Seward). Those framers recognized the interactive element that underpinned their efforts: citizens (in modern parlance, a category of "stakeholders") completed the input cycle by voting, paying taxes, and sacrificing their lives for the constitutional-republican order. The Civil War-era *FRUS* branded not only policies, but also governance processes, government organizations, and government officials. The constitutional-republic system lauded in its pages suffused the essence of a nineteenth-century version of the "Union brand." The Department of State, the Office of the President, and the executive and legislative branches featured prominently in both the production and the content of the volumes. Seward's predominant role as chief architect and principal author of documents in the series left an indelible impression on contemporaries.

Consequently, the case presented here primarily extrapolates "inward" from the information, perspectives, and context provided by published official correspondence. US diplomats and politicians contributed to a corporate branding effort—each believed themselves responsible for presenting, representing, embodying, and contributing to both the identity-(re)definition as well as the practice of republican values.[11] This chapter makes no distinction between nation branding, "Competitive Identity," and public diplomacy because Civil War-era federal officials, had they encountered such language, would have treated them as part of a holistic package.[12] Because Seward featured as the lynchpin correspondent in the inaugural *FRUS* volumes, the diplomatic instructions he sent and the dispatches he received comprise the principal evidence of intent and assumptions.

The "Union Brand" and Branding the Union: Achieving Credibility and Binding by "Living" the Constitution

Defining the nation-branding task facing Civil War-era government officials can be readily conveyed using Anholt's admonition that governments and citizens must "live the brand."[13] Federal leaders conceived the Union as consisting of a constitutional-republican form of government that comprised the highest expression of popular sovereignty. They believed their authority derived from the consent of the populace exemplified by responsible government: citizens voted and their representatives held the executive branch accountable by requiring, inter alia, frequent reports. The president's officials routinely responded quickly by releasing information about government operations or policies. Congress regularly published the

contents of executive branch documents, which informed the citizenry in a timely manner and enabled them to influence subsequent
policy discussions.[14] Executive branch leaders recognized that for
the nation to survive they must pursue a multifaceted strategy
to promote and embody the "Union brand" to an array of domestic and foreign audiences. Their task entailed not only explaining,
but also doing—the functioning of the system comprised both the
how and the why of the motivating action to preserve the Union.
FRUS volumes served as an integral component of the system that
generated support among the domestic populace by exemplifying
responsible government. Simultaneously, the books aimed to influence foreign governments' diplomatic policies, as well as to promote
the benefits of representative-responsible government to ordinary
people in other countries. The contents of the early *FRUS* volumes
indicate the importance Civil War-era officials ascribed to the
strategy Anholt recommends in the quote that heads this chapter:
replicating representative regimes abroad comprised the best way
to advance US interests. Demonstrating how a republic operated
to benefit "the people" proved the attractiveness of the "Union
brand," and encouraged inhabitants of other countries to demand
similar forms of representative-responsible government. The *Foreign
Relations of the United States* publication, therefore, served as both
an instrument of nation branding and an integral element of the
constitutional-republic brand.

Nation branding advocates have increasingly stressed the
primacy of the political sphere by noting that even a good public
relations campaign cannot make up for "bad policy."[15] This movement represents an important shift because the essential task of government is not to generate profit. Most fundamentally, states require
recognition; they must be "seen" as legitimate performers on the
world stage. Otherwise, states, such as those of the Armenians, the
Kurds, or the German polities denied a return to independent status
at the Congress of Vienna, literally do not exist. States require both
internal and external assent to their being in order to exercise any of
the faculties attendant to government. In practice, this often means
not profit, but loss. For example, although Norway[16] and Austria[17]
had very different international reputations in 1945, governmental leaders in both countries committed their states to significant
involvement in UN peacekeeping operations. This policy certainly
depleted national coffers—peacekeeping is intrinsically unprof-
itable. Nevertheless, both states judged the gain in transnational
political capital worth the expenditure. Current-day nation branders

advise clients that to support revenue accretion, governments must conform to international norms about best-practice standards, policies, and procedures.[18] To receive recognition, states require credibility, which depends on a complex interplay of relationships across domestic constituencies and recognized external actors taking place on a shifting playing field of expectations about state behavior.

This chapter highlights the centrality of state cohesion to the nation branding enterprise. The assumption of modern nation branding is that a recognized state already exists and that some modicum of agreement also exists about the goal of the campaign, at least among those who wield authority to project an image of the country. *FRUS*, however, emerged in an extraordinary moment when the very nature and existence of the nation was at issue. The Civil War represented, at its essence, a multifaceted dispute about what the country stood for, including the fundamental purpose of the system and the process by which government and constituents interacted. The 1861–65 *FRUS* volumes demonstrate the importance federal officials ascribed to exemplifying the nation through the exercise of responsible government.[19]

For example, at the outset of the conflict Union officials blockaded cotton exports, a policy inimical to the modern normative nation branding approach. Branding advocates today would typically prescribe capitalizing on the country's principal commodity and best-known product abroad. The US government, however, aimed to eliminate a major Confederate revenue stream, even though doing so hurt domestic shipping interests and disrupted foreign factory workers, who were otherwise well-disposed to support the Union cause.

Given these unique circumstances, the founders of *FRUS* implicitly apprehended the essential objective identified by modern nation branding advocates: binding. To support the state with their tax money, their votes, and their lives on the field of battle, citizens must have the experience of constructing and participating in government. Both foreign and domestic stakeholders expect government policies and governance processes to reflect their values. Put negatively, the goal was to avoid any further domestic or international "brand detachment" because Confederate secession already represented a profound defection from the "Union brand."[20] Seward and his colleagues created an official documentary publication program as a concrete expression of the inclusive, responsible, republican form of government. They succeeded to such an extent that they forged a brand community of adherents well beyond US borders.

Translating Nation Branding to a Nineteenth-Century Setting

The inaugural *FRUS* volumes comprised an important element of the overall federal campaign that promoted constitutional-republicanism in a "brandscape" hostile to representative government. In modern parlance, US officials posited a "country-of-origin" advantage for the "Union brand" because (save small entities such as the Hanseatic Republics and nominally-independent San Marino) the United States claimed a unique system of government.[21] Although leaders pursuing nineteenth-century-European nation building in France, Italy, the German states, and elsewhere often acknowledged the *vox populi* in some fashion, both "democracy" and "republic" remained much-disparaged concepts.[22] From the Union perspective, rebel Confederates illegally rejected the participative processes that defined the United States as a nation. Publishing recent diplomatic correspondence illustrated that a republic operated by maintaining an open dialogue among its citizens, even concerning sensitive, controversial topics. If the essence of nation branding is to enhance binding stakeholder involvement in government and governance processes, *FRUS* volumes exemplified how executive branch transparency-accountability practices engaged citizens.

The books also served politico-strategic purposes beyond US shores. The published correspondence presented a warning to potential adversaries about the magnitude of US power, exemplified by the strength of its governmental institutions and practices. Disseminating diplomatic documents also solicited allies by offering overt encouragement for those abroad who yearned to live under similarly representative systems. Even while facing the greatest crisis in the history of the nation, US officials judged their constitutional arrangements sufficiently robust to launch a worldwide ideological-rhetorical offensive.

Concerning the many examples and lengthy quotes cited below, note that Union officials knew at the time of writing that their correspondence would be published. They made the record available no later than one year (and sometimes as soon as one month) after the originals had been written. Seward and others took advantage of this near-contemporaneous publication practice to generate substantial domestic and international political benefits. Policy makers considered the process by which the United States reported to its citizenry equally important as the content of the correspondence published, cleverly combining information and exemplary practice into a compelling package.

FRUS as Both Brand and Branding-in-Action

Most importantly, the volumes exhibited Union resolve. Seward deployed all manner of persuasion and threat to dissuade foreign powers from recognizing the Confederacy as a legitimate entity. *FRUS* publicized the Secretary's instructions to US representatives around the globe to tout the strength of federal armed forces, to disparage reports of Union military defeats, to counteract the machinations of Confederate diplomatic envoys and military procurement agents, to advocate the exclusion of "pirate" rebel merchant ships from foreign ports, and to explain how the workings of the Constitution served as the bedrock of citizen loyalty.[23]

US officials grasped the importance stressed by modern nation branders of highlighting essentialized national characteristics, enhanced by deploying the differentiation tactic. The volumes emphasized the uniqueness and special strengths of responsible government as exemplified by the Union-republic. In his first circular, Seward instructed ministers to stress, "the people themselves still retain and cherish a profound confidence in our happy Constitution, together with a veneration and affection for it such as no other form of government ever received at the hands of those for whom it was established."[24] Seward's statement to aggressively promote the "Union brand" cited at the beginning of this chapter was bold indeed: he penned it one week after the disastrous 1861 First Manassas battle and approved its release to the world only four months later. In his first missive to Minister William Dayton in Paris, which Seward no doubt constructed for public consumption as well as Dayton's edification, the secretary cheekily highlighted the distinction between the American example and the coup-plebiscite Louis Napoleon engineered to terminate the Second Republic: "The Emperor of France has given abundant proofs that he considers the people in every country the rightful source of authority and that its only legitimate objects are their safety, freedom, and welfare. He is versed in our Constitution, and, therefore, he will not need demonstration that the system which is established by the Constitution is founded strictly on those very principles."[25]

In case readers missed the comparative point, Seward elaborated about the US system: "Not one human life has hitherto been forfeited for disloyalty to the government, nor has martial law ever been established except temporarily in case of invasion. No other people have ever enjoyed so much immunity from the various forms of political casualties and calamities."[26] The secretary contrasted the consensual nature of the federal union with "the central military authority which, in other systems, secures the integrity as well as the peace and harmony of States."[27] Seward also published differentiating reports from his ministers abroad. From Berlin, Minister Norman Judd lamented that the Prussian people had "not yet reached the sublimity of fighting for an idea, viz: constitutional rights—the practical benefits of which are little understood by the masses of the present generation of Prussians."[28]

Union correspondents simultaneously distinguished the US system from the problems commonly associated in the nineteenth-century mind with unfettered democracy. Madrid Legation Secretary Horatio Perry labored to counteract the impression left by his pro-Confederate predecessor that the US government acted as an aggressive, "underbred, *sans cullotte* democracy."[29] Seward also associated US constitutional arrangements with similar government brands of proven repute. To Minister-resident in Switzerland George Fogg, Seward predicted the representative-responsible character of Swiss and US government institutions would "be honored as the founders of the only true and beneficent system of human government—a system that harmonizes needful authority with the preservation of the natural rights of man."[30]

Seward even found a silver lining in divisive partisan politics. During the 1862 congressional campaign, the secretary trumpeted how the "Union brand" derived its strength from robust political debate enabled by the Constitution:

> it is not to be inferred that either party, or any considerable portion of the people of loyal States, is disposed to accept disunion under any circumstances, or upon any terms. It is rather to be understood that the people have become so confident of the stability of the Union that partisan combinations are resuming their sway here, as they do in such cases in all free countries. In this country, especially, it is a habit not only entirely consistent with the Constitution, but even essential to its stability, to regard the administration at any time existing as distinct and separable from the government itself, and to canvass the proceedings of the one without the thought of disloyalty to the other. We might possibly have had quicker success in suppressing the insurrection if this habit could have rested a little longer in abeyance; but, on the

other hand, we are under obligations to save not only the integrity or unity of the country, but also its inestimable and precious Constitution.[31]

News of Lincoln's 1864 re-election prompted Charles Francis Adams in London to report: "It would be difficult to overestimate the importance of this event, in its influence upon the reputation of the nation throughout Europe. Very happily, too, the result has been arrived at without any appearance of popular disturbance."[32] Judd despatched excerpts from leading German-language newspapers indicating that during the campaign, "all deeds and shortcomings, successes and failures, causes and effects, on the part of the administration, have been sifted through" and "that a tribunal, even higher than Congress, has approved of his administration."[33] The routine operation of the Constitution's provisions, even amid insurrection, presented to audiences both domestic and foreign a powerful demonstration-statement about the solidity of the republic.

Federal officials also treated what is now called public diplomacy[34] as an integral element in forging the credibility and legitimacy of the "Union brand." Seward appealed beyond formal diplomatic circles to opinion and organization leaders as well as ordinary people. For example, the secretary instructed Minister to Denmark Bradford Wood to promote the "Union brand" among the smaller states of Europe because "political action even of the more commanding or more active States is influenced by a general opinion that is formed imperceptibly in all parts of the Eastern continent."[35] To Fogg in Berne he wrote, "the sentiments and opinions which influence the conduct and affect the prospects of nations are very often formed in the mountains and dells of Switzerland."[36]

Especially in a context of internecine conflict, federal officials recognized the necessity of defining, exemplifying, and promoting the "Union brand" at home. Members of Congress disseminated multiple copies across their districts to public and private libraries, prominent individuals, and ordinary citizens. To disseminate more documents, the Department of State significantly increased the number of pages published each year, and Congress appropriated funds to produce tens of thousands of volumes. Newspapers and individual readers lauded the strong positions espoused by US diplomats and declared themselves heartened by the volumes' illustration of responsible government in action.[37]

Seward counteracted the natural suspicion that official government publications smack of propaganda by printing very sensitive material, sometimes over the protests of his staff. US diplomats sporadically objected to publishing their messages so quickly, complaining they could hardly be expected to convey honestly to Washington their true assessments only to see them published a few months later. Seward unabashedly supported the openness principle in the name of popular sovereignty, stating: "The Government continually depends upon the support of Congress and the People, and that support can be expected only in the condition of keeping them thoroughly and truthfully informed of the manner in which the powers derived from them are executed."[38] Many preferred that approach to hiring nongovernment intermediaries. In 1864, Congressman Henry Davis applauded the continued publication of official diplomatic correspondence because it comprised

> the only mode that the Government has of stating its case authentically and fully to the nations of Europe. If it is not allowed to state it in that form it will be driven to the very questionable if not disreputable method of buying up the public press of Europe, as the rebels are in the habit of doing continually, for the purpose of manufacturing public opinion. [Seward] thought it better to have an authentic declaration of the opinions of the Government spread before the nations of Europe, official in form, for which we are responsible, and carrying with it the weight of official declarations.[39]

Note the emphasis on process: the way in which the republic's officials enacted responsible government by informing the electorate instilled confidence and credibility, which contributed to the system's legitimacy and strength. In the mid nineteenth century, members of both the executive and legislative branches judged it inappropriate to devolve management of the nation's image upon private contractors specializing in public relations.

Federal officials also used the publication of diplomatic correspondence to influence foreign geopolitical calculations. In presenting his credentials to Tsar Alexander II, Minister Simon Cameron carried a message from President Lincoln stressing the link between popular support for the republic and military prowess. Averring that "my government is able to meet all exigencies" Cameron stated, "the promptitude with which her citizens came to the call of the President, and the existence of our present mighty army, prove that we shall never want soldiers to maintain our domestic security or to defend our national honor."[40] Federal officials understood such missives were also read in more threatening capitals such as London and Paris. Seward signaled US disapproval of any UK move toward recognizing the Confederacy, rendered diplomatically as the Lincoln administration's expectation of "a continued reliance upon the practice of justice and respect for our sovereignty by foreign powers." Moreover, the secretary threatened widening the conflict, "if this reliance fails, this civil war will, without our fault, become a war of continents—a war of the world." He declared that the United States could at any time call upon three hundred thousand men in addition to those already in uniform, and that several hundred thousand more could be enrolled if necessary.[41] Broadcasting such messages in foreign capitals made clear the US government's readiness to use force against other nations if they supported the rebel cause beyond the limits of federal tolerance. Seward's missives indicated that the capacity to follow through stemmed from the constitutional-republican system that generated such exceptional popular support, which illustrated the wellsprings of power underpinning the "Union brand."

Union officials also published *realpolitik* arguments to persuade foreign audiences that supporting the federal cause advanced their interests as well. Perry emphasized to Madrid that leaders of the rebellion had only a few years previously advocated war with Spain to conquer Cuba. Stating that "secession was filibustering struck in," he intimated that Confederate success would lead to attacks on Spanish Caribbean colonies.[42] Seward claimed that if the rebellion succeeded: "The equilibrium of the nations, maintained by this republic, on the one side, against the European system on the other continent, would be lost, and the struggles of nations in that system for dominion in this hemisphere and on the high seas, which constitutes the chief portion of the world's history in the eighteenth century, would be renewed."[43]

To policy makers abroad it may have appeared arrogant to claim that the continued coherence of the United States preserved stability in Europe. For many readers, however, the specter of reproducing a fractious European-style balance of power in the New World provided a powerful argument to support the Union. Governance values underlay state power as the ultimate determinant of legitimacy and profoundly affected international stability; after Union battlefield successes and Lincoln's reelection, *FRUS* editors published Minister to Austria John Motley's November 1863 assessment of the larger implications of the Schleswig-Holstein controversy: "One would have thought that the time had gone by for wars of succession; but they must, perhaps, periodically recur, as results of the European principle, that great countries, with all their inhabitants, are the private property of a small number of privileged families. The probable attitude of the great powers on this question is far more important than the legal aspects of the case."[44]

Recognizing that liberals and laborers across Europe grasped the impact of the contest upon their interests, the editors of *FRUS* published pro-Union declarations from citizen groups, political clubs, and workingmen's associations forwarded by US representatives abroad. At a London Trades Union meeting, Adams reported that one speaker characterized the issue as "a question of free labor, the result of which must directly affect their own cause by raising or lowering the price of labor and the condition of laboring men socially and politically all over the world."[45] The Union and Emancipation Society of Manchester railed against pro-Confederate agents as "the enemies of free government, free labor, and free education."[46] Whether one wishes to apply retroactively categories of analysis such as soft/hard power to these nineteenth-century rhetorical deployments, today's nation branders would certainly acknowledge the value of highlighting crucial similarities of interest to constituencies in other countries. Union communications conveyed a potent package of values and incentives attractive to many audiences.

The volumes also engaged in reverse counterbranding by parrying Confederate efforts to legitimize their secessionist state.[47] In marketing terms, the Richmond government represented a challenger brand that attempted to authenticate its existence by redefining public sector values.[48] Confederate apologists emphasized carefully circumscribed definitions of "freedom," states' rights, and unimpeded trade. Federal officials promoted the Union government as a dominant brand by claiming the legal and moral high ground. Stressing the illegitimacy of rebellion resonated with European governments, many of which feared insurrection. Antislavery arguments appealed to religious, liberal, and laboring constituencies, and the United States recognized Liberia and Haiti in 1862.[49] In a telling example of the Union's domination of the message market, UK officials judged the 1861 publication so important that they reprinted the entire volume and reproduced the three-hundred-page section of British correspondence from the 1862 book.[50]

Measuring Success: How the "Union Brand" Played in Peoria, Pomerania, and Peking

One extraordinary Civil War-era *FRUS* volume provides uniquely valuable evidence about audience reception, the most vexing question of governance, diplomacy, and branding. After President Lincoln's assassination, Washington received messages of condolence and support for the Union from all over the world. Congress judged the missives so compelling that they approved two substantial print runs of a special *FRUS* volume to commemorate this global outpouring of grief and favor for constitutional government. The book's 717 pages featured 1,411 messages from all levels of government, media outlets, nongovernment organizations, and individuals across the six inhabited continents. This "Lincoln Volume" demonstrates federal success in promoting the constitutional-republic as both a system and a process.[51] In Anholt's terms, the "Lincoln Volume" clearly illustrates the coalescence of "Union brand" identity, image, equity, and purpose into a powerful resource supporting the US government's credibility.

The volume's official correspondence far exceeded the traditional state-to-state domain of diplomatic communications. Over forty countries, practically all those generally recognized as independent states, conveyed their condolences.[52] The administrations of European dependencies in British Guiana, Canada, Cuba, Macao, and St Croix communicated independently. The superior legislatures of most European and Latin American states promulgated proclamations. Moreover, the book's editors included letters from municipal councils across Latin America, Europe, and the United States. The Union's branding efforts penetrated well beyond the national level of government.

Additionally, the "Lincoln Volume" is the only book in the series that includes a large number of messages from nongovernment actors, which highlights the success of what might today be called the "Union brand" marketing and customer mobilization efforts. Within the United States, benevolent societies, spontaneous assemblies of citizens, religious organizations, chambers of commerce, corporate boards of directors, college trustees, social clubs, and veterans' organizations submitted declarations, resolutions, and even poems memorializing Lincoln. Missives came from American expatriates abroad and foreign nationals residing in the United States, including immigrants so recently arrived that their letters required translation into English. Condolences even arrived from southern cities, including a resolution approved by an overflow crowd in Savannah, which had been occupied by Federal troops only four months before the assassination.[53] The volume featured similar missives from a plethora of foreign nongovernmental groups. In addition to numerous articles from the periodical press, the editors included communications from voluntary associations such as Masonic lodges in France and Belgium, the Working Men's Club of Berlin, the Turners Society of Kappel am Rhein in the Grand Duchy of Baden, local evangelical alliances, students at the Paris School of Medicine, the Union of Operatives in Genoa, the working classes of Tarare, Swiss residents of Ottoman Bucharest, and inhabitants of municipalities across Europe and the Americas. This array of audiences represented a significant departure for a publication designed to convey government-to-government communications; the global response indicates the success of direct US appeals to ordinary people, promoting the US view that popular sovereignty should serve as the basis of government.

Many condolences also lauded the US governance system and American political values. The Spanish Democratic Committee of Buenos Aires hoped that "republican principles may triumph wherever the want of liberty is felt."[54] Belgian parliamentarians declared they had already judged US institutions worthy of emulation: "We have followed their example in all that regards public liberty, the distribution of power, the election of representatives and decentralization of rule."[55] The *Ulster Observer* (Belfast) opined:

> It is the privilege of republics to be free from the perils which beset countries in which power is centered in an individual or a dynasty. The loss of the President of the United States is great, but the Constitution can repair it . . . those who have steadily watched the history of the past cannot doubt that the future will prove the stability of the institutions that have survived so many rude and awful shocks.[56]

Observers also recognized that the Constitution addressed the greatest challenge of government: ensuring the orderly, legitimate succession of power. Despite the assassination, the US political system suffered no appreciable disruption. The editors of four leading French newspapers jointly wrote: "The Constitution of your country has forever put American democracy beyond the possibility of being affected by the violence done to persons. Where liberty reigns, where the law alone governs, the first magistrates may perish without shaking or even threatening the institutions."[57] Minister Resident in Brussels Henry Sanford reinforced the credibility and differentiation of the constitutional-republic "Union brand," contrasting the "calm transition" with that likely to occur in most European states, which confirmed "the power, fitness, and durability of our system of government."[58] Chinese Foreign Minister Prince Kung noted that "the Vice-President succeeded to the position without any disturbance, and the assassin had been arrested, so that the affairs of government were going on quietly as usual."[59] One can hardly imagine a more powerful international advertisement for US governance institutions; the compilers of this special *FRUS* volume no doubt understood the value of such statements for audiences both domestic and foreign.

The "Lincoln Volume" exemplifies the constellation of attributes that comprise Anholt's concept of "citizen value."[60] A nineteenth-century version of "brand ambassadors" reshaped a preexisting national identity and embodied its institutional-systemic operation. Those federal efforts, including *FRUS*, activated what Dinnie describes as a "diaspora"—a "pre-existing network" of potential "Union brand" supporters.[61] Anholt describes the result as "positive bias";[62] these "consumers," both at home and abroad, derived an image of the "Union brand" that elicited "affective loyalty" as discussed by Dinnie.[63] This volume demonstrates how closely officials and ordinary people, even in remote locales, followed events in the United States; many of their homages recounted the late president's policies and pronouncements in great detail. Many communications also decried the simultaneous attacks that wounded the Secretary and his son Frederick, who served as Assistant Secretary of State. Readers of the volumes might reasonably conclude that William Seward embodied the republic nearly as much as the president; he received good wishes for a full recovery (and for his son as well) from around the world. Minister Resident George Yeaman described this "affective loyalty," reporting from Denmark: "Of the views expressed as to the result of the war, in establishing our nationality and bestowing freedom on a race, [King Christian IX] manifested a clear appreciation and approval ... he hoped [the United States] would now forever remain one people and one nation."[64]

Nation Branding: Not So New Under the Sun

Civil wars present the ultimate test of legitimacy. Seward understood the equation, supporting his pronouncements about the credibility of the constitutional-republic "Union brand" with the acid test of creditworthiness. With the outcome very much in doubt, the secretary published an 1862 communication to Adams sure to impress European financial centers: "Neither the government nor the country has experienced exhaustion, or even financial pressure, but in the midst of wars and campaigns the fiscal condition of both is satisfactory, and superior to that of any other government and people . . . we invite a premature return of all our bonds and stocks, and will pay and redeem in gold."[65]

Union branding efforts succeeded sufficiently to support such rhetoric. Despite the fragility of federal funding arrangements through at least 1864, creditors continued to loan money and greenback dollars retained value far in excess of the ruinous inflation that wrecked Confederate finances. The lack of recognition—not merely diplomatic but more generally of their "brand" as a credible entity— doomed the Confederacy. Put in modern nation branding terms, Richmond failed to secure sufficient binding from domestic constituencies and international audiences because neither their ideology nor their praxis proved supportable.

In the iterative "living" of the mid-nineteenth-century constitutional-republican "Union brand," *FRUS* volumes operated an *ikon* in the sense utilized by Eastern Orthodox churches. More than mere representations, *ikons* claim to serve as a portal into, and a manifestation of, true reality. *FRUS* acted as a mechanism to address the "encapsulation problem": how to present the essence of a multidimensional socio-cultural-economic polity.[66] The Civil War *FRUS* conforms to Anholt's depiction of the distillate function: "The true art of nation-branding is distillation: the art of extracting the concentrated essence of something complex, so that its complexity can always be extracted back out of the distillate, but it remains portable and easily memorable. The distillate, rather than actually attempting to contain all the detail of the country in question, is simply the common thread, the genetic constant, which underlies the basic commonality between the different parts of the brand."[67]

Had Seward and his colleagues read such a definition, one can easily imagine their response would have been "of course!"

William B. McAllister is Special Projects Division Chief in the Office of the Historian, Department of State, and adjunct associate professor at the Georgetown University Graduate School of Foreign Service. McAllister has published widely on the history of international drug control, compiled volumes for the *Foreign Relations of the United States* series, served as Acting General Editor of the series, and directed, edited, and contributed to *Toward "Thorough, Accurate, and Reliable": A History of the "Foreign Relations of the United States"*

Series, which won the 2015 George Pendleton Prize awarded by the Society for History in the Federal Government.

The interpretations of this chapter are the author's and do not necessarily represent any official position of the Office of the Historian or the Department of State.

Notes

Epigraph: Secretary of State Seward to Charles Francis Adams, US Minister to the United Kingdom, 29 July 1861, *Message of the President of the United States to the Two Houses of Congress at the Commencement of the Second Session of the Thirty-Seventh Congress* (Washington: Government Printing Office, 1861), 124 (hereafter *Message, 1861*).

1. William B. McAllister, Joshua Botts, Peter Cozzens, and Aaron Marrs, *Toward "Thorough, Accurate, and Reliable": A History of the Foreign Relations of the United States Series* (Washington, DC: GPO, 2015) (hereafter *TTAR*), especially Chapter 2. I am indebted to Aaron Marrs for his pioneering work on this topic. For *FRUS* volumes online, see http://history.state.gov/historicaldocuments.
2. Simon Anholt, *Competitive Identity: The New Brand Management for Nations, Cities, and Regions* (Houndmills: Palgrave Macmillan, 2007), chapter 1, quote from 21.
3. Anholt, *Competitive Identity*, chapter 2; Simon Anholt, *Brand New Justice: How Branding Places and Products Can Help the Developing World*, rev. ed. (Oxford: Butterworth-Heinemann, 2005), 1–30. This chapter disputes Anholt's claim that the concept of "Competitive Identity" constitutes a "new approach to statecraft" (*Places*, 8); many elements of nineteenth-century US inclusive-responsive-cooperative-functional practice consisted of the strategy + substance + symbolic action model that he describes (*Places*, 13–19).
4. Nadia Kaneva, "Nation Branding: Toward an Agenda for Critical Research," *International Journal of Communication* 5 (2011): 118, 126, emphasis in original.
5. Fiona Gilmore, quoted in Keith Dinnie, *Nation Branding: Concepts, Issues, Practice* (Oxford: Butterworth-Heinemann 2008), 18n23.
6. Dinnie, *Nation Branding*, 4–5.
7. For a constructivist analytical approach that emphasizes theoretical considerations distinct from the functionalism of Anholt, Dinnie, etc., see Ian Somerville, Owen Hargie, Maureen Taylor, and Margalit Toledano, eds., *International Public Relations: Perspectives from Deeply Divided Societies* (New York: Routledge, 2017). This book focuses on societies in conflict, useful in considering the American Civil War example, and highlights potentially applicable concepts such as "entiativity," "actorhood," "agnetic capacity," and "entity-agent frameworks."
8. Anholt, *Competitive Identity*, 5–7.
9. https://history.state.gov/about/faq/department-personnel;   https://history.state.gov/about/faq/diplomatic-and-consular-posts; https://history.state.gov/departmenthistory/short-history/reorganized.
10. Jasper Eshuis and Erik-Hans Klijn, eds., *Branding in Governance and Public Management* (New York: Routledge, 2012) overviews concepts of modern nation

branding including governance definitions, branding in governance processes, distinctions between instrumental and horizontal approaches to branding, counterbranding, and functional and symbolic elements of branding.

11. Dinnie, *Nation Branding*, 72, provides a roughly analogous example of brand networks.

12. Anholt describes the most advanced ("Stage III") type of public diplomacy as an "instrument of policy" (*Places*, 100–1). This chapter argues that nineteenth-century US government officials utilized *FRUS* as part of their strategy to embody and promote a similar iterative dynamic. Dinnie's, *Nation Branding*, 127, description of public diplomacy (news management, strategic communications, and relationship building) comports with much of the approach deployed by Civil War era officials to forge and promote the "Union brand."

13. Anholt, *Competitive Identity*, chapter 1, 56 (quote from 16); Anholt, *Places*, 109.

14. *FRUS* emerged from longstanding responsible government practices: *TTAR*, chapter 1.

15. Lee Hudson Teslik, "Nation Branding Explained," Council on Foreign Relations, 2007.

16. "Norway in the UN."

17. "The participation in peacekeeping operations represents one of Austria's most essential contributions to the United Nations' efforts to maintain peace and international security." "The Vienna International Centre," 5.

18. Anholt, *Places*, 20–23, 45–47.

19. For a recent publication that applies nation branding concepts to societies in conflict, see Somerville, et al., *International Public Relations*.

20. Dinnie, *Nation Branding*, 66.

21. Anholt, *Competitive Identity*, 9–10, Dinnie, *Nation Branding*, chapter 4.

22. Joanna Innes and Mark Philip, eds., *Re-Imagining Democracy in the Age of Revolutions: America, France, Britain, Ireland 1750–1850* (Oxford: Oxford University Press, 2013).

23. *TTAR*, 22–26.

24. Seward to All Ministers of the United States, 9 March 1861, *Message*, 1861, 23. Sent to Madrid, Brussels, Berne, Berlin, Vienna, Constantinople, London, Paris, St Petersburg, and The Hague.

25. Seward to Dayton, 22 April 1861, *Message*, 1861, 196.

26. Seward to Dayton.

27. Seward to Dayton, 199.

28. Judd to Seward, 2 February 1864, *Papers Relating to Foreign Affairs, Accompanying the Annual Message of the President to the Second Session Thirty-Eighth Congress*, Part IV (Washington, DC: Government Printing Office, 1864), 200 (hereafter *FRUS* 1864:IV).

29. Perry to Seward, 21 September 1862, *Message of the President of the United States to the Two Houses of Congress at the Commencement of the Third Session of the Thirty-Seventh Congress* (Washington, DC: Government Printing Office, 1862), 515 (hereafter *Message*, 1862).

30. Seward to Fogg, 15 May 1861, *Message*, 1861, 330.

31. Seward to Adams, 10 November 1862, *Message*, 1862, 233–34.

32. Adams to Seward, 25 November 1864, *Papers Relating to Foreign Affairs, Accompanying the Annual Message of the President to the First Session Thirty-Ninth Congress*, Part I (Washington, DC: Government Printing Office, 1865), 1 (hereafter *FRUS* 1864:I).

33. Judd to Seward, 12 January 1865, *Executive Documents Printed by Order of the House of Representatives during the First Session of the Thirty-Ninth Congress, 1865–66,* Part III (Washington, DC: Government Printing Office, 1866), 42–43 (hereafter *FRUS* 1865:III).

34. Public diplomacy is generally defined today as government attempts to influence foreign audiences and foreign public opinion directly rather than communicating solely through official state-to-state channels.

35. Seward to Wood, 1 May 1861, *Message,* 1861, 311.

36. Seward to Fogg, 15 May 1861, *Message,* 1861, 329.

37. *TTAR,* 35–39, Appendix B.

38. Seward to Adams, 2 March 1864, *TTAR,* 18.

39. *TTAR,* 37. This passage indicates that Richmond also grasped the imperatives of nation branding.

40. Cameron to Seward, 26 June 1862, *Message,* 1862, 447.

41. Seward to Adams, 28 July 1862, *Message,* 1862, 157.

42. Perry to Seward, 13 June 1861, *Message,* 1861, 261.

43. Seward to Cassius Clay, US Minister to St Petersburg, 6 May 1861, *Message,* 1861, 296.

44. Motley to Seward, 24 November 1863, *FRUS* 1864:IV, 131.

45. Adams to Seward, 27 March 1863, *Message of the President of the United States, and Accompanying Documents, to the Two Houses of Congress, at the Commencement of the First Session of the Thirty-Eighth Congress,* Part I (Washington, DC: Government Printing Office, 1863), 186 (hereafter *Message,* 1863); Adams to Seward, 26 February 1863, *Message,* 1863, 144, 146; Adams to Seward, 18 March 1864, *FRUS* 1864:I, 345.

46. Adams to Seward, 29 September 1864, *Papers Relating to Foreign Affairs, Accompanying the Annual Message of the President to the Second Session Thirty-Eighth Congress,* Part II (Washington, DC: GPO, 1864), 316 (hereafter *FRUS* 1864); *FRUS* 1864, 322; Secretary of London Legation Benjamin Moran to Seward, 14 October 1864, *FRUS* 1864, 331.

47. Anholt, *Competitive Identity,* 41–42, discussion of "belligerent branding"; Dinnie, *Nation Branding,* 99–100, discussion of "negative country-of-origin bias."

48. Dinnie, *Nation Branding,* 33–37.

49. https://history.state.gov/countries/haiti;   https://history.state.gov/countries/liberia; *Message,* 1862, 5, 38, 141, 158, 228; multiple references to "Hayti" and Liberia in subsequent volumes.

50. *Extract of a despatch from her Majesty's minister at Washington, dated December 6th 1861, inclosing papers relating to foreign affairs laid before the Congress of the United States at the opening of the session in 1861,* Command Papers, State Papers (North America No. 2), Paper No. 2910, Vol. LXII (London: HMSO, 6 February 1862); *Despatch from Her Majesty's Minister at Washington, dated 8th December 1862, enclosing Extracts of Papers relating to Foreign Affairs presented to Congress, December 1862,* Command Papers, State Papers (North America No. 4), Paper No. 3119, Vol. LXXII (London: HMSO, 19 March 1863).

51. *Papers Relating to Foreign Affairs, Accompanying the Annual Message of the President to the Second Session Thirty-Eighth Congress,* Part IV, *Appendix to diplomatic correspondence of 1865; The Assassination of Abraham Lincoln, Late President of the United States of America, and the Attempted Assassination of William H. Seward, Secretary of State, and Frederick W. Seward, Assistant Secretary, on the Evening of the 14th of April, 1865* (Washington, DC: Government Printing Office, 1866) (hereafter *Assassination*). In 1867, Congress ordered a

subsequent edition including three additional documents from the government of Bavaria. The GPO printed at least 28,550 copies of these editions, constituting the largest print run in the history of the series, and commercial publishers produced an unknown number of additional volumes in subsequent years. *TTAR,* 39–41.

52. The exact count depends on the definition of an independent government. In addition to the Sublime Porte, the governments of Egypt, Morocco, and Tunis conveyed condolences separately. The Hanseatic Republics government sent a message, as did the governments of Bremen, Hamburg, and Luebeck.
53. *Assassination,* 709–10.
54. *Assassination,* 10.
55. *Assassination,* 15.
56. *Assassination,* 419–20.
57. *Assassination,* 88. Editors Alphonse Peyrat of *l'Avenir national,* Adolphe Guerault of *l'Opinion nationale,* Léonor-Joseph Havin of *Le Siècle,* and Auguste Nefftzer of *Le Temps* submitted the text jointly.
58. *Assassination,* 17.
59. *Assassination,* 41.
60. Anholt, *Competitive Identity,* 21.
61. Dinnie, *Nation Branding,* 72.
62. Anholt, *Competitive Identity,* 48.
63. Dinnie, *Nation Branding,* 35, 65.
64. Yeaman to Seward, 20 November 1865, *FRUS* 1865:III, 183.
65. Seward to Adams, 28 July 1862, *Message,* 1862, 157.
66. Dinnie, *Nation Branding,* 35–35, 65–73, 149–51; Anholt's discussion of "playing chess with reality against perception," *Competitive Identity,* 33–34.
67. Simon Anholt, *Brand New Justice: How Branding Places and Products Can Help the Developing World* (Oxford: Butterworth-Heinemann, 2005), 128; Anholt, *Places,* 40.

Bibliography

Anholt, Simon. *Brand New Justice: How Branding Places and Products Can Help the Developing World,* rev. ed. Oxford: Butterworth-Heinemann, 2005.

———. *Competitive Identity: The New Brand Management for Nations, Cities, and Regions.* Houndmills: Palgrave Macmillan, 2007.

———. *Places: Identity, Image, and Reputation.* Houndmills: Palgrave Macmillan, 2010.

Dinnie, Keith. *Nation Branding: Concepts, Issues, Practice.* Oxford: Butterworth-Heinemann, 2008.

Eshuis, Jasper, and Erik-Hans Klijn, eds. *Branding in Governance and Public Management.* New York: Routledge, 2012.

Hasse, Adelaide Rosalia. *Index to United States Documents Relating to Foreign Affairs, 1828–1861.* Washington, DC: Carnegie Institution of Washington, 1914–21.

Innes, Joanna, and Mark Philip, eds. *Re-Imagining Democracy in the Age of Revolutions: America, France, Britain, Ireland 1750–1850.* Oxford: Oxford University Press, 2013.

Kaneva, Nadia. "Nation Branding: Toward an Agenda for Critical Research." *International Journal of Communication* 5 (2011): 117–41.

Kingdom of Norway, "Norway in the UN." Retrieved 8 April 2018 from https://www.norway.no/en/missions/un/values-priorities/peace-stability-sec/.

McAllister, William B., Joshua Botts, Peter Cozzens, and Aaron Marrs. *Toward "Thorough, Accurate, and Reliable": A History of the Foreign Relations of the United States Series.* Washington, DC: Government Printing Office, 2015. Retrieved 8 April 2018from http://history.state.gov/historicaldocuments/frus-history.

Republic of Austria, City of Vienna, Publications issued by the Chief Executive Office—European and International Affairs, "The Vienna International Centre" (2014). Retrieved 8 April 2018 from https://www.wien.gv.at/english/politics/international/mdeui/publications/index.html.

Somerville, Ian, Owen Hargie, Maureen Taylor, and Margalit Toledano, eds. *International Public Relations: Perspectives from Deeply Divided Societies.* New York: Routledge, 2017.

Teslik, Lee Hudson. "Nation Branding Explained." Council on Foreign Relations, 2007. Retrieved 8 April 2018 from http://www.cfr.org/diplomacy-and-statecraft/nation-branding-explained/p14776.

United Kingdom, Command Papers, State Papers (North America No. 2), Paper No. 2910, Vol. LXII. *Extract of a despatch from her Majesty's minister at Washington, dated December 6th 1861, inclosing papers relating to foreign affairs laid before the Congress of the United States at the opening of the session in 1861.* London: Her Majesty's Stationery Office, 6 February 1862.

———. Command Papers, State Papers (North America No. 4), Paper No. 3119, Vol. LXXII. *Despatch from Her Majesty's Minister at Washington, dated 8th December 1862, enclosing Extracts of Papers Relating to Foreign Affairs Presented to Congress, December 1862.* London: Her Majesty's Stationery Office, 19 March 1863.

United States. *American State Papers.* Retrieved 8 April 2018 from https://memory.loc.gov/ammem/amlaw/lwsp.html.

———. *US Serial Set.* Retrieved 8 April 2018 from https://memory.loc.gov/ammem/amlaw/lwss.html.

United States, Department of State. *The Assassination of Abraham Lincoln, Late President of the United States of America, and the Attempted Assassination of William H. Seward, Secretary of State, and Frederick W. Seward, Assistant Secretary, on the Evening of the 14th of April, 1865.* Washington, DC: Government Printing Office, 1866.

———. *Executive Documents Printed by Order of the House of Representatives during the First Session of the Thirty-Ninth Congress, 1865–66,* Part III. Washington, DC: Government Printing Office, 1866.

———. *Message of the President of the United States to the Two Houses of Congress at the Commencement of the Second Session of the Thirty-Seventh Congress.* Washington, DC: Government Printing Office, 1861.

———. *Message of the President of the United States to the Two Houses of Congress at the Commencement of the Third Session of the Thirty-Seventh Congress.* Washington, DC: Government Printing Office, 1862.

———. *Message of the President of the United States, and Accompanying Documents, to the Two Houses of Congress, at the Commencement of the First Session of the Thirty-Eighth Congress,* Part I. Washington, DC: Government Printing Office, 1863.

———. *Papers Relating to Foreign Affairs, Accompanying the Annual Message of the President to the Second Session Thirty-Eighth Congress,* Part I. Washington, DC: Government Printing Office, 1864.

———. *Papers Relating to Foreign Affairs, Accompanying the Annual Message of the President to the Second Session Thirty-Eighth Congress,* Part II. Washington, DC: Government Printing Office, 1864.

———. *Papers Relating to Foreign Affairs, Accompanying the Annual Message of the President to the Second Session Thirty-Eighth Congress,* Part IV. Washington, DC: Government Printing Office, 1864.

———. *Papers Relating to Foreign Affairs, Accompanying the Annual Message of the President to the First Session Thirty-Ninth Congress,* Part I. Washington, DC: Government Printing Office, 1865.

United States, Department of State, Office of the Historian. Retrieved 8 April 2018 from https://history.state.gov/.

Chapter 2

From the Moralizing Appeal for Patriotic Consumption to Nation Branding
Austria and Switzerland

Oliver Kühschelm

In June 2011, members of parliament from the Freedom Party (Freiheitliche Partei Österreichs, FPÖ) submitted an interpellation on "brand Austria." The short text began by explaining:

> In an international context each and every country constitutes a brand, which should convey a country's identity at home and abroad. While the former "Made in Austria" brand had been one of the few logos that represented Austria abroad, Switzerland with its brand "Switzerland" and the Swiss Cross as a symbol has already built up an impressive brand.[1]

This interpellation from the recent past illustrates a well-known fact: for some time now, political and economic elites have found it plausible to think of countries as brands in a competitive world of nations. Additionally, we learn from it that Austria—one of the wealthiest countries in the world—regards its even wealthier neighbor to the west as a model to emulate, and perhaps even to envy. This interpellation lamented the deficiency of Austria's current branding efforts. The government thereupon responded that it was planning to engage in nation branding in order to strengthen the image of the country. Although the term *nation branding* first made its appearance in Austrian media in the mid-2000s, it was only now that it came to the attention of a broader public. The Freedom Party wanted to know what "serious 'nation branding'" would look like.

The Ministry of the Economy answered curtly, telling the rightwing opposition that the government was on top of it.

Fretting about how best to "brand" a country is in some respects quite new, in others not so much, as this chapter will show. It investigates twentieth-century promotional campaigns in Austria and Switzerland that highlighted the connection between products and their country of origin. Rather than focusing on individual brands or companies, I will examine the history of efforts to create goodwill for Swiss and Austrian products and services. After introducing the subject of my research, I will trace in a second section the emergence and ensuing development of promotional activities that staged the relation of products and nations. A third section will discuss the intricate relations between communication that targets a foreign public and messages that are crafted for a domestic audience.

My central hypothesis is that there was significant change in how promotional communication on a country level connected the nation to its products and services. In Austria and Switzerland—like in other Western countries—a moralizing discourse about the nation, the national economy, and the need for patriotic consumption dominated during the interwar era. After World War II, this discourse gave way to managing the international image of the country so as to boost exports and increase tourism. Contemporary practices of nation branding emerged on the basis of this second, younger set of discourses, institutions, and practices. Sketching this development, I will move from the 1920s and 1930s to observations on nation branding in the early twenty-first century. Examples from the 1950s and 1960s, when export promotion became a dominant concern, will give an impression of a transitional period.

Nation branding today suggests a playful staging of countries for the consumption of tourists and investors. Practices of nation branding can be traced further back but the concept itself emerged in the 1990s and early 2000s. Globalization then was in full swing and the dawning of a postnationalist age looked like just a matter of time. The only way the nation seemed to fit into this cosmopolitan context was as a brand for marketing purposes. This stood in sharp contrast to earlier propaganda for nationally minded consumption that appeared hopelessly outdated. In the interwar years the situation had been different. Buy national campaigns were at the heart of promotional communication about the nation. Since the global economic crisis that began in 2007–08 the situation has again changed. Calls for nationally minded consumption have made a comeback, which tells us something important about our current moment. The

Brexit referendum, the election of Donald Trump, and the surge of rightwing populism in many countries around the world, Switzerland and Austria among them, suggest that chauvinism is back with a vengeance. This makes it a good time to renew historical reflection on nations and on how they are staged for the benefit of domestic and foreign audiences.

In a process that began in the nineteenth century but quickened in the 1920s and 1930s, a varied set of new promotional institutions placed their activities at the intersection of business interests with the nation-state and aimed at honing the image of the nation as well as harnessing it in the service of commercial goals. If these institutions were a symbolic expression of the importance that political, cultural, and economic elites already attributed to the nation, they were also aimed at increasing the nation's prestige through a broad array of promotional activities. Looking at the Austrian and Swiss cases, we can distinguish three areas of promotional expertise that were most prominent in fusing business interests with the cultivation or glorification of the nation: tourism advertising, export promotion, and buy national campaigns. Each of them was connected to cultural propaganda, for each had ties to cultural diplomacy directed at foreigners as well as to the educational and promotional efforts that would convey the importance of national traditions and values to citizens.

Export promotion and buy national communication target different audiences: the former addresses foreigners while the latter speaks to co-nationals. Tourist advertising occupies a middle position. Tourism is a service that can have the character of a "hidden export," but national consumption makes up a large portion of demand in the sector in any consumer society with a middle stratum affluent enough to go on holidays. Therefore, tourist promotion has to find ways of addressing both non- and co-nationals. Foreign and co-national audiences differ enormously in their level of knowledge about a country and their emotional involvement with it. Consequently, export promotion and buy national campaigns tend to use different promotional strategies. However, we will also see that export promotion and national/ist pride in production interact and feed on each other. This adds a layer of complexity to the task of reconstructing the shift from a moralizing appeal for patriotic consumption toward an emphasis on the attractiveness of a "nation brand."

Small industrialized states, such as Switzerland and Austria, are ideally suited to corroborate an argument that promotional communication to foreign audiences and messages for co-national recipients are often entwined. Small countries are more reliant on exports than big states with comparatively large interior markets.[2] Consequently, business elites and policy makers have every incentive to think hard about how to boost exports and whether crafting a country image might help to achieve such a goal. Small countries are also more vulnerable to external demand shocks than big countries. Even in the 1930s, during the heyday of protectionism, Austrian and Swiss campaigns that exhorted citizens to mind the national origin of products had to mitigate the risk that their messages would be perceived abroad as a call for the boycott of foreign products. In addition, the Austrian and Swiss cases testify to the fact that acknowledgment by significant "others" is a crucial issue for small states vis-à-vis larger and more powerful countries.

I will focus my account on the similarity between Austria and Switzerland, two small, heavily industrialized countries that share an alpine landscape in Central Europe. However, I will also point to some differences in the history and the current status of the Austrian and the Swiss country brands. Furthermore, it is worth noting that the relation between Austria and Switzerland was asymmetric throughout the twentieth century: while diplomats, advertisers, and others who were engaged in branding Austria often referred to Switzerland as a model to follow, Swiss actors exhibited less interest in their eastern neighbor, which for a long time was a much poorer country. Small prosperous nation-states such as Sweden or the Netherlands seemed to offer more useful lessons for Switzerland.

In his famous treatise "What is a Nation?" Ernest Renan asked: "How is it that Switzerland, which has three languages, two religions, and three or four races, is a nation? . . . Why is Austria a state and not a nation?"[3] Austria was then a multiethnic monarchical state. After 1918, it became a small republic with German-speaking citizens as its dominant language group. But if Renan had lived to the interwar years, he could still have juxtaposed the two neighboring countries and asked the same questions. In Switzerland, liberal-conservative elites emphasized civic values of freedom and democracy in order to overcome religious and linguistic cleavages. They shaped the nation according to middle class values and eventually integrated the working classes, if in a subaltern position. To reach the same point, it took Austria two calamitous wars on the one hand and a long economic boom starting from the 1950s on the other. Switzerland is often considered the typical case of civic as opposed to ethnic or cultural nationalism. On closer examination,

this scholarly distinction gets blurry: Swiss discourses on the
nation, especially in its conservative guises, included essentialist
elements and relied on visions of organic community.[4] The same
goes for Austria after 1945, which its elites conceived as a civic
nation while also emphasizing cultural distinctness from Germany.[5]
Ever more Austrians now considered their small country a viable
nation, yet nostalgia for the imperial past never disappeared alto-
gether. It survives, for example, in the claim to great power status
in the area of high culture. Although this distinguishes Austria from
Switzerland, among the Swiss the idea has proven popular that their
entrepreneurs have built a "hidden empire."[6] Commercial success
harbors the promise of subtle power that does not need military-
political might to achieve greatness.

The study proposed here cuts across some longstanding sub-
disciplinary divisions in the historical sciences. It does not belong
exclusively to economic or business history, or to social or cultural
history alone, or to political history. It instead tries to speak to all of
these research fields. More precisely, it combines multiple strands
of historical research in order to provide insight into promotional
culture as an essential part of how national collectivities have elaborated and communicated notions about themselves. Since the
1980s, constructivist scholarship on nations and national identities
has boomed. Concepts such as Benedict Anderson's "imagined
communities," Eric Hobsbawm and Terence Ranger's "invention of
tradition," or Pierre Nora's "sites of memory" inspired new lines of
research.[7] Swiss and Austrian researchers adopted these perspectives in the early to mid 1990s.[8] The boom has ebbed but for an
analysis of nation branding as a discursive practice constructivist
approaches have still the most to offer.

Advertising has received some attention as part of the burgeon-
ing scholarly interest in the history of consumption. Research on
British and US consumer culture started earlier, but German-speaking
academia has caught up, having now done significant work on the
history of propaganda and advertising in Germany.[9] Far less is known
about the Austrian and Swiss cases, even though "Red Vienna" was a
hotbed for innovation in market research[10] and Switzerland has been
home to exceptionally successful consumer brands like Nestlé and
Swatch as well as global players in branches as diverse as pharma-
ceuticals and machinery.[11] Those who are interested in advertisers
and other protagonists of national joint advertising can profit from
the perspective of a history of knowledge that proposes to analyze
the circulation of knowledge in discourses and practices.[12] It allows

us to situate the professionalization of advertising within the larger story of trust in "experts" and their social techniques that has characterized societies of high modernity and postmodernity.[13]

Advertising and the Nation

In some ways nation branding is the latest twist in a story that began centuries ago. Nationalism typically legitimizes the goal of establishing and maintaining nation-states.[14] It presents itself as bridging the rift between communities and society, between small-scale social units and a large unit that subsumes them all. Nationalism promises shelter against the disembedding forces of modernity while promoting a homogeneous national culture over local and regional loyalties.[15] A long string of scholars has observed that the workings of the nation involve a paradox: It is typically small, closely knit communities that instill "affective attitudes of solidarity."[16] The nation achieves this effect for an imagined community that can include millions of people.

Nationalism accompanied the formation of modern states because they needed new forms of legitimacy as they interacted ever more closely with the lives of ordinary people. This process started in early modern times but the second half of the nineteenth century witnessed its acceleration, and quantitative and qualitative changes. Industrialization, urbanization, novel communication technologies, mass media, mass consumption, and indeed nationalism have coevolved with the newly empowered state and given it shape along the way.[17] In this context, advertising and marketing emerged as social technologies that promised control and management capacities on an unprecedented scale. Like any new professional group, advertisers longed for respectability; being of service to the state could provide official recognition of their usefulness.[18] Fortunately for them, much as businesses discovered their need to manage consumers, states needed to manage citizens; both roles have been linked ever since.[19] As a result, advertising experts succeeded in carving out a place for themselves and their expertise close to the levers of state and corporate power.[20] For that same reason, it is hard to neatly separate commercial advertising from political propaganda. In spite of many attempts to clarify the different types of promotional communication, words such as *Reklame*, *Propaganda*, and *Werbung* were used almost interchangeably in the nineteenth and early twentieth centuries.[21]

Tourist advertising, export promotion, and buy national campaigns differ in important ways, yet they all connect services and products to the country or the nation. In this respect, they operate on common ground. Sources from Switzerland provide ample proof that actors from these fields thought so themselves as early as the interwar years. In addition, the federal state nudged them toward coordinating their activities. In 1932, representatives of different promotional organizations met and established a Central Commission of Swiss Propaganda Organizations. It brought together representatives from the Swiss Center for Export Promotion (Schweizerische Zentrale für Handelsförderung) and the Swiss Center for Tourist Promotion (Schweizerische Zentrale für Verkehrsförderung). It also enlisted the Swiss Week Association (Schweizerwoche-Verband), which exhorted Swiss consumers to behave as patriots; the Central Agency for the Swiss Trademark (Zentralstelle für das Schweizerische Ursprungszeichen), which promoted the use of the crossbow—the weapon of William Tell—for labeling Swiss products; the foundation Pro Helvetia; and the Auslandschweizerwerk, a section of the New Helvetian Society (Neue Helvetische Gesellschaft). It addressed Swiss citizens abroad and specialized in cultural advertising.[22] Furthermore, the central commission counted among its members trade fairs, the federal railway company, and organizations representing the sectoral interests of milk production, forestry, agriculture, gas, and electricity.[23]

When companies from the same sector of trade or industry joined forces to advertise a product category, or to stress their importance in society and the national economy, it was designated as "joint advertising" (Gemeinschaftswerbung).[24] While this type of advertising had already existed in the late nineteenth century, it became much more frequent in the interwar years, providing a link between business interests and promotion of the common good. The broader the interest group backing the advertising campaign, and the broader the concept it gathered around, the more it resembled political or cultural propaganda. Such advertising mostly lacked the feedback of dropping or rising sales; at the same time, it was heavy on ideological content and bold statements. It typically claimed a moral high ground either because of its edifying content, or because its stated goal was to benefit a large social group. Export promotion was an example of the latter case because it allegedly benefited not just exporters but the entire nation. Buy national campaigns similarly claimed to be in the service of the entire nation and were built around a normative core: the appeal to engage in patriotic shopping behavior. The organizers of such campaigns thus liked to argue that their promotional communication moved on a different moral level than commercial advertising. Their claim entailed questioning the urgency or even appropriateness of involving professional advertisers.

In the interwar years, advertising was nonetheless making advances onto the terrain of mass communication about the nation. However, in neither Switzerland nor Austria did advertising expertise occupy as central a place as professional advertisers thought it deserved.[25] Advertising professionals were just one group of actors among many others, such as bureaucrats, journalists, economists, jurists, entrepreneurs, or politicians. All these different actors could fulfill the roles of dedicated sympathizers, employees, or representatives of an organization with a stake in promoting tourism, exports, or national consumption. In 1931, the renowned Swiss advertiser and publisher Adolph Guggenbühl contended that the people in charge of attracting foreign tourists still did not regard themselves as advertising men, although "advertising remains advertising whether it concerns soap, shoes, or a country."[26] There is reason to feel ambivalent about such statements. They represent a curious but typical mix of oversimplification with the allure of expertise. A country is considerably more complex than a bar of soap. An analytical approach on how best to communicate a country's qualities still makes sense nonetheless, and Guggenbühl's assessment is therefore not entirely without merit. It brings to mind an argument of Paul Lazarsfeld, the Viennese sociologist and pioneer of market research, who emphasized the "methodological equivalence" of deciding to vote socialist and deciding to buy soap.[27] Such claims are still provocative, but no longer to the same extent. Today the proposition of branding the nation may not be uncontroversial, yet as a policy suggestion it is commonplace.

In interwar Austria and Switzerland, a number of binary oppositions still had a firm hold on social imaginaries: the distinction between high and low culture, the sacred and the profane, the deep and the superficial, the European and the American way of life, and the difference between the nation and private business. These oppositions aligned into a chain of dichotomies that shaped the understanding of society as a hierarchical totality. In contrast, the contemporary idea of nation branding presupposes a sociocultural situation in which such oppositions might not have disappeared but are submerged into a broad array of hybrid values and lifestyles.[28]

If in the 1920s and 1930s the nation and private business were thought to belong to separate spheres, and if profane business interests should not sully the sacred nation, how did such cultural preferences go together with the notion of "national economy" (*Nationalökonomie*)? Economists, most famously Friedrich List, had already established this concept in the early nineteenth century.[29] Explicitly tying the economy, and thus business activities, to the nation, "national economy" opposed the more cosmopolitan line of thinking represented by "political economy" in the tradition of Adam Smith. Yet, although the "national economy" linked the nation and the commercial sphere conceptually, it put the emphasis more on the nationalization of the economy than the commercialization of the nation. This determined the conditions for any promotional attempt at fusing business ambitions with the national imaginary. Buy national campaigns were a conspicuous example of this trend: not only did they claim to speak on behalf of the entire nation, downplaying the business side of their promotional effort, but they also celebrated their cultural value and stressed their educational mission.

Around the globe, protectionism and nationalism were on the rise since the late nineteenth century.[30] And, after World War I, the combination of the two asserted itself even in small export-oriented countries like Switzerland and even in the new Republic of Austria, where it was hard to reconcile nationalism with economic protectionism.[31] A call to favor Austrian products could not feed on the broadly shared conviction that there were distinct character traits, traditions, and historical events that formed the basis of an Austrian nation. Moreover, at that time, Austrian political and cultural elites considered Austria part of the German nation.[32] This attitude began to change only after the experience of joining Nazi Germany and losing a disastrous war. In the 1950s, appeals for patriotic consumption finally dovetailed nicely with an effort at nation building that centered on re-establishing a small Austrian state rather than a large German nation.

When the nationalist high tide of the 1930s and 1940s receded, it became more problematic to commend nationally minded consumption as the appropriate behavior of good citizens. For the reasons outlined above, this happened sooner in Switzerland than in Austria, but buy national campaigns gradually lost their former prominence in both countries. Tellingly, in the 1960s these campaigns shifted their messages toward highlighting the superior quality of national products. Calls for patriotic consumption had always implied that national products were good, but now they were less premised on national solidarity than billed as a way to acquire services and products of supreme quality.

In the first half of the twentieth century, it seemed natural to align the economic sphere with the national space to the highest degree possible. Yet nation branding, as its present-day practitioners understand it, thrives in a different ideological environment. It is indebted to the neoliberal sea change that has greatly increased the prestige of the market and free trade since the 1970s. Accordingly, ever more institutions are conceived of as acting on markets that are competing for customers. That is what constitutes the conceptual core of nation branding.[33] As practiced, it treats the state as yet another company that needs public relations and wants to sell its products. The principal focus lies on increasing tourism, inward investment, and exports; and the principal target audience is non-nationals. In his much-quoted textbook, Keith Dinnie also envisages a role for the "nation brand" in nation building but dwells mainly on the economic potential of nation branding.[34] Although the rise of neoliberalism laid the ideological foundations, it was not until the 1990s that the idea of branding as an all-purpose communication technology became pervasive. By the end of that decade, its upsurge had inspired Naomi Klein to warn that branding was encroaching on the public sphere. Her book *No Logo* found a worried audience and garnered huge success.[35] Yet as had happened before in the history of marketing, the critique increased the prestige of the new social technique.[36] When compared with the early twentieth century, the suggestion that anything can be a marketable item has lost much of its potential to irritate the public. In liberal, affluent consumer societies, the vast pretenses of branding fit in easily with the population's routine experiences of consumer culture.

In Switzerland, the institutionalization of nation branding started long before the label itself existed. The Central Commission of Swiss Propaganda Organizations had remained a paper tiger. But, in the late 1960s, the federal government gave coordination another try and initiated a new commission to cultivate the image of Switzerland abroad. This led eventually to the founding of Presence Switzerland in 2000—a full-fledged nation-branding agency. Austria was once again lagging behind. Nonetheless, the idea of nation branding had caught on with the institutional actors that worried about Austria's competitiveness, i.e., its economic and cultural place in the world. In 2012, the Ministry of Economy commissioned Simon Anholt to assess the outlook for Austria. Anholt, the inventor of the "Nation Brands Index," warned that the country might get stuck in the uncomfortable position of being the "other small German-speaking country—but not Switzerland."[37] This sounds more dramatic than it is. Both countries enjoy a high reputation, about as good as is possible for small states. The Nation Brands Index of 2011 showed Switzerland in eighth place while Austria ranked thirteenth. Anholt is of course right in concluding that Switzerland has the higher profile of the two. While Austria resembles Switzerland in many crucial respects, Swiss elites have worked on their "brand" far longer than their Austrian counterparts, and with far more continuity. Thus, Austria is placed second in many features that Switzerland had already tied to its brand. This holds true for concepts such as "neutrality" or "humanitarian commitment." Perhaps most importantly, Switzerland has successfully nationalized the notion of an alpine landscape.[38] High culture, however, has not become an essential feature of the Swiss brand. This is quite the opposite of the Austrian image that, apart from staging alpine beauty, includes the idea of a privileged place for theatrical and musical traditions.[39] The touristic exploitation of these tangible and intangible remnants of the former "empire" has worked very well. The items associated with this image are also at the heart of how many Austrians themselves prefer to see their nation.

Promoting the Nation and Its Products at Home and Abroad: Interaction, Discrepancy, and Convergence

The distinctions between export promotion and buy national communication—and to a lesser degree between these and tourist advertising—seem clear-cut enough. Hence it may not surprise us to find that export promotion and buy national communication use different strategies and themes. Yet we can find instances where the goals of attracting non-nationals and pleasing co-nationals have proved compatible. Sometimes the same images and the same strategies can be used for both purposes. Furthermore, identity formation implies a longing for recognition from significant "Others." This results in a broad variety of intricate relations between self-perception and image abroad, between messages for domestic consumption and messages that target foreigners. It further complicates the picture that communication practices often have secondary audiences: export promotion at home, buy national promotion abroad. Starting with such general remarks, I will now provide some examples and embed them in the contemporary history of Austria and Switzerland, respectively.

In 1935, a slogan from Austria summed up the appropriate behavior of good citizens: "Love for the country, self-confidence, loyalty toward the national economy. Buy Austrian goods."[40] In neighboring Switzerland, a slogan of the same year maintained: "He who gives products with the Crossbow [as a Christmas present], shows that he really thinks Swiss."[41] Such messages not only targeted Swiss and Austrian consumers, but also excluded anyone who did not consider himself a co-national. The example from Switzerland has the linguistic form of a declarative sentence; it nevertheless conveys a normative message, as does the imperative in the Austrian example. Both signified calls to duty. What was absent, however, was the hedonist streak that is so typical of contemporary advertising, and so central to modern societies of mass consumption. Therefore, since the second half of the twentieth century buy national campaigns in affluent Western societies have often invited sharp criticism, and—more damagingly—they have been the object of ridicule. From the 1950s onward, the liberal and liberal-conservative media in Switzerland, which acted as loudspeakers for the growing middle classes, heaped scorn on an obsolete approach to international trade. That approach also seemed culturally awkward—a narrow-minded provincialism that had to give way to a more cosmopolitan spirit. Much the same occurred in Austria, albeit at a later moment. Since the 1990s, to celebrate a return to a "small Austria" was deemed at odds with the hegemonic discourse on the country's upbeat European outlook—on the necessity of opening up economically, politically, and culturally.

Export promotion typically makes the case for national products by emphasizing attractive qualities that it associates with the country of origin. This approach is the more broadly applicable than a moralizing appeal. Buy national campaigns have often resorted to this strategy in addition to the didactic calls that constitute their ideological core. Every year in autumn from 1917 into the 1960s, the Swiss Week Association organized a broad array of events to remind citizens of their patriotic duty as consumers. From its beginnings, the Swiss Week Association also used visuals that linked its normative messages to imagery that in many respects resembled tourist advertising: the posters of the campaign literally placed the exhortation to honor Swiss products in the Swiss mountains. In this era, export promotion, tourist advertising, and buy national campaigns fitted together seamlessly. In interwar Austria, though, it was more difficult to achieve this feat because of the insecurity about what Austria should aspire to be. Was it the southernmost part of the "German nation"? An alternative—Catholic—version of Germany? A province of the economically more advanced German Reich? Or, a sovereign state with its eyes set on Central European regions that the Habsburgs had ruled? Promoting images tied to a regional imaginary below the state level could avoid these quandaries. Austrian economic and cultural propaganda agreed that the Viennese enjoyed worldwide fame for their fine taste. Fashion, furniture, and tableware from Vienna were hailed as products that embodied an essential trait of the *homo viennensis*. After World War II, this claim became a prominent element of Austrian nation building. In a 1949 promotional brochure, the Vienna Trade Fair Company told the story of how God had endowed the Viennese with exceptional taste at the beginning of time. Not even a disastrous twentieth century, it seems, was able to eradicate this divine gift. This nationalizing myth converted the luxury demands of the imperial court into a character trait of Austrians. But the cultural and economic basis for luxury craft goods eroded with the dissolution of the Empire at the end of World War I. In addition, Viennese furniture, tableware, and fashion of the eighteenth and nineteenth centuries embodied a conservative taste. This prevented modern design from being considered as authentically Viennese although Austrian designers neither missed out on international trends nor refrained from exploring new forms.[42] Hence it comes as no surprise that, for all the propagandistic efforts of the postwar period, research on the country's image in the 1980s revealed that foreigners associated quality design more readily with Switzerland or Germany than with Austria.[43] In fact, not even Austrians could be persuaded that Austrian products were generally better looking or of superior design when compared to products from abroad.[44]

Although the 1949 brochure was written in German, it bore an English title: *Made in Austria*. This choice betrayed a desire to gain recognition abroad. Another Austrian promotional brochure from 1961 provides an example of how this desire served to instill pride in national production while concurrently encouraging nationally minded consumption. In boldfaced letters, the brochure asked Austrian consumers to consider that "[t]he world appreciates Austrian quality. Let us also trust in our economy, its achievements, and its products."[45] It seemed to matter a great deal how foreigners perceived Austria; it mattered if they bought its products, for business reasons as well as for having something to be proud of. In turn, it was hoped that this pride might enhance the products' reputation in the domestic market, thereby adding the flavor of national self-respect to the act of buying them. Artifacts like this brochure represented and sought to promote the relationship between the nation and its products as a mix of mutually reinforcing economic goals and cultural satisfactions. These promotional artifacts also signalled the increased attention paid to the symbolic value of exports in the second half of the twentieth century.

Promotional communication needs to have a grip on who the target audience is but it cannot prevent others from eavesdropping. The organizers of buy national campaigns were keenly aware of the fact that an appeal to patriotism was unable to transcend the imaginary boundaries of the nation. Worse still, if companies, media, and governments abroad interpreted the campaign messages as a call to boycott imported products, the buy national idea could easily backfire. Export-oriented companies and liberal economists warned of such unintended consequences, even in the interwar years when protectionism was everywhere on the rise. At the same time, a country image that is conducive to export does not necessarily make a domestic audience feel comfortable with the way the country, its people, and traditions are being portrayed abroad. If the metaphor is permitted, a country brand has to be like a Swiss Army knife: it has to permit a variety of different uses.

In the early twentieth century, Switzerland already had a firmly established reputation as a producer of consumer goods. In an editorial from 1930 for the trade journal of Swiss advertisers, Adolph Guggenbühl explained the cultural and political importance of this fact: "Ovomaltine, Switzerland Cheese, and Peter Chocolate have contributed more to making Switzerland well-known and respected in America than even the most accomplished envoy would ever be able to achieve."[46] Today, some eighty years later, the country is still very well-regarded as a producer of high quality products. A 2000 survey asked Americans what they knew about Switzerland: 43 percent of the respondents mentioned the scenic alpine landscape while 37 percent referred to products made in Switzerland.[47] This has been good for business. Yet early on it was clear that such a country image created by exports has its downsides as well.

In 1928, an article in the *New York Times* profiled the Swiss writer and Nobel laureate Carl Spitteler, starting with an assertion: "Of Swiss literature, when we think of it at all, we think much as we do of the Swiss navy—as non-existent. And we are not so far wrong. For surely the Swiss are the least literary people in Europe. They are more apt to express themselves in cheese, chocolate and hotels than in literature."[48] In another article from the *New York Times*, published in 1931, a literary scholar offered a Swiss perspective on the issue. That author wished to enlighten the US public about the importance of Swiss literature. At the outset, he put himself in the shoes of a foreigner whose lack of familiarity with Switzerland might prompt him to ask: "Does Switzerland produce anything but cheese, chocolate, Diesel engines and watches? Are any books written in Switzerland?"[49] While radically differing in their assessment of Swiss literary culture, both articles spoke to the ideas about this small European country that readers of a high quality newspaper (in the largest US city) were supposed to have. Nor was it only cultural elites from far away North America who could be expected to take a dim view of Swiss culture. The passage from the article about Spitteler belonged to a string of unflattering characterizations that prominent foreign voices had been leveling at Switzerland. For success in exports and tourism did not earn the Swiss unanimous sympathy.[50] There is little doubt that the image of Switzerland as a producer of high-quality products helped it find customers abroad. However, parts of the domestic audience clearly did not like being represented as business-minded cheese eaters. There were also non-Swiss who believed in the stereotype, yet found it less a reason to buy Swiss products than to abhor the Swiss. To complicate things even further, there were Swiss intellectuals who shared the opinion that the Swiss paid too much attention to business and not nearly enough to cultural matters.

If we think of Switzerland as a brand, as the nation branding approach suggests, we also have to consider the significant challenge that lies in the relational dynamics of any attempt to steer the attention of recipients. Foregrounding one set of characteristics relegates others to the background, which is not always welcome. This holds true even for Switzerland with its carefully cultivated image and global reputation. Switzerland may well represent the perfect example to make the case for systematic nation branding as a tool for enhancing business interests, but it is still hard to balance a nation's image in ways that suit a diverse array of interests.

Conclusion

The contemporary rhetoric of nation branding is mostly used to signal a marketing-savvy understanding of the nation in a world of open markets. It suggests being at ease with an unrestricted global flux of products, ideas, and people. There are, of course, significant political forces, on both the left and the right side of the spectrum, that are wary of globalization. Let us look again at the interpellation from 2011 that the Freedom Party submitted to the Austrian government. The rightwing party added a nationalist undercurrent to its demand for "serious 'nation branding,'" as implied in the reference to the logo "Made in Austria," whose disappearance the party lamented. The owner of this brand had been a homonymous organization founded in the late 1970s amid worries about the negative trade balance. The parastatal association tried to raise the patriotic awareness of consumers about Austrian products. It was dismantled in 2002 when any hint of economic nationalism seemed at odds with the spirit of membership in the European Union. In addition, at that time, Austrian companies were reaping huge profits in the former socialist countries of Central Eastern Europe.[51] Not accidentally, the rightwing Freedom party displayed fondness for an approach to "brand Austria" that had originated as a defensive strategy and could easily be integrated into an openly chauvinist rhetoric. The "Made in Austria" promotion had come to look outdated in the optimistic mood of the 1990s and early 2000s. However, economic stagnation in the wake of the financial meltdown in 2007, the crisis of the European Union, and fears about migratory flows have since resulted in a resurgence of nationalism in many European countries, and Austria is no exception.

The example from Austria points to several aspects that I have elaborated on: I have stressed that the language of nation branding is new, whereas promotional efforts to connect a nation to its products and services are not. Today, advertising and marketing experts dominate the stage. By discussing the interwar years in some detail, I have shown that at the time these experts still had to explain why the nation needed them. Another difference is the prominent role that the call for patriotic, nationally minded consumption played in that era. Current nation branding is geared toward persuading foreigners. It therefore sells an image instead of appealing to solidarity among co-nationals. The change I have identified in the history of promoting the nation and national products correlates to the rising importance of foreign audiences since the 1950s, after the heyday of nationalism and protectionist economic policies had ended. However, for all the dreams about national self-reliance, foreign audiences had mattered in the 1930s as well. Conversely, the nation branding experts of today emphasize that a country's citizens have to identify with the national brand; otherwise, it will fail to attract foreigners and foreign investment.

In the interwar years, the proponents of exports, tourist promotion, and buy national campaigns already considered addressing co-nationals and persuading foreigners as different yet related tasks.

I have discerned two basic options: first, a moralizing approach, which is characteristic of (and limited to) buy national campaigns; and second, an attempt to associate distinct qualities, or a comprehensive notion of superior quality, with the nation. Export promotion has always had to employ the latter strategy, but buy national promotion was also able to make use of it. Targeting foreigners was sometimes contrasted with talking to co-nationals. And, buy national campaigns typically provoked concerned reactions among non-nationals who regarded such promotion as a way of excluding them or their products. But often messages for foreign audiences and co-nationals could be made compatible: since the 1960s, buy national promotion in Austria tried to make the capacity to export a reason for pride in the country and a motivation to buy national products.

In historical perspective, the term *nation branding* is most useful when serving the genealogical reconstruction of how advertising as a specific field of expertise connected with the nation-state. In the nineteenth and early twentieth centuries private companies drew on the language of bureaucracy and the military to explain business strategies. In neoliberal times it has become plausible to invert the direction of the conceptual transfer and to project onto the state concepts that have taken shape in a business environment. This clearly applies to ideas about branding—that quintessential corporate activity. Although branding expertise has thus gained a central place in the communication about countries and nations, the current return of nationalism poses the concept of nation branding in a new light. It is now easier than only a few years ago to see that in important respects the concept is indebted to its origins in a period when globalization under neoliberal auspices was on the rise. It may belong to a moment in history that has passed already. For historians at least, this makes it all the more interesting to investigate the concept and the related practices.

Oliver Kühschelm is currently a visiting professor at the Department of Economic and Social History of the University of Vienna. His work concerns the history of the middle classes, consumption, and advertising. He has developed a methodological focus on historical discourse analysis and specifically the role of language-image-texts. He co-edited the volumes *Bilder in historischen Diskursen* (Springer, 2014) and *Konsum und Nation* (transcript, 2012). He has recently finished his second book on buy national campaigns in Austria and Switzerland. His latest publication is "(Mis)Understanding Consumption. Expertise and Consumer Policies in Vienna, 1918–1938," in *Émigré Cultures in Design and Architecture*, edited by Alison Clarke and Elana Shapira, 45–61 (London: Bloomsbury, 2017).

Notes

1. Roman Haider (FPÖ), "Parlamentarische Anfrage an den Bundesminister für Wirtschaft, Familie und Jugend betreffend die Marke Österreich," 9 June 2011. All translations are my own unless otherwise stated.
2. See Margrit Müller and Timo Myllyntaus, eds., *Pathbreakers: Small European Countries Responding to Globalisation and Deglobalisation* (Bern: Lang, 2008); Peter J. Katzenstein, *Small States in World Markets: Industrial Policy in Europe* (Ithaca, NY: Cornell University Press, 1985).
3. Ernest Renan, "What is a Nation?," in *Nation and Narration*, ed. Homi Bhaba (London: Routledge, 1990), 8–22.
4. Oliver Zimmer, *A Contested Nation: History, Memory and Nationalism in Switzerland, 1761–1891* (Cambridge: Cambridge University Press, 2003).
5. Ruth Wodak, Rudolf de Cillia, Martin Reisigl, Karin Liebhart, Klaus Hofstätter, and Maria Kargl, *Zur diskursiven Konstruktion nationaler Identität*, Suhrkamp-Taschenbuch Wissenschaft (Frankfurt am Main: Suhrkamp, 1998).
6. This was the title of a bestselling book by a Swiss journalist: Lorenz Stucki, *Das heimliche Imperium: Wie die Schweiz reich wurde* (Bern: Scherz, 1969).
7. Nora's work triggered a cascade of publications on different European countries, for example Emil Brix, Ernst Bruckmüller, and Hannes Stekl, eds., *Memoria Austriae*, 3 vols. (Vienna: Verlag für Geschichte u. Politik, 2004–05); Georg Kreis, *Schweizer Erinnerungsorte: Aus dem Speicher der Swissness* (Zürich: Verlag Neue Zürcher Zeitung, 2010).
8. See Guy Marchal and Aram Mattioli, eds., *Erfundene Schweiz: Konstruktionen nationaler Identität*, Clio Lucernensis 1 (Zürich: Chronos, 1992); Susanne Breuss, Karin Liebhart, and Andreas Pribersky, *Inszenierungen: Stichwörter zu Österreich*, 2nd rev. ed. (Vienna: Sonderzahl, 1995).
9. Gerulf Hirt, *Verkannte Propheten? Zur "Expertenkultur" (west-)deutscher Werbekommunikatoren bis zur Rezession 1966/67* (Leipzig: Leipziger Universitätsverlag, 2013); Pamela E. Swett, Jonathan S. Wiesen, and Jonathan R. Zatlin, eds., *Selling Modernity: Advertising in Twentieth-Century Germany* (Durham, NC: Duke University Press, 2007); Claudia Regnery, *Die deutsche Werbeforschung 1900–1945* (Münster: Verlagshaus Monsenstein und Vannerdat, 2003); Rainer Gries, *Produkte als Medien: Kulturgeschichte der Produktkommunikation in der Bundesrepublik und der DDR* (Leipzig: Leipziger Univ.-Verlag, 2003).
10. Siegfried Mattl, "Die Marke 'Rotes Wien': Politik aus dem Geist der Reklame," in *Kampf um die Stadt: 361. Sonderausstellung des Wien Museums*, ed. Wolfgang Kos (Vienna: Czernin, 2010), 54–63; political and racist persecution forced some of the protagonists to leave for the United States where they pursued highly successful careers. See Jan Logemann, "European Imports? European Immigrants and the Transformation of American Consumer Culture from the 1920s to the 1960s," *Bulletin of the German Historical Institute Washington DC* no. 52 (2013): 117–24.

11. For the advertising and marketing of consumer goods, see Roman Rossfeld, *Schweizer Schokolade: Industrielle Produktion und kulturelle Konstruktion eines nationalen Symbols 1860–1920* (Baden: Hier + Jetzt Verlag für Kultur und Geschichte, 2007); Yvonne Zimmermann, "Heimatpflege zwecks Suppenpromotion: Zum Einsatz von Lichtbildern und Filmen in der Schweizer Lebensmittelbranche am Beispiel von Maggi," *Zeitschrift für Unternehmensgeschichte* 52, no. 2 (2008).

12. Philipp Sarasin, "Was ist Wissensgeschichte?," *Internationales Archiv für Sozialgeschichte der deutschen Literatur (IASL)* 36, no. 1 (2011).

13. James C. Scott, *Seeing Like a State: How Certain Schemes to Improve the Human Condition Have Failed* (New Haven, CT: Yale University Press, 1998); Lutz Raphael, "Embedding the Human and Social Sciences in Western Societies, 1880–1980: Reflections on Trends and Methods of Current Research," in *Engineering Society: The Role of the Human and Social Sciences in Modern Societies, 1880–1980*, ed. Kerstin Brückweh et al. (Basingstoke: Palgrave Macmillan, 2012).

14. John Breuilly, *Nationalism and the State*, 2nd ed. (Manchester: Manchester University Press, 1993).

15. Ernest Gellner, *Nations and Nationalism: New Perspectives on the Past*, 2nd ed. (Ithaca, NY: Cornell University Press, 1983); Anthony Giddens, *The Consequences of Modernity* (Cambridge: Polity Press, 1991).

16. Talcott Parsons, *The Social System*, Routledge sociology classics (London: Routledge, 1991), 129; see also Benedict Anderson, *Imagined Communities: Reflections on the Origin and Spread of Nationalism*. London: Verso, 1983; Ernest Gellner, *Nationalism* (London: Weidenfeld and Nicolson, 1997), 74.

17. Charles S. Maier, "Leviathan 2.0: Inventing Modern Statehood," in *A World Connecting, 1870–1945*, ed. Emily Rosenberg (Cambridge, MA: Belknap Press, 2012); Gellner, *Nations and Nationalism*.

18. Stefan Schwarzkopf, "Respectable Persuaders: the Advertising Industry and British Society, 1900–1939," Ph.D. dissertation, Birkbeck: University of London, 2008; Charles McGovern, *Sold American: Consumption and Citizenship, 1890–1945* (Chapel Hill: University of North Carolina Press, 2006), 25–31; Holm Priebe, "Branding Germany: Hans Domizlaff's Markentechnik and Its Ideological Impact," in *Selling Modernity: Advertising in Twentieth Century Germany*, ed. Pamela E. Swett, Jonathan S. Wiesen, and Jonathan R. Zatlin (Durham, NC: Duke University Press, 2007); Hirt, *Propheten*, 180–216.

19. Sheryl Kroen, "A Political History of the Consumer," *The Historical Journal* 47, no. 3 (2004); Lizabeth Cohen, *A Consumers' Republic: The Politics of Mass Consumption in Postwar America* (New York: Vintage Books, 2004); Kate Soper and Frank Trentmann, eds., *Citizenship and Consumption* (Basingstoke: Palgrave Macmillan, 2008); Hartmut Berghoff, "Consumption Politics and Politicized Consumption: Monarchy, Republic, and Dictatorship in Germany, 1900–1939," in *Decoding Modern Consumer Societies*, ed. Hartmut Berghoff and Uwe Spiekermann (Basingstoke: Palgrave Macmillan, 2012); Claudius Torp, *Konsum und Politik in der Weimarer Republik* (Göttingen: Vandenhoeck & Ruprecht, 2011); Sibylle Brändli, *Der Supermarkt im Kopf: Konsumkultur und Wohlstand in der Schweiz nach 1945* (Vienna: Böhlau, 2000).

20. McGovern, *Sold American*; Stefan Schwarzkopf, "Markets, Consumers, and the State: The Uses of Market Research in Government and the Public Sector in Britain, 1925–1955," in *The Rise of Marketing and Market Research*, ed. Hartmut Berghoff, Philip Scranton, and Uwe Spiekermann (Basingstoke: Palgrave Macmillan, 2012).

21. Thymian Bussemer, "Propaganda. Theoretisches Konzept und geschichtliche Bedeutung, Version: 1.0," *Docupedia-Zeitgeschichte* 2 August 2013.

22. There is significant recent scholarship on Swiss cultural diplomacy: Thomas Kadelbach, *Swiss Made: Pro Helvetia et l'image de la Suisse à l'étranger (1945– 1990)* (Neuchâtel: Editions Alphil—Presses universitaires suisses, 2013); Matthieu Gillabert, *Dans les coulisses de la diplomatie culturelle suisse: Objectifs, réseaux et réalisations (1938–1984)* (Neuchâtel: Editions Alphil—Presses universitaires suisses, 2013); Pauline Milani, *Le diplomate et l'artiste: Construction d'une politique culturelle suisse à l'étranger (1938–1985)* (Neuchâtel: Editions Alphil— Presses universitaires suisses, 2013); a recent publication about the cultural dimension of export promotion: Claire-Luise Debluë, *Exposer pour exporter: culture visuelle et expansion commerciale en Suisse* (1908–1939) (Neuchâtel: Editions Alphil, 2015).

23. [René Kaestlin], *Schweizer Gemeinschaftswerbung im Dienste des Landes* (Lausanne: Schweizerische Zentrale für Handelsförderung, n.d. [1949]).

24. Dirk Schindelbeck, "Werbung für alle? Kleine Geschichte der Gemeinschaftswerbung von der Weimarer Republik bis zur Bundesrepublik Deutschland," in *Unternehmenskommunikation im 19. und 20. Jahrhundert: Neue Wege der Unternehmensgeschichte*, ed. Clemens Wischermann, Peter Borscheid, and Karl-Peter Ellerbrock (Dortmund: Gesellschaft für Westfälische Wirtschaftsgeschichte E.V., 2000); Dirk Reinhardt, *Von der Reklame zum Marketing: Geschichte der Wirtschaftswerbung in Deutschland* (Berlin: Akademie-Verlag, 1993); Erwin Paneth, *Entwicklung der Reklame von Altertum bis zur Gegenwart: Erfolgreiche Mittel der Geschäfts-, Personen- und Ideenreklame aus allen Zeiten und Ländern* (Munich: R. Oldenbourg, 1926), 175–78.

25. See, for example, Th. Häusler, "Konjunktur für Gemeinschaftswerbung," *Schweizer Reklame* no. 5 (December 1935): 116–19.

26. Adolph Guggenbühl, "Verkehrspropaganda und Reklame," *Schweizer Reklame* no. 4 (October 1931), 113.

27. Mattl, "Rotes Wien," 63.

28. There are mountains of research into the "postmodern condition." I therefore limit myself to a few references and to German-speaking scholarship. In the early 1990s, the sociologist Gerhard Schulze published an illuminating study on what he called the experience-driven society: *Die Erlebnisgesellschaft: Kultursoziologie der Gegenwart* (Frankfurt am Main: Campus, 1992). He observed changes in consumption patterns that formed part of far-reaching social transformations since the 1970s. They have by now also become a topic of historical research: Anselm Doering-Manteuffel, Lutz Raphael, and Thomas Schlemmer, eds., *Vorgeschichte der Gegenwart: Dimensionen des Strukturbruchs nach dem Boom* (Göttingen: Vandenhoeck & Ruprecht, 2016).

29. Daniel Speich Chassé, "Nation," in *Auf der Suche nach der Ökonomie: Historische Annäherungen*, ed. Christof Dejung, Monika Dommann, and Daniel Speich Chassé (Tübingen: Mohr Siebeck, 2014); Keith Tribe, *Strategies of Economic Order: German Economic Discourse, 1750–1950* (Cambridge: Cambridge University Press, 1995).

30. Stephen Broadberry and Kevin O'Rourke, eds. *The Cambridge Economic History of Modern Europe, vol. 2: 1870 to the Present* (Cambridge: Cambridge University Press, 2010), 26–27; Maier, "Leviathan 2.0," 179.

31. Oliver Kühschelm, "Implicit Boycott: The Call for Patriotic Consumption in Austria in the Interwar Period," *Management & Organizational History* 5, no. 2 (2010). On the rise of economic nationalism during the interwar years, see, for

example, the contemporary accounts of William Rappard and Wilhelm Röpke. Both economists worked in Geneva and took a liberal stance on matters of trade: Wilhelm Röpke, *International Economic Disintegration* (London: Hodge, 1942); William E. Rappard, "Economic Nationalism," in *Authority and the Individual* (Cambridge, MA: Harvard University Press, 1937).

32. Julie Thorpe, "Pan-Germanism after Empire: Austrian 'Germandom' at Home and Abroad," in *From Empire to Republic: Post-World War I Austria*, ed. Günter Bischof, Fritz Plasser, and Peter Berger (New Orleans: UNO Press/Innsbruck University Press, 2010).

33. Melissa Aronczyk and Devon Powers, "Introduction: Blowing Up the Brand," in *Blowing Up the Brand: Critical Perspectives on Promotional Culture*, ed. Melissa Aronczyk and Devon Powers (New York: Peter Lang, 2010), 1–3; Magdalena Kania-Lundholm, "Nation in Market Times: Connecting the National and the Commercial. A Research Overview," *Sociology Compass* 8, no. 6 (2014).

34. Keith Dinnie, *Nation Branding: Concepts, Issues, Practice* (Oxford: Butterworth-Heinemann, 2008), 15.

35. Naomi Klein, *No Logo, No Space, No Choice, No Jobs: Taking Aim at the Brand Bullies* (New York: Picador, 1999).

36. Aronczyk and Powers, "Introduction," 1. This unintended effect that *No Logo* produced recalls Vance Packard's critical bestseller *Hidden Persuaders* from the 1950s, which greatly benefitted the prestige of motivation research. See Stefan Schwarzkopf and Rainer Gries, eds., *Ernest Dichter and Motivation Research: New Perspectives on the Making of Post-war Consumer Culture* (New York: Palgrave Macmillan, 2010).

37. Simon Anholt, "Kompetitive Identität Österreichs: Schlussbericht," (2013).

38. Laurent Tissot, "From Alpine Tourism to the 'Alpinization' of Tourism," in *Touring Beyond the Nation: A Transnational Approach to European Tourism History*, ed. Eric G. E. Zuelow (Farnham: Ashgate, 2011), 9–10.

39. Günter Schweiger, *Österreichs Image in der Welt: Ein weltweiter Vergleich mit Deutschland und der Schweiz* (Vienna: Service-Fachverlag, 1992), 25–79.

40. "Liebe zur Heimat, Vertrauen auf sich selbst, Treue zur heimischen Wirtschaft. Kauft österreichische Waren."

41. This is a rough translation of the actual slogan: "Wer Gaben mit dem Armbrustzeichen schenkt, zeigt, daß er eidgenössisch denkt."

42. Eva Ottilinger, "Kontinuität und Neubeginn: Wiener Möbeldesign im internationalen Kontext," in *Möbeldesign der 50er Jahre: Wien im internationalen Kontext*, ed. Eva Ottilinger (Vienna: Böhlau, 2005).

43. Schweiger, *Image*, 212.

44. Österreichisches Gallup-Institut, "Made in Austria," Survey January/February 1996 (includes data from a survey done in 1984), Made in Austria Collection, Archive of the Austrian Chamber of Commerce.

45. *Die Welt kauft österreichische Qualität*, Leaflet, n.d. [1961], Made in Austria Collection, Archive of the Austrian Chamber of Commerce.

46. Adolph Guggenbühl, "Der Markenartikel als Friedenstaube," *Schweizer Reklame*, no. 5 (January 1930), 217.

47. Institut für Marketing und Unternehmungsführung (IMB) der Universität Bern, "Image der Schweiz in den USA: Die wichtigsten Ergebnisse im Überblick." 20 November 2000.

48. Henry James Forman, "Spitteler is 'the Greatest German Poet since Goethe,'" *New York Times*, 4 March 1928, 64.

49. René Rapin, "A Letter on Literature in Switzerland," *New York Times*, 3 August 1931, 65.
50. Peter Katzenstein, *Corporatism and Change: Austria, Switzerland, and the Politics of Industry* (Ithaca, NY: Cornell University Press, 1984), 20–23; Jakob Tanner, *Geschichte der Schweiz im 20. Jahrhundert* (Munich: C.H. Beck, 2015), 14–16.
51. Wilfried Altzinger, "On the Profitability of Austrian Firms in the New EU Member States," *The Vienna Institute Monthly Report* no. 3 (2006): 4–10; Andreas Resch, "Austrian Foreign Trade and Austrian Companies' Economic Engagement in Eastern Europe," in *Austria's International Position after the End of the Cold War*, ed. Günter Bischof and Ferdinand Karlhofer (New Orleans: Uno Press/Innsbruck University Press, 2013).

Bibliography

Altzinger, Wilfried. "On the Profitability of Austrian Firms in the New EU Member States." *The Vienna Institute Monthly Report* no. 3 (2006): 4–10.

Anderson, Benedict. *Imagined Communities: Reflections on the Origin and Spread of Nationalism*. London: Verso, 1983.

Anholt, Simon. "Kompetitive Identität Österreichs. Schlussbericht" (2013). Retrieved 1 October 2015 from http://www.bmwfw.gv.at/ Aussenwirtschaft/nationbrandingaustria/Documents/Austria%20 Competitive%20Identity%20Project%20-%20Final%20Report%20GER. pdf.

Aronczyk, Melissa, and Devon Powers. "Introduction: Blowing Up the Brand." In *Blowing Up the Brand: Critical Perspectives on Promotional Culture*, edited by Melissa Aronczyk and Devon Powers, 1–3. New York: Peter Lang, 2010.

Berghoff, Hartmut. "Consumption Politics and Politicized Consumption: Monarchy, Republic, and Dictatorship in Germany, 1900–1939." In *Decoding Modern Consumer Societies*, edited by Hartmut Berghoff and Uwe Spiekermann, 125–48. Basingstoke: Palgrave Macmillan, 2012.

Brändli, Sibylle. *Der Supermarkt im Kopf: Konsumkultur und Wohlstand in der Schweiz nach 1945*. Vienna: Böhlau, 2000.

Breuilly, John. *Nationalism and the State*. 2nd ed. Manchester: Manchester University Press, 1993.

Breuilly, John, ed. *The Oxford Handbook of the History of Nationalism*. Oxford: Oxford University Press, 2013.

Breuss, Susanne, Karin Liebhart, and Andreas Pribersky. *Inszenierungen: Stichwörter zu Österreich*. 2nd rev. ed. Vienna: Sonderzahl, 1995.

Brix, Emil, Ernst Bruckmüller, and Hannes Stekl, eds. *Memoria Austriae*. 3 vols. Vienna: Verlag für Geschichte u. Politik, 2004–05.

Broadberry, Stephen, and Kevin O'Rourke, eds. *The Cambridge Economic History of Modern Europe, vol. 2: 1870 to the Present*. Cambridge: Cambridge University Press, 2010.

Bussemer, Thymian. "Propaganda. Theoretisches Konzept und geschichtliche Bedeutung, Version: 1.0." *Docupedia-Zeitgeschichte*, 2 August 2013. Retrieved 1 October 2015 from http://docupedia.de/zg/Propaganda.

Cohen, Lizabeth. *A Consumers' Republic: The Politics of Mass Consumption in Postwar America*. New York: Vintage Books, 2004.

Die Welt kauft österreichische Qualität, Leaflet, n.d. [1961], Made in Austria Collection, Archive of the Austrian Chamber of Commerce.

Debluë, Claire-Luise. *Exposer pour exporter: culture visuelle et expansion commerciale en Suisse (1908–1939)*. Neuchâtel: Editions Alphil, 2015.

Dinnie, Keith. *Nation Branding: Concepts, Issues, Practice*. Oxford: Butterworth-Heinemann, 2008.

Doering-Manteuffel, Anselm, Lutz Raphael, and Thomas Schlemmer, eds. *Vorgeschichte der Gegenwart: Dimensionen des Strukturbruchs nach dem Boom*. Göttingen: Vandenhoeck & Ruprecht, 2016.

Forman, Henry James. "Spitteler is 'the Greatest German Poet since Goethe.'" *New York Times*, 4 March 1928, 64.

Gellner, Ernest. *Nationalism*. London: Weidenfeld and Nicolson, 1997.

———. *Nations and Nationalism: New Perspectives on the Past*. 2nd ed. Ithaca, NY: Cornell University Press, 1983.

Giddens, Anthony. *The Consequences of Modernity*. Cambridge: Polity Press, 1991.

Gillabert, Matthieu. *Dans les coulisses de la diplomatie culturelle suisse: Objectifs, réseaux et réalisations (1938–1984)*. Neuchâtel: Editions Alphil—Presses universitaires suisses, 2013.

Gries, Rainer. *Produkte als Medien: Kulturgeschichte der Produktkommunikation in der Bundesrepublik und der DDR*. Leipzig: Leipziger Univ.-Verlag, 2003.

Guggenbühl, Adolph. "Der Markenartikel als Friedenstaube." *Schweizer Reklame* no. 5 (January 1930), 217.

———. "Verkehrspropaganda und Reklame." *Schweizer Reklame* no. 4 (October 1931), 113.

Haider, Roman (FPÖ). "Parlamentarische Anfrage an den Bundesminister für Wirtschaft, Familie und Jugend betreffend die Marke Österreich," 9 June 2011. Retrieved 25 January 2016 from http://www.parlament. gv.at/PAKT/VHG/XXIV/J/J_08730/fnameorig_222571.html.

Häusler, Th. "Konjunktur für Gemeinschaftswerbung." *Schweizer Reklame* no. 5 (December 1935): 116–19.

Hirt, Gerulf. *Verkannte Propheten? Zur "Expertenkultur" (west-)deutscher Werbekommunikatoren bis zur Rezession 1966/67*. Leipzig: Leipziger Universitätsverlag, 2013.

Institut für Marketing und Unternehmungsführung (IMB) der Universität Bern. "Image der Schweiz in den USA: Die wichtigsten Ergebnisse im Überblick." 20 November 2000, retrieved 1 October 2015 from https:// www.eda.admin.ch/eda/de/home/das-eda/landeskommunikation/ monitoring-und-analyse/archiv.html.

Kadelbach, Thomas. *Swiss Made: Pro Helvetia et l'image de la Suisse à l'étranger (1945–1990)*. Neuchâtel: Editions Alphil—Presses universitaires suisses, 2013.

[Kaestlin, René]. *Schweizer Gemeinschaftswerbung im Dienste des Landes*. Lausanne: Schweizerische Zentrale für Handelsförderung, n.d. [1949].

Kania-Lundholm, Magdalena. "Nation in Market Times: Connecting the National and the Commercial: A Research Overview." *Sociology Compass* 8, no. 6 (2014): 603–13.

Katzenstein, Peter J. *Corporatism and Change: Austria, Switzerland, and the Politics of Industry*. Ithaca, NY: Cornell University Press, 1984.

———. *Small States in World Markets: Industrial Policy in Europe*. Ithaca, NY: Cornell University Press, 1985.

Klein, Naomi. *No Logo, No Space, No Choice, No Jobs: Taking Aim at the Brand Bullies*. New York: Picador, 1999.

Kreis, Georg. *Schweizer Erinnerungsorte: Aus dem Speicher der Swissness*. Zürich: Verlag Neue Zürcher Zeitung, 2010.

Kroen, Sheryl. "A Political History of the Consumer." *The Historical Journal* 47, no. 3 (2004): 709–36.

Kühschelm, Oliver. "Implicit Boycott: The Call for Patriotic Consumption in Austria in the Interwar Period." *Management & Organizational History* 5, no. 2 (2010): 165–95.

Logemann, Jan. "European Imports? European Immigrants and the Transformation of American Consumer Culture from the 1920s to the 1960s." *Bulletin of the German Historical Institute Washington DC* no. 52 (2013): 113–33.

Maier, Charles S. "Leviathan 2.0: Inventing Modern Statehood." In *A World Connecting, 1870–1945*, edited by Emily Rosenberg, 27–282. Cambridge, MA: Belknap Press, 2012.

Marchal, Guy, and Aram Mattioli, eds. *Erfundene Schweiz: Konstruktionen nationaler Identität*, Clio Lucernensis 1. Zürich: Chronos, 1992.

Mattl, Siegfried. "Die Marke 'Rotes Wien': Politik aus dem Geist der Reklame." In *Kampf um die Stadt: 361. Sonderausstellung des Wien Museums*, edited by Wolfgang Kos, 54–63. Vienna: Czernin, 2010.

McGovern, Charles. *Sold American: Consumption and Citizenship, 1890–1945*. Chapel Hill: University of North Carolina Press, 2006.

Milani, Pauline. *Le diplomate et l'artiste: Construction d'une politique culturelle suisse à l'étranger (1938–1985)*. Neuchâtel: Editions Alphil—Presses universitaires suisses, 2013.

Müller, Margrit, and Timo Myllyntaus, eds. *Pathbreakers: Small European Countries Responding to Globalisation and Deglobalisation*. Bern: Lang, 2008.

Österreichisches Gallup-Institut. "Made in Austria," Survey January/February 1996 (includes data from a survey done in 1984), Made in Austria Collection, Archive of the Austrian Chamber of Commerce.

Ottilinger, Eva. "Kontinuität und Neubeginn: Wiener Möbeldesign im internationalen Kontext." In *Möbeldesign der 50er Jahre: Wien im internationalen Kontext*, edited by Eva Ottilinger, 41–87. Vienna: Böhlau, 2005.

Paneth, Erwin. *Entwicklung der Reklame von Altertum bis zur Gegenwart: Erfolgreiche Mittel der Geschäfts-, Personen- und Ideenreklame aus allen Zeiten und Ländern*. Munich: R. Oldenbourg, 1926.

Parsons, Talcott. *The Social System*. Routledge Sociology Classics. London: Routledge, 1991.

Priebe, Holm. "Branding Germany: Hans Domizlaff's Markentechnik and Its Ideological Impact." In *Selling Modernity: Advertising in Twentieth Century Germany*, edited by Pamela E. Swett, Jonathan S. Wiesen, and Jonathan R. Zatlin, 78–99. Durham, NC: Duke University Press, 2007.

Raphael, Lutz. "Embedding the Human and Social Sciences in Western Societies, 1880–1980: Reflections on Trends and Methods of Current Research." In *Engineering Society: The Role of the Human and Social Sciences in Modern Societies, 1880–1980*, edited by Kerstin Brückweh et al., 41–56. Basingstoke: Palgrave Macmillan, 2012.

Rapin, René. "A Letter on Literature in Switzerland." *New York Times*, 3 August 1931, 65.

Rappard, William E. "Economic Nationalism." In *Authority and the Individual*, 74–112. Cambridge, MA: Harvard University Press, 1937.

Regnery, Claudia. *Die deutsche Werbeforschung 1900–1945*. Münster: Verlagshaus Monsenstein und Vannerdat, 2003.

Reinhardt, Dirk. *Von der Reklame zum Marketing: Geschichte der Wirtschaftswerbung in Deutschland*. Berlin: Akademie-Verlag, 1993.

Renan, Ernest. "What is a Nation?" In *Nation and Narration*, edited by Homi Bhaba, 8–22. London: Routledge, 1990.

Resch, Andreas. "Austrian Foreign Trade and Austrian Companies' Economic Engagement in Eastern Europe." In *Austria's International Position after the End of the Cold War*, edited by Günter Bischof and Ferdinand Karlhofer, 198–223. New Orleans, LA: Uno Press/Innsbruck University Press, 2013.

Röpke, Wilhelm. *International Economic Disintegration*. London: Hodge, 1942.

Rossfeld, Roman. *Schweizer Schokolade: Industrielle Produktion und kulturelle Konstruktion eines nationalen Symbols 1860–1920*. Baden: Hier + Jetzt Verlag für Kultur und Geschichte, 2007.

Sarasin, Philipp. "Was ist Wissensgeschichte?" *Internationales Archiv für Sozialgeschichte der deutschen Literatur (IASL)* 36, no. 1 (2011): 159–72.

Schindelbeck, Dirk. "Werbung für alle? Kleine Geschichte der Gemeinschaftswerbung von der Weimarer Republik bis zur Bundesrepublik Deutschland." In *Unternehmenskommunikation im 19. und 20. Jahrhundert: Neue Wege der Unternehmensgeschichte*, edited by Clemens Wischermann, Peter Borscheid, and Karl-Peter Ellerbrock,

63–97. Dortmund: Gesellschaft für Westfälische Wirtschaftsgeschichte E.V., 2000.

Schulze, Gerhard. *Die Erlebnisgesellschaft: Kultursoziologie der Gegenwart.* Frankfurt am Main: Campus, 1995.

Schwarzkopf, Stefan. "Markets, Consumers, and the State: The Uses of Market Research in Government and the Public Sector in Britain, 1925–1955." In *The Rise of Marketing and Market Research*, edited by Hartmut Berghoff, Philip Scranton, and Uwe Spiekermann, 171–92. Basingstoke: Palgrave Macmillan, 2012.

———. "Respectable Persuaders: The Advertising Industry and British Society, 1900–1939." Ph.D. dissertation. Birkbeck: University of London, 2008.

Schwarzkopf, Stefan, and Rainer Gries, eds. *Ernest Dichter and Motivation Research: New Perspectives on the Making of Post-war Consumer Culture.* New York: Palgrave Macmillan, 2010.

Schweiger, Günter. *Österreichs Image in der Welt: Ein weltweiter Vergleich mit Deutschland und der Schweiz.* Vienna: Service-Fachverlag, 1992.

Scott, James C. *Seeing Like a State: How Certain Schemes to Improve the Human Condition Have Failed.* New Haven, CT: Yale University Press, 1998.

Soper, Kate, and Frank Trentmann, eds. *Citizenship and Consumption.* Basingstoke: Palgrave Macmillan, 2008.

Speich Chassé, Daniel. "Nation." In *Auf der Suche nach der Ökonomie: Historische Annäherungen*, edited by Christof Dejung, Monika Dommann, and Daniel Speich Chassé, 207–33. Tübingen: Mohr Siebeck, 2014.

Swett, Pamela E., Jonathan S. Wiesen, and Jonathan R. Zatlin, eds. *Selling Modernity: Advertising in Twentieth-Century Germany.* Durham, NC: Duke University Press, 2007.

Stucki, Lorenz. *Das heimliche Imperium: Wie die Schweiz reich wurde.* Bern: Scherz, 1969.

Tanner, Jakob. *Geschichte der Schweiz im 20. Jahrhundert: Europäische Geschichte im 20. Jahrhundert.* Munich: C.H. Beck, 2015.

Thorpe, Julie. "Pan-Germanism after Empire: Austrian 'Germandom' at Home and Abroad." In *From Empire to Republic: Post-World War I Austria*, edited by Günter Bischof, Fritz Plasser, and Peter Berger, 254–72. New Orleans: UNO Press/Innsbruck University Press, 2010.

Tissot, Laurent. "From Alpine Tourism to the 'Alpinization' of Tourism." In *Touring Beyond the Nation: A Transnational Approach to European Tourism History*, edited by Eric G. E. Zuelow, 59–78. Farnham: Ashgate, 2011.

Torp, Claudius. *Konsum und Politik in der Weimarer Republik.* Göttingen: Vandenhoeck & Ruprecht, 2011.

Tribe, Keith. *Strategies of Economic Order: German Economic Discourse, 1750–1950.* Cambridge: Cambridge University Press, 1995.

Wodak, Ruth, Rudolf de Cillia, Martin Reisigl, Karin Liebhart, Klaus
Hofstätter, and Maria Kargl. *Zur diskursiven Konstruktion nationaler
Identität*. Suhrkamp-Taschenbuch Wissenschaft. Frankfurt am Main:
Suhrkamp, 1998.
Zimmer, Oliver. *A Contested Nation: History, Memory and Nationalism in
Switzerland, 1761–1891*. Cambridge: Cambridge University Press, 2003.
Zimmermann, Yvonne. "Heimatpflege zwecks Suppenpromotion:
Zum Einsatz von Lichtbildern und Filmen in der Schweizer
Lebensmittelbranche am Beispiel von Maggi." *Zeitschrift für
Unternehmensgeschichte* 52, no. 2 (2008): 203–26.

Chapter 3

BRANDING INTERNATIONALISM
Displaying Art and International Cooperation in the Interwar Period

Ilaria Scaglia

This chapter examines the case of the 1935–36 International Exhibition of Chinese Art in London to explore how the histories of nation branding and internationalism came to be intertwined during the interwar period. This landmark exhibition, hosted by the prestigious Royal Academy of Arts, was "the largest Chinese cultural event ever mounted" and the first to be co-organized by both the British and the Chinese governments.[1] Attracting nearly 422,000 visitors, it showcased more than three thousand works of art lent by individuals, institutions, and governments from all over the world. By all accounts, this was a transformative event, one that greatly fostered interest in China by displaying five thousand years of its artistic production.[2] This was also an unprecedented show of international cooperation, one whose success is remembered and celebrated to this day.[3]

More importantly, this exhibition provided many governments with the opportunity to brand themselves and others in the eyes of both domestic and foreign audiences through public displays of internationalism. In turn, internationalist ideas and practices came to be defined by nation branding, the process through which countries tried to build their reputations. In this context, culture—and art in particular—played an important role in representing power and in shaping both internationalism and nation branding in this period.

Notes for this section begin on page 93.

In this chapter, I define "internationalism" as a complex set of ideas and practices based on the premise that international cooperation represented the most viable solution to shared problems. At its core was what Glenda Sluga called "twentieth century internationalism," an ideology not antithetical to nationalism that envisioned representatives from different countries engaging in peaceful international exchanges while remaining proud of their own national—and sometimes even racial—differences.[4] Along with international cooperation, there were also universalistic notions of internationalism that downplayed national differences and sought to transcend geographic, economic, and racial distinctions. As this chapter demonstrates, the result was the development of various—and sometimes even contradictory—forms of international cooperation in various fields, including the preservation and display of art.

The term *nation branding* is used here to refer to two interconnected ideas. First, nation branding is a set of practices followed not only by governments, businesses, and corporations, but also by a wide variety of actors in the fields of politics and culture to change their perception and improve their reputation.[5] It is separate from propaganda (a form of mass persuasion defined by its intent and disseminated—or propagated—by a central agency or political authority), because nation branding encompasses the dynamic process of creating positive associations with a product—in this case, the nation—and accounts for the multiple actors, motivations, and driving forces that contributed to shaping it.[6] It is also distinct from public relations, as its primary goal is not to establish relationships with others, but to create perceptions and images, and its scope includes the complex processes through which these images are shaped. Nation branding also differs from public and cultural diplomacy, as it is not primarily concerned with the conduct of foreign policy or the management of international relations.[7] Instead, it exists independently from the state as the process through which a wide variety of actors—which may include states—try to change the perceptions of a country (either their own or another) while pursuing various agendas that may be in contradiction with one another.[8]

Second, nation branding is a concept to explore the historical processes by which visibility, perceptions, and emotions became central to political and cultural practices in the twentieth century. Like commercial advertisement, nation branding reveals the aspirations of its target audience as it seeks to cater to its wishes. As such, it allows historians to draw connections between how and why people were enticed by advertising/branding agents to consume a product—in this case, the nation—and what they coveted, feared, or dreamt.[9] Nation branding thus serves as a window onto consumer tastes and desires, and how these shaped the products offered to them. In the case of the art exhibition analyzed in this study, thinking about nation branding makes explicit how publicity and visibility became increasingly important in the 1930s; how the popularity of internationalism played a big part in the nation branding process; and how internationalist ideas and practices evolved to become what their own brands dictated they should be.[10]

The 1935–36 International Exhibition of Chinese Art well illustrates this complex interplay of nation branding and internationalism. The Republic of China used this event—and the internationalism it entailed—to present and legitimize itself as the lawful heir of the Chinese past, as the rightful representative of the Chinese present, and as an "open" player in the international arena. This exhibition also allowed the host, the United Kingdom, to affirm itself as an entrepôt for international cooperation; and the numerous countries who participated by lending objects (including Germany and Japan), to build their own reputations as respectable members of the international community. Most notably, this exhibition was the product of the work of a very heterogeneous group of individuals and institutions that pursued the common goal of staging a public display of international cooperation in the form of an international exhibition of Chinese art, and in doing so deliberately created or promoted a set of images, perceptions, and associations with various countries.[11]

So far, historians have examined these various actors in isolation from one another. The story has been either about the British government and the staging of "national" events in this period;[12] or the Republic of China and its uneasy relationship with the United Kingdom;[13] or the development of networks of art collectors and institutions.[14] As a consequence, the spotlight has often been on conflict rather than on places and moments of intersection and collaboration. Without dismissing the differences and disagreements examined in previous scholarship, this study adopts an alternative framework by looking at all the actors involved in the staging of this exhibition as members of what Melissa Aronczyk called a "transnational promotional class," a group of individuals and institutions with different agendas who were committed to the same nation branding project.[15] This categorization is hardly a stretch, as many of these people were no strangers to business and marketing strategies. In fact, many of them were administrators, financiers, and collectors at a time when advertisement and branding practices were expanding in all fields. At once exhibitors and spectators, they all contributed to crafting and disseminating the message that this exhibition was different from all others that had preceded it because of its "international" and "internationalist" character.

As this chapter demonstrates, internationalism itself came to be defined by the nation branding process. People involved in internationalism became increasingly concerned with the symbolic and the visible, catering to the needs of public display. In this context, they often incorporated universalist arguments about the need to transcend national and racial borders, as well as anti-modernist rhetoric and widespread critiques of the capitalist system. As a result of its being used for nation branding, internationalism evolved into a complex set of ideas and practices increasingly in contradiction with one another. It also played an essential role in representing and communicating power in the global marketplace of ideas of the post-1919 world.

An Exhibition for Nation Branding Purposes

The idea for the 1935–36 International Exhibition of Chinese Art in London originated from a heterogeneous group of people interested in Chinese art: financier and collector Sir Percival David; magnate, collector, and co-founder of the Oriental Ceramic Society George Eumorfopoulos; Sir George Hill and Robert Hobson, the Director and the Keeper of Oriental Antiquities of the British Museum respectively; and retired major general of the British Army Sir Neill Malcolm. These five individuals contacted the British Foreign Office in 1934 asking for "support and patronage" for the idea of a major Chinese exhibition in London. In their minds, Chinese participation was necessary to ensure a show of the highest artistic quality.[16]

As they worked to secure Chinese support for their plan, these individuals presented the event as a means to transmit the "Chinese spirit" to Western audiences and as a vehicle to improve the image of China as a whole.[17] "The direct and the transmitted influence of the ideals of that spirit," they argued in a memorandum to the Chinese government, "are becoming in an increasing measure a ponderable factor in the relations of China with the West." China's message thus mattered greatly to its standing in the world. The memorandum pointed out that the Chinese exhibition would be part of a series that had previously included shows of Flemish, Dutch, Italian, Persian, and French art, which had "succeeded in fostering closer cultural relations between those countries and Britain than would otherwise have been possible." By participating, China would brand itself as a member of a select group of world powers whose artistic production was universally admired.[18]

This document also made explicit how the show would allow China to shape foreign perceptions:

> It is difficult to deny that the impression made on the world by international exhibitions of art go far beyond the events themselves. They enhance the admiration and the respect felt for the people to whose artistic genius the exhibit owes its origin, and they have been proved to result in enormous material benefits, not only politically but commercially and economically as well.[19]

Undeniably, "every country occupying a prominent place in the world to-day is growing increasingly conscious of the desirability of expressing its character and its national ideals through the medium of its art on all occasions when other nations have expressed theirs."[20] The Chinese exhibition, the organizers contended, would serve as a tool for shaping foreign perceptions in the international arena (or for what later would be called nation branding).[21]

Although the idea for the exhibition did not come from a government but from a group of non-state individuals and institutions, very quickly the British Foreign Office and the Chinese Ministry of Education became involved, approved the plan, and used the event for their own nation branding purposes. The British Foreign Office insisted that this exhibition allow the host, Great Britain, to affirm itself as a center for international cooperation; and for the numerous countries who participated by lending objects (which deliberately included Japan), to build their own reputations as willing and respectable members of the international community. For this reason, the Foreign Office, in line with its policy of strengthening China without antagonizing Japan, granted "auspices" only on the condition that the event would not be contentious; accordingly, no conflicts were to arise from the occasion, either within China (over who owned or held authority over the artifacts) or in the international arena. And under no circumstances could it become an anti-Japanese show. In fact, the British Foreign Office took meaningful steps to ensure that Japan would figure in the list of lenders. Stephen Gaselee of the British Foreign Office contacted both the British and the Japanese ambassadors for help to secure loans from the Imperial Household, the Imperial Household Museum in Tokyo, the Tokyo Fine Arts School, and the Kyoto Imperial University, as well as from several Japanese private collectors. As Percival David later acknowledged, it was thanks to the Foreign Office that Japan had been included in the list of participating countries.[22] Consequently, the exhibition publicized the idea that London—and the United Kingdom—served as a center for amicable exchange among different countries.[23]

For the Republic of China, too, participating in the 1935–36 International Exhibition of Chinese Art in London was as a powerful nation branding tool to legitimize itself as the lawful heir of the Chinese past and as the rightful representative of the Chinese present. If the Nanjing government could choose what, when, where, and how Chinese artifacts would be displayed, it would advance its claims to rule the entire Chinese territory including the northeast. Moreover, the Nanjing regime could show itself as "open" to international cooperation. Effectively a tool for nation building, this event branded China—and the republican regime that ruled it—as legitimate, successful, civilized, and engaged in the international community. Undoubtedly, for both the British and the Chinese governments, this exhibition—and the international cooperation that had made it possible—improved their reputations at home and abroad.[24]

As soon as the plan was set in motion, the organizing committee was expanded to include diplomat and League of Nations representative Victor Bulwer-Lytton (chairman); the Chinese ambassador in London, Guo Taiqi; the president of the London Royal Academy, Sir William Llewellyn (vice-chairman); F. T. Cheng (special commissioner of the Chinese government); W. R. M. Lamb (secretary); and F. J. P. Richter (secretary of the Lecture Committee). Other members included a select group of artists and people interested in Chinese art.[25] In China, a Planning and Preparatory Committee was soon set up to coordinate the loan of the objects from the imperial collection. At its head was the Chinese Minister of Education, Wang Shijie. Other members included several representatives of the major branches of government, as well as renowned artist and poet Chen Shuren. In addition, there were executives from the most prestigious Chinese cultural institutions: Ma Heng, who served as director of the Palace Museum, and Yuan Tongli, the president of the National Library of Peiping.[26] Furthermore, a distinguished group of lecturers was invited to address the public on subjects related to the Chinese exhibition. This included several members of the British and the Chinese committees, along with famous sinologists, archeologists, and scholars from various countries around the world (most notably, Langdon

Warner from the United States and Yashiro Yukio from Japan). Finally, a long list of generous sponsors and honorary members offered auspices for the occasion.

The name of Victor Bulwer-Lytton (1876–1947) as the Chairman did much to brand the exhibition as an international—and an internationalist—event.[27] His work as representative of the League of Nations in the context of the 1931 Manchurian crisis had made him famous around the world and in Britain especially. As the author of the "Lytton Report," adopted by the League Council on 24 February 1933, he symbolized the League and its faith in the power of legal arbitration. Although the report itself had become known as a failed attempt at reconciling two parties that ended up leaving both unsatisfied, Lord Lytton continued to write, speak, and rally indefatigably in support of the League. In a series of pamphlets and lectures, he kept discussing his experience in Manchuria, arguing against the inevitability of failure for the League of Nations. Contemporaries thus associated his name with internationalism, its challenges, and its promises.[28]

As a group, the numerous individuals and organizations from all over the world that collaborated in staging the Chinese exhibition served as proof that despite ongoing tensions, international cooperation was possible. This point was conveyed effectively in the official poster of the exhibition. The title, which included the adjective "international," qualified the entire event as such. The long span of time covered by the exhibition, "1700 BC–1800 AD," together with the venerable figure of Emperor Taizong of the Song dynasty, evoked the long artistic tradition of "Old Masters" who could be universally appreciated by people from all over the world.[29] Similarly, the official catalog of the exhibition overtly put on display the international composition of the organizing committee of the exhibition. On the title page, "His Majesty the King, Her Majesty Queen Mary, and the President of the Republic of China" appeared together as the official patrons. The list of honorary presidents, followed by a "committee of honour" and the many subcommittees that had made the event possible, extended several pages.[30] Countless languages were represented in both names and honorary titles. The same was true in the "Index of Lenders," which also occupied several pages. The prominent display of British and Chinese titles and authorities next to one another and the endless roll of political and scholarly authorities that had cooperated for the occasion provided a concrete image of international "practical cooperation" of the kind promoted by the League of Nations in this period.

The preface, co-authored by the President of the Royal Academy Sir William Llewellyn and by Lord Lytton, pointed out that the exhibition had been staged with "the willing support of the Chinese Government." Here too the message was that the exhibition opened a new era, one in which individual nations interacted as equal partners. In the past, objects from China had been simply taken and displayed in Europe regardless of the wishes of the Chinese government; now the situation was different. For the first time, the Chinese government had participated willingly; and the objects had been lent, not acquired permanently. An "Editorial Note" at the beginning of the volume also explained that in some cases the British and the Chinese committees disagreed on the attribution of certain pieces; in such cases, both versions had been included. The volume made it clear that all opinions had been taken into account, providing a concrete image of what a peaceful international exchange looked like in the post-1919 world.[31]

The catalog was a tool to brand internationalism as a successful and promising set of ideas and practices, thus improving the reputation of all those who engaged in it. The preface listed all the governments that had lent pieces for the occasion, including "Austria, Egypt, France, Germany, Japan, Russia, Sweden, Turkey and the City of Danzig, as well as museums and private collectors throughout the world."[32] Here the presence of Germany and Japan provided great reassurance to readers. Even if relationships had been strained, these countries enthusiastically participated in the event. In the context of this exhibition, the City of Danzig and Germany coexisted as two authorities that respected each other and seemingly collaborated in a common endeavor. And the Soviet Union—which appeared under the less threatening name of Russia—seemed to be fully integrated into the international system. At the time these pages were printed, such a roster would not have been possible in any other form of political collaboration. Indeed, Germany and Japan were no longer members of the League, and tensions were rapidly arising in the political realm. Yet the catalog provided a counterargument to this grim reality, portraying international cooperation in the field of culture as an alternative—and significant—reality.

The quality of the artifacts and the sheer size of the exhibition further strengthened this point. By all accounts, visitors went on an unforgettable journey through centuries of Chinese cultural productions: recently excavated pieces from the prehistoric village of Yangshao, in Henan; Shang and Zhou bronzes; works from the Han period; Buddhist sculptures; paintings from Dunhuang; vases, dishes, and porcelains; eighteenth-century lacquers; books; and examples of calligraphy. Every medium of art and craft ever produced in China seemed to be represented within the confines of Burlington House, on display with the international cooperation that had made it possible. Even outside, both during and after the exhibition, admiration for Chinese art quickly turned into an unprecedented "Chinese Art Fever": "Chinese style hats" were in fashion, with "cerulean blue" as the season's preferred color, and the "Chinese wave theme" as the favorite pattern. Crowds were allured by anything Chinese, whether it be a cone-shaped hat or a charm in jade or a movie that promised to feature the real home life of a Chinese family.[33] And if this kind of consumption was connected with imperialism and self-identity formation,[34] its increase in the mid 1930s in conjunction with the exhibition confirms that the event had succeeded in creating positive associations with China and with the policies that had made it possible for all to admire its treasures.

Chinese Art in the Nation Branding Formula

Wally Olins, author of a number of seminal works on nation branding, points out how starting from the 1920s a new "scientific" formula emerged to entice people to buy products. It later became known as a USP (or Unique Selling Proposition), and—simply summarized—it went as follows: a product is better because it contains a magic ingredient X; and the consumer should buy it because ultimately, he/she will be better off.[35] During the same period, international cooperation in the field of culture followed the same formula: according to its promoters it would work because it contained a magic ingredient (in this case, art), which had a universal value. Thanks to this element, international cooperation in the field of culture could go where politics could not, extending to all realms of interaction and leading to peace and stability for all.[36]

Chinese art worked particularly well in this context. Its long history placed it solidly in the canon of "old art" that people from all nations would appreciate (in contrast to modern art, for instance, which would be controversial). Long-standing orientalist notions also contributed to the perception of Chinese art as the quintessential expression of peace. This fueled the argument that every person—regardless of nationality or political views—would be touched by it; this feeling would be transferred from the cultural to the political realm; and the world would be more peaceful for the benefit of the international community as a whole.

The introduction to the catalog made this point most effectively. According to Laurence Binyon, curator at the British Museum and author of several books, Chinese art reflected an alternative "mental world," one which all people could come to appreciate "with little trouble." Nature, not the individual, was at its center. As a result of "genial humanity," Chinese art spoke a universal language: "appealing to the senses alike of sight and touch the finest of the bowls and vases seem at the same time to transcend the world of sense and to speak in some subtle and secret way to the emotions of the spirit."[37] This emotive quality was the secret ingredient that would allow it to work. By studying and viewing Chinese art, he hoped, Europeans might incorporate the values it exuded into their own worldview.[38] As a consequence, their governments would abandon their greedy imperialist policies, and peace would ensue.[39]

Emotions played an important role in the branding process. Chinese art fit well for this purpose because contemporaries thought it expressed sentiments such as "brotherhood," "fraternity," and "love" more than the art of other traditions did. F. T. Cheng, who served as the special commissioner of the Chinese government for the Chinese Exhibition, explained in a lecture delivered at the London Royal Academy that Chinese art—because of its capacity to calm the mind and unite people in harmony—could serve as a powerful tool of governance. He then stressed how peace and harmony were engrained in Chinese cultural history: Chinese art was "not created by the bayonet, but produced by the desire of those things which make perfect beauty: peace, virtue, righteousness, and love." If applied on an international scale, these "things which make perfect beauty" could also bring about peace.[40]

Internationalism, Branded

A close look at the staging of the 1935–36 International Exhibition of Chinese Art reveals that visibility was of paramount importance. Because internationalism was to serve as a tool for nation branding, the transportation and the selection of the objects to be put on display were conducted publicly, and the media devoted much attention to them. Newspapers around the world published photographs of the HMS *Suffolk* carrying the Chinese artifacts from Shanghai to Portsmouth; the British bluejackets carefully transferring each case;

the lorries taking the precious cargo to Burlington House, in the heart of London; and experts from different countries working together to unpack each object and install it in its proper location. Seen against this backdrop, the Chinese exhibition showcased not only artifacts, but also the peoples, the institutions, the governments, and the policies that had led to their display. Concerns about visibility and public perceptions dominated the organizational process, as details about transportation and installation, for instance, were often determined by factors other than the safety or the artistic value of the artifacts. Both the Chinese and the British organizing committees made sure to convey that the Chinese objects were handled with care, and public performance determined not only what international cooperation looked like but also what it was on this occasion.[41]

Much emphasis was placed on the visible and symbolic aspects of international cooperation. The surviving documents relating to the organizational process of the exhibition seldom mention technical meetings among experts from various countries. Instead, file after file reveals an array of press showings, public lectures, luncheons, and banquets held with a frequency that never seemed to slow down throughout the four months in which the exhibition was open. Long lists of attending guests made it to the press; the actual artifacts seemed to be relegated to the background, while the names and titles of those who owned them, lent them, and engaged in international cooperation in order to display them stole the show.

If advertising exposes and shapes what consumers think and want at a given time, then the case of the Chinese exhibition speaks of an audience increasingly convinced that the power of the British Empire—and of "the West" as a whole—was quickly fading. Both a desirable and an inevitable feature of the twentieth century, international cooperation had thus become both a duty and a promise. Professor Walter Perceval Yetts provocatively asked while presenting the exhibition to a wide audience of BBC listeners: "Do you know that nearly a quarter of mankind is Chinese? Do you know that China was civilized more than three thousand years ago?" Yetts pointed out how throughout history, "the Chinese have never failed to assimilate and re-interpret whatever they have borrowed, giving it qualities of their own." Exposure to the cultural production of others had inspired China to execute masterpieces, and a similar effort was now required from British spectators. The message was that Chinese art was worth incorporating into one's cache of cultural knowledge, or perhaps artistic repertoire. In this context, China and its art were branded as indispensable cultural references; and Britain and its people as a well-rounded, cultivated audience.[42]

In a post-imperial world (or one that was soon to be), one could not afford to be ignorant about China.[43] Every school child, but also every adult, should make an effort to understand this world. For this reason, reduced tickets were offered to schools and workers' associations.[44] Unfamiliarity with Chinese art and culture should not discourage potential visitors. Speaking on BBC Radio, Leigh Ashton (who had played a major role in situating each artifact in the galleries of Burlington House) vividly described the richness of the collection on display and assured the public that they ought not to be intimidated by it, because "it is essentially an exhibition for everyone."[45]

The several pages of advertisements at the end of the catalog conveyed the idea that China and its culture were at once desirable and within anybody's reach. Art dealers such as Spink & Son, Frank Partridge, John Sparks, Yamanaka & Co., and C. T. Loo & Co. offered Chinese artifacts for sale; and a subscription to the art magazine *The Connoisseur* would easily provide buyers with the necessary know-how to make wise purchases. Chinese-style jewels and interior designs were all the rage and widely available, and Chinese-style theater plays were in town. And for those who sought a first-hand experience, the Peninsular and Oriental Steam Navigation Company (P&O) offered "Direct fortnightly Passenger and Freight Service by large modern mail steamer from London and Marseilles to Penang, Singapore, Hong Kong, Shanghai, Kobe and Yokohama." At £150 for a round-trip, first-class ticket, China seemed to be around the corner.

Ultimately, this internationalist exhibition was not something to be missed. It was different from all the other events that had preceded it because of its size, and especially because this time China had willingly participated in the event. While previous displays had included objects brought back by European collectors, these artifacts had been delivered directly by the Chinese, thus allowing Western audiences to experience China first-hand. On sale was the "authentic" experience of China, one that still maintained its "aura." This show also represented a once-in-a-lifetime opportunity. This was not only because of the aesthetic value of the objects on display, but also because of the unprecedented degree of international collaboration that it had required in order to be staged. As Leigh Ashton told BBC listeners, these works of art had come from all over the world, and "[t]hey will never come again."[46]

There was also a cosmopolitan, experiential aspect to the exhibition that only visitors could understand.[47] Artist Edward Halliday, who joined Leigh Ashton in a BBC radio program, described the magic atmosphere at the Royal Academy on the day the press and a few VIPs were allowed a first tour of the galleries. "Long shiny cars have been inconveniencing the normal traffic of Piccadilly all day long, as they turned and slid under the dark archway of Burlington House. Photographers before the portico snapped famous faces, and fashion reporters recorded who was wearing what and how."[48] British, Chinese, German, and Japanese exhibitors and visitors alike made their way to Burlington House to admire the same artifacts, to celebrate their love for beauty, and to add to the ambiance.[49] As remarked in an article published in the *Daily Representatives* of Queenstown, South Africa, "Apart from the beauty of the exhibits, the most striking feature at the private viewing of the Chinese exhibition was the Babel of foreign tongues. An English voice was an exception rather than the rule." [50] Such images branded all those who participated in it—and the internationalism that made it possible—as cosmopolitan and modern. As a result, driven by its branding potential, internationalism became dominated by its visible, symbolic aspects. Thus, nation branding and internationalism fueled one another while appealing to the same crowd of participants, exhibitors, and spectators.

Conclusion

As Simon Anholt recently pointed out, nation branding per se does not improve reputation. Ultimately, "countries are judged by what they do, not by what they say."[51] Yet, as this study shows, the act of saying involved much doing on the part of all actors involved. Indeed, while engaging in nation branding the governments of the United Kingdom and China did collaborate in the staging of the exhibition of Chinese art, establishing a precedent that proved influential in the subsequent decades. More work is needed to shed light on this continuity, and particularly on how internationalism and nation branding continued to influence one another throughout the twentieth century.

In the case of the 1935–36 International Exhibition of Chinese Art in London, internationalism served as a powerful tool for nation branding as participants used this public display of international cooperation to build their reputations as open, respectable, and benevolent members of the international community. As a consequence, the growing importance of nation branding led to the increasing predominance of symbolic, visible forms of international cooperation at the expense of less overt ones (e.g., joint insurance for the artifacts, or less conspicuous modes of transportation). Concerns about what internationalism looked like (along with its branding power and potential) dominated all others at Burlington House. The committees in charge of the exhibition made decisions regarding the selection, transportation, and display of Chinese artifacts while paying much consideration to their effect on each participant's reputation. On this occasion, nation branding dictated internationalist practices, shaping international cooperation in ways thus far unexplored.

This study also revealed complexities in the history of nation branding that have been neglected until now by historians and scholars of nation branding alike. In this case, nation branding was not initiated by a country that sought to improve its reputation. Instead, the idea for the exhibition came from a group of actors (collectors and people interested in Chinese art) who used the promise of nation branding to achieve different goals. The Republic of China acted in response to their request and embraced the opportunity to brand itself as the heir to Chinese culture and as a legitimate authority engaged in the international community. Great Britain seized the opportunity to brand itself as a mediator among countries and as a quintessential site for international cooperation. Moreover, other countries served not only as targets, but also as nation branders; and the same can be said about the international crowd of people who visited the exhibition. At once exhibitors and spectators, they too influenced both internationalism and nation branding on this occasion, adding to the wide array of actors involved in defining this event.

We know that consumers and spectators play a major role in shaping both the branding process and the products offered to them. As historians, we may be skeptical of Wally Olins's contention that "the brand is controlled by us—the customers"; that "we, the public, we consumers" have the power of rewarding good brands and punishing bad ones; and that "if we can't be bothered to do that, we will get what we deserve."[52] But keeping his words in mind and shifting focus from the sellers to the consumers of nations and their ideologies might prove a useful exercise for historians of this period. It might allow them to investigate how the desires of the audience might have shaped what was offered to them. How did people's wishes and aspirations affect the efforts to appeal to them, either through internationalism or through nation branding? How did consumers contribute to defining the nations and the ideologies that tried to allure them?

One may question the effectiveness of the branding efforts described in this chapter. To be sure, despite numerous internationalist initiatives, the 1930s remain a decade filled with international tensions. Yet the point stands that at the 1935–36 International Exhibition of Chinese Art numerous countries—including China and the United Kingdom—devoted much energy to building their reputations through international cooperation. The emphasis they placed on symbolic, visible actions proved long-lasting, and still persists in practices of nation branding and internationalism alike.

Our understanding of foreign policy and international relations can also be refined by seeing nations as products defined by the multiple actors who held a stake in their sale and purchase on the global market. Given the centrality of emotions in the branding process, scholars from a broad range of disciplines might be able to delve deeper into the influence of shared notions and feelings (such as friendship, care, pride, and anger) on international relations. By opening a new line of inquiry, nation branding may prove helpful to investigating the role of aspirations in shaping international history and to analyzing how people expressed and endeavored to realize who and what they wanted to be in the international arena.

Ilaria Scaglia is a lecturer in Modern History at Aston University in Birmingham, UK. She is the author of "The Aesthetics of Internationalism: Culture and Politics on Display at the 1935–1936 International Exhibition of Chinese Art," *Journal of World History* 26, no. 1 (March 2015): 105–37. She is also the recipient of the 2016–2017 Volkswagen-Mellon Postdoctoral Fellowship for Research in Germany.

Notes

I thank John Abromeit, Nicholas Cull, Andreas Daum, Steven Gill, Georg Iggers, Jaeho Kang, Michael Krenn, Kristin Stapleton, the editors of this volume for their generous help and the anonymous reviewers who provided valuable feedback on this piece.

1. Jason Steuber, "The Exhibition of Chinese Art at Burlington House, London, 1935–36," *The Burlington Magazine* 148, no. 1241 (August 2006): 528. See also Ilaria Scaglia, "The Aesthetics of Internationalism: Culture and Politics on Display at the 1935–1936 International Exhibition of Chinese Art," *Journal of World History* 26, 1 (March 2015): 105–137.

2. According to the Royal Academy's *Annual Report*, 401,768 paying visitors walked through the turnstiles of Burlington House, and 2,531 season tickets were sold. *Annual Report from the Council of the Royal Academy to the General Assembly of Academicians and Associates for the Year 1936* (London: William Clowes and Sons, 1937), 23, 40. The figure of over 422,000, widely reported by the press, included private viewings and non-paying visitors. This number placed the Chinese exhibition second only to the 1930 Italian exhibition, which attracted 537,968 people. I thank Mark Pomeroy, archivist of the London Royal Academy, for providing me with these figures from the institution's internal database.

3. Most notably, in 2005, the Royal Academy celebrated this landmark event with a commemorative exhibition titled "From Peking to Piccadilly 70 Years Ago: A Display of Press Photographs Showing the Preparation of the Royal Academy's First Chinese Art Exhibition in 1935–6."

4. Glenda Sluga, *Internationalism in the Age of Nationalism* (Philadelphia: University of Pennsylvania Press, 2013), 5.

5. Wally Olins, *On Brand* (New York: Thames & Hudson, 2004), 11. This is in contrast with nation branding as the work of a group of marketing experts formally hired by individual governments to improve their own image, which did not emerge until after 1945. See Melissa Aronczyk, *Branding the Nation: The Global Business of National Identity* (Oxford: Oxford University Press, 2013), 4.

6. On propaganda, see Nicholas J. Cull, *Selling War: The British Propaganda Campaign against American "Neutrality" in World War II* (New York: Oxford University Press, 1995), and *The Cold War and the United States Information Agency: American Propaganda and Public Diplomacy, 1945–1989* (Cambridge: Cambridge University Press, 2008). See also Laura A. Belmonte, *Selling the American Way: U.S. Propaganda and the Cold War* (Philadelphia: University of Pennsylvania Press, 2008).

7. See Nicholas J. Cull, "Public Diplomacy: Taxonomies and Histories," *The Annals of the American Academy of Political and Social Science* 616, no. 1 (March 2008): 31–54. On the distinction between public diplomacy and cultural diplomacy, see Jessica C. E. Gienow-Hecht, "The Anomaly of the Cold War: Cultural Diplomacy and Civil Society since 1850," in *The United States and Public Diplomacy: New Directions in Cultural and International History*, ed. Kenneth Alan Osgood and Brian Craig Etheridge (Leiden: Martinus Nijhoff Publishers, 2010), 32. On public diplomacy, see also Justin Hart, *Empire of Ideas: The Origins of Public Diplomacy and the Transformation of U.S. Foreign Policy* (Oxford: Oxford University Press, 2013).

8. On how to conceptualize this process, and on the distinction between the concept of brand and branding as a practice, see Keith Dinnie, *Nation Branding: Concepts, Issues, Practice* (Oxford: Butterworth-Heinemann, 2008), 14–16.

9. See Nadia Kaneva, ed., *Branding Post-Communist Nations: Marketizing National Identities in the "New" Europe* (New York: Routledge, 2012).

10. On the distinction between a country's brand (or its reputation) and the branding process, see Simon Anholt, *Places: Identity, Image and Reputation* (Houndmills: Palgrave Macmillan, 2010), especially the introduction and chapter 2.

11. On how transnational connections (exchanges among nonstate actors, or individuals and institutions outside of government) constituted an integral part of internationalist ideas and practices, see Daniel Laqua, ed., *Internationalism Reconfigured: Transnational Ideas and Movements between the World Wars* (New York: Palgrave Macmillan, 2011).

12. See aforementioned article by Jason Steuber, "The Exhibition of Chinese Art at Burlington House, London, 1935–36"; see also, Francis Haskell, "Botticelli, Fascism and Burlington House—The 'Italian Exhibition' of 1930," *The Burlington Magazine* 141, no. 1157 (August 1999): 462–72.

13. Ellen Huang, "There and Back Again: Material Objects at the First International Exhibition of Chinese Art in Shanghai, London, and Nanjing, 1935–1936," in *Collecting China: The World, China, and a History of Collecting*, ed. Vimalin Rujivacharakul (Newark: University of Delaware Press, 2011), 138–52.

14. Stacey Pierson, "From Market and Exhibition to University: Percival David and the Institutionalization of Chinese Art History in England," in *Collecting China: The World, China, and a History of Collecting*, ed. Vimalin Rujivacharakul (Newark: University of Delaware Press, 2011), 130–37.

15. Aronczyk, *Branding the Nation*, 11, 38.

16. The National Archives of the UK (hereafter TNA), FO 370/452, L 308/308/405. Letter, dated 14 January 1934, from Major General Neill Malcolm to Charles Orde. See also "Draft of a Memorandum on an International Exhibition of Chinese Art in London," attached to TNA, FO 370/452, L 516/308/405.

17. Royal Academy Archives in London (hereafter RAA), SEC/24/25/1. "Memorandum on an International Exhibition of Chinese Art in London," dated 3 February 1934, signed by Sir George Hill, Sir Neill Malcolm, Sir Percival David, Mr. George Eumorfopoulos, and Mr. R. L. Hobson.

18. Interestingly, this same argument emerged again much later in the literature about nation branding. See, for example, Simon Anholt's "National Brand Pentagon" and "competitive identity." Simon Anholt, *Brand New Justice: The Upside of Global Branding* (Oxford: Butterworth-Heinemann, 2003), 16–17, 122, 170–71; and Simon Anholt, *Competitive Identity: The New Brand Management for Nations, Cities and Regions* (Houndmills: Palgrave MacMillan, 2007), 97.

19. RAA/SEC/24/25/1, "Memorandum on an International Exhibition of Chinese Art in London," dated 3 February 1934, signed by Sir George Hill, Sir Neill Malcolm, Sir Percival David, Mr. George Eumorfopoulos, and Mr. R. L. Hobson, 1–2.

20. RAA/SEC/24/25/1, "Memorandum on an International Exhibition of Chinese Art in London," dated 3 February 1934, signed by Sir George Hill, Sir Neill Malcolm, Sir Percival David, Mr. George Eumorfopoulos, and Mr. R. L. Hobson, 1–2.

21. RAA/SEC/24/25/1, "Memorandum on an International Exhibition of Chinese Art in London," dated 3 February 1934, signed by Sir George Hill, Sir Neill Malcolm, Sir Percival David, Mr. George Eumorfopoulos, and Mr. R. L. Hobson, 1–2.

22. See correspondence in TNA, FO 370/452, L 7491/308/405 and FO 370/477, L 5632/198/405. See also Royal Academy Handwritten Minutes, Meeting 7 January 1935.

23. See correspondence in TNA, FO 370/452. Of particular relevance are: L308/308/405; handwritten comments by Sir Cecil Harcourt Smith, dated 19 January 1934, L308/308/405; handwritten comments by A.W.G. Randall, dated 19 January 1934, L 6779/308/405; note, dated 28 November 1934, from Stephen Gaselee to the Private Secretary; L 6779/308/40. On internal divisions within the Foreign Office with regard to this policy, see Michael Hughes, *British Foreign Secretaries in an Uncertain World, 1919–1939* (London: Routledge, 2006).

24. On the Chinese strife for "equality," see Guoqi Xu, *China and the Great War: China's Pursuit of a New National Identity and Internationalization* (New York: Cambridge University Press, 2005). See also William Kirby, "The Internationalization of China: Foreign Relations at Home and Abroad in the Republican Era," in *Reappraising Republican China*, ed. Frederic Wakeman, Jr. and Richard Louis

Edmonds (Oxford: Oxford University Press, 2000), 179–204; Frank Dikötter, *The Age of Openness: China before Mao* (Berkeley: University of California Press, 2008). On the importance of "symbols" in Republican China, see Henrietta Harrison, *The Making of the Republican Citizen: Political Ceremonies and Symbols in China, 1911–1929* (Oxford: Oxford University Press, 2000).

25. These were the scholar and curator of the Victoria and Albert Museum Leigh Ashton; poet, art historian, and curator of the British Museum Laurence Binyon; Dr. W. C. Chen of the Chinese Embassy; museum philanthropist Dr. J. S. Lee (also known as Bei Shan Tang); the Academy's treasurer, painter Sydney Lee; Victoria & Albert Museum curator Bernard Rackham; art collector Oscar Raphael; young Chinese artist and collector C. C. Wang; and Professor Walter Perceval Yetts. Finally, the renowned French sinologist Paul Pelliot was engaged as a consultant for the selection of the objects to be put on display. *Annual Report from the Council of the Royal Academy to the General Assembly of Academicians and Associates for the Year 1934* (William Clowes and Sons, limited, Printers to the Royal Academy, 1935), 19–20. See also Press Announcement, (January 1935) RAA/SEC/24/25/1.

26. For further details, see RAA/SEC/24/25/1, Telegram, dated 12 December 1934, from Wang Shih-chieh (Minister of Education).

27. There is no published biography of Lord Victor Bulwer-Lytton. An account of his life, written by his son-in-law C. M. Woodhouse, is held at the archive of the historical Lytton residence, Knebworth House, in Hertfordshire. C. M. Woodhouse, *A Biography of Victor Lytton, Second Earl of Lytton* (Unpublished).

28. Due to its conciliatory nature, the report has been described as a step along the inevitable path toward "appeasement" and World War II. For a judicious account and a recent bibliography on these events, see Thomas Burkman, *Japan and the League of Nations: Empire and World Order, 1914–1938* (Honolulu: University of Hawai'i Press, 2008).

29. The poster reproduced exhibition item #2296 Unknown artist; Sung dynasty. Portrait of the Emperor T'ai Tsung (reigned 976–996 AD). Painting in colour on silk. H. 74 cm. W. 47 cm. Probably Ming. Lent by the Chinese government. Displayed in the Central Hall. *Catalogue of the International Exhibition of Chinese Art, 1935–6* (London: Royal Academy of Arts, 1935), 197. I thank Craig Benjamin, Kristin Stapleton, and Mark Pomeroy for their help in attributing this image.

30. *Catalogue*, vi–x.

31. *Catalogue*, xxiv.

32. *Catalogue*, iv–v.

33. These quotes come from a collection of newspaper and magazine clippings about the exhibition preserved by the London Royal Academy collected by Alleyne Clarice Zander. I thank the archivist of the academy, Mr Mark Pomeroy, who kindly allowed me to access this archive when it was still in the process of being preserved and catalogued.

34. On how the consumption of such objects influenced self-identity, see Kristin L. Hoganson, *Consumers' Imperium: The Global Production of American Domesticity, 1865–1920* (Chapel Hill: University of North Carolina Press, 2007). Although Hoganson discussed the case of the United States, I see the same mechanics at play in the United Kingdom.

35. Olins, *On Brand*, 58–59. The concept of "Unique Selling Proposition" was first introduced by Rosser Reeves, *Reality in Advertising* (New York: Alfred A. Knopf, 1961).

36. On the philosophical aspects of the history of the search for a universal language, see Umberto Eco, *The Search for the Perfect Language*, trans. James

Fentress (Cambridge, MA: Blackwell, 1995; orig. *Ricerca della lingua perfetta nella cultura europea*, Roma: Laterza, 1993). On the history of standardization in this context, see Martin H. Geyer, "One Language for the World: The Metric System, International Coinage, Gold Standard, and the Rise of Internationalism, 1850–1900," in *The Mechanics of Internationalism*, ed. Martin H. Geyer and Johannes Paulmann (London: Oxford University Press, 2001), 55–92.

37. *Catalogue,* xviii–xvii.

38. Hatcher noted how Binyon's interest in Asia (and especially his fascination for Taoism) did not constitute a form of "modish spiritual posturing," nor did it provide a means for accumulating fame or material wealth (in fact, his friends often expressed concern for his and his family's well-being). Instead they were the expression of a man's search for a deeper understanding of himself, his own society, and the complexities of the "modern" world in which he lived. John Hatcher, *Laurence Binyon: Poet, Scholar of East and West* (Oxford: Clarendon Press, 1995), 134.

39. *Catalogue,* xiii–xvii.

40. F. T. Cheng, "Some Cultural and Historical Aspects of Chinese Art," delivered at the London Royal Academy on 6 December 1935, in F. T. Cheng, *Reflections at Eighty* (London: Luzac and Co. Ltd., 1966), 70.

41. I analyze some of these materials in depth in chapter II of the section "Annotated Sources."

42. BBC Written Archive Center (hereafter WAC), Programme Records: 1935. Prof. W. P. Yetts, "The Exhibition of Chinese Art at Burlington House," 1.

43. As Melissa Aronczyk pointed out, arguments about the inevitability of globalization accompanied many forms of nation branding and can be seen as a byproduct of the nation branding process. Aronczyk, *Branding the Nation,* 85.

44. *Catalogue,* iii.

45. BBC WAC, Radio Talks Scripts. Edward Halliday and Leigh Ashton, "The International Chinese Art Exhibition," broadcasted regionally on Wednesday, 27 November 1935, 10:00–10:30 pm.

46. BBC WAC, Radio Talks Scripts. Edward Halliday and Leigh Ashton.

47. On cosmopolitanism at the Royal Academy, see Holger Hoock, *The King's Artists: The Royal Academy of Arts and the Politics of British Culture 1760–1840* (Oxford: Clarendon Press, 2003). It is important to note that—as Craig Calhoun has argued—"cosmopolitanism and nationalism are mutually constitutive and to oppose them sharply is misleading." See Craig Calhoun, *Nations Matter: Culture, History, and the Cosmopolitan Dream* (London: Routledge, 2007), 13.

48. BBC WAC, Radio Talks Scripts. Edward Halliday and Leigh Ashton.

49. BBC WAC, Radio Talks Scripts. Edward Halliday and Leigh Ashton.

50. *Daily Representatives,* undated, ca. 27 November 1935. The article is part of the clipping collection on the exhibition preserved at the RAA archives.

51. Simon Anholt, "Beyond the Nation Brand: The Role of Image and Identity in International Relations," *The Journal of Public Diplomacy* 2, no. 1 (2011): 1.

52. Olins, *On Brand,* 16, 220, 233.

Bibliography

Anholt, Simon. *Brand New Justice: The Upside of Global Branding.* Oxford: Butterworth-Heinemann, 2003.

————. "Beyond the Nation Brand: The Role of Image and Identity in International Relations." *The Journal of Public Diplomacy* 2, no. 1 (2011). Retrieved 13 July 2015 from http://surface.syr.edu/exchange/vol2/iss1/1.

————. *Competitive Identity: The New Brand Management for Nations, Cities and Regions.* Houndmills: Palgrave Macmillan, 2007.

————. *Places: Identity, Image and Reputation.* Houndmills: Palgrave Macmillan, 2010.

Annual Report from the Council of the Royal Academy to the General Assembly of Academicians and Associates. William Clowes and Sons, Limited, Printers to the Royal Academy, 1932–1941.

Aronczyk, Melissa. *Branding the Nation: The Global Business of National Identity.* Oxford: Oxford University Press, 2013.

Belmonte, Laura A. *Selling the American Way: U.S. Propaganda and the Cold War.* Philadelphia, PA: University of Pennsylvania Press, 2008.

Burkman, Thomas. *Japan and the League of Nations: Empire and World Order, 1914–1938.* Honolulu, HI: University of Hawai'i Press, 2008.

Calhoun, Craig. *Nations Matter: Culture, History, and the Cosmopolitan Dream.* London: Routledge, 2007.

Catalogue of the International Exhibition of Chinese Art, 1935–6. London: Royal Academy of Arts, 1935.

Cheng, F. T. *Reflections at Eighty.* London: Luzac and Co. Ltd., 1966.

Cull, Nicholas J. *The Cold War and the United States Information Agency: American Propaganda and Public Diplomacy, 1945–1989.* Cambridge: Cambridge University Press, 2008.

————. "Public Diplomacy: Taxonomies and Histories." *The Annals of the American Academy of Political and Social Science* 616, no. 1 (March 2008): 31–54.

————. *Selling War: The British Propaganda Campaign against American "Neutrality" in World War II.* New York: Oxford University Press, 1995.

Dikötter, Frank. *The Age of Openness: China before Mao.* Berkeley, CA: University of California Press, 2008.

Dinnie, Keith. *Nation Branding: Concepts, Issues, Practice.* Oxford: Butterworth-Heinemann, 2008.

Eco, Umberto. *The Search for the Perfect Language.* Trans. James Fentress. Cambridge, MA: Blackwell, 1995; orig. *Ricerca della lingua perfetta nella cultura europea.* Roma: Laterza, 1993.

Geyer, Martin H. "One Language for the World: The Metric System, International Coinage, Gold Standard, and the Rise of Internationalism, 1850–1900." In *The Mechanics of Internationalism,* edited by Martin H. Geyer and Johannes Paulmann, 55–92. London: Oxford University Press, 2001.

Gienow-Hecht, Jessica C. E. "The Anomaly of the Cold War: Cultural Diplomacy and Civil Society since 1850." In *The United States and Public Diplomacy: New Directions in Cultural and International History,* edited by Kenneth Alan Osgood and Brian Craig Etheridge, 27–56. Leiden: Martinus Nijhoff Publishers, 2010.

Harrison, Henrietta. *The Making of the Republican Citizen: Political Ceremonies and Symbols in China, 1911–1929.* Oxford: Oxford University Press, 2000.

Hart, Justin. *Empire of Ideas: The Origins of Public Diplomacy and the Transformation of U.S. Foreign Policy.* Oxford: Oxford University Press, 2013.

Haskell, Francis. "Botticelli, Fascism and Burlington House—The 'Italian Exhibition' of 1930." *Burlington Magazine* 141, no. 1157 (August 1999): 462–72.

Hatcher, John. *Laurence Binyon: Poet, Scholar of East and West.* Oxford: Clarendon Press, 1995.

Hoganson, Kristin L. *Consumers' Imperium: The Global Production of American Domesticity, 1865–1920.* Chapel Hill, NC: University of North Carolina Press, 2007.

Hoock, Holger. *The King's Artists: The Royal Academy of Arts and the Politics of British Culture 1760–1840.* Oxford: Clarendon Press, 2003.

Huang, Ellen. "There and Back Again: Material Objects at the First International Exhibition of Chinese Art in Shanghai, London, and Nanjing, 1935–1936." In *Collecting China: The World, China, and a History of Collecting,* edited by Vimalin Rujivacharakul, 138–52. Newark, DE: University of Delaware Press, 2011.

Hughes, Michael. *British Foreign Secretaries in an Uncertain World, 1919–1939.* London: Routledge, 2006.

Kaneva, Nadia, ed. *Branding Post-Communist Nations: Marketizing National Identities in the "New" Europe.* New York: Routledge, 2012.

Kirby, William. "The Internationalization of China: Foreign Relations at Home and Abroad in the Republican Era." In *Reappraising Republican China,* edited by Frederic Wakeman, Jr. and Richard Louis Edmonds, 179–204. Oxford: Oxford University Press, 2000.

Laqua, Daniel, ed. *Internationalism Reconfigured: Transnational Ideas and Movements between the World Wars.* New York: Palgrave Macmillan, 2011.

Olins, Wally. *On Brand.* 2nd ed. New York: Thames & Hudson, 2004.

Pierson, Stacey. "From Market and Exhibition to University: Percival David and the Institutionalization of Chinese Art History in England." In *Collecting China: The World, China, and a History of Collecting,* edited by Vimalin Rujivacharakul, 130–137. Newark, DE: University of Delaware Press, 2011.

Scaglia, Ilaria. "The Aesthetics of Internationalism: Culture and Politics on Display at the 1935–1936 International Exhibition of Chinese Art," *Journal of World History* 26, 1 (March 2015): 105–137.

Sluga, Glenda. *Internationalism in the Age of Nationalism.* Philadelphia, PA: University of Pennsylvania Press, 2013.

Steuber, Jason. "The Exhibition of Chinese Art at Burlington House, London, 1935–36." *The Burlington Magazine* 148, no. 1241 (August 2006): 528–36.

Woodhouse, C. M. *A Biography of Victor Lytton, Second Earl of Lytton.* Unpublished.

Xu, Guoqi. *China and the Great War: China's Pursuit of a New National Identity and Internationalization.* New York: Cambridge University Press, 2005.

Chapter 4

HIGH CULTURE TO THE RESCUE
Japan's Nation Branding in the United States, 1934–40

John Gripentrog

On 25 February 1933, on the eve of his departure from Geneva, Matsuoka Yōsuke, Japan's chief plenipotentiary at the League of Nations, told news reporters, "I am still hoping that someday Japan will be understood." For nearly three months, Matsuoka had endeavored to convince the world of Japan's just cause for her military actions in Manchuria (1931–33). Despite such entreaties, both the United States and the League of Nations rejected Japan's explanation for hostilities in Manchuria and the creation of the state of "Manchukuo." The US press meanwhile widely condemned Japan's aggression and its pretense of adhering to the post-World War I peace machinery. Renowned columnist Walter Lippmann warned Japan's leaders of a severe blow to their nation's "credit and prestige throughout the world"; the *New York Times* declared Japan to be "morally isolated."[1]

Undercut by the near unanimity of world opinion and facing the prospect of protracted international isolation, in 1934 Japan's leaders established the Society for International Cultural Relations (Kokusai Bunka Shinkōkai, or KBS). Comprised of prominent Japanese politicians, businessmen, academics, and members of the Foreign Service, the state-sponsored organization set out to promote a distinctive image of Japan abroad by foregrounding the nation's culture. Specifically, the KBS sought to brand Japan as a highly refined and cultivated nation. Through the theatrical display of its cultural riches, Japanese officials hoped to restore international credibility and advance the nation's foreign policy goals. As the KBS prospectus delicately explained, "As international relations of the world grow in complexity," it was imperative for Japan "to promote the value and prestige of its own culture . . . so as to merit greater respect, affection, and sympathy on the part of other peoples."[2]

The KBS's decision to tap the nation's perceived cultural assets revealed the group's convictions about the value and emotional impact of culture, especially its seeming authenticity. According to KBS president and rising political star Prince Konoe Fumimaro, "The culture of a nation [was] the key to an understanding of its people and their institutions." From Konoe's perspective, culture could be equated with "correct knowledge." And this, it was assumed, led to a series of positive associations. Once other peoples acquired a "correct understanding" of Japan, said Konoe, "amity and goodwill" would follow.[3] To be sure, in Konoe's simplified rendering, the path from cultural branding to improved foreign relations is presented as axiomatic. Still, in light of recent scholarly interpretations of nation branding, KBS programs were intuitive regarding the enabling possibilities of culture. Simon Anholt, for example, has described culture as having the "power to communicate a country's true spirit and essence."[4] Keith Dinnie similarly argues that a nation's culture "represents a truly unique and authentic facet of national identity," and suggests that negative images associated with a nation's political and military activities "may be offset by more positive associations with the same country's contemporary culture."[5]

The notion that a nation's culture offers rarified insight into national character carried the KBS's strategy to its logical conclusion: the efficacy of Japan's nation branding hinged not only on promoting the grandeur of Japanese culture, but also on convincing the world of Japan's status as a great civilization. To this end, the KBS's nation brand was politically significant because it was ideologically malleable—it could simultaneously indulge the underlying assumptions of diverse political values. On one level, the perceived sophistication of Japanese civilization could be construed as evidence that Japan, despite a detour in Manchuria, remained a leading and respectable member of the international community—a nation whose essential character remained consonant with the norms of international society. On another level—one that aligned most directly with the views of Japanese officials—the greatness of Japanese civilization implied Japanese exceptionalism and constituted evidence of a Japanese mandate to "lift up" Asia. In Geneva, for example, Matsuoka declared, "The good work of my country in Manchuria is on record. . . . In short, we have been a great civilizing and stabilizing force in that wild country."[6] This "harmonious paradox" between messenger and receiver explains the usefulness in politically motivated nation branding to avoid the taint of propaganda.

This chapter utilizes the concept of nation branding to understand Japan's attempt to shape US public opinion in the wake of the Manchurian crisis. In disseminating their nation brand to US audiences, the KBS organized numerous art exhibitions, arranged special tours of Japan, published books and sponsored lectures on a variety of cultural topics, opened libraries and reading rooms, and coordinated cultural events with likeminded transnational organizations. From 1934 to 1937, Japan's carefully crafted display of cultural power in the United States gained the sympathies of myriad American cosmopolitans, many of whom expressed an emotional affinity for the "civilizational" sublimity of Japanese culture. In the end, however, for Imperial Japan, its immediate efforts were in vain. The KBS's attempt to enhance Japan's international standing through sensually accessible cultural images struggled against the contrasting violence of aggression in China. By 1938, the damaging images of warfare and atrocity rendered self-appointed representations of cultural refinement in the United States largely impotent.

By shedding light on the complex dynamics between power, culture, and actors in international relations, this chapter critically engages with branding of the nation in times of crisis and its effectiveness in countering negative foreign images. Particularly striking, considering the absence of branding theory at the time, is the KBS's utilization in the 1930s of modern-day brand management techniques to plant positive ideas about Japan in the minds of foreigners. For one thing, KBS organizers identified an innate national asset: Japanese culture. Dinnie defines innate assets as "enduring elements of national identity," assets that offer a "powerful and authentic means of differentiation for the nation-brand."[7]

The KBS's motivation to brand "the full extent of [Japan's] culture" derived partly from the growing recognition that in recent years there developed among Japanese people "discernible signs of awakening to the value of their own culture." Contributing to this cultural stirring was the nationalist literary movement, the Japan Romantic School (*Nihon Romanha*), which championed the distinctive qualities and authority of Japanese civilization. Just as importantly, KBS officials were cognizant not only of the significant impact Japanese aesthetics first made on foreigners, especially Americans, in the late nineteenth century, but also the central role Americans played at the time in developing the historical canon of Japan as a great civilization.[8]

Indeed, the United States offered the KBS a unique opportunity to draw from a deep cultural well, thanks largely to the efforts of a passionate triumvirate: Edward Morse, Ernest Fenollosa, and Lafcadio Hearn. Morse, a biology professor at Harvard, began teaching at the new Tokyo University in 1877 and became entranced by Japanese aesthetics. Shortly after selling his collection of five thousand ceramic pieces to the Museum of Fine Arts in Boston (MFA), Morse wrote landmark studies on Japanese ceramics and architecture. Fenollosa made Japan his home for twelve years (1878–90), converted to Buddhism, and explored the length and breadth of the country in search of classic Buddhist relics. Fenollosa eventually sold his massive collection of twenty thousand Japanese artifacts to the MFA. In a kind of existential passing of the cultural baton, the same year that Fenollosa packed his bags for Boston, Hearn steamed into the port of Yokohama. Hearn delighted in the role of cultural defense attorney, daring a Western jury to doubt Japan's credentials as a highly civilized nation. He finally declared to an arts editor that "[Japanese] art is as far in advance of our art as old Greek art was superior to that of the earliest European art-gropings. . . . *We* are the barbarians."[9]

Morse and Fenollosa, in particular, helped apprise Meiji officials to the inherent value of their traditional arts, leading to the creation of a national agency to preserve and protect Japan's cultural treasures, and stringent laws that prohibited valued art works from leaving the country. In many respects, then, the KBS endeavor in the 1930s involved brand revival.

Toward this end, the KBS recruited internationally distinguished Japanese as its brand managers. According to Leslie de Chernatony, honorary professor of brand marketing at Aston University, "Successful brands thrive because the people delivering the brand act in a manner that reflects the promised values."[10] In this vein, the KBS's early roster featured a diverse group of cosmopolitan Japanese, including Viscount Ishii Kikujirō (Privy Council member and retired diplomat), Prince Tokugawa Iesato (president of the America-Japan Society and the Japanese Red Cross), Prince Konoe (president of the House of Peers), Anesaki Masaharu (professor emeritus at Tokyo Imperial University), Count Kabayama Aisuke (House of Peers), Baron Dan Inō (former art professor and son of a renowned Mitsui executive), and Foreign Minister Hirota Kōki. Emperor Hirohito's younger brother, Prince Takamatsu Nobuhito, became an honorary patron.

The study of Japan's nation branding and its agents in the 1930s is important for several reasons. First, given the recent scholarly focus on nation branding, the KBS's campaign offers a rare insight into early efforts to institutionalize branding within the state structure and to incorporate, if not pioneer, brand management techniques for the nation-state. Second, the KBS's nation branding provides an excellent case study of a highly politicized endeavor to shape the perceptions of foreign elites and manage a foreign policy crisis. As Nadia Kaneva has explained, a political approach to nation branding is "primarily interested in the impact of national images on nation-states' participation in a global system of international relations." More pointedly, this study aligns with Kaneva's consensus/essentialist research model, in that it views Japan's nation branding "as a form of persuasion that employs the tools of marketing communication with the main purpose of 'representing' national identities to specific audiences, [and] disseminating the 'best' information about [Japan's] policies."[11] In doing so, this study compels scholars to consider the diverse forms and uses of propaganda. Certainly, Japan's branding campaign in the 1930s must be classified as propaganda: it was designed to persuade foreign audiences to think and behave in a desired way, and to serve imperialist aims. But it was also a distinct form of propaganda, one with a decidedly less political character. The choice to market "national refinement"—under ambiguous auspices no less—allowed the KBS to avoid admitting plainly to political pursuits. Indeed, the KBS did the opposite, repeating the benign claim that the KBS's goal was to contribute to "the culture and welfare of all mankind, in happy unison with other nations."[12]

Third, this chapter illuminates the political mutability of a culture-based, nation branding strategy. The story of the KBS makes clear that the "less suspicious" nature of a nation's culture allows such assets to be used to reach different audiences for very different purposes. Importantly, in this case, the nation brand itself—a highly sophisticated Japanese civilization—remained "constant" and existed independent of volatile political values. What changed over time was the intended message to a particular audience. During much of the 1930s, for example, the KBS's nation brand indulged Americans' internationalist assumptions; in the early 1940s, it indulged German assumptions about a new world historical era; during the same time, it attempted to co-opt Asian nationalism by suggesting the primacy of Japan's regional leadership. Moreover, during the occupation of Japan (1945–52), US officials employed the KBS-defined nation brand to help facilitate the "democratization" of Japan.

Lastly, the KBS episode suggests further reflection on the interconnectedness and meaning between the concepts of nation branding and cultural/public diplomacy. As Kaneva notes, two principal schools of thought have emerged, with one side perceiving nation branding as distinct from cultural diplomacy, and the other viewing the concepts as virtually the same thing.[13] This study proceeds from a premise in which the two concepts are distinct, but nonetheless mutually interdependent when guided by a brand management institution. More precisely, this approach views nation branding as the process of designing, planning, and managing a brand, with cultural diplomacy related to the management team's dissemination of the nation brand.

"You Must Know Me As I Know You": KBS's Nation Branding in the United States (1934–37)

The Kokusai Bunka Shinkōkai was founded in April 1934 in Tokyo with an opening ceremony attended by Prime Minister Saitō Makoto. Shortly thereafter, the KBS sent a permanent representative to New York City and set about in earnest to promote the image of a culturally refined Japan. In New York, the KBS could make use of the Japan Society of New York, which was founded in 1907 to promote friendly relations between the two Pacific powers. Indeed, the Japan Society was uniquely positioned to function as a kind of KBS "subsidiary," with many of its enthusiastic, internationally minded members— such as Louis Ledoux and Harold Henderson—primed as proxy publicists for Japan's branding campaign. Japan Society president Henry W. Taft often echoed KBS convictions, stating, for example, that the United States and Japan ought to make themselves "understood to the other" through cultural programs.[14]

Along with the distribution of the first batch of KBS publications (on traditional handicrafts and theatrical masks), the KBS sent one of its directors, Anesaki Masaharu, to the United States to promote his book *Art, Life and Nature in Japan*. In circumstances that presaged the unique relationship between the KBS and the Japan Society, the latter actually had sponsored the book's publication the previous year to commemorate the group's twenty-fifth anniversary. Anesaki now used these auspicious associations to discuss with US audiences his book's principal themes, which dovetailed nicely with KBS nation brand assumptions that the "soul" of a nation is best understood through its culture. In vivid, poetic prose, Anesaki not only provided evidence for the rarified beauty of Japanese art, but also argued that the Japanese nation as a whole was imbued with a highly developed aesthetic sensibility. "To a remarkable degree," wrote Anesaki, "Japanese art enters into the daily life of the people." For the KBS, Anesaki's notion of an embedded cultural heritage became an important element of its nation branding strategy, as it lent credence to the apparent pervasiveness and profundity of Japanese civilization.[15]

Soon after Anesaki's visit, the KBS welcomed eighty-five American college students to Tokyo for the inaugural gathering of a series of US-Japanese student conferences. KBS officials gave financial and moral support to the conference while supplying the Japanese delegates with cultural reference material to share with their American guests. Count Kabayama Aisuke, chair of the KBS's Board of Directors, and Prince Tokugawa Iesato attended the opening along with Joseph C. Grew, the US ambassador to Japan from 1932–41. Revealing the KBS's fundamental concern with calibrating US perceptions, KBS officials extolled the "close personal contacts formed and broader outlook obtained by the younger generation."[16] From the KBS's perspective, doubtless a "broader outlook" referred to a more favorable impression of Japan.

To be sure, the KBS's early initiatives—personal visits to the United States, a student conference, and cultural publications—represented a modest start to the organization's nation branding campaign. This changed, however, in October 1934 with the KBS's sponsorship of a glossy propaganda quarterly, *NIPPON*. Largely the inspiration of Natori Yōnosuke, a 24- year-old photographer who had studied design in Germany, *NIPPON* was a stunning expression of the new photojournalism. In layout, design, and photography, the Bauhaus-influenced *NIPPON* was sophisticated, modern, and stylish. Striking cover designs opened up to attractive photomontages and cultural content that exalted the nation's traditional arts—including pottery, textiles, painting, music, dance, masks, paper-making, literature, temples, and theater—along with modern aspects of Japan, such as rail travel, film, and sports. *NIPPON* thus constituted what one scholar has referred to as a strategically managed vicarious form of nation-brand equity.[17]

KBS officers periodically contributed to *NIPPON*, often to reiterate the importance for foreigners to understand the "real Japan." The quarterly's inaugural issue, for example, introduced the KBS with a photograph of its president, Konoe Fumimaro, and an invitation to Western elites to "acquire a correct grasp of Japan" through the "time-honored culture of which Japan boasts."[18] Cultural theorist Hasegawa Nyōzekan, meanwhile, issued a plea in the form of a command, with an article titled, "You Must Know Me as I Know You." Hasegawa likewise argued that ignorance about Japan was conquered best by understanding her culture.[19]

To help accelerate US understanding of Japan's culture, and thus the "real Japan," in 1935 the KBS vigorously expanded its branding initiatives. In February, Baron Dan worked closely with the Japan Society's Louis Ledoux and curators at the Metropolitan Museum of Art (MET) in New York to launch a two-month exhibition featuring Nō robes. Japanese collectors lent sixteen of the robes on display; the KBS, meanwhile, donated a model of a Nō stage. Such explicit involvement allowed the KBS to carefully craft its civilizational message. To this end, *New York Times* critic Edward Jewell variously described the robes as "radiant," "exquisite," "incredibly beautiful," "brilliant," and a "gorgeous spectacle."[20] The Metropolitan Museum of Art's *Bulletin*, in language that bolstered Japan's nation brand, said that Japanese textiles revealed "a varied and spectacular art in weaving and design as the world has never seen," adding that the exhibit selections were "beauteous in the extreme" and "infallible."[21] Baron Dan alleged to fellow KBS officers that the Nō display was a publicity boon in the United States, producing an "unforeseen degree of sympathy and goodwill."[22]

Shortly after the Nō exhibition, the KBS's campaign to persuade elites in the United States of the sophistication of Japanese civilization veered toward the spectacular. Inspired by a series of ikebana demonstrations organized by Japanese women in New York City, KBS officials conceived of a venture that combined the force of sensually accessible cultural images with attentive personal interaction. On 13 May 1935, the KBS welcomed more than one hundred "socially prominent women" of the Garden Club of America to Japan for a three-week, all-expenses-paid tour of the nation's most prestigious landscape gardens. More than any other KBS program, this Japan-as-exhibit visit—which included stops in Yokohama, Tokyo, Nikko, Hakone, Nagoya, Kyoto, Nara, and Osaka—realized the KBS's goal to brand "the full extent of [Japan's] culture." And it did so within a natural landscape, which, as Dinnie has maintained, contains "extremely powerful emotional and symbolic value."[23]

In addition to daily walking tours of the gardens of private villas and famous public temples, shrines, and monasteries, the KBS also treated the American visitors to Kabuki and Nō plays, a ceramics workshop, a geisha concert, a Bunraku puppet show, and a tea ceremony. The granddaughter of famous Kabuki actor Danjūrō IX, for example, gave Garden Club members a Kabuki makeup demonstration. The KBS also presented each guest with a scholarly work, *Art of the Landscape Garden in Japan*, and a photographic book comprised of high-quality plates of gardens visited on the tour.

In both scope and logistics, the Garden Club tour was unprecedented. To carry out such an ambitious program, the KBS enlisted the help of hundreds of Japanese citizens from across the country either to open up their private villas and gardens, or to perform or demonstrate traditional arts. The KBS also hired and trained seventy-two Japanese women to accompany the American visitors, to attend to their needs, and to answer questions about Japan's cultural heritage. Thus it was not only cultural riches on display, but also "exquisite courtesy and charming cordiality," as one Garden Club member described Japanese hospitality.[24] Significantly, this charm offensive came with an air of official importance: mayors welcomed the Garden Club members in almost every city; Foreign Minister Hirota hosted a reception at his official residence; and Emperor Hirohito's brother, Prince Takamatsu, held a garden party at the Kasumigaseki Palace, which was attended by Prime Minister Okada Keisuke. This was a display of the nation brand on a grand scale.

Speeches by members during the tour reiterated the KBS's underlying assumptions about culture and correct knowledge of a nation. Prince Tokugawa Iesato, for instance, told the visiting Americans "that through the study and appreciation of our gardens" they would come to know Japanese people "more intimately than in any other way." Throughout his address, amity and beauty held sway. But also apparent, in hindsight, was the rhetoric of deception. Drawing a distinction between the garden tour and the apparent political agenda of previous United States-Japanese goodwill missions, Tokugawa said "all thoughts of gain or profit have been submerged by the nobler desire to enjoy the beauties of nature and of artistic achievements of men. . . . To me it seems as if it were the work of Providence that you should be brought here."[25] Far less mysteriously, of course, it was the committed work of Japan's brand management team that made it all happen.

From a twenty-first-century perspective, it may seem peculiar that the leaders of a global power would devote such resources to branding their nation to members of a foreign garden club. KBS officials, however, regarded Garden Club members—many of whom had attended the Nō show at the MET—as women of "high cultural attainment," connected to America's ruling class. This meant that the American visitors, however narrow a constituency, represented a potentially valuable group as KBS brand ambassadors. In fact, shortly after the delegation returned home, the Garden Club's *Bulletin* published a scintillating summary of the trip, declaring that "one hundred enthusiastic pilgrims will carry a message of good will and friendship for Japan to the large organization of seven thousand members."[26] Ambassador Grew's personal secretary, Graham Parsons, addressed a group in Massachusetts a few months after the tour, saying he knew of "no country where the artistic sense is more keenly alive throughout the land [than in Japan]."[27] Such comments, along with the "piles of grateful letters" sent by Garden Club members, prompted KBS officials to conclude that "[the] visit of so many ladies representing the best of America's culture and society has contributed a great deal towards establishing better relations and friendship between the United States and Japan."[28]

To what degree US-Japanese relations were improved by the KBS's nation-branding work, is, of course, difficult to empirically ascertain. Doubtless, the KBS's linkage of the two contained a self-serving bias. Nonetheless, three years after the creation of Manchukuo, Japan's efforts to recover US sympathies seemed to be making genuine headway: United States-Japan relations were "stable," US travel to Japan had surged, Americans bought more Japanese products than any other people in the world, and commentaries in US media increasingly suggested greater tolerance toward Japan. An essay in the *New York Times*, for example, gave tacit recognition to "the new state of Manchukuo," referring to the construction of the new "Japanese Embassy" and raving about miles of new roads "lined with 2,000 American-style homes."[29] Another observer of Far Eastern affairs argued that Japan's absorption of Manchuria was tolerable as long as the empire henceforth adhered to internationalist principles. Officially, the US policy of non-recognition of Manchukuo remained in place, though the Roosevelt administration was mostly a passive observer. According to historian Akira Iriye, by the mid-1930s, the administration in Washington "was by and large willing to leave the new realities alone in Manchuria."[30]

Seemingly encouraged by favorable responses to the Nō exhibit and Garden Club tour, the KBS financed Japanese college students to participate in the second America-Japan Student Conference at Reed College in Portland, published additional books on Japanese culture for English-speaking target audiences, prepared for the presentation of two classic Kabuki plays in select US cities, and produced six hundred lantern slides for public lectures on Japanese painting, sculpture, gardens, and architecture for audiences world-wide.[31] Taking stock of KBS efforts in late 1935, General Secretary Aoki Setsuichi buoyantly reported that the KBS's activities showed "a most gratifying increase."[32]

Most significantly, the KBS prepared for an unprecedented display of Japan as a highly refined, great civilization. On 10 September 1936, amid extraordinary publicity, the Special Loan Exhibition of Japanese Art opened at the Museum of Fine Arts in Boston. The show featured a sweeping display of Japanese art treasures spanning twelve centuries. Museum goers could view more than one hundred objects, primarily wood and bronze sculptures, and painted screens and scrolls—all of which had been painstakingly packed in twenty-six crates and shipped as special cargo from Yokohama. Museum director George H. Edgell called it the "most distinguished exhibition of Japanese art ever held outside Asia." Japanese Ambassador Saitō Hiroshi solemnly declared that such a rare representation of Japan's art would not be repeated.[33]

The timing of the exhibition was not accidental. As early as 1934, KBS officials, several of whom had ties to US academia, were made aware of Harvard's approaching tercentenary anniversary in the fall of 1936. Discussions between representatives of the KBS and the Museum of Fine Arts soon revealed a shared desire to mount a show in conjunction with Harvard's celebration, thereby ensuring KBS officials a grand stage upon which to flaunt Japan's cultural riches. Indeed, Ambassador Grew, who helped to facilitate relations between the KBS, the Museum of Fine Arts, and Harvard University, promised Japanese officials that the show "will be watched with interest by the American public."[34] Grew's words proved to be an understatement.

Over a period of seven weeks, from 10 September to 25 October 1936, more than a hundred thousand visitors came to see the Japanese display. Just as importantly, in art journals, periodicals, and the Sunday editions of major newspapers, art critics unleashed a steady stream of superlatives for Japan's cultural achievements, thereby bolstering the branding of Japan as a great civilization. Sometimes the claim was made point blank, as when a writer for the *Washington Post* observed that the show revealed "the high artistic civilization of [Japan], where, as in Italy during the Renaissance, beauty is nearest to divinity." Director Edgell's introduction to the exhibition in the museum's catalog similarly acclaimed bringing "one important civilization a greater familiarity with another."[35]

The *Boston Herald* extolled the Japanese people's "subtle suavity," while the *New York Herald Tribune's* illustrious critic, Royal Cortissoz, referred to the art treasures as "nothing less than miraculous," "exquisite in detail," and "amazingly beautiful." Despite that semantic bouquet, he ultimately found himself at a loss for words. "I realize the extreme difficulty," said Cortissoz, "of conveying a due sense of the sheer beauty which envelops these paintings." In a similar vein, Edward Jewell of the *New York Times* referred to the works as "indescribably stirring" and "hushed and fresh and exquisite," adding that each picture should have a room to itself. The influential *American Magazine of Art* dedicated thirty photographs to the show and a fifteen-page review by Louis Ledoux, who said the Japanese works on display in Boston were "of such uniformly high rank that any lover of art would have been amply rewarded for crossing a continent and an ocean to see them." Langdon Warner, curator of Oriental Art at Harvard's Fogg Museum, likewise forewarned readers in the *Boston Evening Transcript* that "to miss [the show] would be almost a disaster, to go but once or twice would be almost a shame."[36]

Beyond aesthetic evaluations, some critics declared that the Japanese masterpieces expressed an affinity with Western values and "universal ideas." Warner noted that it was "a matter of absorbing interest for Americans to discover that the ideas behind these strange forms in bronze and wood are precisely our own. . . . They are found to go best in the familiar English of our own Bible." As a result, surmised Warner, "If we foreigners can but begin to comprehend the art of Japan, we shall know a spiritual kinship that treaties and trade fail to inspire." Warner thus alluded to an alleged mutuality of utter importance—a connective cultural tissue between US and Japanese spiritual values, and, implicitly, each nation's core values. The *Washington Post's* Sibilla Skidelsky summoned Greek thinkers and Christian saints, declaring that the works "have behind them the noblest thoughts that humanity ever conceived, teachings equal to those of Plato and St. Francis of Assisi."[37]

Pertinent to KBS branding objectives, such references to shared values and enlightened civilization penetrated the political realm. American critics, for example, alluded to important features of global society, or what historian Frank Ninkovich has called the "deeper attachments to distant others" and an "appreciation of a common human identity." The *Post* believed the show represented "a certain mark of the solidarity of mankind, of the oneness of all true spiritual conceptions." The *Boston Globe* similarly opined that the display "demonstrated over and above the troubled world of international politics" there existed a world "of culture which knows no nationality or ethnological differences." Ledoux called the exhibition "a peculiarly notable example of international cooperation in that universal world which endures beyond the ephemeral changes of political and economic interests."[38] From the Americans' perspective, then, on display in Boston was the visual embodiment of a sophisticated civilization and a respectable member of the so-called family of nations. And, although Japanese views aligned more closely with the old diplomacy, the most important point was that the nation brand should induce friendly and sympathetic feelings as a way to advance foreign policy goals.

Japanese dignitaries explicitly buttressed US assumptions about the seemingly harmonious nexus of culture and internationalism. At the exhibition's opening, for instance, Ambassador Saitō stated that when people identify with past treasures "they may gain an understanding of life and a power for effective action for human welfare and international peace." KBS representatives also sought to differentiate Japan from China. Yashiro Yukio, director of the Tokyo Imperial School of Art, in a piece for the *New York Times*, explained that while much of Japanese art originated in China, what mattered most was "esthetic value" and that Japan had not only "made its own developments" but also preserved them. Alluding to the apparently destructive volatility of Chinese civilization, Yashiro reiterated that "we must turn to Japan" to view preserved Asian works of genius. In terms of artistic preservation, Yashiro's claim was not entirely unfounded, but it was also politically loaded—the alleged turmoil of Chinese civilization was a staple Japanese argument in Geneva to legitimize Japan's "mission" in Asia. Most important, however, was Yashiro's desire to make a distinctive case for Japanese art. As scholars of branding invariably point out, central to the success of a nation branding strategy is the ability to "provide the nation with culturally grounded differentiation."[39]

Ambassador Grew believed a main outcome of the exhibition "was to help [United States-Japan] relations." Grew later conferred with Prime Minister Hirota and Emperor Hirohito, telling them the event had made a deep and lasting impression on Americans. In what way the display positively affected United States-Japan relations is more difficult to assess. The evidence does make clear, however, that Ambassador Grew moved in the KBS's social circles and frequently assessed Japan's immediate political future based on assumptions about cosmopolitan Japanese elites—like many of those who filled the KBS roster and managed Japan's nation brand. As historian John Dower has noted, "Grew, with his clubbish propensity to equate high society with the 'real' Japan and gourmet dining with democracy, linked it all together like a string of pearls: ... civilization, moderation, respectability, comfort, internationalism, peace."[40]

By the spring of 1937, the prevailing bilateral spirit between Japan and the United States was watchful and hopeful. US trade with Japan remained robust, and US travel to the empire promised to be heavy during the upcoming summer. One writer assured readers that it was possible to tour Japan in a week, but that "two weeks is better; three better still." In June, Emperor Hirohito appointed KBS president Konoe Fumimaro as Japan's new premier. Tokyo correspondent Hugh Byas depicted Konoe in culturally familiar categories, noting that he loved golf and appreciated Western music.[41] Other observers described him as a political liberal. Within two months, the Konoe government authorized sending five army divisions to China, a decision that precipitated a war of aggression on the mainland, and an epic challenge to Japan's campaign to promote the nation as pacific cultural jewel rather than a marauding militarist.

The Sino-Japanese War and the Limits of KBS's Nation Branding in the United States (1937–40)

In July 1937, a skirmish between Chinese and Japanese troops on the outskirts of Beijing erupted into full-scale war. Japan's subsequent mobilization and indiscriminate bombing of Chinese cities produced widespread outrage and threw US sympathies overwhelmingly to the Chinese side. Stories in US newspapers told of Japanese planes raining "death and destruction from the skies." Henry Stimson, Secretary of State during the Manchurian crisis, wrote in the *New York Times* that Japan was "terrorizing" Chinese civilians. Sensational photographs—such as the iconic picture of a crying, blackened Chinese baby sitting alone amid railway wreckage—were widely circulated in illustrated journals. All of which engendered an image of Japan grievously at odds with the KBS's civilizational thesis.[42]

Facing protests "of un-heard-of magnitude and determination"—and guided by Count Kabayama's exhortation to serve the nation during wartime from a cultural perspective—on 7 October 1937, the KBS convened a meeting to review the Society's nation-branding efforts in the United States. Baron Dan, explaining the daunting task, fell back on the necessity of proving the "sophistication of

Japanese culture" to the whole United States. Exactly how this was to be accomplished, however, was less clear, beyond the creation of "information offices" in US cities.[43]

In November, the *Asahi Shimbun* quoted Premier Konoe as saying Japan eventually would have to abrogate the Washington treaties.[44] On the heels of Konoe's defiant statement, Japanese troops seized the Guomindang capital at Nanjing. C. Yates McDaniel of the Associated Press, who was in the city during the attack, said his last remembrance of Nanjing was "[d]ead Chinese, dead Chinese, dead Chinese."[45] In an attempt to counter the upsurge in negative images of Japan, the KBS established an information center in New York City, still convinced that the United States' "bad feelings toward Japan" stemmed from ignorance. The Japan Culture Center (Nihon Bunka Kaikan) opened its doors at Rockefeller Center in November 1938. According to Count Kabayama, the center would give Americans a "proper understanding of Japan" by providing accurate and objective information. For the time being, this primarily meant four thousand books and pamphlets on the life and culture of Japan. Concurrently, the KBS endeavored to introduce a traveling library in the United States, but the State Department denied its request, fearing that "some person or group, carried away by feelings against Japan, might seek to do damage to the truck and its occupants."[46]

The KBS also continued to brand Japan through *NIPPON*, though by 1938 the illustrated magazine typically combined stories on Japan's cultural riches with apologias on the Sino-Japanese War. In "Eastern Civilization and Japan" (1938), for example, the author argued that the decline of Chinese civilization had compelled the Japanese to become "cultural crusaders." Japan, he explained, felt "entrusted with a holy mission to renew the life of the spiritual civilization peculiar to the Orient." Not only had China consistently struggled to preserve her cultural riches, but the Japanese army in China had been taking "every precaution to save [cultural artifacts] from damage even at the cost of some strategic disadvantages." Imparting a kind of noblesse oblige, the author said "the Japanese regard it as a great honor to be entrusted with such an important cultural mission."[47] *NIPPON*'s subsequent issue reinforced the image of Japan's allegedly beneficent role in China with a photograph whose caption described "common people in peace-restored Nanking watching juggling in the street."[48] In issues 18 and 19 (1939), *NIPPON* featured Japan's civilizing influence in Korea and Manchuria respectively.

Global political trends meanwhile moved the KBS inexorably into closer relationships with cultural institutions in Germany and

Italy. In 1938, Japan signed a cultural exchange agreement with Nazi Germany, resulting in KBS displays at exhibitions in Leipzig and Berlin in the same year. At the Berlin exhibit, a banner quotation from Premier Konoe promoted the KBS mantra that the "spirit and essence of a people" was best understood through their cultural forms. Cultural relations between the two nations became further formalized in April 1940 with the creation of the German-Japanese culture committee (Deutsch-Japanischer Kulturausschuß). After the signing of the Tripartite Pact in September 1940, in which Japan, Germany, and Italy recognized respective autarkic blocs in Asia and Europe, the KBS's branding campaign in the United States quickly disintegrated. *NIPPON* (24) celebrated the new alliance with a stunning cover headshot of Premier Konoe, six pages of advertisements by large Japanese firms congratulating the new pact, and myriad photographs.[49] After war erupted between Japan and the United States in December 1941, the KBS became an explicit propaganda organ, making use of its resources to help realize the empire's hegemonic aspirations for a Greater East Asia Co-Prosperity Sphere.

Postwar Redux

Japan's surrender in August 1945 and the subsequent occupation by US forces (1945–52) left the Kokusai Bunka Shinkōkai in institutional limbo. US occupation officials in the immediate postwar years were inclined to equate traditional Japanese culture with feudalistic tendencies (leading to censorship, for example, of Kabuki theater). The rising threat of communism in Asia, however, eventually triggered an overhaul of US policies in Japan—including the restoration of cultural institutions. In 1949, the KBS was officially revived, and many prominent KBS officials returned to the fold, including Dan Inō, Kabayama Aisuke, Prince Takamatsu, Maeda Tamon, Anesaki Masaharu, and Tokugawa Yorisada. A mission statement heralded "a fresh start with new ideals and goals" as part of "the rebirth of Japan as a cultural state along democratic lines."[50] Thus began an important part of Japan's makeover from cold-blooded adversary to Cold War ally.

The first postwar branding initiatives grew from a patchwork of public and private institutions, including the KBS, Japan's Ministry of Foreign Affairs and Cultural Properties Protection Commission, the US State Department, and the Japan Society of New York. John D. Rockefeller III, who joined the US Peace Mission to Japan in 1951 as a cultural consultant, played an influential role. In 1952, the year he was elected president of the Japan Society, Rockefeller worked closely with Kabayama Aisuke and Matsumoto Shigeharu (former confidante of Premier Konoe) to establish a center for cross-cultural intellectual exchange. The result was the International House of Japan (I-House), which officially opened in June 1955.

In 1953, Rockefeller also worked with Japanese officials to stage a major touring exhibition of Japanese art treasures at the National Gallery of Art in Washington, DC, the Metropolitan Museum of Art, the Seattle Art Museum, Chicago's Art Institute, and Boston's Museum of Fine Arts. Bearing a striking resemblance to the 1936 MFA show, the loan exhibition must have produced a curious case of déjà vu for individuals who reprised their involvement, including Prince Takamatsu, Joseph Grew, Kabayama Aisuke, Harold Henderson, Langdon Warner, George Edgell, Harada Jiro, and Yashiro Yukio. American critics once again universally hailed Japan's cultural riches, which were viewed by nearly five hundred thousand people. Japan's ambassador to the United States, Araki Eikichi, solemnly intoned that the exhibition "served to draw even closer the bonds of culture and friendship which exist between our countries."[51]

A year later, the Azuma Kabuki Dancers and Musicians toured the United States. Extensive media coverage now praised the traditional Japanese art form as representing the highest of cultural achievements, and President Dwight D. Eisenhower welcomed the troupe to the White House. Around the same time, a noted Far East correspondent for the *New York Times* observed, "After a long and bitter war between us, Japan has now become our ally." Significantly, the writer attributed part of this transformation to cultural programs.[52]

Conclusion

The intentional nation-branding campaign by Japanese officials in the 1930s to promote the attractiveness and power of Japan as a highly sophisticated civilization was striking in its scope and diligence. Under the auspices of the Japanese government, the KBS mobilized numerous "brand managers"—including diplomats, statesmen, academics, and businessmen—to convince targeted foreign cosmopolitans, especially in the United States, of the grandeur of Japanese culture. Through the representation of compelling national assets, Japan's leaders hoped to enhance the nation's credibility and thereby secure a more sympathetic response to the empire's foreign policy goals—in particular, acceptance of greater Japanese control in Manchuria.

In this way, KBS efforts in the 1930s provide a compelling example of a highly politicized form of nation branding, one that sought to serve imperialist aims. That Japanese policy makers saw a vital congruence between nation branding and imperialist ambitions becomes clear from a major address Foreign Minister Hirota gave to the National Diet in 1936. While demanding that China collaborate with Japan and recognize Manchukuo, Hirota, a KBS adviser, simultaneously stressed that it was important for Japan "to introduce our arts and culture to other lands and thus contribute toward international good understanding."[53] Doubtless, the meaning of "good understanding" varied little from Matsuoka's entreaty to reporters in Geneva in 1933 in which he hoped the rest of the world would one day understand Japan.

Nonetheless, the KBS's nation branding strategy in the United States proved ineffectual in the face of blatant aggression and wartime atrocities in China. From a US perspective, starting in late 1937, impressions of a refined and pacific Japan became gravely compromised by contradictory reports and images pouring in from East Asia. The KBS experience in the United States (1934–40) therefore suggests the intended claims of a nation brand must not become severely estranged from actual foreign policy and the worldview of the targeted audience. As Keith Dinnie has noted, nation branding "must co-exist effectively with the prevailing zeitgeist."[54]

And yet, KBS efforts demonstrate that a fluid relationship exists between the brand image and brand message. As indicated in this chapter, while Japan's nation brand (cultural refinement) remained relatively constant, its intended message proved to be ideologically malleable. To American cosmopolitans in the 1930s, the KBS's nation brand connoted that Japan remained a leading and respectable player in the family of nations. When this particular message became meaningless to American elites, the very same nation brand nonetheless suggested to German audiences congruence with the civilizational presumptions of the Tripartite Pact. To Asian peoples during World War II, the message was liberation through Japanese leadership; and under US occupiers, that of a culturally copacetic Cold War ally.

In 1954, the newly sovereign Japanese government renewed its commitment to a cultural nation branding strategy by resuming direct funding for the KBS, which operated until 1972, when it was absorbed by the Japan Foundation. The premises of the KBS-instituted nation brand persist, however, as the Japanese government continues to market the nation's alluring traditional and modern culture. In that sense, the KBS example demonstrates that nation branding is indeed a timeless strategy.

John Gripentrog is associate professor of History at Mars Hill University near Asheville, North Carolina. He received his Ph.D. from the University of Wisconsin-Madison. His work concerns relations between Japan and the United States in the 1930s. Articles and essays include "The Trans-National Pastime: Baseball and American Perceptions of Japan, 1931–1941" in *Diplomatic History* (April 2010); "Pearl Harbor: The Road to Irreconcilable Worldviews" for the *Society for Historians of Foreign Relations*; and a recent article on United States-Japan cultural relations in the *Pacific Historical Review* (November 2015). He is currently completing a book on the political and cultural relations of Japan and the United States in the interwar era.

Notes

1. Matsuoka comments reprinted in *Japan's Case in the Sino-Japanese Dispute as Presented before the Special Session of the Assembly of the League of Nations* (Japanese Delegation to the League of Nations: Geneva, 1933), 49–54, 64. Walter Lippmann, *New York Herald Tribune*, 1 December 1931; "Japan Alone," *New York Times*, 26 February 1933, E4.
2. *Kokusai Bunka Shinkokai: Prospectus and Scheme* (Tokyo: Kokusai Bunka Shinkokai, 1934), 1–2.
3. Prince Fumimaro Konoye [sic], "Foreword," *K.B.S. Quarterly*, 1 (April–June 1935), 1.
4. Simon Anholt, *Competitive Identity: The Brand Management for Nations, Cities and Regions* (Houndmills: Palgrave Macmillan, 2007), 97.
5. Keith Dinnie, *Nation Branding: Concepts, Issues, Practice* (Oxford: Butterworth-Heinemann, 2008), 118.
6. Matsuoka comments, 24 February 1933, reprinted in *Japan's Case*, 55–56.
7. Dinnie, *Nation Branding*, 68.
8. *KBS: Prospectus and Scheme*, 2. On *Romanha*, see Kevin Michael Doak, *Dreams of Difference: The Japan Romantic School and the Crisis of Modernity* (Berkeley: University of California Press, 1994).
9. Hearn quoted in Robert A. Rosenstone, "Learning from Those 'Imitative' Japanese: Another Side of the American Experience in the Mikado's Empire," *The American Historical Review* 85, no. 3 (June 1980): 587. Italics belong to Hearn.
10. Leslie de Chernatony, "Academic Perspective: Adapting Brand Theory to the Context of Nation Branding," in Dinnie, *Nation Branding*, 16.

11. Nadia Kaneva, "Nation Branding: Toward an Agenda for Critical Research," *International Journal of Communication* 5 (2011), 130.
12. *KBS: Prospectus and Scheme*, 2.
13. Kaneva, "Nation Branding," 124.
14. Taft comments cited in *New York Times*, "Japan Shuns War, Says Tokugawa," 28 February 1934, 7.
15. Masaharu Anesaki, *Art, Life, and Nature in Japan* (Boston: Marshall Jones Co., 1933), 5, 178.
16. "America-Japan Student Conference," *K.B.S. Quarterly* 1, no. 2 (July–Sept. 1935): 22–23.
17. Dinnie, *Nation Branding*, 71. *NIPPON* was published by Natori's Nippon Kōbō Company, and appeared from 1934 to 1944. Articles were variously published in English, French, German, and Spanish, though topics presented in English appeared twice as often as all other languages combined.
18. "Movement in Japan for Promotion of Cultural Relations with Foreign Countries," *NIPPON* no. 1 (Oct. 1934): 50.
19. Nyōzekan Hasegawa, "You Must Know Me as I Know You," *NIPPON* no. 5 (1936): 8–9.
20. Edward A. Jewell, "Art of Japanese at Metropolitan," *New York Times*, 19 February 1935, 19.
21. *Bulletin of the Metropolitan Museum of Art* 30 (Feb. 1935): 27–32.
22. Inō Dan, "Broadening Cultural Contacts," *K.B.S. Quarterly*, 1 (Jan.–March 1936): 3.
23. Dinnie, *Nation Branding*, 148.
24. Mrs. Benjamin S. Warren, "The Garden Club of America in Japan," *Bulletin of the Garden Club of America* 17 (Sept. 1935): 25–27.
25. Warren, "The Garden Club," 25–26.
26. Warren, "The Garden Club," 56.
27. *Berkshire Evening Eagle*, 6 September 1935, 4.
28. *K.B.S. Quarterly* (April–June 1935), 29.
29. A. J. Billingham, "Hsinking is Transformed," *New York Times*, 4 August 1935, XX4.
30. George Sokolsky, "Why Fight Japan?" *Current History* (Feb. 1935): 520. Akira Iriye, *The Origins of the Second World War in Asia and the Pacific* (London: Routledge, 1987), 28.
31. Lantern slides were glass photographic slides that projected an image for a mass audience. Their heyday came between the 1870s and 1930s.
32. Setsuichi Aoki, "Quarterly Report," *K.B.S. Quarterly* 1, no. 2 (July–Sept. 1935), 1.
33. George Edgell, "Report of the Director," *Annual Report*, Museum of Fine Arts, Boston, 1936, 17. Saitō quoted in A.J. Philpott, "Exhibition of Japan's Art Opens at Museum," *Boston Globe*, 11 September 1936, 19.
34. Grew Letters, A–J, 1936, Volume 2, Harvard Houghton Library.
35. Sibilla Skidelsky, "Treasures of Art from Japanese Galleries Lent to Boston Museum for Harvard Tercentenary," *Washington Post*, 4 October 1936, 6. George H. Edgell, "Foreword," *Illustrated Catalogue of a Special Loan Exhibition of Art Treasures from Japan* (Tokyo: Sanseido Press, 1936), vi.
36. Irma Whitney, "Emperor's Own Treasures in Japanese Loan Exhibition," *The Boston Herald*, 12 September 1936, 12; Royal Cortissoz, "The Painting and Sculpture of Japan," *New York Herald Tribune*, 27 September 1936, 10; Edward Jewell, "Boston Savors Ageless Japanese Art," *New York Times*, 20 September 1936, X8; Louis Ledoux, "Japanese Painting and Sculpture: The Important Loan Exhibition in Boston," *American Magazine of Art* (September 1936): 561;

Langdon Warner, "Japanese Art Seen in its Full Glory," *Boston Evening Transcript*, 12 September 1936, 3.

37. Warner, *Boston Evening Transcript*, 12 September 1936, 3; Skidelsky, *Washington Post*, 4 October 1936, 6.

38. Frank Ninkovich, *The Global Republic: America's Inadvertent Rise to World Power* (Chicago: University of Chicago Press, 2014), 47. Louis Ledoux, *American Magazine of Art*, September 1936, 572; *Boston Evening Transcript*, 12 September 1936, 4; Skidelsky, *Washington Post*, 4 October 1936, 6; *Boston Globe*, editorial, 11 September 1936, 19.

39. Saitō speech cited in Philpott, *Boston Globe*, 11 September 1936, 19. Yukio Yashiro, "Artists of Japan Speak to the Soul through Symbols," *New York Times*, 6 September 1936, SM 6–7, 19. Dinnie, *Nation Branding*, 15.

40. Grew comment in letter to Edgell, 16 October 1936, Grew Letters, Vol. II, A–J, Harvard Houghton Library. Conversation with Hirota, 30 November 1936, from Joseph C. Grew, *Ten Years in Japan* (New York: Simon and Schuster, 1944), 190; with Hirohito, 1 February 1937, Grew, *Ten Years in Japan*, 204. John Dower, *Empire and Aftermath: Yoshida Shigeru and the Japanese Experience, 1878–1954* (Cambridge, MA: Harvard University Press, 1979), 111–12.

41. "Many Routes to Japan," *New York Times*, 13 December 1936, XX10; Hugh Byas, "Konoye Seeks to Unify Japan," *New York Times*, 11 July 1937, 102.

42. "Japanese Ignore U.S. Protests in Raid on Capital," *New York Post*, 22 September 1937, 1. Grew, 29 August 1937, *Ten Years in Japan*, 216. Henry L. Stimson, text of letter, *New York Times*, 7 October 1937, 12.

43. *Christian Science Monitor*, 30 September 1937, 1. Kabayama and Dan's comments in Shibasaki Atsushi, *Kindai Nihon to kokusai bunka kōryū: Kokusai Bunka Shinkō-kai no sōsetsu to tenkai* [International cultural relations and Modern Japan: History of Kokusai Bunka Shinkōkai, 1934–45] (Tokyo: Yūshindō Kōbunsha, 1999),133–35.

44. Konoe comment in *Asahi Shimbun* cited in Katsumi Usui, "Japanese Approaches to China in the 1930s," in *American, Chinese and Japanese Perspectives on Wartime Asia, 1931–1949,* ed. Akira Iriye and Warren Cohen (Wilmington, DE: SR Books, 1990), 111.

45. C. Yates McDaniel, "Nanking Horror Described in Diary of War Reporter," *Chicago Tribune*, 18 December 1937, 8.

46. "Good-Will Institute Set Up Here By Japan," *New York Times*, 29 March 1939, 17; Kabayama comments cited in Shibasaki, *Kindai Nihon to kokusai bunka kōryū*, 143–44; KBS request to State Department, 12 April 1938 and State Department reply, 15 April 1938, *State Department Central files, 1930–39*, Record Group 59, 811.4279/58, Box 5066, NACP.

47. Kōsaku Hamada, "Eastern Civilization and Japan," *NIPPON* 14 (1938), 3

48. Nanjing photograph, *NIPPON* 15 (1938), 36.

49. Japan signed a cultural agreement with Fascist Italy in 1939. Konoe banner quotation cited in Andrea Germer, "Artists and Wartime Politics: Natori Yōnosuke—A Japanese Riefenstahl?" *Contemporary Japan* 21 (2012): 35.

50. "Kokusai Bunka Shinkokai: Organization and Program," (Tokyo: Kokusai Bunka Shinkokai,1949), 1.

51. "The Best from Japan," *New York Times*, 25 January 1953, SM18; Statement by Ambassador Araki Eikichi at the closing of the exhibition, 11 December 1953, "Japanese Art-MISC," Office of the Secretary Records, The Metropolitan Museum of Art Archives.

52. Otto Tolischus, "Once Enemy, Now Friend," *New York Times*, 24 July 1955, BR10.

53. "Text of Foreign Minister Hirota's Speech to Tokyo Diet," *New York Times*, 21 January 1936, 19.
54. Dinnie, *Nation Branding*, 14.

Bibliography

Abel, Jessamyn R. "Cultural Internationalism and Japan's Wartime Empire: The Turns of the *Kokusai Bunka Shinkōkai*." In *Tumultuous Decade: Empire, Society, and Diplomacy in 1930s Japan*, edited by Masato Kimura and Tosh Minohara, 17–43. Toronto: University of Toronto Press, 2013.

Anesaki, Masaharu *Art, Life, and Nature in Japan*. Boston: Marshall Jones Co., 1933.

Anholt, Simon. *Competitive Identity: The Brand Management for Nations, Cities and Regions*. Houndmills: Palgrave Macmillan, 2007.

Aronczyk, Melissa. *Branding the Nation: The Global Business of National Identity*. Oxford: Oxford University Press, 2013.

Auslin, Michael. *Pacific Cosmopolitans: A Cultural History of U.S.-Japan Relations*. Cambridge, MA: Harvard University Press, 2011.

Burkman, Thomas W. *Japan and the League of Nations: Empire and World Order, 1914–1938*. Honolulu, HI: University of Hawai'i Press, 2008.

Dinnie, Keith. *Nation Branding: Concepts, Issues, Practice*. Oxford: Butterworth-Heinemann, 2008.

Doak, Kevin Michael. *Dreams of Difference*: *The Japan Romantic School and the Crisis of Modernity*. Berkeley, CA: University of California Press 1994.

Dower, John. *Empire and Aftermath: Yoshida Shigeru and the Japanese Experience, 1878–1954*. Cambridge, MA: Harvard University Press, 1979.

Edgell, George H. "Foreword." In *Illustrated Catalogue of a Special Loan Exhibition of Art Treasures from Japan*. Tokyo: Sanseido Press, 1936.

Germer, Andrea. "Artists and Wartime Politics: Natori Yōnosuke—A Japanese Riefenstahl?" *Contemporary Japan* 24, no. 1 (2012): 21–50.

Grew, Joseph C. *Ten Years in Japan*. New York: Simon and Schuster, 1944.

Hasegawa, Nyōzekan. "You Must Know Me as I Know You." *NIPPON* no. 5 (1936): 8–9.

Hotta, Eri. *Pan-Asianism and Japan's War 1931–1945*. London: Palgrave, 2007.

Iriye, Akira. *Cultural Internationalism and World Order*. Baltimore, MD: Johns Hopkins University Press, 1997.

———. *The Origins of the Second World War in Asia and the Pacific*. London: Routledge, 1987.

Kaneva, Nadia. "Nation Branding: Toward an Agenda for Critical Research." *International Journal of Communication* 5 (2011): 117–41.

Ninkovich, Frank. *The Global Republic: America's Inadvertent Rise to World Power*. Chicago, IL: University of Chicago Press, 2014.

Rosenstone, Robert A. "Learning from Those 'Imitative' Japanese: Another Side of the American Experience in the Mikado's Empire." *The American Historical Review* 85, no. 3 (June 1980): 572–595.

Shibasaki, Atsushi. *Kindai Nihon to kokusai bunka kōryū: Kokusai Bunka Shinkōkai no sōsetsu to tenkai* [International cultural relations and modern Japan: History of Kokusai Bunka Shinkōkai, 1934–45]. Tokyo: Yūshindō Kōbunsha, 1999.

Usui, Katsumi. "Japanese Approaches to China in the 1930s." In *American, Chinese and Japanese Perspectives on Wartime Asia, 1931–1949*, edited by Akira Iriye and Warren Cohen, 93–116. Wilmington, DE: SR Books, 1990.

Chapter 5

ALL PUBLICITY IS GOOD PUBLICITY?

Advertising, Public Relations, and the Branding of Spain in the United Kingdom, 1945–69

Carolin Viktorin

> [A]bout the dual significance of tourism: Economically it represents the strongest immaterial export operation that exists and politically it is an equally useful tool to serve the purposes of the state. . . .
>
> Tourism propaganda follows the same line of motivations than commercial advertising does: attract attention, stimulate an interest, inspire sympathy, create a desire and produce a voluntary action.
>
> —Jesús Romeo Gorría,
> General Secretary of the Interministerial Commission
> of Tourism, 1955

This chapter explores how British public relations experts and advertising agencies helped the Franco dictatorship not only to transmit, but also to shape Spain's touristic image in the 1950s and 1960s. In that era, the tourism industry became Spain's most important economic sector to gain foreign currency, lure investors, and create transnational relations. Moreover, tourism promotion offered the dictatorship the opportunity to project national culture and to show Western Europe that Spain was a peaceful, stable, and welcoming country. Success in attracting as many travelers as possible could be interpreted as an acceptance of Franco's authoritarian regime.[1] Hence, advertising campaigns and the expansion of international

Notes for this section begin on page 143.

public relations rebranded Spain from an isolated fascist reminiscence to one of Western Europe's leading holiday destinations.[2]

The process of influencing the country's image was not only the result of efforts by Franco's administration. Foreign advertising agencies, PR consultants, and journalists constituted the driving force behind Spain's branding efforts abroad. Although numerous countries engaging in the promotion of tourism used the help of agencies, these contacts had a special significance for the Spanish government. Of course, there existed political and cultural diplomacy with other Western European countries, but relations with individual states in the region remained cold, chary, or both. The aforementioned media experts opened up a projection screen for the regime it could not resort to in other areas, like official state visits or a flourishing cultural representation, due to its political system. This chapter not only examines the roots of tourism promotion, but also the history of advertising and international public relations in the decades after World War II and how they were intertwined with branding a nation.

Nation branding is a complex process and a technique at the same time. Nadia Kaneva describes it as a "compendium of discourses and practices aimed at reconstituting nationhood through marketing and branding paradigms."[3] Particular characteristics include, according to Melissa Aronczyk, "the rendering of national culture as an auditable form, its reorientation as source of market opportunity . . . and the defanging of diversity in the process."[4] Branding, furthermore, intends the controlled development of all institutional and private activities as well as the communication channels that transmit the country's image.[5]

The promotion of tourism is usually one part, if not the most visible one, of orchestrated nation branding programs. According to Simon Anholt, tourism constitutes one of the six dimensions of nation branding in addition to governance, export, culture and heritage, investment and immigration, and people.[6] These six dimensions are mutually dependent on one another. If tourism leads to a positive image, politics or exports profit as well, and vice versa. Furthermore, the tourism branch is essential for exploring the historical roots of nation branding. The first attempts to consciously create the image of a country and to convert that image into a nation's brand can be traced back to the growth of the tourism industry.[7] Especially in the second half of the twentieth century, countries fiercely competed to attract travelers. To come out on top, they had to emphasize their unique selling point (which may not have been that unique in the end). This process of linking images, goods, slogans, and certain qualities to a nation is at the heart of nation branding. Tourism promotion and nation branding go hand in hand.

Public relations and advertising play an important role in branding. Indeed, they are not only the tools transmitting a branding program or campaign to the world, but they also actively participate in creating the brand itself. The applications of nation branding are certainly not limited to trying to influence public opinion via these two techniques, as Nadia Kaneva points out.[8] A brand, especially the brand of a nation, consists of several elements that are communicated via numerous channels, but may be uncoordinated.[9] Therefore, advertising and public relations should not be regarded as merely a part of the marketing mix, but understood in their broader historical context as well as in their interaction with economy, politics, culture, and society.

Advertising is, as Terence Qualter suggests, "one element in a larger marketing or managerial process that includes packaging, pricing, distribution and retailing."[10] Its aim is to show consumers what commodities and services are available. Furthermore, advertising aims to cultivate a product's image—to convince the consumer to memorize it and then buy it. When the product on sale is a country, this requires a special form of advertising. The consumer needs special trust, as he or she cannot try the product out before buying it. As Cord Pagenstecher states, the product "holiday" has a strong emotional component that is bound up in the perceptions, experiences, feelings, and symbols of touristic mythology.[11] Therefore, tourism advertising usually focuses on creating positive associations. The British professors of tourism Annette Pritchard and Nigel Morgan assert that "[a]dvertising needs not to be complex to be effective—it is simply about creating enough awareness and positive brand associations for it to register as a top-of-the-mind brand when the consumer is faced with a purchase choice."[12] Consequently, advertising concentrates on creating positive associations, awareness, and goodwill.

Besides advertising, public relations are essential to transmitting and shaping an image. Broadly defined, public relations can be understood as the management of communication between the client— who could be an enterprise, a government, or an organization—and the target audiences. Public relations aim to focus attention on a person, institution, city, or country. In contrast to advertising, public relations seek to establish personal relationships. Among other tasks, spin doctors offer thought-out messages to selected media, organize publicity events, and attempt to cultivate relations with decision makers in media or politics. Practitioner Ivo Raza states that public relations "can be used for generating awareness, building recognition, and creating a favorable image." He suggests that public relations hold numerous advantages when compared to advertising, "[b]ecause in advertising you speak about your brand, and in publicity others speak about it. And when others speak, the brand's credibility is infinitely higher."[13] As a consequence, advertising and public relations complement each other because both address the public in different ways.

Throughout the twentieth century, the advertising and public relations industry got more and more professional. With the world being increasingly interconnected, governments discovered the need for explaining their actions to publics inside and outside the country. This implied several branches of state actions including the travel industry. The practice of public relations for foreign governments often remains hardly noticed by the public. Nonetheless, scholars tried to expose attempts to professionally influence public opinion. Two essays in particular on the history of the subject matter relate closely to the study of British public relations for the Spanish government. Scott Cutlip, pioneer and educator of public relations broached the issue of the Carl Byoir agency being in charge of public relations for the German Tourist Bureau in Nazi Germany and propagating the idea that the United States should still maintain trade with Germany and keep traveling there.[14] Lately, communications scholar Natalia Rodríguez Salcedo classified the public relations measures taken to promote Spanish tourism after World War II as precedent of the institutionalization of public relations.[15] Concerning the impact of international public relations on a nation's image, the study of Jarol B. Manheim and Robert B. Albritton provides notable findings. Based on an observation of six nations with varied contexts, the authors concluded that there existed an interrelation between the signing of a contract with a public relations agency and shifts in the image of the nation, in that case in the *New York Times*.[16] This does not necessarily mean that the readership immediately perceives and internalizes such a changed image, but the results of this study strongly indicate the difference PR consulting can make.

Getting Started: Tourism Promotion in Spain and Europe, 1945–62

By the end of the 1940s, it was virtually inconceivable that Europeans would associate Franco's Spain with their most popular travel destination twenty years later. Spain's image was intrinsically tied to fascism and its former collaboration with Italian fascists and German national socialists. As a result, Spain felt internationally isolated while Franco followed an autocratic course. Soon after the end of World War II, parts of the Spanish government endeavored to re-establish relationships in the tourist sector. Luis A. Bolín, who was general director of the Spanish Tourism Board from 1938 until 1952, was intensely committed to alluring travelers. During the Spanish Civil War, Bolín was already engaging in touristic activity by selling battlefield tours.[17] He gained experience in journalism and press work during his time in London as correspondent for the newspaper *ABC* and press counselor for the Spanish embassy. Absolutely loyal to Franco, yet a cosmopolitan at the same time, Bolín was the formative figure of Spain's early efforts in tourism promotion. He untiringly expedited the establishment of relations, in particular with the United States and the United Kingdom, because he recognized the importance of both nations' touristic potential for his country's recovery.[18]

While Bolín acted from within the Ministry, Spanish tourist offices abroad played an important role. This "propaganda exterior" has a tradition dating back to the late 1920s. In 1929, the National Patronage of Tourism, founded during the dictatorship of Miguel Primo de Rivera, opened bureaus in Paris, London, Munich, New York, Buenos Aires, Rome, and Gibraltar. As the *Chicago Tribune* reported, these spaces undertook the task of bringing "Spain out of her isolation and . . . [making] her known in the world."[19] During the Spanish Civil War and World War II, most of the bureaus had to be closed. The office in London officially reopened in 1949 to provide information on Spain.[20] In the following years the government opened numerous branches all over the world. The men and women in these offices not only distributed publicity material, but also operated similarly to a cultural institute or an embassy: the employees observed the country's image in newspapers, organized lectures in adult education centers, established connections to tour operators, and exhibited at fairs. Decorated with cultural artifacts and posters, these outposts morphed into Spanish islands in their own right and often constituted the first personal encounter that potential tourists had with Spain.

Soon after the first offices opened abroad, the presence of the state in tourism increased. In 1951, Franco established the Ministry of Information and Tourism (MIT).[21] This ministry had two main functions: the general directory of information was in charge of censorship (and therefore controlled public discourse), while the other department was responsible for building a tourism industry. As Sasha D. Pack puts it, the promotion of tourism meshed well with the strategy of Spain's foreign minister, Alberto Martín Artajo, whose principal goal was to soften the regime's international image.[22] Franco appointed the ultra-Catholic and conservative Gabriel Arias Salgado as the first Minister of Information and Tourism. During his term in office from 1951 until 1962, Salgado addressed himself to the task of censorship rather than to the movement of travelers. However, whether Franco had intended it or not, he had laid the foundation for the expansion of international tourism and the entrance of Spain into an emerging industry.

Although the state slowly prepared for the attraction of international travelers, the "propaganda exterior" was short of funds. During Bolín's time, in 1951, there was only a limited budget for information material in the United States, and no money for brochures in Europe at all, in spite of several tourist offices already having opened.[23] In the "Studies for a National Tourism Plan," the authors moaned about the limited funds available for the promotion of tourism. They asserted that "[a]ll European nations who are building a tourism industry invested a good deal more on propaganda."[24] In conclusion, the plan demanded that Spain spend more on advertising, while stressing the importance of ads in newspapers and especially in luxury magazines.

When the Spanish technocrats started to boost the tourism industry, other European countries were already well on their way in promoting tourism. Encouraging travel constituted an important measure in the reconstruction of Europe after World War II. The European countries included in the European Recovery Program (ERP) received considerable subsidies to rebuild transport facilities and accommodation in order to encourage tourism and thereby gain foreign currency. Western European countries focused especially on tempting tourists from the United States to visit the Old World. These efforts were flanked by the development of public advertising campaigns. Spain, excluded from the ERP, did not participate in these joint activities of reconstruction and promotion and had to find its own path.

Even so, the administration recognized the need for publicity to impress potential tourists. In the first half of the 1950s, Franco's Spain found its path back into the international community while the tourism branch and Europe's advertising industry boomed. The international competition for tourists became fierce. In 1955, the Interministerial Commission of Tourism discussed the market competition and the efficiency of publicity. The commission's Secretary General Jesús Romeo Gorría bemoaned the lack of an efficient organization of promotion material, and stressed the significance of further publicity—especially the need for foreign advertising experts in addressing their compatriots—in order to survive in a competitive market.[25] Once again, the dictatorship's administration had not been able to accomplish an efficient and modern way of organizing the promotion of Spain abroad. Spanish officials felt overwhelmed by modern advertising techniques and were in desperate need of external advice. Ultimately, despite all efforts made by Spanish officials, the country was a late bloomer in tourism advertising when compared to other nations; and it was foreign experts who played an invaluable role in branding the Spanish nation.

Official Branding of Spain as a United Nation of Tradition, Culture, and Nature

Spanish public servants were confronted with a challenging task after World War II: they had to convert a country with little experience in receiving foreign travelers and a negative political image into a place people yearned to visit. To some extent, the MIT transmitted the touristic image of Spain via posters. Aurelio Orensanz asserted that nature took a back seat in these campaigns. While some posters consisted of photographs of the Spanish landscape and the coast, as well as portrayals of the climate and the country's geography, the majority of posters showed cultural motifs of an eternal Spain.[26] Among them were religious art, motifs showing the "spirit of the country," and symbolic animals. Other illustrations depicted the paintings of Francisco de Goya or El Greco, the statues of Don Quixote and Sancho Panza in Madrid, churches, paradores, villages, uncrowded beaches, or a cliffy mountainside. As Alicia Fuentes Vega has recently shown, in the decade of the 1950s, rural images held great weight in the tourist identity and portrayed Spain's countryside as "rural Eden."[27] The posters' images displayed a preindustrial world—a "classless society, disassociated from the historic pressures and frictions of any time and space."[28] Despite a consistency in the visual representation of Spain, in the posters' images and the texts of brochures, the sender (the advertiser) dominated over the recipient (potential tourist).[29] The Spanish publicity material was so self-involved that it lost sight of its audience.

Although posters formed a significant part of Spain's projection abroad, advertisements in magazines and newspapers reached a greater audience. In the 1950s, these advertisements tended to be rather text heavy and provided certain information. Slogans appealed to the reader to come to "joyful" or "sunny" Spain. In 1955, the MIT launched a campaign showing a map of the Iberian Peninsula with little drawings of regional characteristics—like bullfights or flamenco dancers—pictured on it. Below this, a substantial text illuminated Spain's best assets:

> There's so much to find in Spain—beaches and bullfights, villages and vineyards, old walled towns and crumbling red castles, cathedrals, palaces, and some of the finest picture galleries of the world. Gay fiestas, dancing, processions . . . The beat of the sun against clean white walls . . . Ripe oranges picked sweet from the tree . . . the scented breeze that comes with the sunset. Flamenco-singers . . . Spain gives you history, beauty, warmth and welcome . . . And so little to pay![30]

These writings gave the reader the feeling of Spain being an ideal haven where one could experience what he or she had always dreamed of. On top of everything else, this experience seemed to be affordable. Furthermore, the advertisement showed Spain as a united country without the borders of the former autonomous regions which Franco had abolished after coming to power. Carmen Ortiz found in her analysis that centralism determined the character of the regime, and in the political discourse, Spain's representatives continuously propagated its unity, based on the understanding of the nation as an original and eternal entity.[31] At the same time, in presenting regional characteristics, the advertisement's map showed a diverse Spain. The regime converted regional specifics into an "aesthetic and emotional element"[32] and depicted them as harmless aspects of the nation's unity.

As shown above, the majority of the regime's official advertising did not just focus on the weather, but promoted Spain's traditional culture and quiet landscapes. Accordingly, the target audience was not the sun-seeking philistine, but rather the tourist interested in culture and nature. Yet to answer the question of how advertising helped to brand Spain, it is less important why people eventually flocked to Spain, and more important to explore what image the MIT presented to a broad audience by means of advertising. Posters extolling Spanish art and history appeared at different fairs, exhibitions, travel agencies, and the Spanish tourist offices. Even people who had never visited Spain had access to very specific representations of the country behind the Pyrenees.

Outreach to the Britons: Spain's Negative Reputation and the Help of a British PR Agent and a Journalist in the 1950s

In the early 1950s, Spain's reputation in the United Kingdom was at an all-time low. When the two countries decided to exchange ambassadors in 1951, the British public protested the move loudly. That year, Vincent Tewson, General Secretary of the Trades Union Congress, presented a resolution protesting against the arrival of an ambassador to the Secretary of State for Foreign Affairs, Anthony Eden: "I need hardly remind you of the circumstances in which Franco came to power in Spain, his use of help from Nazis and Italian Fascists and the methods by which he keeps his hold on the country."[33] The resolution demanded that the two countries not exchange ambassadors. Instead, Tewson urged Great Britain to stick to the current practice of keeping a chargé d'affaires. This method would safeguard British interests, but also demonstrate "the disapproval which is shared by the overwhelming majority of people in this country of General Franco and his methods."[34]

Clearly, an intermediary in the shape of a PR consultant was necessary to position positive information about Spain in newspapers, radio, and, later, television in Britain. Luis Bolín, who was determined to encourage tourism to Spain, sought the help of an old buddy he got to know in prewar London. Bolín put E.D. "Toby" O'Brien—according to the *New York Times* a "fabled British public relations man"[35]—in charge of the restoration of the regime's image. O'Brien's biography is closely related to the development of public relations as a profession. In a coeval survey of the British "persuasion industry," John Pearson and Graham Turner even designated O'Brien "pacemaker for the PR business."[36] Edward Donough O'Brien came from a venerable Irish family, he had studied at Exeter College in Oxford and went on to be a journalist afterwards. In 1934, O'Brien became the first director of the British Council's press division, where he countered Joseph Goebbels' anti-British propaganda.[37] Later, O'Brien worked as director of information services at the Conservative Central Office where he led the party's postwar election campaigns. An impetus for his work with Spain was his approval of the regimes installed by Franco in Spain and Salazar in Portugal. O'Brien exclusively supported right-wing authoritarian regimes. When he got the offer to work for Yugoslavia, he turned it down because he did not want to support communists. To make a long story short: O'Brien represented Bolín's loophole.

Toby O'Brien tirelessly worked to generate awareness of Spain in Britain. He knew people of upper class circles as well as members of the parliament, and he constantly tried to take up the cudgels for Spain. By word of mouth O'Brien promoted Spain as a great travel destination. He explained his tactic as follows: "I have thirty whisperers in London . . . I got on to them and set them whispering that Spain was a splendid place for a holiday. In less than no time, the most unexpected people were coming up to me and suggesting that I ought to go to Spain for holiday."[38] O'Brien even claimed, that he coined the expression Costa Blanca for a part of the Spanish Mediterranean coast.[39] To gain free publicity by way of favorable articles, he published in the press and arranged visits of journalists to Spain. A journey of Luis Bolín in 1952 to Britain offered a crucial opportunity for him to gain ground in London's policy and media circles. O'Brien arranged that Bolín socialize with members of parliament, heads of travel agencies, and members of the press. Of special importance was a meeting with the Conservative Party politician Selwyn Lloyd, who was minister in the Foreign Office under Anthony Eden at the time. Selwyn Lloyd and Bolín agreed that tourism already had strengthened Anglo-Spanish relations. O'Brien, when summing up Bolín's agenda, enthusiastically remarked that the visit not only resulted in "invaluable publicity for the Spanish tourist drive, but . . . must have had an important political effect."[40] As O'Brien's résumé illustrates, tourism and politics were deeply intertwined.

Bolín and his successor, Mariano de Urzáiz y Silva, were especially keen to appeal to a prosperous audience. When the article "Andalusian Sunshine" appeared in *Vogue*, Britain's leading fashion magazine of the time—partly due to O'Brien's commitment—Mariano de Urzáiz felt deeply satisfied because the magazine addressed a moneyed readership.[41] Free publicity should not come at any cost however. When Anthony Allfrey, an employee of O'Brien's, arranged that British Pathé, inter alia a producer of newsreels, offered a trip to Spain as a prize in a contest, the organizer suggested running the contest in a popular magazine that often featured photographs of women in slinky dresses on page one. Both Allfrey and the Director General resolutely refused. De Urzáiz wrote to his PR agent that "we do not wish to have this contest run in an awful paper like *Tit-Bits* or something even worse, for God only knows what kind of people would win the prize."[42] *Tit-Bits*, was a popular weekly magazine, whose readership mainly consisted of upper-working-class and lower-middle-class citizens.[43] As we can see, the MIT preferred to woo the well-educated and upper (-middle) class, who could afford to travel overseas, and were more likely to appear morally upright.

Toby O'Brien's efforts proved to be truly successful. The number of bookings increased and he was able to strengthen Spain's presence in British media. In March 1954, the *Sunday Express*, a middle-market British newspaper, printed a letter to the editor from a New Zealand reader titled "Accent on Spain." He wrote:

> An incredible number of recent B.B.C., Third and Home Programmes deal with Spain. Is it possible that someone is trying to "sell" Spain? Does the problem of Gibraltar lie behind it all? If so, as a passionately Empire-minded New Zealander, am I being unduly unfair in thinking somebody may be deliberately using influence in the matter?[44]

O'Brien sent this newspaper cutting to Mariano de Urzáiz, as he proudly saw the reaction of the New Zealander as a clear result of his work: "I am enclosing a copy of a letter . . ., which is about as good a testimonial as your Public Relations Advisor in Britain could desire! We have been working very hard on the BBC, as you know, and I am delighted to see that results are so good."[45]

While O'Brien handled Spain's relations with the British public, a man named Cedric Salter concerned himself with branding postwar Spain in Britain. The prominent British writer and journalist, an old friend of O'Brien, had come to Spain during the Civil War for the first time as a war correspondent. He wrote a book as well as several articles on the pro-Franco side for newspapers like the *Daily Mail* and the *Daily Telegraph*.[46] After World War II, Salter returned to Spain as representative of *The Sunday Times* before he started to work in the service of Franco's government. In 1950, Luis Bolín employed him as a public relations officer in Madrid, based on his assessment of the man as "charming and intelligent."[47] Salter functioned as a contact man who introduced Spain to British personalities visiting the country. Salter also published articles as well as travel guides to encourage British tourism.

Salter's most substantial contribution to rebranding Spain consisted of his travel guide *Introducing Spain*. Luis Bolín, Mariano de Urzáiz, and Antonio Gil-Casares, the Managing Director of the car-hire company ATESA, all assisted Salter in different ways to support his work. When Methuen published the book in 1953, the Spanish National Tourist Office in London celebrated with a press conference organized by Toby O'Brien. This was an important occasion even for diplomats. Besides representatives of the British press, the Spanish ambassador Miguel Primo de Rivera attended the press conference.[48] Salter's portrayal of Spain conveyed the romantic image of a backward country of pre-industrialized times: "Spain, like myself, is more attracted by the past than by the future, and it is nonsense to attribute this to cowardice or lack of ambition. She prefers her age-old folk-dancing to boogie-woogie, and her old, familiar, leisurely round of 'fiestas' to tearing around every week-end from pub to pub in a fast car."[49] The author's perspective on Spain resembled the image of MIT's official tourist advertising. Once again, Spain appeared as a destination from premodern times.

Despite being hired as an advocate of tourism, Salter's motivation to work for the Franco regime was, besides monetary reasons, political. In 1951, he had published a comprehensive article in the *Sunday Times* based on an encounter with Franco. In fact, he was the first British journalist who interviewed Franco after the war. In two articles, he emphasized Franco's hatred of communism and the Spaniards' appreciation of the British character.[50] As Salter later noted, writing about Spain in British newspapers was a very unpopular thing to do during that time, as especially the interview with Franco had earned him some criticism. Once, he got an offer by the *Daily Express* to write articles about Spain. He refused because writing for this newspaper at that time meant writing against the Franco regime.[51] This shows Salter's loyal attitude toward the regime as well as his desire to give the Britons an understanding of the Iberian country.

O'Brien and Salter managed to create a network of Spain-friendly media people and politicians within Britain who helped them to spread the word about Spain as an attractive tourist destination. O'Brien, for one, constantly traveled to Spain himself and also took prominent friends with him. Selwyn Lloyd often accompanied him to the upscale resort S'Agaró on the Costa Brava. Occasionally, Cedric Salter joined them there. After a meeting of the three, he reported to Mariano de Urzáiz: "[T]he Selwyn Lloyd visit to S'Agaró was a tremendous success, and although the dividend may not be either obvious or immediate from 'Turismo's' point of view . . . his visit to San Sebastian indicated that he is something more than what you once called 'another of Toby's political cronies.'"[52] This highlights that Salter not only explained to Bolín's successor the particular importance of Selwyn Lloyd, but also conveyed to him how public relations worked.

As shown above, international public relations created a Spain-friendly atmosphere and tried to convince British media to report about Spain in a more positive light. This started the slow process of rebranding Spain, although the same political system with the same dictator at the top persisted. When Cedric Salter left Spain in 1958, he commented on his work in an interview with a daily newspaper called *Madrid*: "My mission is finished. Spain has enough friends now."[53]

Charming the United Kingdom: The Bundling and Enforcement of Nation Branding Activities in the 1960s

In the 1960s, Spain's nation branding increased once again and its organization became of ministerial importance. At the center of these efforts stood Manuel Fraga Iribarne, Minister of Information and Tourism from 1962 to 1969. Fraga had studied law; he was conservative, but known at the same time as a "liberalizer." Most importantly, Fraga became the major initiator of Spain's effort to charm the world in the 1960s. Fraga used mass media to reach the European public and the production of posters skyrocketed while he was in office. Like the World Bank had suggested, he valorized the DGT (Dirección General de Tráfico, the Spanish transportation authority) to an undersecretary and equipped it with more staff and money. In addition, a newly founded Directorate-General expedited *propaganda turística*, and public relations.[54] Fraga emphasized the connection between touristic propaganda and the international image of a state. In 1965, he stated to the news agency EFE: "The touristic propaganda is, from a political point of view, of great importance. You have to keep in mind that what we are projecting abroad is nothing less than the image of Spain, a pure and genuine one, without making concessions to clichés."[55] This quotation indicates that Fraga saw the projection of Spain's image as a consciously directed process. He supported this development by expanding the use of advertising and public relations.

Since Fraga's reorganization of the ministry, his personnel bundled their further activities and involved new agencies that put tourism branding on firm footing. Toby O'Brien had lost the Spanish account, probably because the newly appointed head of Foreign Services at MIT accused him of misappropriating his travel expenses for private purposes.[56] Pemberton's, an agency founded by Alfred Pemberton in 1924, took over advertising activities, while the Business Press Bureau was put in charge of the public relations program. At that time, the tourism market was developing quickly and competition with other nations was, as the Tourist Office in London observed, "more intense than ever before."[57] Eastern European countries as well as Morocco, Portugal, and Egypt also expanded their tourist interests and became new rivals. By the end of 1964, the London Tourist Office, Pemberton's, and the Business Press Bureau reviewed their campaign of the current year and devised the strategy for the following one. Their aim was to convince potential tourists to visit Spain rather than a competitor state. Research showed that in Britain the target group consisted of middle and upper class households in the age groups 35–44 and 15–24 (and, to a lesser extent, young families).[58] Further measures were supposed to reach the developing market, which also contained lower income groups.[59] The use of market research helped to tailor advertising and PR activities exactly to the needs of the expected audience.

The campaigns that Pemberton's developed in the following years differed markedly in their organization as well as in their motifs of the Ministry's older publicity material. First, Pemberton's and the two airlines, British European Airlines and Iberia, launched several cooperative advertising campaigns. The handshake with the airline industry promised to have a positive effect on the establishment of Spain as a touristic brand. Second, the chosen topics and motifs transmitted a different image than the material produced by the ministry. Pemberton's chose several motifs for advertising that were based on what they felt were specific attractions Spain had to offer: "uncrowded beaches with a clear sea, sunshine, inexpensiveness of Spain for a holiday abroad, restaurants and nightlife of Spain, easiness of getting there, the refreshing and relaxing result of a holiday in Spain."[60] These motifs gave the idea of Spain a new touch. Pictures did not focus on cultural attractions, but emphasized leisure and relaxation. The slogan that accompanied the ads encouraged tourists to "Fall in love with Spain" and addressed the receiver's emotions. In 1966, Pemberton's took out ads showing a woman wearing a straw hat and drinking a glass of wine with a man. The photograph was followed by the slogan "Toast yourself in late Spanish sunshine." Another ad presented a woman in a bikini who held an air mattress under her arm while running toward the ocean. It was underlined with the slogan "Head off for a late Spanish sun" and the logos of Aer Lingus and Iberia.[61] Those ads presented Spain as a modern country ready to welcome tourists interested more in leisure than old-fashioned, romantic culture. Furthermore, in contrast to the regime's official advertising, these joint advertisements involved the receiver.

Whereas the majority of the tourism posters created by the ministry presented an old-fashioned Spain, the advertisements by international advertising agencies used a modern touch to project Spain's image abroad. Since the late 1960s, the MIT called for tenders to execute a large international campaign. In 1969, the Spanish subsidiary of the renowned agency Young and Rubicam won the job. Their advertising specialists intended to change Spain's image abroad in order to "deploy the rich variety of shades and not just some limited clichés."[62] Experts launched a campaign playing with stereotypes of Spain. One version of the advertisements showed a picture of a Spanish torero and was titled "Now, find out how much you *don't* know about Spain." The text was arranged as a quiz about Spain, which should reveal unusual facts, like: "In Galicia (North-western Spain) they play, the guitar, the castanets, the bagpipes? Answer: bagpipes. Which of these pastimes is the most popular in Spain? Jai-alai, soccer or bullfight? Answer: soccer. The first skyscraper in Europe was built in Frankfurt, London, Madrid or Milan? Answer: Madrid."[63] The advertisement was underlined with the slogan "Spain. The biggest surprise in the world." The preceding examples indicate that the advertising agency was working to counter the stereotypical image of Spain—it should not be associated with castanets, bullfights, or technical backwardness any more, but rebranded as a nation of soccer lovers, as architecturally innovative, and similar to another familiar country, where the bagpipes belonged to the national culture. Ironically, the ministry was not satisfied with Young and Rubicam's handling of the campaign and vice versa.[64]

Whereas advertising agencies directly courted the potential traveler, the Business Press Bureau mapped out a strategy to obtain media coverage and engage sympathies for Spain. Stephen Danos, public relations officer in charge, saw press receptions and the individual entertainment of journalists as "necessary to maintain goodwill"; Danos wanted them to be "constantly reminded of the material available on Spain as against all other newsworthy countries." To that end, Danos offered facilities to scores of journalists who were interested in reporting about Spain. Every month, he published the

Spanish Travel News, a newsletter in which he presented efforts of the tourism industry or portrayals of Spain's regions. A picture of a bull, which functioned as a logo, decorated the paper. In addition, travel agents should be "entertained so that close contact could be achieved and an added personal interest given to promoting Spain. Through these personal contacts, travel agents . . . will be enthused about Spain and pass this on to the public by selling Spain."[65] Moreover, the Business Press Bureau provided an information service answering inquiries from the press, television, and radio. For example, in 1968, *The Jewish Chronicle* asked Danos to provide information on vegetarian cooking in Spain, while *Farmers Weekly* inquired about detailed agricultural information.[66] Danos and his colleagues were not only the first contact in touristic matters, but their offices served as a drop-in center for almost any kind of information on the country.

Although the actors involved in Spain's branding efforts abroad avoided being involved in political issues, political and touristic matters overlapped at times, like in the case of Gibraltar. The affiliation of the peninsula's southernmost point had been a controversial issue in Spanish-British relations since the Spanish War of Succession in 1704. In the 1950s, Franco reclaimed sovereignty over Gibraltar. After British newspapers critically covered Franco's claim, several travel agents asserted that bookings were decreasing.[67] Decisions of the British to choose Spain as holiday destination partly depended on the diplomatic relations between both countries. In November 1964, shortly after the inauguration of the Labour Party government, the Spanish government imposed restrictions on entering and leaving Gibraltar. In the following months the problem was aggravated. As a consequence, a politician of the Labour Party, Eirene White, undersecretary at the Colonial Office at that time, advised people not to go to Spain for a holiday in February 1965.[68] Stephen Danos then tried to convince people that Spain still welcomed British citizens. Danos stated that "it is not possible at all times to remain completely aloof from semi-political matters such as Gibraltar, the arrest of British tourists . . . When Mrs. Irene [*sic*] White makes a ridiculous statement in Parliament about advising people not to go to Spain a political matter becomes a tourist one."[69] Though the MIT and their British co-operators intended to build a brand—Spain—that had a positive connotation, sometimes reality intervened. When the police arrested tourists for incomprehensible reasons, the aftermath of Spain's long-lasting isolation cropped up. And the demands for Gibraltar barred Franco's still existing claim to power. Among others, White interpreted the booking of a holiday in

Spain as support of this policy and intertwined touristic and political issues.

Another example shows that in spite of being responsible merely for Spain's touristic image, Stephen Danos tried to counterbalance negative political comments on the dictatorship. In the year following the Gibraltar incident, several unfavorable programs appeared on BBC television's daily news, which showed considerable anti-Spanish bias concerning the political nature of the regime. Danos felt he had to intervene; he talked to the editors of the program and complained to the management of the BBC. Partly as a result of this pressure, the news program, *24 hours*, produced two special films, featuring the tourist strongholds Lloret de Mar and Torremolinos. Both portrayed Spain as a sunny and friendly country.[70] Danos's intervention demonstrates that his job also required that he contend with critical journalists in the course of branding Spain in the press. While opponents of Franco's regime illuminated the political, problematic side, Danos and his PR or advertising colleagues attempted to portray a welcoming country.

In the mid 1960s, Spain had risen to the most popular overseas travel destination. In 1966, 22 percent of the British traveling abroad chose Spain as their destination, followed by Italy (17 percent) and France (14 percent).[71] The influence of public relations on the increase of travel and the process of rebranding was noticed publicly in the BBC's debate radio program *Any Questions?*. On 14 October 1966, host Freddy Grisewood had Gerald Nabarro as a guest on his show. Nabarro was a British businessman and member of the Conservative Party. During the show, Grisewood observed that minority extremist elements in any country could do untold harm to its image abroad. Then, he asked his guest what action could be taken by the majority of more moderate people to counteract this. Gerald Nabarro answered:

> About 15 years ago, very few British people went to Spain for their holidays. In the last few years, hundreds of thousands of British people have gone to Spain. . . . It wasn't because Spain, comparatively, was cheaper for holiday purposes than other countries . . . [T]here was an element of truth in that, but it was most largely due to public relations. I believe in technological application of public relations whenever an image is to be changed abroad. Be it a company, or a public body, or an institution, or a nation.[72]

It goes without saying that Danos and his colleagues did not manage to mute all criticism of Franco's regime. The tourist brand

Spain remained controversial in certain circles. Some organizations and individuals such as trade unionists or leftists still opposed traveling to Spain, arguing that any travel to the country constituted an act of support for Franco's dictatorship. But the fact that whether traveling to Spain or not aroused public interest shows that there already existed competing images of this nation.

Conclusion: Nation Branders and the Battle over Public Opinion

In the tale of Spanish PR and advertising campaigns in the United Kingdom, we see a variety of nation branders at work, and many of them were not Spanish. First, some officials in Spain like Luis Bolín and his successors sought to showcase the country's best assets to the West. Although the MIT developed a large number of posters and brochures, the administration did not spend much on advertising until the 1960s. Second, British public relations agents hired by the MIT sympathized with Spain. Toby O'Brien, Cedric Salter, and Stephen Danos all maintained strong bonds with the administration and therefore showed strong dedication to consulting Spanish actors and positioning Spain in the British media and among politicians. As a result, they achieved public relation's main purpose: they got people to talk about Spain again, and in particular, to do so in a nonpolitical and positive way. Third, the advertising agencies, which launched several campaigns in order to persuade people to travel to Spain, perceived the Spanish ministry as a regular client, not a political actor. The advertisers were primarily interested in meeting the customer's demands and addressing the consumer's needs. The analysis of these two groups indicates that personal commitment, as well as a focus on profit, were pivotal for the realization of the Spanish image campaigns. Foreign co-operators did not care whether Spain was a dictatorship, whether Franco still repressed regional movements, or enforced questionable death sentences. On a personal and professional level, they separated tourism from politics because their work was conceived as apolitical. As advertisers, they simply sought to satisfy their clients' wishes and they did this with extraordinary passion. Their work resulted in helping Spain to constantly appear in the media in a positive way, or, at least, in non-politic sections.

The advertising campaigns and public relations activities described above not only attracted tourists, hard currency, and international investment, but also presented Spain in a positive and apolitical way. It is probably impossible to figure out the concrete impact of these campaigns—increasing numbers of tourists also depended on the influence of tour operators, a low exchange rate, good value for money, and word-of-mouth recommendations. More importantly for our purpose, the actors of the MIT and their co-operators continuously redesigned the "brand Spain," adjusted it to certain target groups, and presented it via different media channels. Advertisements repeatedly mentioned slogans and displayed images. Even without visiting the ballyhooed destination, at least it left its mark in one's awareness. All these factors contributed to branding Spain and to creating new images of that country.

Discussing how a nation branded itself means talking about the actors fighting for control over public opinion at the same time. The efforts to influence public opinion on Spain and draw a specific picture of the nation did not necessarily mirror the actual reality. The actors on the Spanish side were representatives of Franco's regime. As such, they transferred a nationalist view of the country. As the case of Spain in the 1950s and 1960s shows, nation branding in general can usually just express the view of a group of people, often those who govern and pay the bills, especially in a dictatorship. Behind the scenes, Spain still was a nondemocratic state that occasionally arrested tourists for dubious reasons, repressed regional movements, and carried out death sentences. Furthermore, the branding of a nation always simplifies its image. Evidently, in reality multiple subjective images exist. Countries are usually far more complex and pluralistic than single campaigns can ever communicate. In the end, the example of branding Franco's Spain can teach us one important lesson: the brand of a country and its image are never created by representatives of the given nation alone. The brand of a country is always shaped by people of other nations as well, either through the efforts of a go-between or via the recipient's perspective.

Carolin Viktorin is a doctoral candidate at Freie Universität Berlin. Her research project examines the tourism branding of Spain in Western Europe from the 1950s to the 1970s. She focuses on the interrelations of the travel industry and the professionalization of public relations and advertising. The *Stiftung Bildung und Wissenschaft* as well as the German Historical Institute London supported her current project.

Together with Jessica C. E. Gienow-Hecht, she recently co-authored a chapter on nation branding in *International History in Theory and Practice*, edited by Barbara Haider-Wilson, William Godsey, and Wolfgang Müller, 695–720 (Vienna: Verlag Österreichische Akademie der Wissenschaften, 2017).

Notes

Epigraph: Minutes of the meeting of the Interministerial Commission of Tourism, 26 May 1955, (3) 49.02 box 14416, General Archive of the Administration, Alcalá de Henares (AGA). All translations are mine unless otherwise stated.

1. Joan Cals, "El modelo turístico español," *Estudios Turísticos*, no. 80 (1983): 15.
2. In recent literature, Spain's nation branding after the transition to democracy is usually regarded as a prime example of successful branding and repositioning. The internal changes and the success of these campaigns in the 1980s/1990s are undoubtedly significant. However, one should not overlook that Spain under Franco already softened its image and eventually was not that isolated. Please also consult on that topic: Neal M. Rosendorf, "Spain's First 'Re-Branding Effort' in the Postwar Franco Era," in *US Public Diplomacy and Democratization in Spain: Selling Democracy?* ed. Francisco Javier Rodríguez Jiménez, Lorenzo Delgado Gómez-Escalonilla, and Nicolas J. Cull (New York: Palgrave Macmillan, 2015), 177–80.
3. Nadia Kaneva, "Nation Branding: Toward an Agenda for Critical Research," *International Journal of Communication* 5 (2011): 118.
4. Melissa Aronczyk, *Branding the Nation: The Global Business of National Identity* (Oxford: Oxford University Press, 2013), 43.
5. Francisco Javier Montiel Alafont, "Spanische Identität? Spaniens Country Branding seit den 1960er Jahren: Eine kulturhistorische Annäherung," in *Spanien von innen und außen: Eine interkulturelle Perspektive,* ed. Anne Rupp (Berlin: Lit, 2011), 121–41, 124.
6. Simon Anholt, *Competitive Identity: The New Brand Management for Nations, Cities and Regions* (New York: Palgrave Macmillan, 2007).
7. Alafont, "Spanische Identität," 124.
8. Nadia Kaneva, "Nation Branding," 118.
9. Árpad Ference Papp-Váry, "The Marketing Point of View: Countries as Brands," Conference Paper (2006), 6.
10. Terence H. Qualter, *Advertising and Democracy in the Mass Age* (Basingstoke: Palgrave Macmillan, 1991), 85.
11. Cord Pagenstecher, *Der bundesdeutsche Tourismus: Ansätze zu einer Visual History: Urlaubsprospekte, Reiseführer, Fotoalben, 1950–1990* (Hamburg: Verlag Dr. Kovač, 2nd rev. ed., 2012), 169–72.
12. Nigel Morgan and Annette Pritchard, *Advertising in Tourism and Leisure* (Oxford: Butterworth-Heinemann, 2003), 17.
13. Ivo Raza, *Heads in Beds: Hospitality and Tourism Marketing* (Upper Saddle River, NJ: Prentice Hall, 2005), 123.
14. Scott M. Cutlip, "Pioneering Public Relations for Foreign Governments," *Public Relations Review* 13, no. 1 (Spring 1987): 15.

15. Natalia Rodríguez Salcedo, "El comienzo del turismo español: una aproximación a los precedentes de las relaciones públicas institucionales (1900–1950)," *Revista Internacional de Relaciones Públicas* 5, no. 10 (2015): 5–24.
16. Jarol B. Manheim and Robert B. Albritton, "Changing National Images: International Public Relations and Media Agenda Setting," *The American Political Science Review* 78, no. 3 (1984): 655.
17. Sandie Holguín, "'National Spain Invites You': Battlefield Tourism during the Spanish Civil War," *American Historical Review* 110, no. 5 (2005), 1399–426.
18. On the United States, consult Neal M. Rosendorf, "Be El Caudillo's Guest: The Franco Regime's Quest for Rehabilitation and Dollars after World War II via the Promotion of U.S. Tourism to Spain," *Diplomatic History* 30, no. 3 (2006), 367–407. In fact, Bolín as well as other European states overestimated the potential of US tourism, see Ana Moreno Garrido, "Los otros 'años vitales': Luis Bolín y la España turística (1948–1952)," *Ayer* 99 (2015): 153.
19. Mariano de Alarcon, "King Alfonso Takes Lead in Spanish Campaign to Make Nation Attractive to World's Tourists," 3 March 1929, *Chicago Tribune*, in (10) 54/11546, AGA.
20. The first office that reopened was in Buenos Aires, the second one in New York. On the latter consult Neal M. Rosendorf, *Franco Sells Spain to America: Hollywood, Tourism and Public Relations as Postwar Spanish Soft Power* (Basingstoke: Palgrave Macmillan, 2014), 22–24.
21. The so-called Directorate General of Tourism was previously part of the Interior Ministry.
22. Sasha D. Pack, *Tourism and Dictatorship: Europe's Peaceful Invasion of Franco's Spain* (New York: Palgrave Macmillan, 2006), 65.
23. Moreno, "Luis Bolín," 173.
24. Studies for a National Tourism Plan, 1952, p. 111–12, (3) 49.02 box 14415, AGA.
25. Studies, 1952, p. 111–12, (3) 49.02 box 14415, AGA.
26. Aurelio L. Orensanz, "Public Icons and Bourgeois Novels: Cultural Expressions in Francoist Spain," *International Journal of Politics, Culture and Society* 1, no. 2 (1987): 244. Further see Julio Aramberri, "Branding Spain's Tourism Miracle (1959–1979)," in *Tourism Branding: Communities in Action,* ed. Liping A. Cai, William C. Gartner, and Ana M. Munar (Bingley: Emerald Group, 2009), 146.
27. Alicia Fuentes Vega, *Bienvenido, Mr. Turismo: Cultura visual del boom en España* (Madrid: Cátedra, 2017).
28. Orensanz, "Public Icons," 246.
29. José-Luis Febas Borra, "Semiología del lenguaje turístico," *Estudios Turísticos* 57–58 (1978): 202; Orensanz, "Public Icons," 260.
30. Advertising Campaign in Britain, 1955, (3) 49.05 box 23562, AGA.
31. Carmen Ortiz, "The Uses of Folklore by the Franco Regime," *The Journal of American Folklore* 112, no. 446 (1999): 487–88.
32. Ortiz, "Folklore," 488.
33. Vincent Tewson to Anthony Eden, 24 January 1952, FO 371/102016, The National Archives London (TNA).
34. Tewson to Eden, 24 January 1952, FO 371/102016, TNA.
35. Philip H. Dougherty, "Advertising: New Name and Plan at Agency," *New York Times*, 30 December 1983.
36. John Pearson and Graham Turner, *The Persuasion Industry* (London: Eyre & Spottiswoode, 1965), 225.

37. Donough O'Brien, John D. Green, and Patrick Lichfield, *Fringe Benefits: The Good, the Bad, the Beautiful and the O'Briens* (London: Bene Factum Publishing, 2000), 28.
38. Cit. after Pearson and Turner, *Persuasion*, 230.
39. Richard West, "Paid to Persuade," *The Sunday Times*, 7 April 1963, 3.
40. Draft Report on Visit of Luis Bolín, 23 April 1952, (10) 77.02 box 6870.
41. E. D. O'Brien to Mariano de Urzáiz y Silva, 30 April 1954, and reply, May 1954 (3) 49.03 box 16070, AGA.
42. Mariano de Urzáiz y Silva to Anthony Allfrey, 1 February 1957, (3) 49.03 box 16071, AGA.
43. Kate Jackson; "The Tit-Bits Phenomenon: George Newnes, New Journalism and the Periodical Texts," *Victorian Periodicals Review* 30, no. 3 (1997): 201.
44. W. Teed, "Accent on Spain," *Sunday Express*, 28 March 1954: 3.
45. E. D. O'Brien to Mariano de Urzáiz y Silva, 29 March 1954, (3) 49.03 box 16070, AGA.
46. Cedric Salter, *Try-Out in Spain: Where the Axis Strategists Rehearsed the Atrocities That Are Devastating the Free Peoples of Europe* (New York: Harper & Brothers Publishers, 1943).
47. Luis Bolín to E. D. O'Brien, 14 September 1950, (3) 49.22 box 62896, AGA.
48. Spanish National Tourist Office London, Report of June 1953, (10) 77.02 box 6870, AGA.
49. Cedric Salter, *Introducing Spain* (London: Methuen, 1953), 15.
50. Cedric Salter, "General Franco Talks to The Sunday Times on Attitude to Britain," *Sunday Times*, 25 November 1951; Cedric Salter, "New Ally—or the Man With the Poker Face?," *Sunday Chronicle*, 25 November 1951.
51. M. Sanchez Cobos: "Cedric Salter, el periodista inglés que dijo siempre la verdad sobre España," *Madrid*, probably 1957, (3) 49.02 box 9568, AGA.
52. Cedric Salter to Mariano de Urzáiz, 20 September 1954, (3) 49.03 caja 16070, AGA.
53. Sanchez, "Cedric Salter," *Madrid*, probably 1957, (3) 49.02 box 9568, AGA.
54. Ana Moreno Garrido, *Historia del turismo en España en el siglo XX* (Madrid: Editorial Síntesis, 2007), 241–42.
55. Fraga Iribarne towards EFE, 17 September 1965, (3) 49.11 box 42404, AGA.
56. Head of Foreign Services to Director General of Tourism, 11 September 1962, (3) 49.22 box 62897, AGA.
57. Spanish National Tourist Office, Outline Proposal for the Promotion of Tourism from the United Kingdom during 1965, p. 9, (3) 49.04 box 20775, AGA.
58. Outline Proposal 1965, p.8; AGA (3) 49.04 box 20775.
59. Outline Proposal 1965, p. 14; AGA (3) 49.04 box 20775.
60. Outline Proposal 1965, p. 17; AGA (3) 49.04 box 20775.
61. Advertisement of Pemberton's, 1966, (3) 49.07 box 30819, AGA.
62. Promotion of Tourism for 1969, proposal by Young and Rubicam España, 1968 (3) 49.08 box 35474, AGA.
63. Collection of material on advertising campaign, (3) 49.09 box 38843, AGA.
64. A problem for the agencies was that the ministry only gave them a one-year contract. See "Spanish Account Up for the Bidding," *Advertiser's Weekly*, 13 June 1969: 56.
65. Outline Proposal 1965, p. 21; AGA (3) 49.04 box 20775.
66. Public Relations Report on Activity for the Spanish Ministry of Information and Tourism, January 1968, Business Press Bureau, p. 4, (3) 49.08 box 35474, AGA.

67. Activities January 1954, Spanish National Tourist Office, (10) 77.02 box 6870, AGA.
68. "Spain Holidays: Minister Warns," *Daily Mail*, 16 February 1965: 1; "'Don't Holiday in Spain'Advice," *Daily Telegraph*, 16 February 1965: 1.
69. Business Press Bureau, Report on PR activities in the UK and Ireland, December 1965, p. 8, (3) 49.05 box 23550, AGA.
70. PR report for the MIT, October 1966, Business Press Bureau, (3) 49.07 box 30817, AGA.
71. "Section A: The British Travel Industry Today," in *The British Travel Industry: A Survey*, ed. The Association of British Travel Agents (London 1968), 4.
72. Good Public Relations to Improve a Country's Image, 14 October 1966, 8:40 pm, Any Questions; Stephen Danos to Francisco Girón Tena, 25 October 1966, (3) 49.07 box 30817, AGA.

Bibliography

Anholt, Simon. *Competitive Identity: The New Brand Management for Nations, Cities and Regions.* New York: Palgrave Macmillan, 2007.

Aramberri, Julio. "Branding Spain's Tourism Miracle (1959–1979)." In *Tourism Branding: Communities in Action*, edited by Liping A. Cai, William C. Gartner, and Ana M. Munar, 133–47. Bingley: Emerald Group Pub., 2009.

Aronczyk, Melissa. *Branding the Nation: The Global Business of National Identity.* Oxford: Oxford University Press, 2013.

Cals, Joan. "El modelo turístico español." *Estudios Turísticos*, no. 80 (1983): 15–19.

Cutlip, Scott M. "Pioneering Public Relations for Foreign Governments." *Public Relations Review* 13, no. 1 (Spring 1987): 13–34.

Febas Borra, José-Luis. "Semiología del lenguaje turístico." *Estudios Turísticos* 57–58 (1978): 17–205.

Fuentes Vega, Alicia. *Bienvenido, Mr. Turismo: Cultura visual del boom en España.* Madrid: Cátedra, 2017.

Holguín, Sandie. "'National Spain Invites You': Battlefield Tourism during the Spanish Civil War." *American Historical Review* 110, no. 5 (2005): 1399–426.

Jackson, Kate. "The Tit-Bits Phenomenon: George Newnes, New Journalism and the Periodical Texts." *Victorian Periodicals Review* 30, no. 3 (1997): 201–33.

Kaneva, Nadia. "Nation Branding: Toward an Agenda for Critical Research." *International Journal of Communication* 5 (2011): 117–41.

Manheim, Jarol B., and Robert B. Albritton. "Changing National Images: International Public Relations and Media Agenda Setting." *The American Political Science Review* 78, no. 3 (1984): 641–57.

Montiel Alafont, Francisco Javier. "Spanische Identität? Spaniens Country Branding seit den 1960er Jahren: Eine kulturhistorische Annäherung."

In *Spanien von innen und außen: Eine interkulturelle Perspektive*, edited by Anne Rupp, 121–41. Berlin: Lit, 2011.

Moreno Garrido, Ana. *Historia del turismo en España en el siglo XX*. Madrid: Editorial Síntesis, 2007.

———. "Los otros 'años vitales': Luis Bolín y la España turística (1948–1952)." *Ayer* 99 (2015): 151–74.

Morgan, Nigel, and Annette Pritchard. *Advertising in Tourism and Leisure*. Oxford: Butterworth-Heinemann, 2003.

O'Brien, Donough, John D. Green, and Patrick Lichfield. *Fringe Benefits: The Good, the Bad, the Beautiful, and the O'Briens*. London: Bene Factum, 2000.

Orensanz, Aurelio L. "Public Icons and Bourgeois Novels: Cultural Expressions in Francoist Spain." *International Journal of Politics, Culture, and Society* 1, no. 2 (1987): 242–62.

Ortiz, Carmen "The Uses of Folklore by the Franco Regime." *The Journal of American Folklore* 112, no. 446 (1999): 479–96.

Pack, Sasha D. *Tourism and Dictatorship: Europe's Peaceful Invasion of Franco's Spain*. New York: Palgrave Macmillan, 2006.

Pagenstecher, Cord. *Der bundesdeutsche Tourismus: Ansätze zu einer Visual History: Urlaubsprospekte, Reiseführer, Fotoalben 1950—1990*. 2nd rev. ed. Hamburg: Kovač, 2012.

Papp-Váry, Árpad F. "The Marketing Point of View: Countries as Brands." Conference Paper 2006, Retrieved 30 January 2016 from http://www.papp-vary.hu/english/Countries_as_brands_Marketing_point_of_view.pdf.

Pearson, John, and Graham Turner. *The Persuasion Industry*. London: Eyre & Spottiswoode, 1965.

Qualter, Terence H. *Advertising and Democracy in the Mass Age*. Basingstoke: Palgrave Macmillan in association with the London School of Economics and Political Science, 1991.

Raza, Ivo. *Heads in Beds: Hospitality and Tourism Marketing*. Upper Saddle River, NJ: Prentice Hall, 2005.

Rodríguez Salcedo, Natalia. "El comienzo del turismo español: una aproximación a los precedentes de las relaciones públicas institucionales (1900–1950)." *Revista Internacional de Relaciones Públicas* 5, no. 10 (2015): 5–24.

Rosendorf, Neal M. "Be El Caudillo's Guest: The Franco Regime's Quest for Rehabilitation and Dollars after World War II via the Promotion of U.S. Tourism to Spain." *Diplomatic History* 30, no. 3 (2006): 367–407.

———. *Franco Sells Spain to America: Hollywood, Tourism and Public Relations as Postwar Spanish Soft Power*. Basingstoke: Palgrave Macmillan, 2014.

———. "Spain's First 'Re-Branding Effort' in the Postwar Franco Era." In *US Public Diplomacy and Democratization in Spain: Selling Democracy?*, edited by Francisco Javier Rodríguez Jiménez, Lorenzo Delgado

Gómez-Escalonilla, and Nicolas J. Cull, 155–89. New York: Palgrave Macmillan, 2015.

Salter, Cedric. *Introducing Spain*. London: Methuen, 1953.

———. *Try-Out in Spain: Where the Axis Strategists Rehearsed the Atrocities That Are Devastating the Free Peoples of Europe*. New York: Harper & Brothers Publishers, 1943.

"Section A: The British Travel Industry Today," in *The British Travel Industry: A Survey*, ed. The Association of British Travel Agents (London 1968): 1–4.

Chapter 6

THE ART OF BRANDING

Rethinking American Cultural Diplomacy during the Cold War

Michael L. Krenn

Nearly a quarter of a century ago, when the first edition of *Explaining the History of American Foreign Relations* appeared, there was but one contributor pleading the case for culture as an essential element of the study of US diplomacy: Akira Iriye. By 2004 and the second edition, Iriye was joined in that effort by a young scholar from Germany—Jessica C. E. Gienow-Hecht. By that time, the scholarship dealing with US cultural diplomacy was in full bloom, and the field continues to find new areas for investigation. Focused almost entirely on the Cold War era, this new vein of research closely examined the United States' cultural output for the foreign audience: music (mostly rock and roll and jazz), sports, movies, theater, dance, art, and a host of other genres. Studies have also looked at the bureaucratic side of the picture by examining the efforts of the Department of State and United States Information Agency, in particular, in terms of designing and implementing cultural diplomacy programs.[1] Despite this wealth of invaluable scholarship, however, the field of US cultural diplomacy has yet to reach a point whereby we more clearly understand its place within the larger frameworks of either US diplomatic history or the much larger picture of international cultural relations.

In recent years, however, the theory of nation branding has been put forward as one possible avenue for more effectively grasping the larger and deeper context of cultural relations among nations.

Notes for this section begin on page 167.

The theory itself is hardly new, but its application to the study of cultural diplomacy has gained traction only in the past few years. I propose to take a rather unique approach to testing the usefulness of the theory of nation branding in the study of US cultural diplomacy by utilizing it as a tool for a re-examination of my 2005 book, *Fall-Out Shelters for the Human Spirit: American Art and the Cold War.* The purpose is not to "prove" or "disprove" my earlier findings, but rather to illustrate how nation branding can help scholars to reframe and re-conceptualize their work (past, present, and future) in ways that move the field of cultural diplomacy from a distinct (or even peripheral) role to a more central and interconnected role in the study of international relations.

Defining Nation Branding

As even the devotees of nation branding admit, a primary problem that confronts the theory is the uncertainty concerning the precise definition of the concept. As Nadia Kaneva concludes, "Despite nation branding's growing popularity, there is much disagreement about its meaning and scope." This is amply demonstrated in Keith Dinnie's recent work in which he first divides the definition of nation branding into "two camps": "definitions that focus upon the visual manifestation of a brand" and "deeper definitions that go beyond the visual aspects of a brand and attempt to capture the essence of a brand." Even the term itself—nation branding—is more complex than perhaps first imagined: one must "distinguish between a *national brand* . . . and a *nation brand*."[2] Given the fact that the application of nation branding to the study of diplomacy is relatively new, however, such confusion and disagreement is not unusual. Scholars of cultural diplomacy well understand the problems arising from definitions: what is cultural diplomacy; what is culture; is culture, by any definition, really part of diplomacy? For the purposes of this chapter, I will be relying on the definitions offered by scholars such as Dinnie: "the unique, multi-dimensional blend of elements that provide the nation with culturally grounded differentiation and relevance for all of its target audiences."[3] Kaneva offers a more detailed analysis:

> In terms of practical manifestations, nation branding includes a wide variety of activities, ranging from "cosmetic" state structures by creating governmental and quasi-governmental bodies

that oversee long-term nation branding efforts. The most ambitious architects of nation branding envision it as "*a component of national policy*, never as a 'campaign' that is separate from planning, governance or economic development."[4]

At first glance, these might appear to be definitions so wide-ranging as to fit almost any theory or circumstance. There is perhaps some validity in this observation, but the strength and value of nation branding lies in the very fact that instead of consistently narrowing the focus for scholars by invoking an ever-constricting range of terms and/or exclusionary definitions of "fields" and "theories," nation branding seeks to expand the research agenda by pushing beyond such definitional wrangling and seeking to construct a more inclusionary, yet still intellectually rigorous, approach to the study of diplomatic history and cultural diplomacy. Ilaria Scaglia, in her chapter in this collection, quite rightly points out that in dealing with events involving the transmission of ideas and national identity (in the case of her own study, the idea of internationalism), the historian is often faced with "a complex set of ideas and practices increasingly in contradiction with one another [that] played an essential role in representing and communicating power."[5] In addition, Scaglia notes that the actual means of transmitting such ideas (the International Exhibition of Chinese Art) was indeed a multidimensional undertaking in the sense that it was not merely a manifestation of state-directed propaganda. Instead, the branding process is conducted by a diverse collection of individual and institutional actors, often operating with very different agendas.[6] From this wider perspective I will draw upon several elements that seem to consistently present themselves in the discussions of nation branding and apply them to a re-examination of one of my older works.

Studies of Cultural Diplomacy: Strengths and Limitations

When I began the research for *Fall-Out Shelters for the Human Spirit: American Art and the Cold War* in the early-2000s, I understood very little about the cultural side of cultural diplomacy. My preceding book, dealing with African Americans and US foreign policy, introduced me more fully to the propaganda battle for "hearts and minds" during the Cold War period and so, in examining US art displays sent overseas after World War II, I followed the traditional pattern of looking first at the Department of State and United States

Information Agency. Cultural diplomacy, it seemed to me at the time, was merely the "cultural" manifestation of traditional diplomacy, and it therefore seemed inevitable that my study would concentrate on how various offices and officers in the State Department and the United States Information Agency (USIA) went about their business of using art (and music, movies, theater, dance, and literature) as a weapon in the war of ideas with the Soviet Union.

I soon became aware that other, nonstate players were also involved—the American Federation of Arts (AFA), the Museum of Modern Art (MOMA), and the Smithsonian, for example, but my interpretation of the relationship between state and nonstate actors hinged on two distinct (but nevertheless intertwined) ideas. First, the nonstate actors were "different." The distinction was a simple one—art exhibits organized and sponsored by the US government were "official" examples of cultural diplomacy, whereas those exhibits sent abroad by AFA or MOMA were private initiatives with no larger aims in mind than sharing American art with the world. Second, the differences between state and nonstate actors naturally led to conflicts. In both their means and their goals, private organizations, museums, and even individual artists and curators saw the art exhibits in ways that often seemed to be diametrically opposed to what the State Department and USIA wished to accomplish. In short, the nonstate players saw art as an important means of building an international language of understanding and providing an important counterweight of culture in a world increasingly focused on the military, political, and economic ramifications of living in the dangerous postwar world. For the government, art was merely another tool, another weapon in a propaganda arsenal that sought to disparage the communist bloc and show the United States in the best light possible.

The struggle between these state and nonstate participants was exacerbated by the fact that both sides eventually recognized that they needed each other in order to build a substantial and meaningful overseas art program. The US government had the resources, but it lacked the expertise that only the museums, artists, and art institutions could provide. In addition, the focus on abstract expressionism as the preferred art form—at least for the major international exhibits—was another source of friction. This new artistic approach did strike a chord with certain elements of the foreign audience (the young and the more educated), but some of the artists themselves were soon found to have "suspect" political backgrounds. Both the art and the artists became lightning rods for domestic criticism as

some US congressmen and officials from more traditional art organizations argued that abstract expressionism was most definitely
not an acceptable means of representing the United States abroad.
In the end, such criticisms finally put an end to the large-scale
US-government sponsored art exhibits by the mid-1970s.

When all was said and done, I believed that the book made a
significant contribution to the study of US cultural diplomacy
during the Cold War. It was only years after its publication that I first
became acquainted with the theory of nation branding. Overcoming
my initial skepticism about any theory that appeared to have its
origins in the world of business and advertising, I began to wonder
whether the theory could assist me in my continuing study of United
States' cultural diplomacy. My first tentative foray into nation branding came while presenting a paper at the Culture and International
History V Conference.[7] At the time, I felt that focusing on a rather
small example—one particular US exhibit in 1907—would be a valuable testing ground for the theory. Utilizing a single event—and a
very small chronological window—did have its advantages, especially given the confines of a conference presentation. However, as
I began to conceptualize my contribution to this present volume, I
realized that in the same way that nation branding helped to broaden
and deepen the theoretical framework for the study of US cultural
diplomacy, I also needed to start from a larger canvas. Thus, my
decision to look back to my earlier work on US art exhibits during
the Cold War.

According to many of the advocates of the theory of nation
branding, one of its primary benefits is that it allows scholars to
place instances of cultural (or other forms of public) diplomacy in a
much longer chronology of national identity building.[8] In his spirited
defense of the theory, Wally Olins argues that:

> All the historians and political scientists who have studied
> the subject, Hobsbawm, Geller, Kedourie, Benedict Anderson,
> Dominic Lieven and many others share more or less similar views.
> As nations emerge they create self-sustaining myths to build
> coherent identities. When political upheavals take place, colonial
> masters are overthrown or a new regime emerges as in Eastern
> Europe in the 90's of the last century, the nation reinvents itself.[9]

He points out that France and Germany, from their very beginnings
as nations, have engaged in both branding and, when necessary
or desirable, rebranding themselves as nations and peoples.[10]
Examining US cultural diplomacy as part of international cultural

history by using the nation-branding approach, Jessica C. E. Gienow-Hecht reinforces Olins's conclusions by noting that the United States during the Cold War was hardly the first country to engage in more sophisticated efforts at self-representation: "In a timeless fashion, programs echoed the desire to inform people at home and abroad what was special and important about the US identity and what legitimized the United States' international ascent to the top."[11] Trying to portray these programs as simply "Cold War propaganda" completely misses the point: "Cold War propaganda developed in the context of a continuum spanning centuries. It had less to do with the Cold War proper than with the development of the modern nation state and its desire to display power in an iconic and marketable fashion."[12]

However, most of the studies of US cultural diplomacy—my own included—locate such efforts by the US government squarely during the years 1945 to the 1960s or 1970s, the hottest part of the Cold War. In this fashion, the cultural programs developed during that timeframe are seen largely as specific responses to a specific challenge—the threat of communism. As such, it is not surprising that the focus is on the late-1940s, 1950s, and 1960s, the years in which the struggle between East and West was at its most dramatic. It is also not surprising to find that the majority of the research for these projects is done among the "usual suspects"—Department of State and USIA records. When other sources are consulted it is usually to find out the ways in which this or that organization or individual worked with (or had conflicts with) the government offices running the show. I devoted a total of four and a half pages in my book to the pre-1945 history of the use of art as part of international relations; just three of those pages dealt with pre-World War II efforts by the US government to utilize art as part of its official diplomacy. My reasoning was clear: prior to the Cold War the "United States . . . was much slower in developing direct connections between the state and arts."[13] Even the prewar program directed at cultural exchanges with Latin America (as part of President Franklin Delano Roosevelt's Good Neighbor Policy) was glossed over because of the effort's "tiny budget and a rather narrow charge." In short, my study suggested that prior to 1945, lacking any substantial or sustained "state" direction of art exhibits overseas, nothing in the way of an effective or coherent program to "sell" American culture abroad was able to gain much traction. And while my bibliography included records from the Archives of American Art, the Phillips Collection, the National Gallery of Art, the Smithsonian Institution, and the Museum of

Modern Art, my focus while examining these sources was to locate the specific connections these organizations or museums had with the State Department and USIA. I purposely excluded from consideration, or marginalized, those art exhibits sent abroad without the official imprimatur of the US government; those, after all, were not components of the "official" cultural diplomacy effort.[14]

There is nothing inherently wrong with this approach taken by many scholars looking at US cultural diplomacy. Indeed, it resulted in some excellent work that has succeeded in bringing culture into the diplomatic history discussion in ways never before imagined. Yet even the most ardent defenders of this subfield must admit that it does create a rather constricting field of view. While the focus is on "official" (i.e., state-financed, directed, and/or operated) examples of cultural diplomacy activities, the work of nonstate actors is often pushed behind the scenes or relegated to subsidiary roles in support of the more meaningful work of the US government. The relationship between the state and nonstate players is very often portrayed as combative, with the government adopting a narrow and practical view of the use of culture (i.e., as simply another propaganda weapon) and the nongovernmental participants arguing for a more "positive" or "humanistic" approach (i.e., art for art's sake). Furthermore, by bookending the discussion between the end of World War II and the waning of East-West tensions by the 1970s and 1980s, the timeframe is itself fairly compact. In this fashion, cultural diplomacy is (perhaps inadvertently) portrayed as a creature of the Cold War, with no discernible antecedents or impact on the post-Cold War world.

As I started work on my new project, a comprehensive study of the history of US cultural diplomacy, the limitations of much of the current research became rapidly apparent.[15] How was I to more fully and carefully consider the overseas activities of private US citizens and groups that were undertaken during the nineteenth and early twentieth century? Was Frederick Douglass's speaking tour through the United Kingdom cultural diplomacy? What about the American baseball teams that toured the world in the 1880s and 1890s? American art was shown abroad prior to the Cold War, but if this was done via private groups, did it "count" as cultural diplomacy? After some lengthy research and consideration, I came to the conclusion that there was, so to speak, ideological "connective tissue" binding all of these early efforts into a more comprehensive national effort at identity. And as I drew these conclusions about the 1800s and early-1900s, it also became clear that my understanding of the post-1945 cultural diplomacy of the United States would need to be seriously reconsidered. I decided to start this process of reinvestigation with my own work on US art exhibits sent abroad during the Cold War.

Nation Branding: Expanding the Chronological Framework

If we apply some of the basic premises of nation branding to these studies—most particularly my own book—we begin to see the outlines of a much different story. First, we begin with the assumption that the art exhibits sent overseas during the Cold War were neither unique nor unprecedented. To do so, however, we must understand a central tenet of the nation branding theory: it does not truly matter whether the cultural diplomacy comes from "official" (i.e., governmental) sources or from private concerns. In her contribution to this collection, Ilaria Scaglia takes into account all of the contributors to the formation of the 1935–36 art exhibit and concludes that, "So far, historians have examined these various actors in isolation from one another." She argues, instead, for a more inclusive study that pulls together the entire "group of individuals and institutions with different agendas who were committed to the same nation branding project."[16]

Taking this one step further, if we understand the nation-branding mission as composed of various constituencies then we need not limit our examination of cultural diplomacy to only those efforts undertaken by the US government. In short, we push beyond the confines of the Cold War and in so doing locate the cultural diplomacy efforts of that time period in a broader chronological framework. To be sure, scholars have already attempted to do just that. Justin Hart recently looked back to the 1920s and 1930s to find the antecedents of what eventually blossomed after 1945. Frank Ninkovich, Thomas Zeiler, and Jessica C. E. Gienow-Hecht all look back to the nineteenth century for clues to the longer history of US cultural relations with the world. To a large degree, however, studies of earlier periods are lumped by many reviewers into the category of "precursors" to the fully developed cultural diplomacy of the Cold War period or, even worse in the case of studies from the nineteenth and early twentieth centuries, dismissed as not being "real" cultural diplomacy at all because of a lack of active and focused state actors in the process. The analysis from the world of nation branding allows us to see such episodes not as mere precursors to the *real* cultural diplomacy of the post-World War II period, but as an essential step in the much longer history of the United States' efforts to portray an image of itself on the international stage.[17]

In this regard, therefore, the use of American art as part of the nation's cultural arsenal begins not with the disastrous *Advancing American Art* exhibit of 1946–47 but nearly one hundred years earlier. As Carol Troyen explains, in 1867 at the Exposition Universelle in Paris, "there was the American section of the Fine Arts Department designed to present to an international audience the achievements of American culture and to demonstrate that American art was the equal of its machinery and inventions." Eventually including nearly 120 pieces of American art (ranging from sketches, to sculpture, and over eighty paintings), the collection was evidence that a "new, patriotic self-assurance had for the moment displaced the nation's deep-seated cultural insecurity and, full of naïve enthusiasm, America in 1867 sent its best contemporary art to be measured against Europe's greatest modern masters."[18] And it was, indeed, an awe-inspiring exhibit of works by artists such as Winslow Homer, Frederic Church, and Albert Bierstadt. However, the foreign reception was decidedly mixed. Church's grand painting of Niagara Falls managed to secure a silver medal from the awards jury, but by and large the French and British critics virtually ignored the American works or dismissed them as pale imitations of superior European works. There was plenty of finger-pointing in the wake of the disappointing showing by American art, including accusations that the French purposely relegated the works by the upstart Americans to less than prestigious settings in the exhibit hall. However, "It was the selection of works that was most frequently blamed for the failure of the American display." The most pointed criticism charged that "the entries from the United States were neither native nor descriptive enough, and insufficiently documented the characteristic aspects of certain typical American scenes."[19]

Troyen's article did not appear in one of the journals concerned with diplomatic history or international relations. Had it done so, there would most certainly have been questions about its relevance to those fields, most particularly the area of cultural diplomacy. The crucial issue would be provenance: the 1867 exhibit was organized and funded by private US organizations and individuals. The National Academy of Design in New York City was the primary force behind establishing the US exhibition. An appeal to the US government for assistance was met with a good deal of hemming and hawing by Congress. Impatient with the delay, the National Academy of Design eventually appointed its own committee to oversee the work, and ultimately relied on a selection committee made up of artists, art dealers, critics, and several industrialists who collected art. The committee relied on appeals to collectors, individual artists, and museums to secure the works ultimately shown in Paris.[20] Therefore, while the "cultural" aspect of the undertaking is self-evident, the "diplomacy" part of the equation appears to be absent.

For example, a comparison of the 1867 exhibit, and the State Department funded, organized, and exhibited showing of the *Advancing American Art* collection in 1946–47, might at first glance be classified as an illustration of the old "apples and oranges" adage. Both were exhibits of art shown overseas, but in the traditional viewpoint espoused in so much of the cultural diplomacy literature, the similarities begin and end there since the Cold War exhibit was "official" cultural diplomacy (i.e., government-sponsored), while the 1867 show was very much a "private" matter and, thus, without a larger meaning for understanding America's international relations. Nation branding, however, argues for broadening the outlook by focusing on similarities rather than differences.

Nation Branding: Dismissing the State versus Nonstate Dichotomy

If we consider both shows as part of a continuum, as nation branding theory posits, rather than two distinct events the similarities quickly become apparent. First and foremost, the delineation between "official" and "unofficial" cultural diplomacy evaporates when we focus on aims and goals rather than the organizational or bureaucratic environment in which the exhibits took place.

Both the nineteenth-century and Cold War art exhibits shared one important element common to any analysis that utilizes nation branding: the purpose of both shows was defining (or, perhaps more accurately, redefining) the United States. In short, both exhibitions sought to "brand" the United States with an identity that would be both understandable and appealing to the foreign audience. The impetus for the two exhibits came largely from the same source—a belief that the world did not fully understand or appreciate the cultural productivity and strength of the American republic, and that this lack of understanding undercut the United States' international standing. Troyen explains that the American art on display in Paris was "designed to present to an international audience the achievements of American culture and to demonstrate that American art was the equal of its machinery and inventions." Landscape paintings were chosen to send a particular message: they "immortalized the optimistic spirit of antebellum America, and proclaimed the country to be expansive, unspoiled, and indomitable." In arguing for Congressional support, the organizers of the American art exhibit declared that funding was necessary in order to "secure a proper representation of the art of the country in Paris."[21]

That the 1867 exhibit received no state support does nothing to diminish the fact that the "private" organizers very clearly and articulately expressed their desire to have the works of art serve as instruments to construct an image of the United States in the eyes of the foreign audience and fully believed that in doing so this would enhance America's prestige and influence. One of the great values of nation branding theory is, as Gienow-Hecht observes, that it "does not prioritize either state or nonstate actors but allows for a fluid interaction between the two."[22] In the mid nineteenth century, the interaction was necessarily limited; the United States had not achieved a sufficient level of modernization or sophistication that would support such cultural undertakings. Nor had US business (and advertising) reached the stage of advanced industrialization characteristic of the late nineteenth and early twentieth century. By the time World War II ended, the pieces were in place for a deeper involvement between governmental and nongovernmental players. Indeed, the support for the Cold War exhibit effectively erased the lines between "official" and "unofficial" actors. For example, William Benton, who served as Assistant Secretary of State for Public Affairs from 1945 to 1947 and oversaw the development and exhibition of the *Advancing American Art* show came to government work only after a long career in advertising. Alfred Frankfurter, editor of *Art News*, argued just prior to the initial showing of *Advancing American Art* in the United States that the exhibition of the best of America's modern art would be a useful antidote to European perceptions of US culture as being encapsulated in "such luxuries as chewing gum and comic books."[23] Representatives from the Department of State agreed. One official declared that, "It is the sort of thing which helps to counter propaganda which tries to label us as cultural barbarians."[24] His ideas were echoed by a colleague: "The United States has demonstrated its superb ability to manufacture tanks, airplanes, guns, and all the other implements of war. . . . The United States must demonstrate that it also has an interest in and a vigorous movement in the fields of art, music, and allied fields."[25]

Nation Branding: Understanding the Domestic Context

The similarities do not end there, nor does the importance of those similarities. As with the 1867 show, criticisms from the US side soon rang out. The denunciations of *Advancing American Art* did not come about because of the foreign reception of the exhibit. In both Europe and Latin America the show was generally well received. Like the domestic critics of nearly a century before, most of the negative comments were aimed at the selection of the art sent abroad, centering on the idea that the artwork did not truly represent "America." Almost as soon as the modern art in the collection was shown at the Metropolitan Museum of Art prior to going overseas the bricks were flying. Congressmen argued that not only was the art "un-American," but so were the artists—many of whom had not even been born in the United States. *Look* skewered the show, as did radio personality Fulton Lewis; both fumed about US taxpayers' money being used to exhibit such awful and un-American art. Other artists joined in the attacks, including the more conservative American Artists Professional League, which charged that there had been a "one-sided selection of works" that was "manifestly unfair and unrepresentative."[26]

In my study of the post-World War II international art program, I interpreted these attacks on modern art as part of a more intense domestic debate over what was, and what was not, art. Certainly, Presidents Harry S. Truman and Dwight D. Eisenhower expressed very real concerns about the nature of the more abstract art being produced at that time. Truman famously declared, after seeing one of the paintings from *Advancing American Art*, "If that's art, I'm a Hottentot." Eisenhower was a bit more temperate when he discussed the American art show at the 1959 American National Exhibition in Moscow, calling the abstract works "unintelligible to the average eye."[27] In the white-hot cauldron of the Cold War, critiques of the art were rapidly transformed into criticisms of the art's "message" and the political allegiances of the artists themselves. In short, the heated debates over American art during the 1940s, 1950s, and 1960s were merely one more example of how the Cold War mindset poisoned discussions of even something so apparently harmless as a painting.

Nation branding, however, helps us to understand what was happening on another level. As Kaneva notes, "nation branding programs can be directed at both domestic and international audiences." In fact, the domestic "audiences" must, of necessity, be inextricably involved in the nation branding process. If we re-examine the battles over America's international art program from this theoretical perspective, we begin to comprehend that these fights were not simply domestic manifestations of the Cold War. Instead, we now have to take into account two other important aspects.

First, while there was an effort throughout the life of the programs to send US art overseas to include "business interests, government parties, civil society actors, and citizens" in the formulation and presentation of art exhibits sent abroad, this occurred within a relatively small circle of those entities and purposefully excluded participants who argued for other approaches.[28] There were, to be sure, small exhibits of what might be referred to as more "traditional" American art sponsored by the US government during the Cold War. It is clear, however, that modern art—particularly abstract expressionism, and, in the early 1960s, pop art—was the preferred style. Norman Rockwell may have been the most popular artist in the United States in the postwar period, but for the people who set up the US international art exhibits, this was beside the point. As one of the organizers for the collection of American abstract expressionist art to be shown at the 1958 world's fair argued, visitors from the United States would likely "feel that American art would be better represented by Norman Rockwell and Grandma Moses. Europeans, on the other hand, are far more interested in seeing what is happening in American art today."[29] That may well have been true. Requests from US posts around the world often specifically requested that modern American art be sent for display. Both state and nonstate players believed that abstract expressionist art expressed decidedly American values—freedom of expression and cultural leadership.

Second, there is little doubt that, on the whole, the international audience (particularly in Europe) responded favorably to modern American art. Nation branding, however, asks us to examine this form of diplomacy from both international and domestic viewpoints. When we do so, some of the attacks on the US international art program take on greater meaning. Certainly, there were some critics—Congressman George Dondero, for example—whose attacks on the exhibits of abstract expressionist art were simply handy weapons to use against political opponents, or a means of gaining public notoriety and popularity.[30] The fact that so many of the artists were not born in the United States was also a useful rallying point for those critics who believed that during the Cold War the issue of "loyalty" took on added importance. In short, the brand was

changing, and to some, loyalty and native birth rather than internationalism and cosmopolitanism now constituted primary ingredients
of the national brand. Pushing past all of the Cold War rhetoric, we
also perceive that—like the critics of the 1867 show—one persistent
argument was that modern art did not truly (or, at least, completely)
represent anything distinctly "American." As the American Artists
Professional League lamented in 1958 concerning the modern art at
the US pavilion at the world's fair, most European visitors would not
"realize the continuing strength of the main stream of American Art,
imbued with faith in the verities of our common heritage of great
Art, of and for the Ages, but none the less essentially, vitally, and
contemporaneously American." The United States Committee of the
International Association of Plastic Arts also complained. The use of
art as part of the nation's cultural diplomacy was not in question; it
was simply the fact that the 1958 exhibit contained the work of "just
seventeen young Americans of astonishingly similar aesthetic points
of view."[31]

In my earlier study, it was relatively easy to dismiss or at least
marginalize such criticisms as "sour grapes"—outpourings from
artists who were left out of the exhibits or felt jealous of the new
prestige and prominence accorded to modern American art. There
is little doubt that in both 1867 and 1958, professional animosities
and envy did play some role. But the criticisms from both centuries
also point out something that nation branding helps to illuminate: by
focusing most of the work on US cultural diplomacy on the foreign
reception of such art, we sometimes tend to minimize the domestic
implications. This overlooks the point so clearly made by Sue Curry
Jansen who argues that, "Branding not only explains nations to the
world, but also reinterprets national identity in market terms and
provides new narratives for domestic consumption."[32] Simply put,
nation branding suggests that the foreign reception was, in some
ways, unimportant; i.e., the fact that American art was "liked" or
"admired" by international audiences is not as important as whether
or not the viewers could discern a definitive American identity—or
"brand"—within the art. Since nearly every exhibit of modern or
abstract expressionist art was met with harsh public and congressional criticisms at home in the United States, and since influential
figures such as Truman and Eisenhower very publicly expressed
grave doubts about whether such art was truly "American" art (or art
at all), it is fair to ask two important questions. If significant portions
of the US public (or, at least, very visible and influential portions
of that public) did not believe the art on display to be an accurate

representation of their nation, how did this influence the impact on the foreign audience? And, to take this analysis to its logical conclusion, if the foreign audience perceived that many Americans did not in fact support the art, did the exhibits have the desired impact? Did the art fail to create a national "brand" that influenced foreign audiences and simultaneously met with the approval of domestic audiences? This is, in fact, more than likely. As György Szondi succinctly puts the matter, "Nation branding is successful when the brand is lived by the citizens."[33] This line of thought introduces another important variable into the all-important analysis of the impact of cultural diplomacy efforts: the ability of the cultural product being used to reflect a broad consensus among the domestic stakeholders. Abstract expressionist art, for all of its champions in the art world, never gained acceptance from either the wider American public or many government officials. Thus, while many foreign audiences enjoyed the works of art, with some even perceiving the "hidden" propaganda message of "freedom of expression," this does not mean that the art ever made a tangible impact on those audiences in terms of creating a specific American "brand" in their minds—something that was decidedly different from what other nations might just as easily produce.[34]

Nation Branding: Rethinking the Issue of Impact

And as nation-branding theory argues, the difference is what makes the difference. According to Szondi:

> Differentiation is an inseparable feature of branding, as a strong brand identity can differentiate the actual product or company from its competitors ... A core ideal of nation branding is to identify the "uniqueness" of the country, its people, culture or landscape to identify and draw on features that distinguish and differentiate "us" from "them," as opposed to public diplomacy, which often tries to identify those elements of the history, culture or people that unite, rather than separate, "us." In nation branding, therefore, the appeal factor (the soft power) is the different, the otherness.[35]

In that regard, it is questionable as to whether American art was ever able to establish the kind of sustained "differentiation" that set the United States apart and/or gained for the United States a wider acceptance of US leadership and power on the international stage (which is also what Troyen concludes about the 1867 show: most of the European critics, and many of the domestic critics as well, could not find what was distinctly "American" in the art even if they liked the particular pieces). US success—and failure—at the most important art show in the world, the Venice Biennale, is illustrative of this problem. Throughout the 1950s and early 1960s both state and non-state players representing the United States sent a wide variety of artistic styles to Venice in an attempt to gain international recognition of the power of American art. Exhibits included the starkly realist works of Edward Hopper, the social realism of Ben Shahn, figurative expressionist paintings by Jan Muller, modernist works from Stuart Davis and Yasuo Kuniyoshi, as well as a heavy dose of abstract expressionism from Jackson Pollock, Arshile Gorky, Willem de Kooning, Franz Kline, and Hans Hofmann. None of these painters, however, were sufficiently impressive to win awards at Venice. It was not until 1964, when "Pop Art" went on display at the US pavilion, that an American—Robert Rauschenberg—won the grand prize.[36]

Difficult as it may be to assess the impact of the art on foreign audiences, there are nonetheless some important questions and tantalizing clues. Despite Rauschenberg's victory, and the fact that the United States followed up with more Pop Art at Venice in 1966, did all of this translate into a victory for US cultural diplomacy by establishing either American art as something "different" or American cultural leadership? In other words, did the art gain something for the United States in terms of prestige, reputation, and power? It would be difficult to argue that it did. Even in 1964, many European critics did not see the United States' exhibit at Venice as evidence of an important difference; certainly not a difference in a positive fashion. From around Europe, newspaper headlines screamed, "TREASON AT VENICE." Italian art critics in particular were appalled by Pop Art, claiming that it represented work that "contributes to dividing the world, which continues to pick up all the hateful and stupid inanities of Europe, all the stale materialism and nihilism dreamed up by so-called intellectuals and ignorant enemies of culture." As one US representative in Rome put it, the criticisms made clear that Europeans believed that "the United States is somehow considered the center of 'contagion' and that the 'mechanistic' and 'mass-production' philosophy thought to be typical of American 'pragmatism' has caused the spread of 'this new barbarism' to the rest of the world." Again, mere awards or popularity did not necessarily translate into what the US organizers so badly desired: recognition of US art as a symbol of the discernible difference between American art and the cultural products of other nations. Instead, it continued to be a "hateful" imitation of European culture. Nor was the art able to establish the desired "brand"; in other words, for much of the foreign audience, American art was not a representation of freedom and individualism, but of "materialism and nihilism." Little wonder that just four years after Rauschenberg's great victory Italian student protesters made their way to the Biennale grounds and surrounded the US pavilion, screaming their criticisms of US culture and politics. Even US artists began to turn against the idea that American art could serve as advertising for the US "brand." They boycotted participation of the United States at the 1969 Sao Paulo Biennial, and most of them refused to have their art shown at the 1970 show in Venice.[37] As Szondi argues, efforts at branding are successful only when the citizens "live" that brand. Quite obviously, neither the domestic nor the international audiences were "buying" what US cultural diplomacy was "selling."

Conclusions

The purpose of utilizing nation-branding theory as a new lens through which to view my previous work on US art exhibits sent abroad during the Cold War has not been to "disprove" that earlier work, or to "prove" the validity of the theory. Instead, the goal has been to illustrate some of the ways in which nation branding can assist historians of US cultural diplomacy in expanding both the scope and depth of our studies. Ultimately, the hope is that with the assistance of this relatively new theory, the scholars of US cultural diplomacy can push past some of the roadblocks that sometimes threaten to isolate and marginalize this particular field of study.

First, and foremost, nation branding challenges us to put the study of cultural diplomacy into a much wider chronological framework. While so much of the work on US cultural diplomacy focuses on the space of two decades (1945–65), nation branding asks us to understand these cultural efforts not as isolated events aimed at addressing a particular problem, but as part of the continuum in which the United States has struggled to construct a national identity and project this onto the world stage. To do so, this new theory also pushes those who study America's cultural diplomacy to move beyond the standard conceptualization of exactly what cultural diplomacy is by asking us to consider a much wider range of participants. In short, nation branding urges us not to confine our research efforts solely to those cultural efforts that can be labeled as "official" or state-directed. Nation branding argues that there is more value in looking for the similarities of goals and means between state and nonstate players than there is in focusing on the seemingly more obvious differences. Using this as a starting point we can then begin to draw interesting and significant comparisons between much earlier attempts to use American culture as a tool to shape national identity and increase national prestige in the international realm. The "private" exhibit of American art in Paris in 1867, therefore, is not merely a hazy "precursor" to the more "official" (and, hence, more meaningful) art shows send abroad during the Cold War. It is, in fact, all part of the same story.

This more inclusive view of what constitutes US cultural diplomacy also moves us to more clearly understand that, first, a number of different "agents" (state and nonstate) needed to be involved in any quest to create a truly *national* identity. By focusing on the goals of these various groups—and, again, the similarities—rather than the bureaucratic or institutional means utilized by these players, we get a clearer sense of what they were all trying to accomplish rather than minutely dissecting the more obvious (and often very real) battles between these groups. In addition, we also understand that the critics of the cultural programs—who are very often marginalized as simply malcontents or cultural barbarians—were sometimes making a very valid point: if the cultural products used in this aspect of US diplomacy were not truly representative of a wide cross-section of the American public, then perhaps this explains why things such as exhibits of abstract expressionist art failed to convince either the US or the foreign audience that these forms of art represented the "real" America.

Finally, by enlarging the scope of our study of what truly constitutes US cultural diplomacy, nation branding—with its emphasis on "differentiation" as the ultimate goal, rather than mere popularity (i.e., being "liked" by the international audience)—we also begin to better understand some of the critical problems faced by US cultural efforts abroad. It was not enough that American art was eventually embraced by some European critics and won major international awards. As nation branding theory posits, if that art did not successfully make the argument for a distinct and important difference between American culture being represented through the works and the art that any other culture might also produce, then it ultimately failed to create an American identity (or "brand") that would lead to recognition, respect, and power for the United States.

Scholars of US cultural diplomacy have made important contributions to the field of diplomatic history by expanding the range of topics into such things as art, music, dance, world's fairs, television, food, fashion, and a host of others. The subfield successfully pushed the understanding of international relations beyond the more traditional realms of politics, economics, and military strength. It has also gone beyond the "usual suspects" (the Department of State and USIA) by including a fascinating array of nongovernmental actors. Nearly a quarter century after Akira Iriye asked diplomatic historians to include culture in their range of topics, however, scholars of cultural diplomacy are still struggling to more precisely define exactly what constitutes cultural diplomacy, to place their studies within the larger framework of US diplomatic history, to better understand the domestic context for these cultural activities, and to define the successes and failures of America's cultural endeavors overseas. Nation branding may not be the panacea that miraculously solves all of these critical problems, but it is evident that the theory allows us to explore them from a number of different angles, and to pose questions that get us closer to a more sophisticated and deeper understanding of US cultural diplomacy.

Michael L. Krenn is a professor of history at Appalachian State University. He received his Ph.D. from Rutgers University in 1985 where he studied with Lloyd Gardner. He has published six books, including *The Color of Empire: Race and American Foreign Relations* (2006) and *Fall-Out Shelters for the Human Spirit: American Art and the Cold War* (2005), and *The History of U.S. Cultural Diplomacy: From 1770 to the Present Day* (2017). Currently, he is serving as advisor for a documentary based on his 1999 book, *Black Diplomacy: African Americans and the State Department, 1945–69.*

Notes

1. Akira Iriye, "Culture and International History," in *Explaining the History of American Foreign Relations*, ed. Michael J. Hogan and Thomas G. Paterson (New York: Cambridge University Press, 1991), 214–25; Jessica C. E. Gienow-Hecht, "Cultural Transfer," in *Explaining the History of American Foreign Relations*, ed. Michael J. Hogan and Thomas J. Paterson, 2nd ed., (New York: Cambridge University Press, 2004), 257–78. The literature on US cultural diplomacy and public diplomacy is so vast that the following list must, of necessity, be considered a mere starting point: Jessica C. E. Gienow-Hecht, *Transmission Impossible:*

American Journalism as Cultural Diplomacy in Postwar Germany, 1945–1955 (Baton Rouge: Louisiana State University Press, 1999); Frank Ninkovich, *The Diplomacy of Ideas: U.S. Foreign Policy and Cultural Relations, 1938–1950* (New York: Cambridge University Press, 1981); Uta G. Poiger, *Jazz, Rock, and Rebels: Cold War Politics and American Culture in a Divided Germany* (Berkeley: University of California Press, 2000); Naima Prevots, *Dance for Export: Cultural Diplomacy and the Cold War* (Hanover, NH: University Press of New England, 1998); Robert H. Haddow, *Pavilions of Plenty: Exhibiting American Culture Abroad in the 1950s* (Washington, DC: Smithsonian Institution Press, 1997); Giles Scott-Smith, *The Politics of Apolitical Culture: The Congress for Cultural Freedom, the CIA and Post-War American Hegemony* (London: Routledge, 2002); Nicholas J. Cull, *The Cold War and the United States Information Agency: American Propaganda and Public Diplomacy, 1945–1989* (New York: Cambridge University Press, 2009); Kenneth Osgood, *Total Cold War: Eisenhower's Secret Propaganda Battle at Home and Abroad* (Lawrence: University Press of Kansas, 2006); and Laura Belmonte, *Selling the American Way: U.S. Propaganda and the Cold War* (Philadelphia: University of Pennsylvania Press, 2010).

2. Nadia Kaneva, "Nation Branding: Toward an Agenda for Critical Research," *International Journal of Communication* 5 (2011): 118.

3. Keith Dinnie, *Nation Branding: Concepts, Issues, Practice* (Oxford: Butterworth-Heinemann, 2008): 14–15.

4. Kaneva, "Nation Branding," 118. Passages in quotation marks are from Simon Anholt "Practitioner Insight: From *Nation Branding* to *Competitive Identity*—the Role of Brand Management as a Component of National Policy," in Dinnie, *Nation Branding*, 23 (italics in original).

5. Ilaria Scaglia, "Branding Internationalism: Displaying Art and International Cooperation in the Interwar Period," chapter 3 in this volume.

6. Scaglia, "Branding Internationalism," chapter 3 in this volume.

7. Michael L. Krenn, "Nation Branding before Nation Branding? Reputation and Image at the International Maritime Exposition of 1907," presented at the Culture and International History V Conference, 28 April 2014, Berlin, Germany.

8. Kaneva, "Nation Branding," points out that there are some vigorous disagreements among scholars dealing with nation branding, with some arguing that there is "no clear consensus on the relationship between public diplomacy and nation branding." On one side are those scholars—mostly from the field of marketing—who favor what she calls the "technical-economic approach"; in other words, nation branding is primarily "a strategic tool for enhancing a nation's competitive advantage in a global marketplace." On the other side are researchers who view nation branding in terms of a more "political approach": as a form of public diplomacy (or, in some extreme cases, as merely public diplomacy by another name). Kaneva concludes that despite the differences, "it is clear from the overall reading of the literature that certain assumptions held by the technical-economic approach are also shared by authors in the political approach." (120, 124, 125). This chapter will focus on some of those shared assumptions.

9. Wally Olins, "Branding the Nation—The Historical Context," *Journal of Brand Management* 9 (April 2002): 246.

10. Olins, "Branding the Nation," 241–48.

11. Jessica C. E. Gienow-Hecht, "Nation Branding," in *Explaining the History of American Foreign Relations*, ed. Michael Hogan and Frank Costigliola, 3rd ed. (Cambridge: Cambridge University Press, 2016), 241.

12. Gienow-Hecht, "Nation Branding," 241.

13. Michael L. Krenn, *Fall-Out Shelters for the Human Spirit: American Art and the Cold War* (Chapel Hill: The University of North Carolina Press, 2005): 14–18.

14. Krenn, *Fall-Out Shelters*, 281–83.

15. Michael L. Krenn, *The History of United States Cultural Diplomacy: 1770 to the Present Day* (London: Bloomsbury Academic, 2017).

16. Scaglia, "Branding Internationalism," chapter 3 in this volume.

17. Justin Hart, *Empire of Ideas: The Origins of Public Diplomacy and the Transformation of U.S. Foreign Policy* (New York: Oxford University Press, 2013); Frank Ninkovich, *Global Dawn: The Cultural Foundation of American Internationalism, 1865–1890* (Cambridge, MA: Harvard University Press, 2009); Thomas W. Zeiler, *Ambassadors in Pinstripes: The Spalding World Baseball Tour and the Birth of the American Empire* (Lanham, MD: Rowman & Littlefield Publishers, Inc., 2006); and Jessica C. E. Gienow-Hecht, *Sound Diplomacy: Music and Emotions in Transatlantic Relations, 1850–1920* (Chicago: University of Chicago Press, 2009).

18. Carol Troyen, "Innocents Abroad: American Painters at the 1867 Exposition Universelle, Paris," *American Art Journal* 16, no. 1 (1984): 4–6.

19. Troyen, "Innocents Abroad," 13.

20. Troyen, "Innocents Abroad," 4–5.

21. Troyen, "Innocents Abroad," 4–6.

22. Gienow-Hecht, "Nation Branding," 237.

23. Alfred M. Frankfurter, "American Art Abroad: The State Department Collection," *Art News* (1946): 21–31, 78.

24. William Benton to Fred Busbey, 2 April 1947, Record Group 59, Records of the Assistant Secretary of State for Public Affairs, 1945–1950, Subject File, Box 7, Folder ASNE, National Archives.

25. Kenneth Holland to William T. Stone and William Benton, 10 March 1947, Exhibitions section, Advancing American Art File, United States Information Agency Historical Collection.

26. Krenn, *Fall-Out Shelters*, 35–39; "League Protests to the Department of State," *Art Digest* (15 Dec. 1946): 32. For more on the *Advancing American Art* fiasco, see Margaret Lynne Ausfeld and Virginia M. Mecklenburg, *Advancing American Art: Politics and Aesthetics in the State Department Exhibition, 1946–1948* (Montgomery, AL: Montgomery Museum of Fine Arts, 1984); Taylor D. Littleton and Maltby Sykes, *Advancing American Art: Painting, Politics, and Cultural Confrontation at Mid-Century* (Tuscaloosa: University of Alabama Press, 1989); and Scott Bishop, Robert Ekelund, et al., *Art Interrupted: Advancing American Art and the Politics of Cultural Diplomacy* (Athens: Georgia Museum of Art, 2012).

27. Harry S. Truman to William Benton, 2 April 1947, Exhibitions Section, Advancing American Art file, USIA Historical Collection; Dwight D. Eisenhower to Francis Walter, 16 July 1959, cited in Walter Hixson, *Parting the Curtain: Propaganda, Culture, and the Cold War, 1945–1961* (New York: St. Martin's Press, 1997), 173.

28. Business interests included Philip Morris, S.C. Johnson and Sons, and *Sports Illustrated*; the government was usually represented by the Department of State or the United States Information Agency, although the government-supported National Gallery of Art and the Smithsonian Institution were also involved; the Museum of Modern Art, American Federation of Arts, and the Whitney Museum of American Art; and, finally, numerous private citizens including art critics, museum curators, and the artists themselves.

29. George Staempfli to H. Harvard Arnason, 7 July 1958, Records of the American Federation of Arts, Box 69, Exhibition Files, Misc. Exhibits, 17 Contemporary

American Painters-Brussels, 1957–60 file, Archives of American Art, Washington, DC.

30. Dondero, a Republican from Michigan, happily rode the wave of anticommunist hysteria after World War II, but took a particular delight in focusing in on the art exhibits. His actual knowledge about the art and artists was suspect (he often misspelled artists' names, such as "Jackson Pollack" and "Marc Chagoll"), but this did not stop him from constantly criticizing the US art exhibits until his retirement in 1957.

31. Wheeler Williams to Eisenhower, 10 May 1958, Record Group 43, Brussels-General Records, Box 13, FA-10-Exhibits; Leon Kroll to Howard Cullman, 21 March 1959, RG 43, Files of the Commissioner General, Box 33, FA-00-Comments and Criticisms, National Archives.

32. Sue Curry Jansen, "Designer Nations: Neo-liberal Nation Branding—Brand Estonia," *Social Identities: Journal for the Study of Race, Nation, and Culture* 14, no. 1 (2008): 122.

33. György Szondi, *Public Diplomacy and Nation Branding: Conceptual Similarities and Differences* (The Hague: Clingendael Netherlands Institute of International Relations, 2008): 5.

34. Greg Barnhisel, in his recent study, *Cold War Modernists: Art, Literature, and American Cultural Diplomacy* (New York: Columbia University Press, 2015), makes the argument that "modern" culture never gained a wide foothold among audiences in either the United States or even in Europe. Its impact was largely understood and appreciated by more sophisticated and educated elites. Such an interpretation fits in well with the aims of US cultural diplomats during the 1940s and 1950s who believed that although abstract works were never going to gain popularity with the masses, they would appeal to influential political and intellectual leaders in the foreign audiences.

35. Szondi, "Public Diplomacy," 16.

36. Krenn, *Fall-Out Shelters*, 79–81, 85–86, 103–4, 198–206. Also see Lawrence Alloway, *The Venice Biennale, 1895–1968: From Salon to Goldfish Bowl* (Greenwich, CT: New York Graphic Society, 1968). For Rauschenberg's role in American art on the global stage, see Hiroko Ikegami, *The Great Migrator: Robert Rauschenberg and the Global Rise of American Art* (Cambridge, MA: The MIT Press, 2010).

37. Krenn, *Fall-Out Shelters*, 204–5, 223–24, 225–32.

Bibliography

Alloway, Lawrence. *The Venice Biennale, 1895–1968: From Salon to Goldfish Bowl*. Greenwich, CT: New York Graphic Society, 1968.

Aronczyk, Melissa. "How to Do Things with Brands: Uses of National Identity." *Canadian Journal of Communication* 34 (2009): 291–96.

Ausfeld, Margaret Lynne, and Virginia M. Mecklenburg. *Advancing American Art: Politics and Aesthetics in the State Department Exhibition, 1946–1948*. Montgomery, AL: Montgomery Museum of Fine Arts, 1984.

Barnhisel, Greg. *Cold War Modernists: Art, Literature, and American Cultural Diplomacy*. New York: Columbia University Press, 2015.

Belmonte, Laura. *Selling the American Way: U.S. Propaganda and the Cold War*. Philadelphia, PA: University of Pennsylvania Press, 2010.

Bishop, Scott, Robert Ekelund, et al. *Art Interrupted: Advancing American Art and the Politics of Cultural Diplomacy*. Athens, GA: Georgia Museum of Art, 2012.

Cull, Nicholas J. *The Cold War and the United States Information Agency: American Propaganda and Public Diplomacy, 1945–1989*. Cambridge: Cambridge University Press, 2009.

Dinnie, Keith. *Nation Branding: Concepts, Issues, Practice*. Oxford: Butterworth-Heinemann, 2008.

Frankfurter, Alfred M. "American Art Abroad: The State Department Collection." *Art News* (1946): 21–31, 78.

Gienow-Hecht, Jessica C.E. "Cultural Transfer." In *Explaining the History of American Foreign Relations*, 2nd ed., edited by Michael J. Hogan and Thomas J. Paterson, 257–78. New York: Cambridge University Press, 2004.

———. "Nation Branding." In *Explaining the History of American Foreign Relations*, 3rd ed., edited by Michael Hogan and Frank Costigliola, 232–44. Cambridge: Cambridge University Press, 2016.

———. *Sound Diplomacy: Music and Emotions in Transatlantic Relations, 1850–1920*. Chicago, IL: University of Chicago Press, 2009.

———. *Transmission Impossible: American Journalism as Cultural Diplomacy in Postwar Germany, 1945–1955*. Baton Rouge, LA: Louisiana State University Press, 1999.

Haddow, Robert H. *Pavilions of Plenty: Exhibiting American Culture Abroad in the 1950s*. Washington, DC: Smithsonian Institution Press, 1997.

Hart, Justin. *Empire of Ideas: The Origins of Public Diplomacy and the Transformation of U.S. Foreign Policy*. Oxford: Oxford University Press, 2013.

Hixson, Walter. *Parting the Curtain: Propaganda, Culture, and the Cold War, 1945–1961*. New York: St. Martin's Press, 1997.

Ikegami, Hiroko. *The Great Migrator: Robert Rauschenberg and the Global Rise of American Art*. Cambridge, MA: The MIT Press, 2010.

Iriye, Akira. "Culture and International History." In *Explaining the History of American Foreign Relations*, edited by Michael J. Hogan and Thomas G. Paterson, 214–25. New York: Cambridge University Press, 1991.

Jansen, Sue Curry. "Designer Nations: Neo-liberal Nation Branding—Brand Estonia." *Social Identities: Journal for the Study of Race, Nation, and Culture* 14, no. 1 (2008): 121–42.

Kaneva, Nadia. "Nation Branding: Toward an Agenda for Critical Research." *International Journal of Communication* 5 (2011): 117–41.

Krenn, Michael L. *Fall-Out Shelters for the Human Spirit: American Art and the Cold War*. Chapel Hill, NC: The University of North Carolina Press, 2005.

———. *The History of United States Cultural Diplomacy: 1770 to the Present Day*. London: Bloomsbury Academic, 2017.

————. "Nation Branding before Nation Branding? Reputation and Image at the International Maritime Exposition of 1907." Culture and International History V Conference, 28 April 2014. Berlin, Germany.

Littleton, Taylor D. and Maltby Sykes. *Advancing American Art: Painting, Politics, and Cultural Confrontation at Mid-Century*. Tuscaloosa, AL: University of Alabama Press, 1989.

Ninkovich, Frank. *The Diplomacy of Ideas: U.S. Foreign Policy and Cultural Relations, 1938–1950*. New York: Cambridge University Press, 1981.

————. *Global Dawn: The Cultural Foundation of American Internationalism, 1865–1890*. Cambridge, MA: Harvard University Press, 2009.

Olins, Wally. "Branding the Nation—The Historical Context." *Journal of Brand Management* 9 (April 2002): 241–48.

Osgood, Kenneth. *Total Cold War: Eisenhower's Secret Propaganda Battle at Home and Abroad*. Lawrence, KS: University Press of Kansas, 2006.

Poiger, Uta G. *Jazz, Rock, and Rebels: Cold War Politics and American Culture in a Divided Germany*. Berkeley, CA: University of California Press, 2000.

Prevots, Naima. *Dance for Export: Cultural Diplomacy and the Cold War*. Hanover, NH: University Press of New England, 1998.

Scott-Smith, Giles. *The Politics of Apolitical Culture: The Congress for Cultural Freedom, the CIA and Post-War American Hegemony*. London: Routledge, 2002.

Szondi, György. *Public Diplomacy and Nation Branding: Conceptual Similarities and Differences*. The Hague: Clingendael Netherlands Institute of International Relations, 2008.

Troyen, Carol. "Innocents Abroad: American Painters at the 1867 Exposition Universelle, Paris." *American Art Journal* 16, no. 1 (1984): 2–29.

Zeiler, Thomas W. *Ambassadors in Pinstripes: The Spalding World Baseball Tour and the Birth of the American Empire*. Lanham, MD: Rowman & Littlefield Publishers, Inc., 2006.

Chapter 7

SURINAME

Nation Building and Nation Branding in a Postcolonial State, 1945–2015

Rosemarijn Hoefte

> Our cultural diversity and how we live and work together peacefully, regardless of religion or ethnic roots, can be a model for the world.
> —Desiré Delano Bouterse

These words by Surinamese president Desiré (Desi) Delano Bouterse cherish the country's diversity as a source of pride and as an example for the entire world. It is the cornerstone of Suriname's image that is projected both at home (internal marketing) and abroad (external marketing). Suriname is a case study showing how processes of nation building and nation branding can be interwoven. It took the country more than half a century to come to grips with its multicultural society, to address the question of how it sees itself, and to find a way to present the nation to its citizens at home and abroad.[1] Suriname is one of the countries that only make the news when disaster strikes. It is an unknown quantity, except in the Netherlands, its former colonizer, and it is a small country trying to find a space in a crowded field. Since 2000, Suriname has made attempts to change this by trying to put itself on the map as a dynamic, multicultural country welcoming trade, foreign investment, and tourists, while mitigating its complex, heterogeneous sociocultural and political identity.

I view nation branding as a "set of discourses and practices located at the intersection of the economy, culture, and politics."[2]

Referring to the term in 1996, Simon Anholt, stated that "brand has become the dominant genre by which the nation is expressed."[3] Of course, nations have long branded themselves through—often rather meaningless—symbols such as flags or anthems, but the use of commercial branding techniques to reach international audiences is new.[4] In the words of Sue Curry Jansen, nation branding transforms civic space into a commercial space.[5] The state uses nation branding to introduce itself or to enhance its positioning within the global economy by creating a recognizable image. The state hires branding experts to advise on how to create and sell this image at home and abroad. They use extant images, products, and places to sculpt a coherent brand, which is disseminated through strategic marketing campaigns. The goal is to (re)shape the image of the country and to transfer the brand to the country's products in order to (re)charge the economy by attracting foreign visitors and investors, promoting trade, and establishing or enhancing the country's profile in regional or international organizations.[6] Equally important, branding also addresses the domestic population: it is a tool to mobilize pride in the nation and its accomplishments.[7] In other words, emotions are tied to the commercial enterprise of selling the nation. It almost goes without saying that in such campaigns a positive image is of paramount importance. Conflict or dissenting opinions are not part of the package that is presented to the world.[8] In short, nation branding is a commercial tool, but also an expression of symbolic power in the ideological quest to build a nation.

It is not my intention to analyze the marketing effectiveness of nation branding campaigns. My focus is rather on how nation branding serves as a vehicle to (re)define the nation and national belonging in a postcolonial society in the twenty-first century. I follow Melissa Aronczyk in viewing nation branding as a "logical extension" of the ways in which national identity is constructed and communicated.[9] In recently independent countries, nation building is often a complex and ongoing process, and this is even more intricate when different population groups, cultures, religions, and languages are involved. In a constructed society such as Suriname, rhetoric, (invented) traditions, micro myths, images, rituals, and symbols are crucial elements to involve the country's inhabitants more deeply in order to legitimize and perpetuate the nation.[10] My interest is in showing how in Suriname nation building and nation branding intersect in a globalizing world.

I use two case studies—the most recent campaigns by the Tourism Foundation Suriname and the 2015 *We Are Suriname* campaign by the

Ministry of Foreign Affairs—to analyze which elements of Suriname's culture, nature and natural resources, and economy these institutions select to show the world what the country has to offer. I study audiovisual and printed sources by these (semi)government agencies and use interviews with key informants to address the following questions: How does Suriname brand itself? What are the special or even exclusive characteristics that the branding agents believe define Suriname and its inhabitants? Who is involved in these branding efforts, who coordinates or leads these projects, and who are the (intended) audiences?[11] These answers will inform my analysis of the intersection of nation building and nation branding in Suriname. But first, I will provide a brief overview of nation building in Suriname, a process in which writers and artists, rather than politicians, played a prominent role.

The Challenge of Nation Building

Suriname is South America's smallest country, located on the northern shoulder of the continent.[12] Approximately the size of the US state of Georgia, it counts some 540,000 inhabitants, the great majority of whom live in the coastal area, especially in and around the capital of Paramaribo. Another 350,000 people of Surinamese descent live in the Netherlands as a result of postcolonial migrations. Given its history of plantations and forced labor, the country is considered part of the Caribbean, despite its location on the mainland. Suriname is a prime example of a Caribbean colonial creation, built under European hegemony by enslaved Africans and Asian indentured laborers, and their descendants (British Indians or Hindustani, Javanese, and Chinese). Capitalism and (forced) labor migration determined the colonial hierarchy and consequently the development of ethnic relations. According to the most recent census, held in 2012, the Hindustani are the largest group (27.4 percent), followed by Maroons (descendants of runaway slaves; 21.7 percent), Creoles or Afro-Surinamese (15.7 percent), Javanese (13.7 percent), and people of mixed descent (13.4 percent). Approximately half of the population is Christian, the next largest religions are Hinduism and Islam.[13]

Economically, Suriname has traditionally been dependent on the supply and demand of European and North American markets, including investments. The import of consumer goods and food stuffs has frustrated the development of local production. Natural resource exploitation has long been the basis of the country's economy, leading to regular boom-and-bust cycles. In the twentieth century, bauxite mining generated foreign exchange revenues and financed a rapid increase in state expenditure. In the postwar period, respective governments have expanded the large state bureaucracy, employing tens of thousands of party supporters. In the first decade of the current century, the economy was booming on account of the exploitation of gold, oil, and timber. In 2015, falling oil and gold prices caused another bust.[14] Efforts to move beyond natural resource exploitation have not been very successful thus far.

As in many postcolonial societies, the state preceded the nation: sovereignty came first, followed by the building of a nation. History plays an important socioeconomic and political role, and in the words of historian Bridget Brereton who described this process of creating a "universal" narrative in the multicultural Caribbean country of Trinidad and Tobago, the past is "a key arena for contestation" in a dynamic and complex society.[15] In both Trinidad and Tobago and Suriname, original presence—or the time of arrival—trials and tribulations, economic input, and loyalty are arguments to support claims on the nation by different groups. Ethnic hierarchizing and positive self-ascription, while disparaging other groups, are all part of ethnic strategies to advance the socioeconomic and cultural interests of one group over another.[16]

The decades between World War II and 1975, when Suriname gained independence, were a time of economic growth and increasing political and cultural awareness in Suriname. In his analysis of nationalism in Suriname, historian Peter Meel bases himself on concepts developed by Anthony Smith in his volume *National Identity* (1991).[17] Meel concludes that territorial nationalism is very much part of the country's postwar history. Integration nationalism has been less prominent, mainly because of the overwhelming role that ethnicity has played, and still plays, in Surinamese society. With the introduction of universal suffrage in 1948, ethnicity rather than ideology formed the basis of the dozens of political parties.[18] The main goal was to guard the interests of the "own" population group. Ernest Gellner has suggested that economic progress may ease ethnic tensions.[19] Elsewhere I have argued that the so-called fraternization politics, a pragmatic alliance between Javanese, Hindustani, and working-class Afro-Surinamese parties in the period 1958–67, only worked when the economy was expanding, as it allowed the participating groups to increase their share of the economic pie.[20]

In the late 1950s, the first nationalist ideas filtered through to the ruling ethnic parties who adopted a more nationalist stance. In 1959, the administration for the first time actively promoted nation building by adopting a flag, a national anthem, and a coat of arms. However, these symbols that transcended ethnicity were not part of a coherent cultural or nation building policy. On the contrary, at the same time non-African and non-Christian groups demanded and received cultural and religious equality, they thus undermined the Surinamese nationalist movement.[21] Politically, this sociocultural emancipation translated into the slogan "Unity in diversity."[22]

The first nationalist political party (Partij van de Nationalistische Republiek, Nationalist Republic Party), founded in 1961, failed to attract a multi-ethnic following as it was seen as an Afro-Surinamese party. In hindsight, Dutch journalist Gerard van Westerloo concluded "among other population groups nationalism entrenches itself as nightmare."[23]

Given this situation, it is not surprising that Prime Minister Henck Arron's unexpected announcement of a speedy independence caused bitter political fights between opponents and nationalists: only the smallest possible parliamentary majority supported independence. Independence was seen as a "Creole thing" and fiercely opposed by the majority of Hindustani and Javanese. The fear of racial violence that had rocked neighboring Guyana in the 1960s led to a massive increase in emigration to the Netherlands. In the period from 1970 to 1980, 120,000 migrants—about a quarter of the population—boarded a plane to Amsterdam.[24]

There existed no official vision for how the new republic was to proceed as a nation. Independence in 1975 was merely a constitutional break with the past. Suriname was a case study of an uneasy marriage between decolonization and nation building. In his dissertation with the telling English subtitle "nation building as a challenge," social scientist Edwin Marshall concluded that the nationalists had been naïve: "They also had the simple belief that nation building was an autonomous process that would develop itself after independence."[25]

The only concerted political effort at nation building took place during the military regime (1980–87) headed by Desi Bouterse.[26] At Paramaribo's Independence Square, Cuban-style propaganda signs depicted the nation's history of struggle and resistance, and stressed national unity rather than ethnic difference. The creation of a true "Surinamese man," somewhat analogous to Che Guevara's "New Man" after the Cuban Revolution, was an example of this

new ideology. After the return to democracy, and to ethnic politics, these nation-building attempts were immediately halted and
Surinamization became a contaminated issue that many people still
linked to the economic misery and human rights violations of the
dictatorship.

Whereas most politicians focused on the constitutional process
of attaining—or opposing—sovereignty, artists, writers, and poets
played a prominent role in developing nationalism and building the
nation.[27] Probably the most quoted Surinamese poem is "Wan bon"
(One tree) by Dobru (Robin Ravales):

> One tree
> So many leaves
> One tree
> . . .
> One Suriname
> So many hair types
> So many skin colours
> So many tongues
> One people.[28]

Another much loved expression of cultural nationalism is theatre
maker Henk Tjon's Ala Kondre Dron (a musical ensemble playing
drums of all ethnic groups). Through percussion and dance the
ensemble shows "the many different cultures in Suriname . . . From
all the way from Africa till India we are One [*sic*]."[29] This cultural
expression inspired Jack Menke, a sociologist at the Anton de Kom
University of Suriname, to coin the concept of nation creation. He
defines nation creation as "the collective efforts of (cultural) groups
in the nation-state to develop a society based on solidarity, mutual
respect, and a harmonic interaction between ethnic groups and their
cultures."[30] Menke uses Ala Kondre Dron as a literal example of this
harmony and of nation creation.[31] He stressed that nation creation is
a positive, bottom-up, creative, fairly organic evolution undermining
the state's top-down strategy aimed at monocultural uniformity.[32]
That perhaps explains why the contest to design a national symbol,
announced by the president at the Independence Day celebrations
in 2014 and set to be unveiled a year later at the fortieth anniversary
of independence, never took place.[33] In contrast to Smith's model in
Suriname anticolonial and integration nationalism "do not converge
seamlessly with the country's pre- and postindependence nationalist movements" as the pre-independence nationalism was equaled
to Creole not Surinamese nationalism.[34] Consequently, integration

nationalism is still a work in progress. Nationalism in Suriname is the creation of a cultural ideology rather than a natural given.

Both Dobru's poem and Ala Kondre Dron express how different cultures exist together in Suriname. In the twenty-first century, this cultural diversity has become the national identity.[35] The old political slogan "unity in diversity" has become a national mantra. For example, the Hindustani VHP (Vooruitstrevende Hervormings Partij, Progressive Reform Party) proclaimed at Independence Day 2014 that ethnic groups should proudly celebrate their own culture, tradition, and language: "Diversity should be maintained, while we continue with creating national unity."[36] Diversity is a source of pride. Suriname likes to portray itself as a United Nations in miniature, pointing to its peaceful and harmonious relations. This was also the message of President Bouterse on World Diversity Day 2015.

Case 1: Branding Suriname as a Tourist Destination

The Tourism Foundation Suriname, a government-private partnership founded in 1996 by the Ministry of Transport, Communication, and Tourism and the Chamber of Commerce and Industry, is in charge of tourism promotion and development to "optimize the tourism potential of our country." Its major goal is to "create an attractive image for Suriname and 'branding' Suriname as a tourist destination."[37] Traditionally, visitors "from the diaspora" (the Netherlands) constitute the majority of tourists. However, given that they often reside with family, they are not the most commercially attractive group to the local economy. Therefore, the Tourism Foundation wants to attract tourists from all over the world, but from the US East Coast and Germany in particular.[38] The division of labor seems clear as the government is to provide the infrastructure and safety, while the business sector provides amenities. The confusion starts with the different messages communicated by the Tourism Foundation.

The Foundation's website—in English and German—leads with the slogan: "Suriname, A Colorful Experience . . . Exotic beyond Words."[39] The button "Discover Suriname," assures:

Authentic cultures, an enchanting nature and unique people from many different origins.
    That is what every traveler who visits Suriname will experience with absolute certainty. The diversity of people from various parts of the world who retained most of their original customs and

habits, mark Suriname with a cultural blend that is one of its own kind in the entire world.

The 41-second, fast-paced video "Suriname: A Colorful Experience" presents touristic highlights in the jungle and the capital.

In the 2012 "Official Tourist Destination Guide" titled "Green Caribbean," Minister of Tourism Falisie Pinas lauded the country's "many colours, cultures, cordiality and exuberance!" He promised a unique holiday experience: "you will profusely enjoy our traditional cultures, the wonderful nature and the culinary diversity of the different Suriname populations." In the following pages the Tourism Board explained that "Suriname is also called a large melting pot of different cultures where the roots from their own soil are mixed with those from far away, which have merged to become the harmonious people of Suriname. Indigenous, African, Indian, Chinese, Indonesian and European descendants all live together in peaceful harmony."[40] The concept of harmony thus features in two consecutive sentences. Harmony is also a keyword in internal communication from the state to the nation, as was shown during the fortieth anniversary of independence in November 2015, when banners signed by His Excellency President Desire [*sic*] Delano Bouterse urging "unity and harmony," adorned government buildings.

In a later guide, with the same title at the Foundation's website—but without a date—the same minister promised that

> You will experience a vacation in Suriname as an inimitable medley of authenticity, nature, culture, heritage, and events . . . The natural resources we have at our disposal as a vacation destination are plentiful but above all authentic and nearly untouched. In Suriname you encounter jungle that has not previously been entered, Amerindian and Maroon populations that have retained their centuries-old traditions, impressive rapids, rigged mountain scenery, and rare animal and plant species.[41]

Whereas in 2012 the Foundation highlighted Suriname's multiculturalism, in later years it has chosen to focus more on the country's authenticity and natural assets. Talisha van Leeuwaarde of the marketing department of the Tourism Foundation states that the new keywords are "authentic," "unspoiled," and "no mass tourism." Activities are geared toward the promotion of nature, culture, heritage, events, and Paramaribo's nightlife.[42] Nature is supposed to appeal to US and European visitors, heritage to the Dutch, and festivals, music, and nightlife to neighbors in French Guiana. However, the second foreword in the "Suriname: A Colorful Experience" guide by the acting director of the Foundation, Faridy Lila, does not follow the new direction; instead, the second foreword returns to the previous message of friendliness, culinary experience, and cultural diversity to praise the country's uniqueness:

> Suriname's hospitable population is known for its exuberance and cheerfulness. Sociability, good food, the country life and merrymaking are part of the daily life of the Surinamer. The various cultures, the pluralistic culinary tours de force, the variegated dress, the diverse festivities, the eventful history and the plethora of flora and fauna make. for a colorful ensemble qualifying Suriname as a unique destination.[43]

Martin Panday, a former manager of the Foundation, confirms that there is no consistency in the branding of Suriname. Without an agreement on slogans, Suriname used several simultaneously, including "Beating Heart of the Amazon," "The Other Caribbean," "A Colorful Experience," and "The Green Caribbean." Summing up, Panday states, "At every tourism fair or market we show a different face."[44] Suriname presents itself as Caribbean in the Netherlands, and South American in Germany.[45] Besides this lack of consistency, both Van Leeuwaarde and Panday point to the interrelated problems of poor coordination between the Foundation and the state and the Foundation's small budget, which makes promotion very difficult.[46] Germany is the one exception to the problem of budgetary restrictions—in Germany, promotion of Suriname by the German firm Noble Communications is not funded by Suriname but by the Netherlands through the CBI program (Centre for the Promotion of Imports from developing countries, which is a part of the Netherlands Enterprise Agency and commissioned by the Dutch Ministry of Foreign Affairs).[47]

However, as Van Leeuwaarde notes, it is debatable whether reaching out to Germany is a logical move—communication with German tourists is problematic because few Surinamese representatives or guides speak German.[48] Panday puts this problem in a larger perspective by questioning whether the product matches the brand: "Suriname presents itself as 'green,' but in reality it shows very few signs of ecological sustainability: the so-called unspoiled rainforest is exploited by miners and the timber industry, while the inner city—a UNESCO world heritage site—features dilapidated buildings and heavy traffic."[49] The inconsistencies noted in tourism promotion also trouble a nation branding effort by the Suriname Ministry of Foreign Affairs.

Case 2: *We Are Suriname*

In March 2015, Foreign Minister Winston Lackin proudly presented a
new branding campaign, *We Are Suriname* (or #WEARESURINAME).
"We want to show the world who we are, why we are as we are, where
we want to go, and why we want to do so. Branding is a process. In
the past we were recognized, but now they know us [referring to
Suriname's regional diplomatic efforts]."[50] Lackin explained that the
campaign had been in the making for two and a half years, and that
this was an all-out effort in cooperation with Suriname's embassies
around the world. The minister emphasized that the real asset of
Suriname is "its harmonious and peaceful society," and that during
the forty years of independence "divisions have been transformed
into positive energy . . . we have to invest in our best resource: the
Suriname people." New York City as the center of the world was to
be the focus of the campaign. A video, a website, a Facebook page,
and a number of activities—including Suriname billboards in Times
Square—were to wow Wall Street and the rest of the world.[51] In
addition, Lackin announced that the ministry had flown in editors
of *Vogue* to write and publish a "magnificent" article on Suriname.[52]
Other influential people would also be invited to experience the
country. He expected the campaign to climax on 25 November 2015,
the fortieth anniversary of independence.

Minister Lackin's press conference focused heavily on image
("who we are") rather than content ("where we want to go" and how).
He seemed to suggest that billboards would be sufficient to convince
the world to come to Suriname and to invest in the country. Apart
from a few clichés like "people are our best resource," the minister
did not have much to say about Suriname or its people. The minster
echoed the sentiments of the firm selected to create the brand, and
on its website Everard Findlay explains that the *We Are Suriname*
concept

> highlights the connection between Suriname's varied cultures, its
> unsurpassed natural resources and its future economic oppor-
> tunities. We used a prominent tree in the Suriname rainforest,
> called the Kankantrie, to carry the brand image. We designed the
> tree's leaves as vivid green geometric-shapes. The shapes are rem-
> iniscent of the weavings and patterns of Suriname's indigenous
> artisans and also embrace the symbolism of form and function in
> modern development.[53]

The site also features six virtual billboards, each with one keyword: adventure, uncharted, sensation, majesty, harmony, and balance respectively. Images and symbolism rather than facts are the message.

The most prominent part of the campaign is a four minute and thirty second long video produced by Dutch company DK Productions, featuring Surinamese artists Lakeli, Benaja, and Enver while depicting the rainforest and the rivers, downtown Paramaribo, flora and fauna, and people in ethnic dress. In short, the video shows stereotypical images in a modern, international setting; the theme song "We Are One" has an international sound (R&B and rap) and does not include traditional Surinamese music such as kawina or kaseko, Hindustani baithak gana, pop Jawa or Javanese gamelan. Given its prominence, I will analyze the lyrics, the intended audience, and the staging.

The first part of the song (in English) summarizes the history of colonialism, plantations, and forced labor in five words: "been through lots of tribulation." It also celebrates Suriname's natural beauty and resources. This is followed by a rap extolling a can-do mentality. The third part, in Dutch, again praises the country's unique natural qualities and also the different cultures that live in peace. The last sentence is inclusive: "my Suriname, your Suriname, our Suriname." In short: we are Suriname. The second rap is in Dutch, English, and Sranan Tongo. Pride in being born in Suriname is the key here; it is the best country in the world. The finale calls for Suriname to be unified as one nation, to build for the future, and it invites others to come and meet.

What to make of this song and video that are central to the campaign? The first observation is that these lyrics are exceedingly generic. Replace the name (Suriname) and the text could be used by almost any country that gained its independence in the post-World War II period. Second, the songs seem more geared toward Surinamese people in Suriname rather than outsiders as evidenced by lyrics like "Born and raised / Tied to where I am" and "our" Suriname. Repeatedly, the listener is urged "to make a plan." Only in the last lines are outsiders invited to come and meet, but it is not exactly clear what the purpose of the visit would be. The use of three languages is also confusing: why the use of Dutch and Sranan Tongo when the video is aimed at an international audience? This video suggests that the Ministry of Foreign Affairs is acting more like a Ministry of Home Affairs or of Culture and Education by engaging in nation building.

The third observation concerns the staging. The images are consistent with the lyrics, showing Suriname as an environmental "treasure," depicting ethnic diversity, and so on. The final frames feature children and adults in Amerindian, Chinese, Afro-Surinamese, Hindustani, and Javanese costumes. The final shot focuses on six women in traditional dresses made from the Surinamese flag. This is a traditional way of staging Suriname's diversity and resembles how the state prefers to present itself in performances for foreign visitors or at international festivals. According to theater maker Sharda Ganga:

> The following characteristics can be found in most, if not all of these performances: the central element is the display of our wealth of ethnicities; each ethnic group is depicted separately through a parade of traditional costumes, song and dance—each group gets a chance to demonstrate their culture separate from the rest; in the end there is a coming together in a climax of all ethnic groups—a spectacle of unity.[54]

Ganga's conclusion is that the depiction of ethnic costumes, culture, and symbols with only a "thin storyline" holding it together, underlines the fact that "our national governments over the past 30 years" make "the conservation of the ethnic cultural expression" the central issue.[55] The video *We Are Suriname* confirms this "ethnic conservation." Summing up, *We Are Suriname* communicates images and sentiments in lyrics and visuals mainly intended for the Surinamese people, rather than facts to convince the world outside of Suriname.

Minister Lackin expected that the campaign would "have a positive effect on Suriname and the Surinamese in general, and boost specific sectors such as tourism. In addition, Suriname has to be presented as positively as possible to interest investors and to establish sustainable relationships with foreign companies."[56] Two issues make this statement questionable. First, the Tourism Foundation Suriname was not involved in this campaign to boost tourism, much to the frustration of Talisha van Leeuwaarde, who was "in shock" to find out that scarce resources were spent on another branding campaign that, moreover, was contrary to what the Tourism Foundation was trying to accomplish.[57]

Second, other government policies do not back up the goal of attracting investors. To lure foreign businesses many things— including fast and cheap transportation, adequate property and contract laws, an attractive fiscal regime, and above all an efficient and transparent government—have to be in place. In the words of

branding expert György Szondi: "Having a country brand is necessary to attract investors, but not enough; there must be an infrastructure, a skilled workforce, favorable tax policies and returns
on investment."[58] If a country intends to become a serious player
in the globalizing neoliberal world, facts have to trump sentiments.
Suriname does not yet have a good reputation for doing business. In
a 2015 report of the World Bank, *Doing Business 2016*, the country
ranked 156th (out of 189 countries in total) in terms of ease of doing
business. And Suriname, along with Guinea-Bissau and Afghanistan,
ranked as the countries with the slowest process to resolve commercial disputes.[59] In order to improve the country's performance,
the Investment and Development Corporation Suriname (IDCS), was
founded by the first Bouterse administration in 2010 to administra-
tively facilitate foreign investment. A lack of government backing,
however, forced the IDCS to close its doors in 2011, only to begin
operations anew one year later. Funded by the Ministry of Finance,
the IDCS faced new financial cutbacks (in 2016, it lost approximately
two-thirds of its budget) and has been unable to open offices abroad.
Director Winston Caldeira concluded: "everything is divided into
pigeon holes, there is not enough communication."[60]

The *We Are Suriname* campaign sends mixed messages about
purpose, audience, and process. In his press conference, Minister
Lackin seemed unclear about the purpose of the campaign, stating
on the one hand that "We want to show the world who we are," while
claiming on the other hand that "now they know us" after Suriname
has enhanced its international profile in regional organizations. The
logic of showing the world who you are if you are already known is
not clear. The intended audience is "the world," but, as discussed
above, the campaign seems to focus primarily on evoking patriotism. Lackin also stated that "branding is a process." He ignored that
it is a complex process that requires cooperation and support at the
"front" and at the "back." Backing up the branding effort are agencies
that facilitate foreign investments or economic activities, such as
the IDCS. All agencies interested in branding, not only the Tourism
Foundation, but also the Chamber of Commerce and the Ministry of
Economic Affairs form the front. Lackin specifically mentioned the
role of the Surinamese embassies. However, Gilmar Macnack of the
Suriname Embassy in the Netherlands declared that he "had never
seen anything from the campaign; nothing was sent to us."[61]

This may explain why none of the websites of Surinamese
embassies mentioned the *We Are Suriname* campaign or showed
a link to the video. Searches of websites of Surinamese embassies

around the world in March 2014, February 2015, and January 2016 revealed that few embassies had up-to-date websites. During this period, the website of the Suriname embassy in the United States, which was the focal point of the campaign, was a work in progress.[62] In contrast, the official website of the Suriname embassy in New Delhi displayed visually attractive pages on symbols of nationhood, general facts, a map, national holidays, Suriname-India relations, and consular services. The media section featured a video, two minutes and forty seconds long, by the IDCS on investment opportunities in Suriname and three tourism videos: *Suriname: The World at Your Feet*, a seventeen-minute video by the Tourism Foundation Suriname, and a two-part eighteen-minute film *Destination Suriname* produced originally as inflight entertainment for KLM/Royal Dutch Airlines.[63] There was no sign of *We Are Suriname*. Clearly, the Foreign Ministry did not reach out to its embassies to help brand the nation abroad. Finally, the anticipated climax on 25 November 2015 did not occur. In the words of diplomat Macnack, "The campaign did not get the expected media boost."[64] It is unclear whether the fact that Lackin did not return as Foreign Minister after the elections of May 2015 or financial cutbacks contributed to the fizzling out of the campaign.

The campaign reinforces the idea that Suriname lacks a unified vision and a clear strategy for promoting the country. In the analysis of Gilmar Macnack, "the intentions of Minister Lackin were very good, but he lacked the right people in his team to pro-actively get the job done."[65] As a result, different actors were working past each other or at cross purposes.[66] The Tourism Foundation said to have been caught unaware by the *We Are Suriname* campaign; this maybe a result of incompetence or bureaucratic infighting in a struggle for limited funds, but it may also be a sign of a political struggle to increase the visibility of the Foreign Ministry in general or the minister in particular. It should be borne in mind that Minister Lackin—a prominent member of President Bouterse's party—launched the campaign in March 2015 when general elections were two months away.

In addition, it seems that in all campaigns so far there are no thoughts on or investments in work beyond the projected images. Creating an image is one thing, but it needs to be grounded in society and supported by actual practices to make these campaigns work. In the words of Nadia Kaneva and Delia Popescu, there exists a tension "between national realities and aspirations."[67]

Conclusion: What is the Story?

Steven Ma-Ajong, General Manager of Suriname Alcoholic Beverages, related how a foreign visitor at an international trade fair approached him with the question "What is your story?"[68] In this case: what makes Surinamese rum different from all the other Caribbean rums? But the larger question is: what are the "unique" characteristics of Suriname?

The branding campaign *We Are Suriname* and the videos, website, and guides produced by the Tourism Foundation define Suriname and its people in a rather stereotypical way: the unspoiled rainforest, the picturesque inner city of Paramaribo, the capital's temples, mosques, churches, and synagogue, as well as Suriname's unique culture and the friendliness of its people. In short, the campaigns borrow known images that are tropicalized for Western consumption.[69] The struggle to represent what is unique about the country is not a challenge faced by Suriname alone—many countries struggle to find a truly distinctive voice with which to communicate their message. Aronczyk quotes from five government-sponsored tourism websites (Poland, Ireland, Jamaica, Turkey, and Senegal) to show the similarities in these texts, despite the historical, cultural, and geographical differences between the five countries. Each of the websites praise the country's natural beauty, the hospitality of the inhabitants, and, first and foremost, the nation's diversity.[70] Martin Panday and Steven Ma-Ajong note the same problem: what Suriname presents as its assets are not unique; they may not even be attractive to visitors. Moreover, Suriname lacks internationally known sites, stars, or cultural expressions that are familiar to outsiders. In the words of Ma-Ajong: "I envy Jamaica, with Usain Bolt, reggae, and the Blue Mountains."[71] In contrast to Jamaica, Suriname still needs more time and effort to put itself on the map. Or in Ma-Ajong's answer to his inquisitive visitor "we are still working on our story."[72]

The image that Suriname presents is positive and predictable, but not apolitical or without ideological influences. The campaigns discussed here whitewash existing sociocultural, political, and economic tensions; the message of harmonious unity and looking forward is ideological. In his seminal work *Nations and Nationalism since 1780*, Eric Hobsbawm stated that propaganda is an essential element in national identity construction or nation building. Obviously, the line between propaganda and branding is diffuse. The video *We Are Suriname*, the heart of the branding campaign, is an example of emotional branding propaganda for internal use, even though the government minister responsible for the campaign and the company creating the brand emphasized that it was made to attract foreign tourists and investments by showing the country's "future economic opportunities." It is very much located in the civic space, rather than the commercial space.[73] The clear message of the government campaign *We Are Suriname* is harmony and pride in the nation. According to Jansen, nation branding provides a reinterpretation of national identity and new narratives for domestic consumption,[74] but that is not the case in Suriname. Here, well-known images and rhetoric are reified to impart that the strength and attractiveness of Suriname is to be found in its diversity, harmony, and peacefulness. These are the same key words that the government uses in its communications with the Surinamese people. The result is a cheery, optimistic, post-political, but culturally diverse patriotism.[75] Political ideology trumps economic motives, and this ideology is not focused on homogenization but rather on diversity.

In Suriname nation building (internal marketing) and nation branding (external marketing) are not only extensions of one another—they actually overlap. The idea of Suriname as a harmonious and ethnically diverse country figures prominently in the country's public imagination. Nation branding in Suriname is still in its infancy. The first attempts at nation branding seem very much geared toward the hearts of the domestic population by promoting a young, patriotic, forward-looking image. It is part of a long and complex process of creating positive (self-)images of the people and the country. Suriname is still developing its own story for internal and external use.

Rosemarijn Hoefte is a professor of the history of Suriname at the University of Amsterdam and a senior researcher at KITLV / Royal Netherlands Institute of Southeast Asian and Caribbean Studies in Leiden, the Netherlands. Her main research interests are the history of postabolition Suriname, migration and unfree labor, and Caribbean contemporary history. Her most recent monograph, *Suriname in the Long Twentieth Century,* was published by Palgrave Macmillan in 2014. She is the managing editor of *New West Indian Guide.* Currently she serves as president of the Association of Caribbean Historians.

Notes

Epigraph: Desiré Delano Bouterse, Speech on the occasion of the UN World Day for Cultural Diversity for Dialogue and Development, 21 May 2015.

1. Jessica C. E. Gienow-Hecht, "Nation Branding," in *Explaining the History of American Foreign Relations*, ed. Michael J. Hogan and Frank Costigliola (Cambridge: Cambridge University Press, 2016), 232–44.
2. Nadia Kaneva, "Nation Branding in Post-Communist Europe: Identities, Markets, and Democracy," in *Branding Post-Communist Nations: Marketizing National Identities in the "New" Europe*, ed. Nadia Kaneva (New York: Routledge, 2012), 5.
3. Simon Anholt, "Foreword," *Journal of Brand Management* 9, no. 4–5 (2002): 233.
4. Keith Dinnie, "More than Tourism: The Challenges of Nation Branding in Asia," *Global Asia* 7, no. 3 (2012): 13.
5. Sue Curry Jansen, "Designer Nations: Neo-Liberal Nation Branding—Brand Estonia," *Social Identities: Journal for the Study of Race, Nation, and Culture* 14, no. 1 (2008): 122; Sue Curry Jansen, "Redesigning a Nation: Welcome to E-stonia, 2001–2018," in *Branding Post-Communist Nations: Marketizing National Identities in the "New" Europe*, ed. Nadia Kaneva (New York: Routledge, 2012), 81.
6. See, for example, Dinnie, "More than Tourism," 14.
7. Cf. Zala Volčič, "Branding Slovenia: 'You Can't Spell Slovenia Without Love . . .,'" in *Branding Post-Communist Nations: Marketizing National Identities in the "New" Europe*, ed. Nadia Kaneva (New York: Routledge, 2012), 147.
8. Cf. Jansen, "Designer Nations," 79; Melissa Aronczyk, "New and Improved Nations: Branding National Identity," in *Practicing Culture*, ed. Craig Calhoun and Richard Sennett (London: Routledge, 2007), 121–24.
9. Aronczyk, "New and Improved Nations," 109.
10. Aronczyk, "New and Improved Nations," 109; Eric Hobsbawm, "Introduction: Inventing Traditions," in *The Invention of Tradition*, ed. Eric Hobsbawm and Terence Ranger (Cambridge: Cambridge University Press, 1993), 1–14; Peter Meel, "Towards a Typology of Suriname Nationalism," *New West Indian Guide* 72 (1998): 257–81. According to Hobsbawm (1), an invented tradition is "a set of practices, normally governed by overtly or tacitly accepted rules and of a ritual or symbolic nature, which seek to inculcate certain values and norms of behaviour by repetition, which automatically implies continuity with the past."
11. I want to thank Sharda Ganga, Virginia Gould, Talisha van Leeuwaarde, Steven Ma-Ajong, Gilmar Macnack, Martin Panday, Peter Sanches, and Sjoerd Zanen as well as two informants who were interviewed "off the record" for their time and insights.
12. This section is based on Rosemarijn Hoefte, "Mama Sranan's Children: Ethnicity and Nation Building in Postcolonial Suriname," *Journal of Caribbean History* 48, no. 1–2 (2014): 128–48.
13. Algemeen Bureau voor de Statistiek-Suriname, *Definitieve resultaten Achtste Algemene Volkstelling* (Paramaribo: ABS, 2014).
14. According to the World Bank, Suriname belongs to the Upper Middle Income countries, comparable to, for example, Brazil and Mexico (www.worldbank.org). GDP per capita was last recorded at US$ 7,661.80 in 2016, the all-time high was US$ 9,008.80 in 2013. Retrieved 16 November 2017 from https://www.trading economics.com/suriname/gdp-per-capita.

15. Bridget Brereton, "Contesting the Past: Narratives of Trinidad & Tobago History," *New West Indian Guide* 81 (2007): 170.

16. Brereton, "Contesting the Past"; Thomas Hylland Eriksen, *Ethnicity and Nationalism: Anthropological Perspectives* (London: Pluto Press, 2010), 56, 77; Anouk de Koning, "Beyond Ethnicity: Writing Caribbean Histories through Social Spaces," *Latin American and Caribbean Ethnic Studies* 6 (2011): 260; Meel, "Towards a Typology of Suriname Nationalism."

17. Meel, "Towards a Typology of Suriname Nationalism."

18. For analyses of Suriname's political history in English, see Edward Dew, *The Difficult Flowering of Surinam: Ethnicity and Politics in a Plural Society* (The Hague: Martinus Nijhoff, 1978), or Hans Ramsoedh, "Playing Politics: Ethnicity, Clientelism and the Struggle for Power," in *Twentieth-Century Suriname: Continuities and Discontinuities in a New World Society*, ed. Rosemarijn Hoefte and Peter Meel (Kingston: Ian Randle / Leiden: KITLV Press, 2001). See Ruben Gowricharn, "Ethnogenesis: The Case of British Indians in the Caribbean," *Comparative Studies in Society and History* 55 (2013): 388–418, for the importance of leadership in the ethnogenesis of immigrant groups in the Caribbean.

19. Ernest Gellner, *Encounters with Nationalism* (Oxford: Blackwell, 1994), 46.

20. Rosemarijn Hoefte, *Suriname in the Long Twentieth Century: Domination, Contestation, Globalization* (New York: Palgrave, 2014), 105.

21. Harold Jap-A-Joe, Peter Sjak Shie, and Joop Vernooij. "The Quest for Respect: Religion and Emancipation in Twentieth-Century Suriname," in *Twentieth-Century Suriname: Continuities and Discontinuities in a New World Society*, ed. Rosemarijn Hoefte and Peter Meel (Kingston: Ian Randle / Leiden: KITLV Press, 2001), 208–10.

22. Jnan Adhin, a leading Hindustani intellectual, introduced this notion/ideology in Suriname. It is also the motto of, for example, Indonesia, South Africa, and the European Union. Recently, Surinamese politician Wim Bakker made a case for "diversity in unity" thus stressing unity rather than diversity, Wim Bakker, *Srefidensi: De politiek van natievorming* (Paramaribo: by author, 2015).

23. Gerard van Westerloo, "Suriname, acht jaar onafhankelijk: Een modeldekoloni-satie met dodelijke afloop," in *De schele onafhankelijkheid*, ed. Glenn Willemsen (Amsterdam: Meulenhoff, 1983), 220.

24. Simona Vezzoli, "Migration in the Three Guianas: Evolution, Similarities and Differences," in *Caribbean Pathways from Post-Colonialism: The Three Guianas in Amazonian South America*, ed. Rosemarijn Hoefte, Matthew L. Bishop, and Peter Clegg (Abingdon: Routledge, 2017), 72–91.

25. Edwin Marshall, *Ontstaan en ontwikkeling van het Surinaams nationalisme: Natievorming als opgave* (Delft: Eburon, 2003), 267.

26. One could argue that the military coup d'état of 25 February 1980 was a more significant political rupture than independence five years earlier, see Hoefte, *Suriname in the Long Twentieth Century*, 133–58.

27. See, for example, Jerome Egger, "Een 'Creoolse Onafhankelijkheid' in Suriname?" *His/HerTori* 6 (2015): 29–47; Marshall, *Ontstaan en ontwikkeling van het Surinaams nationalisme*; Meel, "Towards a Typology of Suriname Nationalism"; Jos de Roo, "De stem van Wie Eegie Sanie via de Wereldomroep," *Oso* 34, no. 1–2 (2015): 74–86.

28. Retrieved 17 January 2016 from http://www.suriname.nu/701vips/belangrijke45.html.

29. See https://www.youtube.com/watch?v=GDkJhPR3j4g for a performance of Ala Kondre Dron. Henk Tjon founded the ensemble in 1971.

30 Jack Menke, "Ethnicity between Nation-building and Nation-creation," in *M.G. Smith: Social Theory and Anthropology in the Caribbean and Beyond*, ed. Brian Meeks (Kingston: Ian Randle, 2011), 197. Menke rejected nation building as a Eurocentric concept. For a discussion of Eurocentric creationism and hybridity, see also Frederick Buell, *National Culture and the New Global System* (Baltimore, MD: Johns Hopkins University Press, 1994), 223–35.

31. Menke, "Ethnicity between Nation-building and Nation-creation," 214–15.

32. See also Bakker, *Srefidensi*, 69–113; and Egger, "Een 'Creoolse Onafhankelijkheid' in Suriname" on the concept of nation creation.

33. "Bouterse kondigt prijsvraag aan voor een nationaal symbool," retrieved 26 November 2014 from http://www.starnieuws.com/index.php/welcome/index/nieuwsitem/26309.

34. Meel, "Towards a Typology of Suriname Nationalism," 274

35. Hans Ramsoedh,"Van samenleving in een grensgebied naar integratie in Suriname," *Oso* 33, no. 1–2 (2014): 27–30.

36. "VHP: Diversiteit behouden en werken aan nationale eenheid," retrieved 26 November 2014 from http://www.starnieuws.com/index.php/welcome/index/nieuwsitem/26273.

37. "Suriname: A Colorful Experience . . . Exotic Beyond Words: The Official Tourist Destination Guide," 39.

38. Consultants identified Germany and the New York and Atlanta areas as potentially interesting for Surinamese tourism, interviews with Talisha van Leeuwaarde, Marketing Department Tourism Foundation Suriname, Paramaribo, 20 November 2015 and Martin Panday, tourism expert, Paramaribo, 29 November 2015.

39. Retrieved 9 September 2015 from http://www.surinametourism.sr.

40. "Suriname, 'The Green Caribbean': The Official Tourist Destination Guide 2012" by the Tourism Foundation Suriname.

41. "Suriname: A Colorful Experience," 5.

42. Interview with Van Leeuwaarde, Paramaribo, 20 November 2015.

43. "Suriname: A Colorful Experience," 7.

44. Interview with Panday, Paramaribo, 29 November 2015. For Panday's version of this interview see his article "Een gesprek over branding," retrieved 6 December 2015 from http://unitednews.sr/news/blik-op-toerisme/.

45. Interview with Van Leeuwaarde, 20 November 2015.

46. Van Leeuwaarde explained that since 2012 the government has cut the Foundation's budget by two-thirds. In late November 2015, the budget for 2016 was still unknown, making it impossible to plan any activities for 2016.

47. Interviews with Panday, 29 November 2015 and Van Leeuwaarde, 20 November 2015.

48. The efforts in Germany are supposedly based on the presence of German planters and missionaries in colonial Suriname, see interview with Surinamese tour operator Liesbeth Gummels in Fineke van der Veen and Dick ter Steege, *Commewijne: Plantages, Javanen en andere verhalen* (Volendam: LM Publishers, 2016), 93.

49. Interview with Panday, 29 November 2015; for a similar observation in post-communist Bulgaria see Nadia Kaneva, "Who Can Play this Game? The Rise of Nation Branding in Bulgaria, 2001–2005," in *Branding Post-Communist Nations: Marketizing National Identities in the "New" Europe*, ed. Nadia Kaneva (New York: Routledge, 2012), 115.

50. *Dagblad Suriname*, "Buza lanceert 'We are Suriname,'" 14 March 2015.

51. Facebook: https://www.facebook.com/We-Are-Suriname-772789739437515/; video: http://www.bigtunes.nl/bigtunes/wearesuriname/. It is unclear whether the plans for the billboards ever materialized. Diplomat Gilmar Macnack of the Surinamese Embassy in The Hague declared that he was not aware that the billboards made it to Times Square. According to him it was "an ambitious, opportunistic plan" (telephone interview with Macnack, 19 January 2016).

52. Unfortunately, I have not been able to locate this article yet. Macnack stated that he had never seen the article and did not know whether it had been published at all (telephone interview 19 January 2016).

53. The website continues: "The trees also carry a mythical significance as a communication tool. By drumming the roots, the sound was said to carry from Paramaribo to the interior villages. The tree's mythical place in history and its current relevance in the rainforest made it a strong visual representation for the interconnectedness of Surinamese people to each other, the environment and the world beyond," retrieved 6 December 2015 from http://everardfindlay.com/projects/we-are-suriname-branding-campaign/.

54. Sharda Ganga, "Contemporary Theatre in Suriname: Lost in the Search for a National Culture," Conference "Globalisation, Diaspora and Identity Formation," University of Suriname, 26–29 February 2004, 7.

55. Ganga, "Contemporary Theatre in Suriname," 8.

56. *Dagblad Suriname*, "Buza lanceert 'We are Suriname,'" 14 March 2015. According to Macnack, the promotion of tourism was the main goal of the campaign (telephone interview 19 January 2016).

57. Interview with Van Leeuwaarde, 20 November 2015.

58. Szondi quoted in Gerald Sussman, "Systematic Propaganda and State Branding in Post-Soviet Eastern Europe," in *Branding Post-Communist Nations: Marketizing National Identities in the "New" Europe*, ed. Nadia Kaneva (New York: Routledge, 2012), 29.

59. Retrieved 27 December 2015 from http://www.doingbusiness.org/~/media/GIA WB/Doing%20Business/Documents/Annual-Reports/English/DB16-Chapters/DB16-Mini-Book.pdf, 5 and 7.

60. Theo Ruyter, "Erop of eronder voor IDCS," *Parbode* 10, no. 116 (2015): 51.

61. Telephone interview with Macnack, 19 January 2016.

62. Retrieved 11 January 2016 from http://www.surinameembassy.org.

63. Retrieved 11 January 2016 from http://www.surinameembassy.in.

64. Telephone interview with Macnack, 19 January 2016.

65. "If you want to brand, you need a marketing team." Macnack also questioned the choice of media outlets; according to him, the National Geographic Channel or the Travel Channel would have been better choices (telephone interview 19 January 2016).

66. See Kaneva ("Who Can Play this Game?," 110) for analyses by her informants of the "chaotic nature of nation branding in Bulgaria": "everyone is doing something," "lack of funds," a "bureaucratic mindset," or "lack of sufficiently evolved political and business thinking." See also the analysis of branding expert Charles Brymer who states that "creating a branding program for a country demands an integration policy that most countries do not possess—the ability to act and speak in a coordinated and repetitive way about themes that are the most motivating and differentiating a country can make" (Brymer quoted in Aronczyk "New and Improved Nations," 113).

67. Nadia Kaneva and Delia Popescu. "National Identity Lite: Nation Branding in Post-communist Romania and Bulgaria," *International Journal of Cultural Studies* 14, no. 2 (2011): 193.
68. Interview with Steven Ma-Ajong, General Manager of Suriname Alcoholic Beverages, Paramaribo, 30 November 2015.
69. On the portrayal of picturesque, supposedly pre-modern paradises for tourist consumption, see Krista A. Thompson, *An Eye for the Tropics: Tourism, Photography, and the Framing of the Caribbean Picturesque* (Durham, NC: Duke University Press, 2006); Jefferson Dillman in *Colonizing Paradise: Landscape and Empire in the British West Indies* (Tuscaloosa: The University of Alabama Press, 2015) points at "the persistence of landscape as an important and powerful means of both reflecting and driving perceptions about place" (185). In contrast, Kaneva notes that in Bulgaria "a modern vision of life" replaced older campaign themes such as folk costumes and pristine nature, Nadia Kaneva, "Meet the Europeans: EU Accession and the Branding of Bulgaria," *Advertising & Society Review* 8, no. 4 (2007): 10.
70. Aronczyk, "New and Improved Nations,"119–20.
71. Interviews with Ma-Ajong, 30 November 2015; and Panday, 29 November 2015.
72. Interview with Ma-Ajong, 30 November 2015.
73. Jansen, "Designer Nations," 122.
74. Jansen, "Designer Nations," 122.
75. Cf. Aronczyk, "New and Improved Nations."

Bibliography

Algemeen Bureau voor de Statistiek-Suriname, *Definitieve resultaten Achtste Algemene Volkstelling*. Paramaribo: ABS, 2014.
Anholt, Simon. "Foreword." *Journal of Brand Management* 9, no. 4–5 (2002): 229–39.
Aronczyk, Melissa. "New and Improved Nations: Branding National Identity." In *Practicing Culture*, edited by Craig Calhoun and Richard Sennett, 105–28. London: Routledge, 2007.
Bakker, Wim. *Srefidensi: De politiek van natievorming*. Paramaribo: by author, 2015.
Brereton, Bridget. "Contesting the Past: Narratives of Trinidad & Tobago History." *New West Indian Guide* 81 (2007): 169–97.
Buell, Frederick. *National Culture and the New Global System*. Baltimore, MD: Johns Hopkins University Press, 1994.
Dew, Edward. *The Difficult Flowering of Surinam: Ethnicity and Politics in a Plural Society*. The Hague: Martinus Nijhoff, 1978.
Dillman, Jefferson. *Colonizing Paradise: Landscape and Empire in the British West Indies*. Tuscaloosa, AL: The University of Alabama Press, 2015.
Dinnie, Keith. "More than Tourism: The Challenges of Nation Branding in Asia." *Global Asia* 7, no. 3 (2012): 13–17.
Egger, Jerome. "Een 'Creoolse Onafhankelijkheid' in Suriname?" *His/ HerTori* 6 (2015): 29–47.

Eriksen, Thomas Hylland. *Ethnicity and Nationalism: Anthropological Perspectives*. London: Pluto Press, (1994) 2010.

Ganga, Sharda. "Contemporary Theatre in Suriname: Lost in the Search for a National Culture." Globalisation, Diaspora and Identity Formation Conference, University of Suriname, 26–29 February 2004.

Gellner, Ernest. *Encounters with Nationalism*. Oxford: Blackwell, 1994.

Gienow-Hecht, Jessica C. E. "Nation Branding." In *Explaining the History of American Foreign Relations*, edited by Michael J. Hogan and Frank Costigliola, 232–44. Cambridge: Cambridge University Press, 2016.

Gowricharn, Ruben. "Ethnogenesis: The Case of British Indians in the Caribbean." *Comparative Studies in Society and History* 55 (2013): 388–418.

Hobsbawm, Eric. "Introduction: Inventing Traditions." In *The Invention of Tradition,* edited by Eric Hobsbawm and Terence Ranger, 1–14. Cambridge: Cambridge University Press, (1983) 1993.

———. *Nations and Nationalism since 1780*. Cambridge: Cambridge University Press, 1990.

Hoefte, Rosemarijn. "Mama Sranan's Children: Ethnicity and Nation Building in Postcolonial Suriname." *Journal of Caribbean History* 48, no. 1–2 (2014): 128–48.

———. *Suriname in the Long Twentieth Century: Domination, Contestation, Globalization*. New York: Palgrave, 2014.

Jap-A-Joe, Harold, Peter Sjak Shie, and Joop Vernooij. "The Quest for Respect: Religion and Emancipation in Twentieth-Century Suriname." In *Twentieth-Century Suriname: Continuities and Discontinuities in a New World Society,* edited by Rosemarijn Hoefte and Peter Meel, 198–219. Kingston: Ian Randle / Leiden: KITLV Press, 2001.

Jansen, Sue Curry. "Designer Nations: Neo-Liberal Nation Branding—Brand Estonia." *Social Identities: Journal for the Study of Race, Nation, and Culture* 14, no. 1 (2008): 121–42.

———. "Redesigning a Nation: Welcome to E-stonia, 2001–2018." In *Branding Post-Communist Nations: Marketizing National Identities in the "New" Europe*, edited by Nadia Kaneva, 79–98. New York: Routledge, 2012.

Kaneva, Nadia. "Meet the Europeans: EU Accession and the Branding of Bulgaria." *Advertising & Society Review* 8, no. 4 (2007). Retrieved 4 December 2015 from http://muse.jhu.edu/journals/advertising_and_society_review/v008/8.4kaneva.html.

———. "Nation Branding in Post-Communist Europe: Identities, Markets, and Democracy." In *Branding Post-Communist Nations: Marketizing National Identities in the "New" Europe*, edited by Nadia Kaneva, 3–22. New York: Routledge, 2012.

———. "Who Can Play this Game? The Rise of Nation Branding in Bulgaria, 2001–2005." In *Branding Post-Communist Nations: Marketizing National*

Identities in the "New" Europe, edited by Nadia Kaneva, 99–123. New York: Routledge, 2012.

Kaneva, Nadia, and Delia Popescu. "National Identity Lite: Nation Branding in Post-communist Romania and Bulgaria." *International Journal of Cultural Studies* 14, no. 2 (2011): 191–207.

Koning, Anouk de. "Beyond Ethnicity: Writing Caribbean Histories through Social Spaces." *Latin American and Caribbean Ethnic Studies* 6 (2011): 259–82.

Marshall, Edwin. *Ontstaan en ontwikkeling van het Surinaams nationalisme: Natievorming als opgave*. Delft: Eburon, 2003.

Meel, Peter. "Towards a Typology of Suriname Nationalism." *New West Indian Guide* 72 (1998): 257–81.

Menke, Jack. "Ethnicity between Nation-building and Nation-creation." In *M.G. Smith: Social Theory and Anthropology in the Caribbean and Beyond*, edited by Brian Meeks, 196–220. Kingston: Ian Randle, 2011.

Ramsoedh, Hans. "Playing Politics: Ethnicity, Clientelism and the Struggle for Power." In *Twentieth-Century Suriname: Continuities and Discontinuities in a New World Society*, edited by Rosemarijn Hoefte and Peter Meel, 91–110. Kingston: Ian Randle / Leiden: KITLV Press, 2001.

———. "Van samenleving in een grensgebied naar integratie in Suriname." *Oso* 33, no. 1–2 (2014): 11–35.

Roo, Jos de. "De stem van Wie Eegie Sanie via de Wereldomroep." *Oso* 34, no. 1–2 (2015): 74–86.

Ruyter, Theo. "Erop of eronder voor IDCS." *Parbode* 10, no. 116 (2015): 50–51.

Smith, Anthony D. *National Identity*. Harmondsworth: Penguin, 1991.

Sussman, Gerald. "Systematic Propaganda and State Branding in Post-Soviet Eastern Europe." In *Branding Post-Communist Nations: Marketizing National Identities in the "New" Europe*, edited by Nadia Kaneva, 23–48. New York: Routledge, 2012.

Thompson, Krista A. *An Eye for the Tropics: Tourism, Photography, and the Framing of the Caribbean Picturesque*. Durham, NC: Duke University Press, 2006.

Veen, Fineke van der, and Dick ter Steege. *Commewijne: Plantages, Javanen en andere verhalen*. Volendam: LM Publishers, 2016.

Vezzoli, Simona. "Migration in the Three Guianas: Evolution, Similarities and Differences." In *Caribbean Pathways from Post-Colonialism: The Three Guianas in Amazonian South America,* edited by Rosemarijn Hoefte, Matthew L. Bishop, and Peter Clegg, 72–91. Abingdon: Routledge, 2017.

Volčič, Zala. "Branding Slovenia: 'You Can't Spell Slovenia Without Love. . . .'" In *Branding Post-Communist Nations: Marketizing National Identities in the "New" Europe*, edited by Nadia Kaneva, 147–67. New York: Routledge, 2012.

Westerloo, Gerard van. "Suriname, acht jaar onafhankelijk: Een modeldekolonisatie met dodelijke afloop." In *De schele onafhankelijkheid*, edited by Glenn Willemsen, 218–37. Amsterdam: Meulenhoff, 1983.

Chapter 8

A NEW BRAND FOR POSTCOMMUNIST EUROPE

Beata Ociepka

After the collapse of communism, the countries of Central and Eastern Europe (CEE) underwent a very quick modernization process.[1] The changes were profound. Several of the countries gained or regained independence, and all of them transformed their political systems and built a market economy from the bottom up. Some countries improved their international position by joining the European Union (EU) and the North Atlantic Treaty Organization (NATO). Approximately ten years after the 1989 revolutions, CEE governments realized the necessity of informing the world about their existence and thus jumped on the bandwagon of nation branding.

This chapter will analyze nation branding as governmental efforts to make the CEE countries recognizable using the positive values of their people, the places where they live, the products they provide, and the politics they conduct. In this way, nation branding squeezes national identity into a brand story. Branding—following the taxonomy of Rhonda Zaharna[2]—is one of the asymmetric, informational types of external communication. National brands stand for competition among countries but, at the domestic level, they have an integrating and mobilizing potential.

For a better understanding of the phenomenon of governmental branding, this chapter will focus on the cases of Poland, Lithuania, Latvia, and Estonia. All four shared the difficulties of a transition to democracy and employed soft-power[3] tools to overcome their international invisibility at the same time. Nation branding was essential to providing these countries with more international security. As they are medium-sized or small states, their marginal position in the international community created a difficult context for their rebranding campaigns.

According to the hypothesis of this study, the geopolitical positions of Poland, and the Baltic states of Lithuania, Latvia, and Estonia were one of the most relevant conditions for the development of their nation branding. These countries became members of the EU in 2004. Poland joined NATO in 1999; and the Baltic states followed in 2004. Poland, which is middle-sized and located centrally in Europe, borders the Russian Federation, Ukraine, Lithuania, and Belarus on the east and Germany to the west. Lithuania, Latvia, and Estonia are small countries that became independent after the collapse of the Soviet Union and still suffer from (fading) perceptions as former Soviet republics. With many Russian-speaking citizens and members of the Russian minority (Lithuania: 5.8 percent of the population; Latvia: 26.9 percent, and Estonia: 25.2 percent in 2011[4]), some members of the citizenry share media narratives and construct a single information space with the Russian Federation.

According to Immanuel Wallerstein's approach,[5] because of their geographical position and their limited hard assets, Poland, Lithuania, Latvia, and Estonia play the role of informational peripheries in international communication. Germany as the regional big power is among their relevant economic partners (first among top trading partners for Poland, fourth for Latvia and Lithuania, and fifth for Estonia in 2015) and, for Poland, Germany is one of the most important targets of branding and politics of memory. In contrast, the four countries' history of conflict with Russia (first among top trading partners for Lithuania, third for Latvia, fourth for Estonia, and the seventh for Poland in 2015[6]) contributed to a perception of the nations as "Western Russophobe Neophytes" within the EU, a perception that dominated their image during the accession process to the EU, but gained an explanation throughout the Ukrainian–Russian conflict since 2014. The four countries are linked by targeting their branding efforts at Russia and simultaneously against Russia. Their relations with the Russian Federation often define the context of their campaigns aimed at EU member states. Although all four border the Baltic Sea, the Baltic identity and image are more relevant for Lithuania, Latvia, and Estonia than for Poland. Still, the Baltic identity as a value is not a primary concern. Cooperation among the Baltic states has provided them with more international visibility and recognition, but, at the same time, all three countries have tried to replace the perception of them as Baltic with the idea of being Nordic,[7] which in political and economic terms is more favorable. Last but not least, all four countries achieved substantial economic success as a result of transformation and, in spite of the 2008 global financial crisis, Lithuania, Latvia, and Estonia are now members of the Eurozone.

Despite being newcomers to postmodern nation branding,[8] Poland, Lithuania, Latvia, and Estonia have long traditions in international public relations and destination branding, as conducted by Lithuania in 1919 and by Poland's state tourism agencies before 1989. After 1991, Poland, Lithuania, Latvia, and Estonia suffered from dark and gloomy images abroad. One of the branding consultancies described them as "unhappy perceptions."[9] All four had been striving against their image as a postcommunist, backward region for a long time.

The weak position of all four countries in the international community forced their governments to be more proactive in nation branding. As early as the mid-1990s, their governments were conscious of the countries' weak images, and undertook efforts to analyze perceptions abroad. The surveys conducted by the Polish Institute for Public Affairs from 1998 to 2001 in select Eastern and Western European countries, for example, revealed little knowledge and a negative perception of Poland dominated by poverty and a strong religious bent, World War II, concentration camps, the Holocaust, and more recently the Solidarity movement and transition to democracy.[10] The ideas associated with Lithuania in 1997 were "Catholicism, family, and mafia."[11] Meanwhile, the research undertaken by Interbrand about Estonia revealed that the country was confused with its neighbors.[12]

Two decades after the 1989 revolutions, all four countries were still suffering from persistent negative perceptions abroad.[13] From the early stages of their transformation, the countries could not have relied on their products as brands, as they were unknown or associated with low quality. The same applied to tourism. According to Anholt's *Nation Brands Index* from the year 2006, Poland and Estonia were ranked by Americans as the "most boring" destinations among the thirty-eight countries included in the research.[14] Poland had also been suffering from persistent negative public sentiments in neighboring Germany, which were rooted in the history of conflict between the countries and barriers in intercultural communication. The indifference of potential audiences and negative perceptions defined the initial context for the development of their branding campaigns. Governments expected that by implementing branding they could reverse negative stereotypes, present the countries as destinations worthy of a visit, and attract the attention of the public abroad. Branding also played an important internal role, improving the self-image of the societies, and in some cases expressing their euphoria about Europe.

It should not be overlooked that postcommunist countries in the process of transforming their economies adopted nation branding in order to attract foreign direct investment (FDI). The promise of EU accession initially triggered campaigns of economic diplomacy and consultation on strategies for nation branding. The first Estonian initiative in nation branding (Brand Estonia) was launched by Enterprise Estonia, which was established for the economic promotion of the country.[15] The focus on the economic dimension is still present in all four countries. Deprived of brand products, the countries built their reputations on their outstanding economic growth from 2004 to 2008 and after 2010. In 2005 alone, Estonian gross domestic product (GDP) grew by 10.5 percent. In 2009, Polish Prime Minister Donald Tusk mentioned that the Polish GDP had been growing consistently despite the 2008 crisis, and dubbed Poland a "green island" in Europe.[16] The growth of Polish, Lithuanian, Latvian, and Estonian markets and GDP in all the countries turned out to be the most positive message about them, albeit a message that was hardly heard by mass audiences abroad. Still, some of the economic messages from the region were ambiguous, such as promoting not only well-educated but also cheap labor while attracting FDI.

Branding, Visibility, and International Security

The first campaigns in economic promotion did not contribute to more international visibility for the four countries given that they were targeted mainly at potential investors. For small and medium-sized countries, international visibility is not automatically a given. The phenomenon—following John Thompson's idea of mediated visibility[17]—can be understood as one of the dimensions of the international environment. Visibility—a "pervasive feature" for Thompson—also relates to states. The phenomenon is not limited to the visual presence or visual representation of the state in international communication (as in Thompson), but includes also the status of being recognized internationally as an independent entity with a unique international identity for the state and cultural identity of its people. A country's sound international visibility is one of the pre-requisites for its international recognition and even provides for its security. The international visibility of states is closely related to their prestige and position in international communication, and thus has a geopolitical context. Negative international presence is strength-ened by the infrequent appearance of "products or promotions . . . in the market."[18] The stronger a country's position in international communication and the greater the presence of its products in the market, the more international visibility the country gains. A small or medium-sized country deprived of both can manage to punch above its weight by implementing soft tools of foreign policy. This chapter is thus based on the assumption that a country's international visi-bility is a result of its participation in international communication as a mediated process, and its impact on the international environ-ment while smartly combining the means of hard and soft power in its foreign policy. For small countries, sound international visibility is a prerequisite for security, as explicitly stated by President of Lithuania Dalia Grybauskaite in 2014[19] in response to the Ukrainian crisis.

In Poland, Estonia, Latvia, and Lithuania, governmental nation branding is conducted by the Ministries of Foreign Affairs, Ministries of Culture, and Ministries of Economy as state actors. Their efforts are supported by governmental tourism agencies such as the Polish Tourist Organization (POT), the Lithuanian State Department of Tourism (a department operating within Lithuania's Ministry of the Economy), the Latvian Tourism Development Agency (LTDA), and the Estonian Tourism Board. As country branding in the region is closely related to economic diplomacy, governmental development or foreign investment agencies must also be seen as relevant actors: in Poland, the Polish Information and Foreign Investment Agency; in Lithuania, Invest Lithuania (which replaced the Lithuanian Development Agency, from 1997 to 2010); in Latvia, the Latvian Development Agency; and in Estonia, the Estonian Investment Agency, a facet of Enterprise Estonia. Last but not least, govern-mental cultural institutes (such as the network of Polish Institutes and the Adam Mickiewicz Institute [IAM], the Latvian Institute, the Estonian Institute, and the Lithuanian Culture Institute) complete the picture. Governmental agencies cooperate in the field with nongovernmental cultural and business organizations such as the Polish Chamber of Commerce; however, nation branding is first and foremost a governmental responsibility in the region under investigation.

All four countries expressed narratives that are fundamental
for national identities, and defined the tools necessary to achieve
international recognition and prestige. The central images and
messages of Poland, Lithuania, Latvia, and Estonia reflected the
fact that the countries (re)gained and lost their independence
again in the twentieth century. In each case, the relation between
nation branding and national identity can be elucidated in the light
of Benedict Anderson's idea of the nation. According to Anderson,
a nation "is imagined because the members of even the smallest
nation will never know most of their fellow-members, meet them, or
even hear of them, yet in the minds of each lives the image of their
communion."[20] "The image of their communion" is the foundation
for branding—this image includes the values and narratives that
constitute the nation brand. Still, place marketing researchers such
as Nicolas Papadopoulos add "the unity of purpose" to the "image
of the communion." Papadopoulos stressed that this unity should
not be expected to be given automatically, because governments
have to "satisfy . . . various diverse constituencies" and do not have
the "decision-making authority over any constituency other than
itself."[21] This applies especially to societies under transition, which
are divided also in the imagination of how they should be presented
abroad. This issue was reflected in some of the branding strategies
in the region under research, for instance in the first Estonian branding campaign, Brand Estonia, which "promoted national cohesion"
of Estonians and their Russian or Russian-speaking compatriots.[22]
Poland is yet another example. Wally Olins'[23] key message from 2004
about Poland's "creative tension," reflecting diverging domestic
opinions about Polish identity, was very much abandoned in 2005
after parliamentary elections. Branding in the region must thus
be seen in a wide perspective. As such, it has had an important
domestic dimension and sheds light on diverging approaches to
self-identification.

In all four countries, the governments relied on the experience of
foreign advisors in the field. The strength of their brands was eval-
uated on the basis of Simon Anholt's *Nation Brands Index*, *Country
Brand Index* by Future Brand, or *Brand Finance Index*. The countries were advised by Wally Olins and Simon Anholt, Interbrand,
and Saffron Brand Consulting. Some authors see the strong impact
of foreign advisors in nation branding as an outcome of Western
normative power in CEE.[24] While elaborating on key messages and
logos, the advisors cooperated with, or consulted, local businesses.
In Poland, as a bigger economy than the Baltic states, business

organizations turned to the Polish government's autonomous partners in their efforts to build a Polish brand.

Nation branding in the region has not yet reached a global scale.
The EU was chosen as the first target of branding campaigns, with a
focus on Germany, France, and the United Kingdom, while the Baltic
states added Scandinavian countries to their target list. Their closest
neighbors to the east came second. In the basic document from 2009
on promoting Poland, Russia was defined as a specific place for
Polish interests ("important political partner of Poland and Europe,
relevant market for business and tourism"), and it was deemed
worth investing in the positive sentiments of many Russians toward
Poland, "despite temporary political tensions."[25] As the "temporary
tensions" turned to EU sanctions against the Russian Federation in
2014, and with all the countries in question supporting Ukraine in
its conflict with Russia, the big neighbor to the east ceased to be
considered a target of any branding campaign. Poland canceled the
Polish–Russian Year of Culture that had been planned for 2015.

Key Messages of Branding Strategies

Governments launching branding strategies for their countries are
responsible for key messages that are the core of any campaign. The
countries in question illustrate very well how complicated the elabo-
ration of a key message is. To follow Polish, Lithuanian, Latvian, and
Estonian efforts in the field, research for this chapter relied on the
basic governmental documents on branding and promotion as well
as the official brochures presenting the countries online,[26] and—if
available—the strategic documents issued by branding consultancies hired to rebrand the countries. Almost all of the documents
and brochures were published not earlier than 2003. This date confirms the expectation that the wakeup call for nation branding in
the region took place shortly before the countries in question joined
the EU. Estonia was the first to launch efforts in nation branding in
about 2000. Lithuania started its first campaign in 2006, advised by
Saffron and Wally Olins, who also advised Poland in 2004 (invited by
the nongovernmental Institute for Brand Poland) and later. Latvia
relied on Simon Anholt's expertise in 2007, but in this case the implementation of nation branding was preceded by accepting the "Basic
Principles of External Communication, 2002–2005" by the Latvian
Ministry of Foreign Affairs in 2002,[27] and by a short cooperation with
Wally Olins in 2003. In all four countries, business organizations or

the domestic audience were involved in the process—the former as cooperators and the latter as verifiers for key messages. The hardships of the governmental search for a key message are reflected in the history of adopting and rejecting the logos and slogans designed for the countries.

In Poland, the actors of nation branding have decided on two main messages since 2004. "Creative tension" from 2004 was followed in 2013 by "Polska Power" and "Polska Empowers" (in a document "Rules for Communicating the POLSKA Brand").[28] A logo designed in 2004 in the form of a flying kite in Poland's national colors of red and white, which was strongly criticized by Polish journalists and did not draw upon a consultation with the domestic audience, was hardly used. When 2005 brought about a change in the government, the incumbent parties barely accepted the key message and new logo. The Polish government eventually agreed on the direction of Polish promotion in 2009 in a document presenting the main trends for promoting Poland from 2009 to 2015. In this document, the very notion of brand and branding the country related only to the Polish Chamber of Commerce's project "Brand for Poland."[29] Polish nation branding gained momentum during the preparations for the first Polish Presidency of the Council of the EU in 2011 and the UEFA Euro 2012 European soccer championship organized in conjunction with Ukraine. Both events demonstrated that a medium-sized country's nation branding was focused on staging events (see below).

The authors of the 2013 "Rules for Communicating the POLSKA Brand" built the new key messages on "national characteristics" that were "most attractive" for foreign stakeholders. The document thus hardly mentioned Poland's communist past. It recommended the use of the Polish name for Poland—Polska— and the unification of the (many) Polish logotypes. "Rules for Communicating the POLSKA Brand" presented the Polish people as the main value of the nation's brand.

The new logo, designed by Wally Olins in 2014, presented a tightly wound "spring"[30] in Polish national colors and in a shape reminiscent of Poland's borders was again strongly criticized by the domestic audience. In this country of thirty-eight million people, not even two hundred thousand took part in the online voting for one of the "spring" versions. The "spring" evidently did not reflect the Polish "image of communion." As a result, the latest official Polish documents and promotional brochures like *Discover Polska*, which are available online, presented the "national characteristics that are most attractive," but no logo. In 2015, business organizations established a new "Polska Brand" Foundation in order to strengthen the Polska brand. The foundation decided to go back to "creative tension" and abandoned the idea of a new logo. It should not be overlooked that the involvement of the Institute of Polish Brand, the Polish Chamber of Commerce, and eventually the "Brand for Poland" Foundation well exemplified the emerging cooperation between government and nonstate actors in the field of national branding.

The Lithuanian government also relied on Wally Olins' and Saffron's advice in the process of developing a nation-branding strategy. Lithuania regained independence in 1991, and the main aim of its early branding efforts was to inform foreign publics about that fact and to fight against notoriety. Lithuania was not a newcomer to nation branding—the country had employed public relations guru Edward Bernays as early as 1919 to gain support in the United States for Lithuanian independence.[31] Before 2009, Lithuanian governments tried to create a favorable image of the country to attract investors, engaging Lithuanians in the process. Yet, it was not until 2003–04 that Lithuania started to receive more positive coverage in the European media. Thanks to its economic growth after 2001, the famous Lithuanian preference for basketball (Lithuania won the European basketball championship in 2003), and political events (such as joining the EU and NATO), Lithuania reversed its negative image as a Baltic laggard. Lithuanian governments have managed to combine positive messages about Lithuania's economy, sport, and politics to attract the attention of foreign publics.[32] In 2005, the government announced a competition—"Vivat, Lithuania"—to select an agency responsible for reshaping Lithuania's image at home and abroad. Although the government selected the consortium, the contract was never signed. Instead, in 2006, the Lithuanian government launched a program for a tourism and business brand for the country. Lithuania's key messages at that time reversed the fears rooted in geopolitics, while claiming that the country had a "great geopolitical location."[33] Eventually, it was Saffron Brand Consulting that presented a strategy for developing Lithuania's national brand. The 2009 document prepared by Saffron—"Selling Lithuania Smartly"—concentrated on "an economic image for the country." The key message rested on the "thoughtful and reliable" and "lively and romantic" Lithuania. The strategy was mainly focused on attracting investors, without negating the impact of culture in the process ("An 'economic image' is inseparable from overall image").[34] Saffron recommended abandoning Lithuania's Baltic identity and replacing it with a northeastern identity. After 2008, southern countries like

Portugal, Ireland, Greece, and Spain were labeled PIGS, unable to deal with their governmental debts. That reputation affected their images significantly, and attracted global media attention to the sound and stable economies of Northern Europe. For Lithuania, Latvia, and Estonia a northern identity was synonymous with a European identity. Using nation branding, the countries wanted to alter perceptions while "shifting" themselves gently from being perceived as a Baltic, post-Soviet region to European and Nordic. Lithuania also showed that the regional (i.e., Baltic) identity was not seen as the most desirable by the country itself. Despite the fact that the Baltic states' cooperation helped them to gain international recognition, the nations also—following the logic of branding—wanted to be perceived as unique and separate from each other. This dichotomy seems to be a characteristic trend for small countries.

Latvia, in turn, and its capital Riga were one of the first destinations in the region for Wally Olins and his students as early as 2003. In 2005, the Latvian government adopted a strategy predicated on "Latvia's Image and Reputation in the World."[35] Latvia shared many difficulties in rebranding with Lithuania and Estonia. The Latvian government explained its understanding of branding in a document published by the Latvian Institute:

> Branding must strengthen most popular elements of the brand. It also must widen the brand in spheres, which potentially could promote the state and make it more recognizable. The rise of Latvia's reputation is a long-term challenge. However, the state has one worldwide recognized brand that is more popular than the state itself—Riga. In order to gain a reasonable balance, it is necessary to establish a communication about elements of the brand of Latvia and to develop communication about Riga.[36]

The government defined the core elements of the Latvian brand as culture, environment, and ecology ("Latvia has one of the least industrialized environments in Europe"); education, science, and technology; as well as Riga and tourism. The inclusion of Riga in the key message suggests that the Latvian government was conscious that the capital—as the best-known city in the Baltics—was more recognized internationally than the Latvian state itself. Even if rebranding efforts in the case of Latvia were less focused on the economy than in the case of Lithuania, the government signaled that encouraging exports is "a question of quality and . . . a question of public relations (getting the message out)."[37] This "getting the message out" seems to be an essential reason for small countries' branding. The promotional brochure published by the Latvian Institute in 2015—"Latvia. Get to Know It!"[38]—situated the country "in Northern Europe, on the coast of the Baltic Sea, linking the East and the West." The idea of a bond or a bridge between East and West is very vivid in the common imagination of the region and is incorporated into key messages.

Finally, Estonia explicitly located itself between the North and the East in its branding-strategy document, "Brand Estonia." "Estonia has four cornerstones: the Northern influence; rootedness; the Eastern influence; and progress."[39] The country defined "key areas" of its brand as education, internal communication, tourism, and business. The significant position of education in the small state (with only approximately 1.3 million inhabitants) is striking. The Estonian government launched "Study in Estonia" as a separate brand for attracting foreign students, who, together with scientists, were targeted as the main audience of the Estonian brand. Still, "Study in Estonia" can only precede the inclusion of education into Estonian public diplomacy. Academic exchanges are usually understood as core elements of the latter, thanks to their dialogical and symmetrical form.

Estonia's key message was that the country was "positively surprising" and (like Poland, because of "creative tensions") full of contradictions. It related consciously to the small size, as there "would be no Goliath . . . without David."[40] The Estonian document on country brand was the only primary source under research that explicitly verbalized "Easternness" in relation to Russia. "Easternness" was reflected in such Estonian values as "accessibility, the abundance of interesting experiences, exotic people and places, surprising, hospitable, multicultural, tempting." This set of "Eastern values" was supported with the desired "Northernness," which was seen as "cleanliness, purity, ruggedness, quality, strength, clarity, naturalness, elegance, straightforwardness."[41]

Estonia put much emphasis on the domestic dimension—that is, convincing Estonians of the importance of their involvement in creating the national brand. Still, the internal message confronted Estonians with their negative self-image and stereotypes in an attempt to convince them to act as more proactive ambassadors of the Estonia brand. The same applied in 2009 to Latvians, who saw their international image as negative,[42] Lithuanians in 2005, and Poles in the IAM campaign from 2013 entitled "Poland. Come and Complain."[43] Estonia launched the first efforts to brand itself in about the year 2000, advised by Interbrand, and soon decided to attract the attention of external publics as an information technology (IT) nation.[44] Estonia was a positive exception among the four countries, as it presented its entire advanced and thoroughly thought-through brand philosophy online. Its exceptionalism rested also on the deliberate inclusion of "Easternness" and its relations with Russia as components of the Estonian brand. Its branding strategy started with a presentation of the unwanted perception of Estonia as "raw post-Soviet." It was the "(Soviet) system that had long confined . . . [Estonia] behind the Iron Curtain," and as Simon Anholt pointed out above, the same system destroyed the public identities of the four countries.

Nation Branding by Staging Events

As we have seen, once they enter the spotlight, albeit shortly, small and medium-sized countries often seize the opportunity to (re) shape their brands; such opportunities may include filling the role of president of the Council of the EU, joining the Eurozone, and staging sporting events. Grasping that chance is small countries' way of attracting the attention of global media and achieving greater visibility. The six-month rotating presidency of the Council of the EU, for example, is relevant as it has agenda-setting powers. During the presidential term, the country coordinates work within the Council of the EU. Poland held the presidency in 2011, Lithuania in 2013, Latvia in 2015, and Estonia in 2017. For each nation, the presidency symbolized the ultimate inclusion in the European Union—the act of "returning to Europe."

The presidencies have added impetus to work undertaken on the new EU members' brands. In Poland, the 2011 presidency was accompanied by a destination branding campaign in Germany, the United Kingdom, and France, as well as external and internal programs of cultural events (called "I, Culture"). In 2012, Poland continued its efforts at destination branding when attracting potential publics to the UEFA soccer championship. Estonia was quite successful at the beginning of 2011 in gaining positive coverage from the European media when it entered the Eurozone, stressing prospects for its growing economy and effective cuts in the state's budget. At the same time, the media reported on Tallinn as the European Capital of Culture. Estonia thus implemented a kind of interdisciplinary strategy as the introduction of the new currency was linked with a major event in European cultural life. The same was repeated by Latvia in

2014 when it joined the Eurozone and Riga was the European Capital of Culture. Meanwhile, Lithuania consciously built on the fame won by Lithuanian basketball players globally. The FIBA EuroBasket basketball championship in 2011 played a similar role for Lithuanian nation branding as the UEFA Euro 2012 soccer championship did for Poland. Latvia also took advantage of organizing the Ice Hockey World Championship in 2006, as hockey is relevant for mass audiences in Russia, the United States, Canada, and the Scandinavian countries. These sporting events gave the governments the opportunity to present their countries not only through their sporting achievements, but also as efficient organizers, enthusiastic hosts, and normal members of the European Union.

Branding campaigns in the region have accompanied such cultural events as festivals, concerts, and exhibitions. The popular Eurovision Song Contest, which was won by Estonia in 2001, is a good example. The following year's contest, held in Tallinn, was widely covered by European media. As the revolutions of 1989–91 in the Baltic states were called "singing revolutions," some of the states, including Latvia, tried to construct the image of a "country that sings." The term "singing revolutions" was coined by Estonian artist Heinz Valk and stressed the peaceful character of the political changes. The term also reflected the simple fact that the events of 1989 were held during festivals where the people of the Baltic states would gather both to listen to music and to sing. At one such event in Estonia, almost a quarter of the country's entire population gathered together.[45]

In 2002, Latvia's LTDA launched a new logo and a slogan, "Latvia—a Land that Sings," for destination branding purposes. The logo and slogan were used until 2010, but, as the LTDA admitted, there was no real concept behind it. The slogan was abandoned because the message was difficult to translate for foreign audiences that were unfamiliar with the history of Latvian song and dance festivals and the concept of the "singing revolutions."[46] In 2014, Latvia organized the World Choir Games, once again building a narrative based on Latvia's long tradition of song contests and the "singing revolution." Unfortunately, small and medium-sized countries are usually deprived of many popular artists who would serve as their soft-power icons. Moreover, these countries' messages, which are built on classical music and performing arts, gain only niche audiences. Only sporting events gave them more than European visibility and reached not only niche but also mass audiences.

Nation Branding and the Politics of Memory

International public relations research classifies societies such as in Poland, Lithuania, Latvia, and Estonia as past-oriented.[47] This orientation is crucial for social and political behavior, and it shapes, to some extent, economic policy in these countries. Given that the Iron Curtain excluded Polish, Lithuanian, Latvian, and Estonian narratives of the twentieth century from the Western mainstream, and from the Eastern because of the predominance of Russian interpretations, nation branding became one of the tools implemented by the four countries for their inclusion. This policy was rather unsuccessful, however, as the past-oriented political culture was hardly accepted in the "old countries" of the EU and its messages were almost untranslatable, as illustrated by the example of the "singing revolutions" presented above. The "landscapes of memory" in the Western and Eastern EU are still very different.[48] The year 2014 provided a good example of these differences. While Germany, France, and the United Kingdom focused on the centenary of 1914 and the start of World War I as a turning point in their histories, for Poland, Lithuania, Latvia, and Estonia the anniversary was not of much relevance.[49] Instead, all four countries are expected to focus on celebrating the centenary of their (re)births in 2018.

The key messages of Eastern European countries comprise the basic facts such as the key dates and dominating interpretations of history. The Latvian brochure about the country's history explained in this context that "History [is]—an ever present force."[50] Political elites in the region perceived the politics of memory as the agenda of the state. The inclusion of Eastern European interpretations of history into the mainstream in Europe was emphasized as an essential precondition for reshaping European identity after the countries joined the EU. All four countries expressed their close links to their history in their nation-branding strategies. For all four, their capital cities are meaningful places of memory.

In accordance with this trend, the Polish brochure *Discover Polska*, which is aimed at foreigners, includes basic facts about Polish history. Poland presented itself as the victim of two large neighbors—Germany and Russia—with some striking exceptions. The brochure told the story of the year 1610, when Poland was "one of the only foreign powers, apart from the Mongols and the French Empire under Napoleon, to have ever occupied Moscow." That observation was included in the narrative because, since 2005, the Russian Federation has been celebrating the day of the expulsion of Poles from the Kremlin as a national holiday (Union Day on 4 November), replacing the Day of the Revolution. World War II was also illustrated in the *Discover Polska* brochure, with a picture of German *Wehrmacht* and Soviet Red Army soldiers "chatting . . . during the joint victory parade" after both armies met in occupied Poland on 22 September 1939.[51] Poland joined the Baltic states in their narrative of the double—German and Soviet—occupation and presented it in basic brochures in a similar way. The history of the Soviet occupation during the twentieth century is one of the main fields where the memories of Poland, Lithuania, Latvia, Estonia, and their neighbor Russia clash. The interpretation of the Ribbentrop–Molotov pact from August 1939—as mentioned in the Latvian brochure *From Tribe to Nation*—is one of the main bones of contention between the four countries and Russia. Indeed, it played a symbolic role in the Baltic states' politics of memory, such as when, for example, the Baltic Way event in 1989[52] was organized on 23 August, the day the pact was signed in 1939.

However, the latest document on the Polska brand, the "Rules for Communicating the Polska Brand," hardly related to history as such. Written by public relations specialists, the document found history and clichés to be relevant elements of the nation brand. Yet the "Rules" was a revolutionary document for a society as oriented toward the past as Poland because its authors recommended sticking to "the here and now, and the past then seen from a present-day perspective," so that Poland would be seen as "a modern and forward-looking nation, so this should be reflected in the way we talk about our country's history."[53] Still, the "Rules" gave only very general recommendations. Neither its authors nor the Polish government, which accepted the document in 2013, filled it with any more detailed content.

The basic Lithuanian document on "Selling Lithuania Smartly," by Saffron and Wally Olins, only slightly related to Lithuania's history. According to the strategy, the "colorful history" of Lithuania should be included as part of the message but at the same time it distinguished the dilemmas of "heavy moments" in Lithuania's past. The document mentioned Lithuanian Jews and Vilna as the Jerusalem of the north in the past, the fact Lithuania—according to Saffron— could not get full credit of because of "the reputational problems it got caught up in as a result of the World War II." Instead of explaining the problem and shedding light on the Holocaust experienced by Lithuanian Jews, the document muted controversies. It returned to history when evoking the memory of Lithuania as the biggest country in Europe in the fifteenth century,[54] a fact unknown to the European public at large. At that time, Poland and Lithuania formed the Polish–Lithuanian Commonwealth (a bi-confederation that was formalized in 1569), but Saffron's recommendations did not mention that fact. The Polish–Lithuanian Commonwealth could be used in the basic narratives of Poland and Lithuania as an early example of European integration, if, that is, both countries were able to agree on a coherent message.

Latvia returned to history in its brochures and presentations, which are available online, while citing basic dates connected to Latvian independence and explaining the role of Latvian traditions (such as singing) for the independence movement. Latvia also underlined the double—Soviet and German—occupation during World War II. The Latvian brochure surprises the reader with information about Riga as the place where the first Christmas tree was decorated, as early as the beginning of the sixteenth century. This is an example of a soft message about Latvia's past that is included in the brochure to make the story more digestible for the average reader who is not interested in political history.

Finally, Estonia presented its ancient roots as a nation and at the same time equated history with rootedness. Still, similarly to the Polish "Rules," Estonia's "One System" includes history as a facet of the Estonian brand, but does not go into detail. The website *Visit Estonia*, which is operated by the Estonian Tourism Board, explained more about the history of the country. While this small IT-based nation presented among its turning points the "Singing Revolution" and the Baltic Way event (as noted above), the website *Visit Estonia* redirected the reader to articles on *Wikipedia* and *Histrodamus*, an interactive platform for the study of Estonian history. A tourist interested in Estonian history can read—and edit—entries on Estonian history that appear on *Wikipedia*, or actively compile news from *Histrodamus*. In this attractive way, *Visit Estonia* combined tradition with modernity, illustrating how branding reflects past experiences of the nation and also projects understanding and expectations of its future.

Conclusion

Governmental nation-branding messages clearly do not explain the history of the countries in a detailed way. All of the documents under research in this study were based on the relevance of history and tradition ("rootedness"), but did not allow for any insightful representations of nuances and in-depth narratives of the past. While muting controversies and presenting mainly one-sided visions, they gave evidence that governmental nation branding was an asymmetrical communication. The cases of Poland, Lithuania, Latvia, and Estonia support the approach of Rhonda Zaharna to nation branding.

Lithuania, Latvia, and Estonia implemented branding in order to abandon their Baltic identity and, together with Poland, stressed the negative impact of their post-Soviet or postcommunist images (equated with being closely linked to Russia) on their international images. Only Estonia included the "Eastern influence" as an asset of the "cornerstones of the Estonian character." Lithuania's and Latvia's key messages worked together with their capital cities' narratives, with both countries building their images on the basis of their capitals' publicity. In Poland, a country with a middle-sized economy, branding also had a positive impact on governmental cooperation with business. At least some of Poland's branding initiatives were developed thanks to this cooperation, while some also served as necessary replacements for otherwise lacking governmental engagement. But while joining the bandwagon of nation branding and hiring consultancies and advisors, the four countries hardly developed any new approaches to re-shaping their images internationally. In all four, the difficulties in achieving "unity of purpose" reveal how complex the process is for governmental nation branding.

Geopolitics has been one of the most important variables to study nation branding in CEE countries. The region's governments had expected that soft-power assets, cleverly implemented through branding, would support the process of gaining national recognition internationally. Middle-sized Poland wanted to achieve higher prestige in the international community, whereas for Lithuania, Latvia, and Estonia, visibility was a precondition for security. The governmental branding was necessary, because without these efforts hardly any message from the region about its economic performance and newly gained political stability would be heard abroad. Eventually, after joining the EU, all four countries achieved a rather positive image in Europe.[55] Still, when foreign policy places too much emphasis on nation branding, it reduces the complexity of national identity and how nations' key messages are perceived (such as with Polska Power), and suggests quick answers to misperceptions about the country abroad. Although governmental nation branding can be a very useful tool for midsized and small countries, it cannot resolve all the perception problems that arise in the international community as a result of geopolitical positioning.

Beata Ociepka works at the Faculty of Social Sciences, Institute of International Relations, University of Wroclaw in Poland. She specializes in studies on public diplomacy and international broadcasting. Beata Ociepka was the editor of the first monograph on public diplomacy in Poland in 2008. Her recent book on "Poland's New Ways of Public Diplomacy" was published in 2017 by Peter Lang.

Notes

1. The research presented in this chapter was funded by Poland's National Science Center, under Research Grant 2013/11/B/HS5/03904.
2. Rhonda Zaharna, "The Public Diplomacy Challenges of Strategic Stakeholder Engagement," in *Trials of Engagement: The Future of US Public Diplomacy*, ed. Ali Fischer and Scott Lucas (Leiden: Martinus Nijhoff, 2011), 209.
3. This chapter's understanding of soft power rests on the concept of Joseph S. Nye Jr., as explained in his book *Soft Power*. According to this approach, nation branding as well as public and cultural diplomacy are tools of soft power.
4. Statistical Office of Estonia, Central Statistical Bureau of Latvia, Statistics Lithuania, "2011 Population and Housing Censuses in Estonia, Latvia and Lithuania," 2015, 25.
5. Immanuel Wallerstein, *The Modern World-System* (New York: Academic Press, 1974).
6. "Lithuania's Top Trading Partners," 2015; Investment and Development Agency of Latvia, "Latvia Foreign Trade Statistics," 2015; "Poland's Top Trading Partners," 2015; "Estonia's Top Trading Partners," 2015.
7. Baltic stood as a political and economic term for postcommunist and East European, whereas Nordic stood for Scandinavian welfare states in Europe. In geographical terms, a Baltic state lies on the coast of the Baltic Sea.
8. The term "postmodern nation branding" comes from Sue Curry Jansen, "Designer Nations: Neo-Liberal Nation Branding—Brand Estonia," *Social Identities: Journal for the Study of Race, Nation, and Culture* 14, no. 1 (2008), and means that "brand itself . . . becomes the focus of promotional efforts" (125).
9. Saffron Brand Consultants, "Selling Lithuania Smartly: A Guide to the Creative–Strategic Development of an Economic Image of the Country," 2009.
10. Lena Kolarska-Bobińska, ed., *Obraz Polski i Polaków w Europie* [The image of Poland and Poles in Europe] (Warsaw: Instytut Spraw Publicznych, 2003), 84.
11. Ausra Park, "'Selling' a Small State to the World: Lithuania's Struggle in Building its National Image," *Place Branding and Public Diplomacy* 5, no. 1 (2009): 73.
12. Jansen, "Designer Nations," 128.
13. Council for the Promotion of Poland, "Kierunki Promocji Polski do 2015" [Directions of Poland's promotion until 2015] (Warsaw, 2009).
14. Jansen, "Designer Nations," 130.

15. Jansen, "Designer Nations," 128.
16. "Poland in the EU: The Green Island."
17. John B. Thompson, *The Media and Modernity: A Social Theory of Media* (Cambridge: Polity, 1995).
18. Nicolas Papadopoulos, "Place Branding: Evolution, Meaning and Implications," *Place Branding* 1, no. 1 (2004): 45.
19. "Lithuania's Ambassadors to Hold Annual Conference in Vilnius," 2014.
20. Benedict Anderson, *Imagined Communities: Reflections on the Origin and Spread of Nationalism,* rev. ed. (London: Verso, 1991), 224.
21. Papadopoulos, "Place Branding," 44.
22. Jansen, "Designer Nations," 129.
23. Wally Olins was an advisor in nation branding employed in 2004 and 2013 by Polish nongovernmental actors to elaborate on the Polish brand.
24. James E. Grunig and Larissa Grunig, "The Role of Public Relations in Transitional Societies," in *Introducing Market Economy Institutions and Instruments: The Role of Public Relations in Transition Economies*, ed. Ryszard Ławniczak (Poznań: Piar. pl, 2005), 4.
25. Council, "Kierunki Promocji Polski do 2015," 44.
26. Basic quantitative content and discourse analysis were the tools.
27. BaltMetPromo, "Place Branding and Place Promotion Efforts in the Baltic Sea Region," 2011, 39.
28. Council for the Promotion of Poland, "Rules for Communicating the POLSKA Brand," 25 October 2013, retrieved 15 April 2018 from https://www.msz.gov. pl/resource/096aa594-87a8-4ba2-9af1-0c713be337a6:JCR. The document was adopted by the Council for the Promotion of Poland, since 2009 coordinating Polish efforts at promotion.
29. Council, "Kierunki Promocji Polski do 2015," 45.
30. The "spring" was closely linked to the campaign "Poland. Spring into New" that took place in the United Kingdom in 2014.
31. Scott M. Cutlip, "Lithuania's First Independence Battle: A PR Footnote," *Public Relations Review* 16, no. 4 (1990): 12.
32. Park, "'Selling' a Small State to the World," 75.
33. Park, "'Selling' a Small State to the World," 77–78.
34. Saffron Brand Consultants, "Selling Lithuania Smartly," 10.
35. David J. Galbreath, "Latvian Foreign Policy after Enlargement: Continuity and Change," *Cooperation and Conflict* 41, no. 4 (2006): 447.
36. Latvian Institute, "Latvian Brand," 2015.
37. Galbreath, "Latvian Foreign Policy after Enlargement," 454.
38. See online at http://www.latvia.eu/sites/default/files/media/latvia._get_to_know_it_0.pdf.
39. "Brand Estonia," 2015.
40. "One Country, One System, Many Stories," 2015, retrieved 18 May 2015 from http://brand.estonia.eu/en/home.
41. "One Country, One System, Many Stories."
42. Andrejs Plakans, "Latvia: Normality and Disappointment," *Eastern European Politics and Societies* 23, no. 4 (2009): 518–25.
43. The humorous campaign confronted Poles with foreigners in six films available on YouTube, with the Polish predilection for complaining as a core Polish value; see https://www.youtube.com/user/ComeAndComplain/videos.
44. BaltMetPromo, "Place Branding and Place Promotion Efforts in the Baltic Sea Region," 2011, 10, 41.

45. Anatol Lieven, *The Baltic Revolution: Estonia, Latvia, Lithuania, and the Path to Independence* (New Haven, CT: Yale University Press, 1993), 113.
46. The Latvian Nationwide Song and Dance Celebration was initiated in 1873 and had an enormous impact on Latvians' identity formation; see "Latvian Tourism Marketing Strategy 2010–2015," 14.
47. Rhonda Zaharna, "'In-awareness' Approach to International Public Relations," *Public Relations Review* 27, no. 2 (2001): 135.
48. I derive this concept from Mälskoo, who introduced four landscapes: Western–Atlantic; German; Central–Eastern European; and Russian. See Maria Mälskoo, "The Memory Politics of Becoming European: The East European Subalterns and the Collective Memory of Europe," *European Journal of International Relations* 15, no. 4 (2009): 654.
49. A good example is Latvia's *From Tribe to Nation: A Brief History of Latvia* by the Latvian Institute. The brochure said in one sentence that "World War I violently swept through Latvia in the spring of 1915" and then concentrated on the Latvian quest for independence (10).
50. Latvian Institute, *From Tribe to Nation: A Brief History of Latvia*, 2015.
51. Ministry of Foreign Affairs of Poland, "Discover Polska," 2014, retrieved 20 March 2015 from www.msz.gov.pl.
52. The Baltic Way was an event organized in Lithuania, Latvia, and Estonia, where two million people gathered on the streets and roads and created a human chain, crossing all three countries. The Baltic Way was a peaceful action directed against Russian occupation. It was widely covered by global media and became a symbol of the nonviolent "singing revolutions."
53. Council for the Promotion of Poland, "Rules for Communicating the POLSKA Brand," 25 October 2013: 3, retrieved 10 October 2014 from http://www.msz.gov.pl/resource/f188d84a-2c10-4ebb-8055-d88eb669c70a:JCR.
54. Saffron, "Selling Lithuania Smartly," 81.
55. In 2012, according to a special issue of *Brand Finance Journal* on nation brands, Poland achieved the highest progress in one year, being placed as the twentieth most valuable nation brand; see *Brand Finance Journal,* August 2012, retrieved 10 September 2012 from www.brandfinance.com/docs.

Bibliography

Anderson, Benedict. *Imagined Communities: Reflections on the Origin and Spread of Nationalism.* Rev. ed. London: Verso, 1991.

Andersson, Marcus. "Region Branding: The Case of the Baltic Sea Region." *Place Branding and Public Diplomacy* 3, no. 2 (2007): 120–30.

BaltMetPromo. "Place Branding and Place Promotion Efforts in the Baltic Sea Region." 2011. Retrieved 16 October 2012 from http://www.onebsr.eu/baltmetpromo/identity-and-branding/wp-content/uploads/2011/04/Branding_report_BDF_Final.pdf.

"Brand Estonia." 2015. Retrieved 12 February 2015 from http://brand.estonia.eu/en/home/brand/.

Brand Finance Journal. August 2012. Retrieved 10 September 2012 from www.brandfinance.com/docs.

Council for the Promotion of Poland. "Kierunki Promocji Polski do 2015" [Directions of Poland's promotion until 2015]. Warsaw, 2009.
———. "Rules for Communicating the Polska Brand." Warsaw, 25 October 2013. Retrieved 10 October 2014 from http://www.msz.gov.pl/resource/f188d84a-2c10-4ebb-8055-d88eb669c70a:JCR.
Cutlip, Scott M. "Lithuania's First Independence Battle: A PR Footnote." *Public Relations Review* 16, no. 4 (1990): 12–16.
Dempsey, Judy. "Poland and France Move toward a Europe Less Dependent on US." *The New York Times*, 18 March 2013. Retrieved 20 December 2013 from www.nytimes.com/2013/03/19/world/eur.
"Estonia's Top Trading Partners." 2015. Retrieved 13 February 2016 from www.tradewithestonia.com/estonian/.
Fischer, Ali, and Lucas, Scott, eds. *Trials of Engagement: The Future of US Public Diplomacy.* Leiden: Martinus Nijhoff, 2011.
Galbreath, David. J. "Latvian Foreign Policy after Enlargement: Continuity and Change." *Cooperation and Conflict* 41, no. 4 (2006): 443–62.
Grunig, James E., and Larissa Grunig. "The Role of Public Relations in Transitional Societies." In *Introducing Market Economy Institutions and Instruments: The Role of Public Relations in Transition Economies*, edited by Ryszard Ławniczak, 3–26. Poznań: Piar. pl, 2005.
Investment and Development Agency of Latvia. "Latvia Foreign Trade Statistics." 2015. Retrieved 13 February 2016 from www.liaa.gov.lv/en/trade/foreign-trade-statistics/.
Jansen, Sue Curry. "Designer Nations: Neo-Liberal Nation Branding—Brand Estonia." *Social Identities: Journal for the Study of Race, Nation, and Culture* 14, no. 1 (2008): 121–42.
Kamps, Klaus. *Politik in Fernsehnachrichten: Struktur und Präsentation internationaler Ereignisse—ein Vergleich.* Baden-Baden: Nomos, 1999.
Kolarska-Bobińska, Lena, ed. *Obraz Polski i Polaków w Europie* [The image of Poland and Poles in Europe]. Warsaw: Instytut Spraw Publicznych, 2003.
Latvian Institute. *From Tribe to Nation: A Brief History of Latvia.* 2015. Retrieved 20 May 2015 from www.li.lv/en.
Latvian Institute. *Latvian Brand.* 2015. Retrieved 20 May 2015 from http://www.li.lv/en/nation-branding.
Latvian Institute. *Latvia. Get to Know It!* 2015. Retrieved 20 May 2015 from http://www.li.lv/en/nation-branding.
"Latvian Tourism Marketing Strategy 2010–2015." 2010. Retrieved 20 May 2015 from http://www.li.lv/en/nation-branding.
Ławniczak, Ryszard, ed. *Introducing Market Economy Institutions and Instruments: The Role of Public Relations in Transition Economies.* Poznań: Piar. pl, 2005.
Lieven, Anatol. *The Baltic Revolution: Estonia, Latvia, Lithuania, and the Path to Independence.* New Haven, CT: Yale University Press, 1993.

"Lithuania's Ambassadors to Hold Annual Conference in Vilnius."
    2014. Retrieved 22 May 2015 from http://en.delfi.lt/archive/article.
    php?id=65306258.
"Lithuania's Top Trading Partners." 2015. Retrieved 13 February 2016 from
    www.worldstopexports.com/lithuania-top-exports/.
Mälskoo, Maria. "The Memory Politics of Becoming European: The East
    European Subalterns and the Collective Memory of Europe." *European
    Journal of International Relations* 15, no. 4 (2009): 653–80.
Ministry of Foreign Affairs of Poland. *Discover Polska.* 2014. Retrieved 20
    March 2015 from www.msz.gov.pl.
Nye, Joseph S., Jr. *Soft Power: The Means to Success in World Politics.* New
    York: Public Affairs, 2004.
"One Country, One System, Many Stories." 2015. Retrieved 18 May 2015
    from http://brand.estonia.eu/en/home.
Papadopoulos, Nicolas. "Place Branding: Evolution, Meaning and
    Implications." *Place Branding* 1, no. 1 (2004): 36–49.
Park, Ausra. "'Selling' a Small State to the World: Lithuania's Struggle in
    Building its National Image." *Place Branding and Public Diplomacy* 5,
    no. 1 (2009): 67–84.
Plakans, Andrejs. "Latvia: Normality and Disappointment." *Eastern
    European Politics and Societies* 23, no. 4 (2009): 518–25.
"Poland in the EU: The Green Island." Retrieved 31 July 2015 from
    http://www.msz.gov.pl/en/foreign_policy/europe/european_union/
    poland_ineu/poland_in_eu/.
"Poland's Top Trading Partners," 2015. Retrieved 13 February 2016 from
    www.worldstopexports.com/polands-top-exports/.
Saffron Brand Consultants. "Selling Lithuania Smartly: A Guide to the
    Creative-Strategic Development of an Economic Image of the Country."
    2009.
Statistical Office of Estonia, Central Statistical Bureau of Latvia, Statistics
    Lithuania. "2011 Population and Housing Censuses in Estonia, Latvia
    and Lithuania," 2015.
Thompson, John B. *The Media and Modernity: A Social Theory of Media.*
    Cambridge: Polity, 1995.
Wallerstein, Immanuel. *The Modern World-System.* New York: Academic
    Press, 1974.
Zaharna, Rhonda. "'In-awareness' Approach to International Public
    Relations." *Public Relations Review* 27, no. 2 (2001): 135–48.
———. "The Public Diplomacy Challenges of Strategic Stakeholder
    Engagement." In *Trials of Engagement: The Future of US Public
    Diplomacy*, edited by Ali Fischer and Scott Lucas, 201–230. Leiden:
    Martinus Nijhoff Publishers, 2011.

Part II

PROMISES AND CHALLENGES OF NATION BRANDING

COMMENTARIES ON CASE STUDIES

Chapter 9

HISTORICIZING THE RELATIONSHIP BETWEEN NATION BRANDING AND PUBLIC DIPLOMACY

Justin Hart

Nation branding, as explored in this volume, functions both as a policy or set of policies and as a category of historical analysis. The former refers to the marketing technique first developed by the British consultant Simon Anholt two decades ago and subsequently embraced by an increasingly large and diverse group of people working for businesses and governments around the world; the latter turns that technique into an analytic used not just to describe contemporary policies, but also to interpret or reinterpret actions that took place decades, if not centuries, ago. The eight case studies presented in this book mostly fit into the latter framework, and they represent the first sustained attempt to interrogate nation branding as a historical phenomenon. In contemplating how—and how well—nation branding works as a category of historical analysis, it is particularly important to consider the ways in which applying a contemporary marketing concept to historical events complicates and revises our understanding of the constellation of activities traditionally labeled as public diplomacy or (at a broader level) international cultural relations. These are the areas of study that correspond most closely to the emerging historical discussion of nation branding, so they will be the focus of this commentary.

In a sign of how new this subject is, both in theory and in practice, all of the essays in this book build on essentially the same discrete body of literature on nation branding. We see, of course, numerous

Notes for this section begin on page 229.

references to Simon Anholt's many publications, but other scholars invoked repeatedly include Keith Dinnie, Wally Olins, Melissa
Aronczyk, Nadia Kaneva, and György Szondi. Although each of these
scholars has touched on the relationship between nation branding
and public diplomacy—none more explicitly than Szondi—for the
most part they have been concerned with defining and theorizing
nation branding for understanding and navigating the contemporary
world, and not for its potential application to historical events.

In considering the similarities and differences between nation
branding and public diplomacy several issues come into play:
connections and/or tensions between public and private efforts to
brand the nation or capitalize upon existing nation brands; the inter-
dependence of domestic and foreign affairs; contradictions between
words and deeds; the intentions and goals of the branding effort;
the methods used for branding; and the very definition of *nation*
in the age of globalization. To date, the most extensive exploration
of the distinctions between public diplomacy and nation branding
comes from an essay by PR guru György Szondi. Reflecting upon the
existing literature on nation branding, Szondi suggests that there
are five possibilities for conceptualizing its relationship to public
diplomacy:

1. Public diplomacy and nation branding are distinct spheres.
2. Public diplomacy is part of nation branding.
3. Nation branding is part of public diplomacy.
4. Public diplomacy and nation branding are distinct but over-
   lapping concepts.
5. Nation branding and public diplomacy are the same concepts.

For the most part, Szondi is reluctant to advance one of these expla-
nations as the "correct" one, noting that individual nations have
approached the subject of branding in different ways at different
times, although he is extremely skeptical of the notion that the two
concepts are interchangeable.[1]

As Szondi points out, at the genesis of the field, Simon Anholt
treated public diplomacy as part of nation branding. However, over
the years, Anholt has seemed to evolve toward the position that the
two concepts overlap in places while largely retaining distinct char-
acters. Meanwhile, Szondi notes, the premier journal in the field—
Anholt's *Place Branding and Public Diplomacy*—is primarily devoted
to branding, publishing few articles on public diplomacy except in
cases when its practitioners utilize branding techniques.[2] All in all,

then, the question of how public diplomacy relates to nation branding remains open—at least in the present context. So how does the historical perspective provided by this volume influence that discussion?

Each of the essays published here speaks to this question, although only Ilaria Scaglia and Michael Krenn explicitly take a position on the relationship between nation branding and public diplomacy. Scaglia distinguishes nation branding from propaganda, public diplomacy, and cultural relations, arguing that:

> [nation branding] is not primarily concerned with the conduct of foreign policy or the management of international relations . . . Instead, it exists independently from the state as the process through which a wide variety of actors—which may include states—try to change the perceptions of a country (either their own or another) while pursuing various agendas that may be in contradiction with one another.[3]

Krenn, on the other hand, treats public diplomacy as a subset of nation branding, suggesting that "one of [nation branding's] primary benefits is that it allows scholars to place instances of cultural (or other forms of public) diplomacy in a much longer chronology of national identity building."[4]

My own view is much closer to Krenn's. I would argue that, while not all nation-branding efforts constitute public diplomacy, all public diplomacy has the ultimate goal of nation branding. As I argued in *Empire of Ideas*, my book on the origins of US public diplomacy during the 1930s and 1940s, the driving force behind the US government's decision to adopt the various techniques that later became known as public diplomacy was a recognition that, moving forward, the nation's image in the world would constitute a central component of US foreign policymaking in a way that it never had before. Therefore, policy makers had no choice but to engage in the global conversation on the image of "America"—a conversation that would take place whether they liked it or not, and whether they participated or not. US public diplomacy should be understood, then, as the US government's official attempt to help shape the image of America projected to the world, even though policy makers understood better than anyone that the government's contribution to that effort would often struggle to compete with the constant flow of information from private sources—whether those might be newspapers, radio, Hollywood movies, or anything else. Like Michael Krenn, participating in this discussion of nation branding has made me rethink some of the things I have written in the past and if I were writing *Empire of Ideas* today, in the wake of this volume, I might substitute the concept of nation branding for the many places I deployed the far less precise term "image."[5]

However, what I would not do is substitute the concept of nation branding for public diplomacy. Even if all public diplomacy represented an attempt to engage in nation branding, collapsing the former into the latter runs the risk of losing much of the nuance attached to our discussion of public diplomacy. As Jessica C. E. Gienow-Hecht has argued in her important new essay on nation branding—written for the most recent edition of the venerable volume *Explaining the History of American Foreign Relations*—the concept of nation branding, when deployed as a historical analytic, "does not distinguish between a presumably 'democratic' or 'positive' cultural diplomacy designed to create 'mutual understanding' and 'manipulative,' 'negative' propaganda. Likewise, it is irrelevant whether a state is pre-modern or modern, democratic or authoritarian. Nation Branding, in other words, is a matter of timeless aspiration."[6] What potentially gets lost, then, if we treat public diplomacy solely as a subset of nation branding (and, to be clear, I am not suggesting that Gienow-Hecht is proposing that we do so) is a sense of motivation and context—*what* public diplomats hoped to accomplish by branding their nation and *why* they chose the methods they chose. For example, the Assistant Secretary of State for Public Affairs and the CEO of Disney both hope to sell a certain vision of the United States, but their goals—and often their methods—are vastly different, and we run the risk of losing sight of those distinctions if we view them solely through the prism of nation branding.

Moreover, in the case of the United States, I would argue that public diplomacy since its inception has been an act not just of nation branding, but also of empire branding and, ultimately, empire building. For most other countries, the branding process functioned quite differently, with different objectives, even when deploying the same methods (although John Gripentrog's essay in this volume on Japan's empire branding efforts during the interwar period offers some intriguing parallels). For some countries, the primary goal of nation branding might be increasing tourism; for others, it might be tipping the regional balance of power by appealing to or distancing oneself from more powerful nations; many, of course, seek to improve negative perceptions that result from questionable policy choices. Whatever the case, the only way to identify the objective of a set of public diplomacy initiatives is to examine policy makers' motives in undertaking them. Often, those motivations have been so different that we cannot simply view nation branding as a continuum, with all countries engaged in roughly the same basic activity. In fact, doing so potentially obscures as much as it reveals.

With these observations in mind, I will now comment on what I see as some of the more significant findings in the essays in this book. The first thing that should be said is that there are, indeed, a remarkable variety of agendas and activities that fall under the nation-branding umbrella. It should also be pointed out that several of these stories would likely not be included in this discussion were we to focus solely on public diplomacy.

Moving through the volume we find: the US Department of State creating a new series of public documents during the US Civil War to assert the legitimacy of a government in crisis at home and abroad; the waxing and waning of efforts to use images of nationalism to promote trade and tourism in Austria and Switzerland during the twentieth century; efforts to advertise China's commitment to internationalism in order to attract sympathy from the West during the Asian crisis of the mid-1930s; Japan's attempt during the same period to ameliorate the damage done to its national brand by its aggression in China; an exploration of how existing scholarship on US cultural diplomacy during the Cold War can be enhanced and potentially reinterpreted by applying a nation-branding framework; the Franco government in Spain trying to repair its reputation in the United Kingdom after its World War II alliances with totalitarian governments in Germany and Italy decimated its national brand; postcolonial Suriname using nation branding not just to assert its independence from its former colonial master, but also to cement the revolution and establish the legitimacy of the government for its citizens at home; and, finally, a study of recent branding efforts in postcommunist Europe, as nations such as Poland, Lithuania, Latvia, and Estonia attempt to recover from the obliteration of their individual national brands under the yoke of Soviet occupation.

Returning to the major issues discussed above that typically come into play in both studies of nation branding and public diplomacy, all are at work here, many in multiple essays. By far the most common theme is the effort to navigate the frequent tensions that emerged in branding for a domestic audience versus an international audience. William McAllister shows how the *Foreign Relations of the United States* series originated in an attempt by the US government to brand itself as transparent and functional—both to its own citizens and to potential diplomatic partners around the world—amid an existential challenge from a Confederate government that also sought to build support for its brand at home and abroad. On a completely different subject a century later, Oliver Kühschelm notes that twentieth century branding efforts by Austria and Switzerland served both domestic and foreign objectives, since the major branding goals of "export promotion and buy national communication target different audiences: the former addresses foreigners while the latter speaks to co-nationals. Tourist advertising occupies a middle position."[7] Ilaria Scaglia focuses on the ways that China's efforts to wrap itself in the cloak of internationalism abroad during the mid-1930s also contained a domestic component of encouraging citizens to "live the brand." As Simon Anholt argues, "countries are judged by what they do, not by what they say," so people at home have to back up what branders are saying about their country, or the branding effort will suffer, if not fail entirely.[8] In the case of the international art exhibition Scaglia writes about, she suggests that "the act of saying involved much doing on the part of all actors" and thinking of words as deeds is an interesting way to conceptualize the act of branding.[9] Meanwhile, Rosemarijn Hoefte demonstrates that government and business efforts to brand postcolonial Suriname as inclusive—and an attractive destination for tourists—also served to legitimize the fledgling country in the eyes of its own citizens. Finally, Beata Ociepka shows how the entire branding process in postcommunist states in Central and Eastern Europe depended upon conveying the "positive values of their people, the places where they live, the products they provide, and the politics they conduct."[10]

In making sense of the connection between domestic and international aspects of branding, it is important to recognize the critical distinction between a nation's brand and the act of nation branding. The brand exists, in other words, independent of efforts to shape it—it may be positive, negative, or neutral; it may be dynamic or banal, exciting or boring; it may even struggle to be recognized. Branding, on the other hand, represents an effort to "improve" the already existing brand—to make it more positive, dynamic, exciting, and/or recognized. International perceptions of a country and its people are formed from myriad sources of information; public and private efforts to improve upon that image depend upon being able to nudge existing conversations in a different direction.

It is here, then, that we see another theme in several of these essays: the interaction between public and private branding efforts. Branders often have a lot of power, but they still face an awesome—and at times overwhelming—challenge in trying to create movement on the nation's brand. Complicating this process is the fact that public and private branders often work at cross-purposes, like the Disney executive and the Assistant Secretary of State who both hope to shape the image of the United States in the world, but have vastly different visions of the image that needs to be conveyed to advance their interests. The public-private rivalry is one place where collapsing public diplomacy into nation branding, or conflating the two as basically the same thing, would severely limit our understanding of the historical dynamics at work. For example, Oliver Kühschelm gives us the case of businesses in Austria and Switzerland that have in recent years used buy national campaigns to sell products at the same time that their governments promote free trade and participation in the European Union. Conflict is not inevitable, as shown in the essays by Carolin Viktorin, Rosemarijn Hoefte, and Beata Ociepka. In each case, public diplomats came together with local business interests to promote tourism, which is perhaps the area most likely to find public and private branders on the same page. However, even here, as with the *We Are Suriname* campaign in Hoefte's essay, public and private officials sometimes disagreed about *how* to generate tourism despite agreeing on the importance of doing so.

Another common theme is the difficulty in synchronizing words and deeds, or, more specifically, the difficulty in crafting a message that is not immediately contradicted and undermined by a government's policies or the actions of its citizens. In the case of US public diplomacy, the most famous example of this process was the way that images of racial violence and discrimination constantly compromised official efforts to portray progress in those areas. In this volume, John Gripentrog explains how the Japanese government torpedoed any attempt to brand Japan as part of the community of nations through its unrelenting aggression in the late 1930s. Likewise, Michael Krenn tells the fascinating story (based on his book *Fall-Out Shelters for the Human Spirit*) of US public diplomats attempting to use modern art to brand the nation as progressive and sophisticated, only to watch others in the US government destroy that effort by denouncing the exhibit as unrepresentative of American culture.

These cases lead me to think about one major issue that often gets overlooked in discussions of both nation branding and public diplomacy: the way that nations and governments brand themselves intentionally and unintentionally through policy choices not just in the cultural realm, but in military, political, and economic realms as well. As discussed above, nation branding happens both consciously and unconsciously, both at home and abroad, and through both public and private efforts—and this process cannot be contained by national boundaries, or by the officially-designated custodians of the nation's "foreign relations." At the same time, foreign policy makers do exert a tremendous influence on their country's brand even, or maybe especially, when branding is not explicitly part of their job; it is critical not to lose sight of that fact by focusing solely upon official branding efforts.

It is particularly important, I would argue, to pay attention to cases where foreign policy makers attempt to brand the nation through the use of hard power rather than soft power. The Iraq War and contemporary US policy in the Middle East are good examples of what I am talking about. One of the primary objectives George W. Bush's administration touted in launching the Iraq War was sending a message to the rest of the region—a reverse domino theory in which toppling one dictatorship would lead to the fall of others and produce a wave of democratic revolutions throughout the region. Here we had an unapologetic attempt to project the nation's brand through bombs and bullets, not just slick salesmanship. This was, needless to say, a really bad idea that went horribly wrong, but regardless of the outcome I wonder if there is a place for war (or, less severely, political and economic sanctions) within the nation-branding framework. In short, hard power speaks too, and we should not ignore its message or its cultural implications.

Overall, I think this volume demonstrates that nation branding considerably enriches our discussion of public diplomacy by providing a new explanation for what public diplomats are trying to accomplish. How much it contributes to the broader category of international cultural relations is somewhat less clear, I would argue. In cases where nations and their leaders tried to capitalize upon international cultural exchanges to improve their own image, it is clearly relevant. However, there are also numerous examples of nongovernmental organizations using communications strategies and exchange programs not for nation branding but for what might be described as "international branding" or "trans-national branding." Understanding the hows and whys of these "international branding" efforts matters a great deal, and the propensity of nation branding to collapse distinctions between different kinds of international cultural activities might actually be unhelpful in this case. Nevertheless, there are indeed a lot of cultural activities— including public diplomacy—focused upon shaping the nation's brand. It can be valuable to put them in conversation with each other, as long as we also remember to examine means and motives to draw important distinctions between them.

Justin Hart is associate chair and associate professor of History at Texas Tech University, where he started teaching in 2005 after completing his Ph.D. in History at Rutgers University. He is the author of *Empire of Ideas* (Oxford University Press, 2013) and numerous articles and book chapters on US public diplomacy and other elements of US foreign relations. He is currently writing a history of President Truman's failed campaign for Universal Military Training in the United States.

Notes

1. György Szondi, "Public Diplomacy and Nation Branding: Conceptual Similarities and Differences," Netherlands Institute of International Relations "Clingendael," October 2008.
2. Szondi, "Public Diplomacy," 20–21.
3. Ilaria Scaglia, "Branding Internationalism: Displaying Art and International Cooperation in the Interwar Period," chapter 3 in this volume.
4. Michael Krenn, "The Art of Branding: Rethinking American Cultural Diplomacy during the Cold War," chapter 6 in this volume.
5. Justin Hart, *Empire of Ideas: The Origins of Public Diplomacy and the Transformation of U.S. Foreign Policy* (New York: Oxford University Press, 2013), 6–12.
6. Jessica C. E. Gienow-Hecht, "Nation Branding," in *Explaining the History of American Foreign Relations*, 3rd ed., ed. Michael J. Hogan and Frank Costigliola (Cambridge: Cambridge University Press, 2016), 237.
7. Oliver Kühschelm, "From the Moralizing Appeal for Patriotic Consumption to Nation Branding: Austria and Switzerland," chapter 2 in this volume.
8. Simon Anholt, "Beyond the Nation Brand: The Role of Image and Identity in International Relations," *Exchange: The Journal of Public Diplomacy* 2, no. 1 (2013): 6.
9. Scaglia, "Branding Internationalism," chapter 3 in this volume.
10. Beata Ociepka, "A New Brand for Postcommunist Europe," chapter 8 in this volume.

Bibliography

Anholt, Simon. *Brand New Justice: How Branding Places and Products Can Help the Developing World*, rev. ed. Oxford: Butterworth-Heinemann, 2005.
———. *Competitive Identity: The New Brand Management for Nations, Cities, and Regions*. Houndmills: Palgrave Macmillan, 2007.

————. *Places: Identity, Image, and Reputation*. Houndmills: Palgrave Macmillan, 2010.

————. "Beyond the Nation Brand: The Role of Image and Identity in International Relations." *Exchange: The Journal of Public Diplomacy* 2, no. 1 (2013): 6–12.

Aronczyk, Melissa. *Branding the Nation: The Global Business of National Identity*. Oxford: Oxford University Press, 2013.

Dinnie, Keith. *Nation Branding: Concepts, Issues, Practice*. Oxford: Butterworth-Heinemann, 2008.

Gienow-Hecht, Jessica C. E. "Nation Branding." In *Explaining the History of American Foreign Relations*, 3rd ed., edited by Michael J. Hogan and Frank Costigliola, 232–44. Cambridge: Cambridge University Press, 2016.

Hart, Justin. *Empire of Ideas: The Origins of Public Diplomacy and the Transformation of U.S. Foreign Policy*. New York: Oxford University Press, 2013.

Kaneva, Nadia. "Nation Branding: Toward an Agenda for Critical Research." *International Journal of Communication* 5 (2011): 117–41.

Kaneva, Nadia, ed. *Branding Post-Communist Nations: Marketizing National Identities in the "New" Europe*. New York: Routledge, 2012.

Krenn, Michael L. *Fall-Out Shelters for the Human Spirit: American Art and the Cold War*. Chapel Hill, NC: The University of North Carolina Press, 2005.

Olins, Wally. "Branding the Nation—The Historical Context." *The Journal of Brand Management* 9 (April 2002): 241–48.

Szondi, György. "Public Diplomacy and Nation Branding: Conceptual Similarities and Differences." Netherlands Institute of International Relations "Clingendael," October 2008. Retrieved 3 June 2016 from http://www.clingendael.nl/sites/default/files/20081022_pap_in_dip_nation_branding.pdf.

Chapter 10

NATION BRANDING
A Twenty-First Century Tradition

Melissa Aronczyk

Nation Branding in Perspective

It was with some reservations that I agreed to contribute a response essay to this volume. Please understand: this has nothing to do with the excellent contributions you will find herein. It has to do, rather, with the intensity of my years of critical study of the phenomenon, and my disappointment that this problematic practice continues to grow. Over the many years I devoted to examining the professional industry of nation branding, I began to feel like a volunteer firefighter at a five-alarm wildfire, trying desperately and with insufficient resources to contain the flames as they blazed unbound across geographic and intellectual territory.

When my book *Branding the Nation* was published in 2013, I hoped it would throw some water on the fire. The heart of my argument in that book was that applying the metaphor of a brand to the form and content of the nation was not a neutral exercise. It was a concerted effort by business and political elites to transfer power from the state and its citizen protections to business concerns and capital-generating industries. The relative failure, over the last twenty-five years, of nation branding campaigns to actually "work" in the long term to improve countries' political, social, or cultural status is a result of the gap between what was continually promised and what was actually taking place: short-term, elite-led, self-serving projects for market reform with few clear beneficiaries, save the nation branding consultants who initiated the projects. Hard-won battles for citizen welfare protections or national redistributive policies in the postwar era were undone by state leaders' fears of being left behind in the competition for footloose international capital, and their subsequent turn toward private industry to help them "win" this zero-sum game.

What I did not expect was that *Branding the Nation* would fan the flames rather than douse the fire. Students of marketing and public relations thanked me for my fine "textbook" that appeared to them to indicate best practices for brands; market researchers followed me on Twitter; academics quoted passages from the book as evidence of the industry's success. In sum, my critical views were taken as excellent lessons for how to build a better brand.

How did this happen? One conclusion we can draw from the overall positive reception of nation branding is that the principles of business today dominate the popular imagination. While this statement could be made over multiple eras, I am referring to the particular set of business principles emerging in the 1970s and early 1980s that extended the precepts and purpose of commercial management across social and political institutions and positioned the corporation as the fulcrum of societal transformation. The success of this transformation is evident in the unquestioning adoption of "brand" as a synonym for political and cultural transformations at the level of the nation-state.

Another possibility is that my work, and that of like-minded colleagues, was insufficiently critical of nation branding. Had I wielded a sharper tongue and a defter hand, I might have had greater success in cutting off future generative discourses at the knees. Yet history has shown that capitalism is surprisingly good at absorbing its own critique. This is true not only for publications about nation branding, but also for actual experiments in nation branding in different countries. Nation branding is used by many national governments as a form of "beta-test"—a systematic exploration of different models of governance, and different appeals to national pride, to ascertain which are most effective for capital generation.[1] Incorporating risk models like nation branding into governance has dramatic implications for culture and politics.[2]

A third possibility, and the one with perhaps the greatest consequences for academic scholarship, is that we have confused ubiquity with universality. Nation branding is presented as everywhere applicable and everywhere accepted. It appears as a corollary to the most uncritical interpretations of globalization: a necessary marker of identification and coherence, a language for all nations on a global stage. But it is important to remember that globalization is not in fact a universal phenomenon, if by universal we mean that it affects all spaces on the globe equally, evenly, and simultaneously. Like nation branding itself, globalization is a Western-dominated, market-oriented process predicated on making winners and losers. It is not applied the same way in all spaces, and it does not benefit all affected parties.

In this volume we have a variety of rather creative and well-researched attempts to reveal aspects of the historical record that correspond to the set of features characterizing nation branding. Some essays reveal a concern with media representation and coordination; others focus on public displays of national culture; still others consider the communicative implications of products wrapped, so to speak, in their national flag. Each of these chapters adds depth and dimension to stories whose endings we thought we already knew. Nonetheless, and at the risk of disappointing those readers who seek to expand the legitimate ground on which the phenomenon may rest, it is my view that nation branding cannot be propelled back in time, avant la lettre. It is not the fault of these thoughtful chapters; it is that this phenomenon, as I understand it, cannot be divorced from the context of its emergence. Neither can it be separated from the specific bases of knowledge and expertise required to power this practice in the international community.

I rest my argument on three foundational pillars, each of which I examine below in terms of the use of the concept for historical analysis: the origins of nation branding in industrial requirements, the genre of branding as a business vernacular, and points of reference for ongoing research.

Origins of Nation Branding

It is notable that each of the chapters in this volume sets up a different definition for nation branding. The polyvalence of the phrase is part of its power. To undo its mythical pull, we require a contextual analysis that digs into the emergence of the specific phenomenon as it was initially conceived and practiced. Put another way, how was nation branding made *thinkable* and *observable* in the modern era?

I have written elsewhere that the nation branding industry appears at the confluence of (a) regulatory industrial transformations in the 1970s and 1980s; (b) the "spatial fix" required by the globalization of capital flows; (c) challenges to the form of the nation amid the rise of sub-, supra-, and transnational forms of affiliation and migration; and (d) processes of mediatization that placed overweening emphasis on communication speed, visuality, and virtuality.[3] Developing a discipline of national identification that could fit these requirements seemed important for state leaders searching for ways to prove their jurisdiction still mattered in a rapidly globalizing context.

But it was not to matter in the same way for all populations, nor for all geographic territories. That the solution of branding the nation emerged from the corporate world is a crucial point. The concept of brand cannot be separated from its origins in business. The commercial aims of nation branding since its development have been clear: nation branding is not only about making the nation meaningful for its populace; it is about making the nation matter in order to attract international capital. The nation's brand clearly communicates value to its "target audience": investors, tourists, and consumers. The message is far less clear for less visible, more fragile, or more needy populations.

It is this history that makes nation branding qualitatively different from, for instance, nineteenth- or twentieth-century art shows; wartime policy making; or international diplomatic missions. Efforts to align national branding with idealized democratic objectives, or with broad notions of visibility and perception, miss the crucial ways in which branding is at its heart a commercial enterprise aligned with profiting some at the expense of others.

This is what discounts the otherwise appealing essays by Ilaria Scaglia on China's 1935–36 international art exhibition in Britain (chapter 3) and Michael L. Krenn on traveling exhibits of American art in the mid twentieth century (chapter 6). The origins, motivations, and ultimate outcomes of these projects, which themselves can be traced back to at least the eighteenth century,[4] are not reducible to the mediatized, monetized, and marketized efforts of the contemporary brand. To situate these art exhibits as prototypical instances of nation branding is to miss the distinctly modern marriage of market and moral ideologies that characterizes the commercial project of nation branding.

A better starting point is found in the history of the commercial corporation. Starting in the early seventeenth century, and formed by royal British decree, entities such as the East India Company and the Russia Company married patriotic sentiment with trade activities.[5] In the mid nineteenth century, as companies grew in size and scope, the design features of corporate holdings gained importance, not merely for aesthetic purposes but as a form of internal synchronization and external communication. Industrial rail and shipping magnates sought to develop a visual identity for their business concerns, coordinating architecture, livery, staff uniforms, logos, and typefaces.[6] These visual designs typically reflected their national homes (even if their owners were non-nationals).

In the 1920s and 1930s, businesses developed, or commissioned from graphic designers, what were then known as "house styles"— logos, slogans, and symbols that spurred instant recognition of the company's products along with its nascent desire for a "relationship" with its consumers—which reflect a form of social value. Ascribing a deliberate social value to the corporate entity was meant to inspire coherent and disciplined identification among employees and investors as well as to convey the corporation's values to the public. Over time, this style became known as "corporate identity." With the name change came a more expansive understanding of its role. First, corporate identity programs involved a more systematic coordination of the "holistic" relationships among a company's products, its production and distribution processes, and its public reputation. Second, corporate identity began to be recognized on accounting balance sheets as a separate line item, meaning that the company's style—its brand—was an asset that could be valued separately from its "brick and mortar" holdings.

It was in wartime that commercial and state purposes were combined most dramatically, and where parallels between national "branding" and business incentives were most disturbingly revealed.[7] Such parallels also provide strong justification for why it is in autocratic regimes that nation branding achieves its greatest efficacy, as Carolin Viktorin's and John Gripentrog's chapters in this volume demonstrate. As Viktorin (chapter 5) points out, the rapid transformation of Spain's image from fascist state into European tourist destination could only have happened under the leadership of one who would brook no opposition. Gripentrog (chapter 4) provides a compelling account of Japan's surprisingly successful pre-World War II cultural outreach in the United States to mask its political alliance with Nazi Germany. Less dramatically, but as relevant, Oliver Kühschelm's (chapter 2) thoughtful examination of campaigns to promote Swiss and Austrian products as part of the national self-image shows the importance of recognizing historical efforts at national cultural representation as resting on particular economic bases.[8]

The Genre of Branding

At the current conjuncture, the brand has become, to borrow a phrase, a "rascal concept": "promiscuously pervasive, yet inconsistently defined, empirically imprecise and frequently contested."[9] The dramatic rise in academic articles and books over the last two decades that place "branding" at their center is not so much attributable to an empirical increase of brands in the world as it is to the expansion of the term to account for a surprisingly heterogeneous range of phenomena. This tendency risks collapsing fine-grained and complex distinctions among terms with robust genealogies and established applications.

The word *brand* has been wielded by scholars as a synonym for image, reputation, style, identity, public opinion, influence, trust, mediatization, exhibition, visualization, self-representation, symbolic value, coordinated messaging, diplomacy, publicity, international cooperation, promotion, and even—with strong implications—culture. This latter application may have roots in the Cold War tendency to see culture as a functional attribute in international relations.[10] This is not to say that culture was not deployed as a foreign policy instrument in different historical periods and world regions. Rather, I wish to argue for a rethinking of culture as context instead of as cause in international relations and its attendant scholarship. The flourishing of cultural approaches to international relations since that time offers multiple resources to expand and nuance the culture concept.

Clearly, brands do have cultural resonance. They reflect and instantiate cultural norms and beliefs. They are designed to achieve popular recognition, create collective meanings, maintain a coherent, consistent message, and, through familiarity, build consumer trust. But to the extent that they tell stories about who we are or what we want to be, brands must be understood as a particular genre. Branding is a form of storytelling conceived primarily to satisfy the needs of the storyteller, and only secondarily (if at all) the needs of the listener. They are indeed designed to incite, motivate, and justify decision-making, but they do so in ways that are not endemic to equal representation or recognition. They are not developed for purposes of mutual understanding, public deliberation, or common goodwill. They are developed as strategic and instrumental tools to achieve a pragmatic goal that benefits the interests of its developers.

In the dominant paradigm of the nation branding industry, culture and identity are conceptualized as highly useful tools of international relations. Nation branding practitioners present their practice as more media-friendly, relatable, and long lasting than the traditional, closed-door, diplomatic means of communication among nations.

This is an appealing argument; but it is inaccurate, in my opinion, for a number of reasons. The way in which marketing strategists have conceptualized identity and culture isolates both concepts as a separate domain, that is, separate from economy and society. This ideological move inhibits the potential for analysis of culture in relation to political economy.[11] It is also a deeply ahistorical perspective on culture and identity, considering the extent to which historical structures of social relations, patterns of exploitation or empire, and the monuments and documents of memory prevail in contemporary political discourse and practice.

In the typical approach adopted by the nation branding industry, culture appears as a modular unit; that is, as elements of an international discourse that can be unproblematically transferred wholesale to different national settings or used to explain transnational relations. But "there is a complex interplay between each local culture and the international discourse,"[12] as well as differences within national cultures. Culture is not a singular or bounded unit anywhere. When state theory is "open to cultural analysis ... the boundary between the state and the nonstate [can] be seen as a variable discursive effect" rather than a concrete barrier.[13]

The nation branding paradigm appears to project a strong distinction between the nation and the state, namely that the nation may be cultural but the state is not. Yet as the international relations scholar Beate Jahn has argued, "the precondition for the establishment of government is some sense of shared values. And it is the presence of these shared values—a common culture—which makes the establishment of states possible in the domestic sphere and its absence which prevents a similar development in the international sphere" (i.e., there is no "world state").[14] Similarly, George Steinmetz observes that state officials engage in cultural practices and discourses that affect their policy decisions.[15]

When we treat brand as technology instead of as ideology, we miss the ways this phenomenon is symptomatic of the social and political role of business in modern society. To brand is neither a neutral nor an easily transposable process. Nation brands cannot be exchanged for national culture by recourse to observations about shared values or meanings. Given its self-interested, commercially minded, and profit-centered orientation, we cannot align nation branding unprob-lematically with democratic or diplomatic objectives, regardless of what its practitioners and proponents might argue.

Writing Nation Branding into History

Research and writing on nation branding are dominated by members of what I have elsewhere called the transnational promotional class: a loosely allied group of individuals who stand to benefit in some way from promoting the nation form.[16] The prolific output of materials by nation branding practitioners, along with their clients' brand books, media campaigns, spokespeople, and administrative conferences, is heavily inflected by these authors' ongoing desire to achieve legiti-macy for their practice while attracting future clients.

By drawing too heavily on practitioner texts as reference points for historical investigation, we risk losing the analytical purchase of the critical academic scholar. Moreover, we become implicit collaborators in promoting business knowledge as intellectually dominant. To describe nation branding as a form of social justice, or to argue that nations have "always" been brands, or to liken nation branding to nation building, as practitioners have done, is to accept the primacy of a social framework embedded in market principles. Indeed, these texts are less sociohistorical accounts than they are valuable data to be mined—evidence of a particular mindset in a particular era about how society should work and what skills and roles are required to achieve this vision. This perspective can help qualify the practitioner claims that William B. McAllister (chapter 1) relies on in his discussion of US Civil War documents. Rosemarijn Hoefte's discussion (chapter 7) of Suriname's misguided branding campaign and Beata Ociepka's (chapter 8) analysis of the brand strategies of European postcommunist regimes would also benefit from greater reflexivity toward the intentions of their interlocutors; but the chapters engage the reader by maintaining a focus on the specific campaigns and the motivations of the actors dedicated to carrying them out.

There is a profound gap between the practice of nation branding and what intellectuals want nation branding to be. In the column marked "potential," we dream of its value as a form of collective identification, a modern expression of deeply felt beliefs and a sense of purpose in a modern globalizing era. But in the "actual" column we find a series of damaging implications: (a) urban and regional attempts at capital generation, often marginalizing or drawing funds away from nonurban spaces; (b) monies moved from welfare projects to capital intensive ones (e.g., tourism attraction, foreign direct investment schemes, tax havens); (c) treating citizens or residents as "stakeholders," with the accompanying attitude that these citizens or residents are not just participants in the future of their home territory but are also responsible for its success or failure. "Living the brand" has drastic consequences when the life choices presented to them involve untenable decisions.

To propel a distinctly modern phenomenon like nation branding back in time compels us to take account of this gap. The study of national culture requires a study of the ways that this culture is made tangible for those who experience it. The separation of society into spheres—political, cultural, economic, and so on—is an analytical project, not a practical one. To assess the reality that members of society experience in everyday life, now or in the past, requires a totalizing assessment. It is for this reason that expressions designed to characterize particular features of this paradigm—"stakeholders," "brand assets," "transparency"—have a cultural valence that cannot be assessed independently of the context of their emergence.

The Nation in the Twenty-First Century

What is the role of the nation in nation branding? This question often gets left out when the analytical lens is too closely trained on branding and its effects. Yet it is a surprising omission at a time when talk of the nation and its futures is particularly prevalent. If there is one uniform outcome to be discerned from the recent political upheavals in the United States and the United Kingdom, it is that we have certainly not moved into a post-national era. From Brexit to border walls, to the eruption of social movements on race and religion, political discourse in the twenty-first century reveals an ongoing preoccupation with the contours of the nation.

When intellectuals argued, in the early part of this century, that the nation still matters in the world, they pointed to instances of collective identification, citizen protections, and forums for free expression.[17] What was not then anticipated was that the concept would be used as a shield for some identifications, protections, and freedoms against the protections and freedoms of other would-be national members. The current waves of anti-immigrant, anti-elite, and anti-cosmopolitan rhetoric illustrate the degree to which the promises of globalization have not been realized for all who are affected by it.

It is evident whose interests nation branding was designed to serve. Nation branding was presented to its potential national clients as a salve for the aches and pains of global transformation. It promised its government adherents continued power and influence in a world where the nation-state seemed to be disappearing. Its promises were far less clearly articulated to the citizens who would be subject to new regimes. But as a form of "global nationalism," nation branding appeared attractive to many constituents.[18] The question now is what role nation branding plays in an atmosphere of renewed nationalism, where the national sentiment in many places is ugly and antagonistic.

Here is where the historical record has much to teach us. Some have argued that the current political rhetoric around the nation reflects an older notion of sovereignty and a desire for tradition—however distorted by nostalgic sentiment.[19] If this is the case, it is the task of the historian to teach us how and why these older conceptions have come to matter again, and with what consequences for our collective future.

Melissa Aronczyk is associate professor in the Department of Journalism & Media Studies at Rutgers University. Her work on globalization, nationalism, place branding, and marketing has been published internationally, including two books: *Branding the Nation: The Global Business of National Identity* (2013) and *Blowing Up the Brand: Critical Perspectives on Promotional Culture* (co-editor, 2010) as well as articles in several media and communications journals.

Notes

1. Neil Brenner, Jamie Peck, and Nik Theodore, "Variegated Neoliberalization: Geographies, Modalities, Pathways," *Global Networks* 10, no. 2 (2009): 182–222.
2. See Arjun Appadurai, *Banking on Words: The Failure of Language in the Age of Derivative Finance* (Chicago: University of Chicago Press, 2015); Benjamin Lee and Edward LiPuma, "The Foundations of Finance: Charisma, Aura and Uncertainty," *Rethinking Capitalism* no. 3 (2012): 2–4.

3. Melissa Aronczyk, *Branding the Nation: The Global Business of National Identity* (Oxford: Oxford University Press, 2013).
4. Linda Colley, *Britons: Forging the Nation 1707–1837* (New Haven, CT: Yale University Press, 1992).
5. Colley, *Britons.*
6. See, for example, David Raizman, *History of Modern Design* (London: Laurence King Publishing, 2003).
7. See, for example, Steven Heller, *Iron Fists: Branding the Twentieth-Century Totalitarian State* (New York: Phaidon Press, 2011).
8. See also Victoria De Grazia, *Irresistible Empire: America's Advance through Twentieth Century Europe* (Cambridge, MA: Harvard University Press, 2005) for evidence of the intricate yet inseparable links between cultural diplomacy and consumerism after World War II.
9. Brenner, Peck, and Theodore, "Variegated Neoliberalization: Geographies, Modalities, Pathways," 184.
10. Jessica C. E. Gienow-Hecht and Frank Schumacher, ed., *Culture and International History* (New York: Berghahn Books, 2003).
11. For a corpus of work on cultural political economy, see the publications of the sociologist Bob Jessop.
12. George Steinmetz, "Introduction: Culture and the State," in *State/Culture: State-formation after the Cultural Turn*, ed. George Steinmetz, (Ithaca, NY: Cornell University Press, 1999), 26.
13. Timothy Mitchell, quoted in Steinmetz, "Introduction: Culture and the State," 26.
14. Beate Jahn, "The Power of Culture in International Relations," in *Culture and International History*, ed. Jessica Gienow-Hecht and Frank Schumacher (New York: Berghahn Books, 2003), 28.
15. Steinmetz, "Introduction: Culture and the State," 24.
16. Aronczyk, *Branding the Nation.*
17. Craig Calhoun, *Nations Matter: Culture, History and the Cosmopolitan Dream* (London: Routledge, 2007).
18. Leslie Sklair, *The Transnational Capitalist Class* (Malden, MA: Blackwell, 2001).
19. Calhoun, *Nations Matter.*

Bibliography

Appadurai, Arjun. *Banking on Words: The Failure of Language in the Age of Derivative Finance.* Chicago, IL: University of Chicago Press, 2015.

Aronczyk, Melissa. *Branding the Nation: The Global Business of National Identity.* Oxford: Oxford University Press, 2013.

Brenner, Neil, Jamie Peck, and Nik Theodore. "Variegated Neoliberalization: Geographies, Modalities, Pathways." *Global Networks* 10, no. 2 (2009): 182–222.

Calhoun, Craig. *Nations Matter: Culture, History and the Cosmopolitan Dream.* London: Routledge, 2007.

———. "Brexit is a Mutiny against the Cosmopolitan Elite." *The World Post.* 27 June 2016. Retrieved 1 August 2016 from http://www.huffingtonpost.com/craig-calhoun/brexit-mutiny-elites_b_10690654.html.

Colley, Linda. *Britons: Forging the Nation 1707–1837*. New Haven, CT: Yale University Press, 1992.

De Grazia, Victoria. *Irresistible Empire: America's Advance through Twentieth Century Europe*. Cambridge, MA: Harvard University Press, 2005.

Gienow-Hecht, Jessica C. E. and Frank Schumacher, ed. *Culture and International History*. New York: Berghahn Books, 2003.

Heller, Steven. *Iron Fists: Branding the Twentieth-Century Totalitarian State*. New York: Phaidon Press, 2011.

Jahn, Beate. "The Power of Culture in International Relations." In *Culture and International History*, edited by Jessica C. E. Gienow-Hecht and Frank Schumacher, 27–41. New York: Berghahn Books, 2003.

Lee, Benjamin, and Edward LiPuma. "The Foundations of Finance: Charisma, Aura and Uncertainty." *Rethinking Capitalism* no. 3 (2012): 2–4.

Raizman, David. *History of Modern Design*. London: Laurence King Publishing, 2003.

Sklair, Leslie. *The Transnational Capitalist Class*. Malden, MA: Blackwell, 2001.

Steinmetz, George. "Introduction: Culture and the State." In *State/Culture: State-formation after the Cultural Turn*, edited by George Steinmetz, 1–49. Ithaca, NY: Cornell University Press, 1999.

Chapter 11

THE HISTORY OF NATION BRANDING AND NATION BRANDING AS HISTORY

Mads Mordhorst

*N*ation Branding in Modern History poses the following question: is nation branding useful as a historical analytical concept? Not surprisingly the book answers affirmatively; nation branding can be useful as an analytical concept in a historical perspective. When you read the book, however, you find that this conclusion is amply supported by eight historical cases and analyses. They show that nations historically practiced nation branding even before the modern concept of nation branding emerged. Furthermore, it is apparent that nations have employed the new practices and tools brought forward under the heading of "nation branding" for decades, if not centuries. In other words, nation-branding praxis precedes the development of the concept. It looks as if nation branding can easily be applied as a descriptive historical concept—perhaps a bit too easily.

Nation Branding: Historical Concept or Practical Tool

Is nation branding a contemporary analytical concept to be used—as the authors put it—as "history avant la lettre," as a time-transcending way to get a better understanding of the past than the past had of itself? Or, is nation branding a time- and context-specific concept, an investigation of which might shed light on the specific time period when it emerges?

Notes for this section begin on page 253.

The answer given in *Nation Branding in Modern History* is that it can be both, and that both are legitimate uses of the concept. I agree, but I must insist on distinguishing firmly between these two perspectives. In this book, nation branding is mainly used in the first sense, and since most of the contributors are historians exploring cases that have a historical focus this is legitimate. However, to balance this and give a complementary perspective—and perhaps to avoid a tendency to anachronism—I will focus on the other perspective, i.e., nation branding as an expression and a concept that emerges at a particular time, in a certain environment, and with a specific purpose.

That nation branding in this volume that is mainly used avant la lettre can be seen from the fact that in most of the cases in the book it is the authors and not the historical actors themselves who categorize the activities they are involved in as nation branding. The two exceptions are the most contemporary contributions. Beata Ociepka's "A New Brand for Postcommunist Europe," and Rosemarijn Hoefte's "Suriname: Nation Building and Nation Branding in a Postcolonial State, 1945–2015." These are not only the chapters that deal with real nation-branding campaigns, but also the most critical of modern nation-branding practices and the consequences of nation branding. They problematize the utilization and commodification of national identity and the use of external branding consultants without deep historical and cultural knowledge of the nations. These chapters see nation branding as naïve, as a way to "whitewash existing sociocultural, political, and economic tensions" to quote Hoefte in her conclusion.[1]

Paradoxically, both analyses focus on contemporary states that for different reasons—postcolonialism and the fall of the Berlin Wall—deal with the preliminary process of nation building just as much as nation branding itself; processes that for the rest of the cases in the book took place from the eighteenth to the twentieth century. So despite the fact that the two chapters are the most contemporary, they cover an earlier stage of nation building—and branding—than the rest of the chapters.

This points to a more overall research question that many of the contributions in *Nation Branding in Modern History* touch upon: what is the relationship between nation building and nation branding historically as well as today? A historical approach to these questions seems to be a central contribution, because the link between nation branding and nation building somehow seems to have slipped into the crack between the community of nation branding experts and the academic field of studies in nations and nationalism.[2]

The Conceptual History of Nation Branding

Chronologically, the rest of the cases in the book stretch from 1861 to the end of the Cold War. The chronological focus is thus a "long twentieth century" that ends with the fall of the Berlin Wall, before the discourses of neoliberalism and globalization became dominant narratives, and concept of nation branding emerged.[3]

Unlike many other concepts, it is relatively easy to trace the origin of the concept of nation branding. It was created in 1996 by the British marketing consultant Simon Anholt and used in print for the first time in the article "Nation-Brands of the Twenty-First Century."[4]

The conceptual breakthrough of nation branding around the year 2000 was more than just good labeling; it was in line with the broader discourses of the time. In *Trading Identities* (1999) corporate branding consultant Wally Olins explained the rationality behind the new interest in nations as objects for branding. Olins observed a change in the relationship between nations and companies—reflected in the term "trading identities"—which he described as follows: "The relationship between countries and companies is changing. In some ways they are becoming more alike. Nations increasingly use business language—growth targets, education targets, health targets; global companies increasingly emphasize soft issues, their value to society and their benevolent influence."[5] In other words, nations and companies had become more alike, and the distinction between nation states and politics on one side, and companies and economics on the other, had become increasingly blurred. From a branding and marketing perspective it was logical to take promotional tools that had been successful in the commercial sector and apply them to nations. Because, as Teslik puts it, "nation branding . . . means applying corporate branding techniques to countries."[6]

Another ongoing theme in the argumentation for nation branding was that the process of globalization and global competition would result in a fundamental change in the institutional landscape of the world. As Anholt formulated it, "[t]he rapid advance of globalisation means that every country must compete with every other for its share of the world's consumers, tourists, investors, students, entrepreneurs, international media, of other governments, and the people of other countries."[7]

The purpose (or end) of nation branding is therefore a hardcore global competition for resources, and the present concept of nation branding is to be seen as a means to achieving this end. By focusing on the avant la lettre perspective, there might be a tendency to focus on continuity and elements that bridge the past and the present, and thus partly overlook the differences. Therefore, while I fully agree with Michael L. Krenn when he concludes in his chapter "The Art of Branding: Rethinking American Cultural Diplomacy during the Cold War" that "nation branding challenges us to put the study of cultural diplomacy into a much wider chronological framework,"[8] I would have liked for this to also have included an analysis of how cultural diplomacy during the Cold War differed from modern nation branding. The same is true in regard to John Gripentrog's chapter "High Culture to the Rescue: Japan's Nation Branding in the United States, 1934–40." In this chapter, Gripentrog convincingly shows that Japanese reputation efforts, which included a broad range of different stakeholders, moved well beyond the bounds of traditional cultural diplomacy or state-sanctioned propaganda and were at least as strategic and efficient as modern nation branding campaigns orchestrated by nation branding consultants.

This historical perspective is again interesting because according to Simon Anholt, Philip Kotler, Wally Olins, Keith Dinnie, and other nation-branding consultants, the winners in this new global competition for resources would be the nations who had invested in creating a positive brand. The losers, on the other hand, would be nations that had not invested in nation-brand management

From this perspective, nation branding is a concept that emerged as a part of the performative influence of the neoliberal globalization discourse around the year 2000. It was created by leading consultants in marketing and branding, and is thus embedded in the discourses of market, economy, and business that became dominant during the 1990s.

Along these lines, the emergence of nation branding can be seen as indication of what Philip Cerny and other scholars have observed as an overall change in the role of the state from nation state to competition state. According to this perspective, states—in their attempt to adapt to and counter the discourses of globalization—do not merely reproduce the historically constructed nation state and the modern welfare state, but transform themselves into a new type of state. The nation state changes from a state whose central aim is to supervise the market, into a competition state that is under the supervision of the market. The competition state focuses on its own competitiveness in global arenas that increasingly bring together disparate political, cultural, and commercial elements. Consequently, states begin to act as "quasi enterprise associations."[9] Thus, the sudden interest in nation branding in the late 1990s can be seen as the globalization of nationalism in two senses. First, it changes the focus of national identity, shifting it from a set of internal concerns about a common horizon of meaning and values among the citizenry, to a more external orientation, in which national branding is used by the state to promote its interests in the global marketplace. Second, nation branding moves nationalism out of its traditional political, cultural, and ideological fields, and into the logics of the marketplace and the domain of the global competition for prosperity. The state develops into a hybrid that must transcend the national/global dichotomy of political and commercial concerns, as well as the distinction between public and private sectors.

While the concept of nation branding thus turns nationalism upside down and exposes the hybridity of the present society, nation branding can be used avant la lettre to analyze the hybrid tensions historically negotiated by modern nation states.

An example of this is Ilaria Scaglia's contribution "Branding Internationalism: Displaying Art and International Cooperation in the Interwar Period." As the title indicates, this study focuses on twentieth-century internationalism, which is genealogically in line with globalism. Besides the chronological difference is the focus of internationalism on peaceful international exchange among nation states rather than the struggles endemic to the competition state and the global marketplace.

Scaglia's study suggests that most of the dichotomies and hybrid tensions that can be observed in the competition state were already embedded in the nation state; the competition state and nation branding just focus on the flip side of the coin. This side has been in the shadow, so to say, and we have become blind to it. By using concepts such as nation branding as part of our historical lens, we become able to see and analyze these tensions and dichotomies.

This is why some of the historical cases in the volume conclude that the nation-branding and nation-building process goes back in time, and that the hybridity is perhaps an integrated part of the nation-building process. This might explain why the cases that apply nation branding avant la lettre find that the use of nation branding opens up new questions about the past. This contrasts with the two contemporary cases that analyze nation branding praxis and conclude that it created one-dimensional national images.

Nation Branding as Practice

Nation branding was not developed as a tool for academic historical analysis, but rather a set of tools and recipes for sale to governments and politicians. As such the product was in high demand. Nation branding gave politicians the means to act against the threatening clouds of globalization by taking domestic narratives and discourses and deploying them in the external competition for resources on the global stage.[10]

Consequently, state after state in Europe launched nation-branding programs and campaigns in the first decade of the twenty-first century—this was the heyday of the nation branding business. Often politicians made direct reference to the logic mentioned above—if we do not brand our nation we risk becoming the losers in the global competition—and often they hired people from nation-branding consultants such as Simon Anholt, Keith Dinnie, and Wally Olins.

It seems, however, as if the buzz around nation branding has ended. In recent years, very few Western countries have launched new programs or campaigns, and many of the countries that had nation branding campaigns have ended their efforts.

There are different individual reasons for this, but I will focus on three more general issues that have contributed to the loss of interest in nation branding: first, the failure of nation-branding programs; second, the financial crisis that began in 2007; and finally, the transformation in global politics and discourse apparent in phenomena such as Brexit and the refugee crisis.

That nation-branding campaigns in general have not succeeded in delivering the results they promised has been accepted for some years, even by some of the consultants themselves. In 2010 Anholt wrote, "[b]etween 2005 when the Anholt *Nation Brands Index* was launched, and the last study in 2009, there has been no detectable correlation between changes in national image and expenditure on 'nation branding campaigns.'"[11] Of course, the fact that it has been nearly impossible to see any significant results of the campaigns makes it difficult to sell nation-branding campaigns to the politicians, and for politicians to legitimize spending taxpayers' money to fund activities that do not seem to have any measurable effect.

This has been reinforced by the financial crisis. In general, concepts such as "branding," "experience economy," and "immaterial economy" are concepts that thrive mainly in times of growth. The financial crisis has not only reduced the public economic scope, it has also occasioned a turn from spending money on intangible matters and soft issues to a focus on more traditional and hardcore welfare issues.

The last global trend that has contributed to the deceleration of the nation-branding bus is a change in global discourse on globalization and the relation between the global and the national. Where nation branding, as argued above, can be seen as a part of globalization and the externalization of nationalism, the Western world has recently taken a turn toward internalization and renationalization, a trend that has manifested in the growth of populist nationalist movements in Europe, the European refugee crisis, Brexit, and Donald Trump's slogan "America First."

Denmark's recent nation-branding efforts serve as an example of both the buzz and the downturn of nation branding. Within a span of ten years Denmark experienced two severe reputation crises. The first was the cartoon crisis in 2006 that followed the publication of cartoons of the prophet Muhammad in a Danish newspaper, which led to riots in Muslim countries. Danish embassies were burned down and more than 150 people lost their lives in the riots. The hostility toward Denmark was not restricted to Muslim countries, however. In the Western media and among Denmark's traditional allies, there was also a significant outpouring of negative press coverage. In the aftermath of this crisis, the Danish government launched a huge nation-branding program in order to reestablish Denmark's tarnished reputation in the short term, and to create a long-term strategic investment.[12] After five years, the nation-branding program was terminated with neither public or nor political discussion.[13]

Then, in the fall of 2015 and the first months of 2016, Denmark again became front-page news internationally, this time due to initiatives and laws to prevent refugees from seeking asylum in Denmark. The so-called "Jewelry Law" received the most attention—this law authorized the Danish police to confiscate asylum seekers' valuables, including jewelry. Prominent Western media like *The Washington Post, CNN, BBC, The Wall Street Journal,* and the *Independent* picked up the story, comparing the law to Nazi confiscation of jewelry and other personal effects from Jews during the Holocaust. Ironically, the so-called "Jewelry Law" also culminated in an outpouring of cartoons; however, these cartoons now appeared in British newspapers portraying the Danish prime minister as a Nazi.[14]

It is striking how differently the Danish government handled these two crises. While the cartoon crisis was used to launch a nation-branding program, there were no such ideas after the second crisis; at least not in the official national rhetoric. In contrast, the government has insisted on focusing on internal national agendas and what is referred to as "national coherency." The rhetorical pendulum has thus swung back, and nation building has replaced nation branding as the dominant political discourse.

However, if we look beyond the official rhetoric at government spending, the Danish government has continued to fund activities that were previously categorized as nation-branding activities, but now without the label of nation branding. These activities include inviting investment delegations to Denmark, sponsoring business-promotion initiatives, and upgrading public diplomacy efforts in order to repair the damage done to the Danish image—i.e., brand—in the wake of the crisis.

This supports the historical argument that national reputation management has to be seen in a broader perspective than the modern concept of nation branding suggests. In fact, the concept of nation branding might sometimes be a straight jacket for analyzing the efforts. An example of this might be Carolin Viktorin's contribution "All Publicity is Good Publicity? Advertising, Public Relations, and the Branding of Spain in the United Kingdom, 1945–69." In this essay, Viktorin demonstrates how the tourism industry entered into what, in branding terminology, would be seen as destination branding, and focuses on how this became a vehicle for legitimizing the Franco dictatorship, developing international public relations, and paving the road for future investments. Furthermore, she shows how this was done through engaging international networks and consultants. All in all, this would be seen as an example of a nation branding campaign. However, maybe this was so efficient on account of the fact that it was not launched as a nation branding campaign. This made it possible to operate under the radar and present Spain in an apolitical way, thereby detaching it from the Franco regime.

The present shift from a globalization discourse to cultural nationalism, political isolationism, and economic protectionism is not new. From a historical perspective it can be seen as a nearly cyclical movement, or as the swing of the pendulum. One example is described in Oliver Kühschelm's chapter in this book, which is a historical analysis of the change in the promotion of countries from inward-looking and protectionist tendencies in the interwar period to the more internationalized economy after World War II.

Kühschelm's case shows that historical studies can be used as parallels and examples for present problems in national reputation management and can support the implicit axiom of this book:

despite the fact that nation branding as a concept emerged and had its heyday in a specific historical time and context, it is relevant to examine a praxis that could be categorized as nation branding in a broader historical perspective. At the same time, this suggests a need for clarifying the difference between nation branding and nations as brands—historical analyses could be helpful in unfolding this distinction.

Nation as Brand versus Nation Branding

Since it takes place in the praxis-oriented realm of marketing, branding, and the consultant business, nation-branding research has logically focused on how to adjust and apply the tools and logics developed in branding products or businesses to branding nations. Nations are thus considered comparable to goods or companies, and sometimes even perceived as un-branded or "virgin" areas that can easily be branded by experts. This book shows that it is in fact the other way around. Nations have "always already" been branded and used as brands. Together the problems mentioned above—that no nation-branding campaigns have been able to deliver proof of measurable long-term effects, and that national governments seem to have lost interest in investing in nation branding—suggest that it might be time to reconsider the research agendas in the field.

A first step could be to change the focus from "branding" to "nation," or, from developing a toolbox for nation branding to understanding the nation as brand. According to Anholt, it is paradoxical that on the one hand nations have brand images, but on the other that nations cannot be branded, at least not with ordinary branding tools. This book points to the historical foundation of this paradox. For a long time, nations have been built as brands, and the "tools" used in this process are more multifaceted and comprehensive than any nation-branding campaign. The book makes it clear that the nation-building process has been going on for centuries concomitantly with an integrated process of what we today call brand building. William B. McAllister's chapter "Nation Branding Amid Civil War: Publishing US Foreign Policy Documents to Define and Defend the Republic, 1861–66" reinforces this point when he concludes that nation building includes nation branding and vice versa. Over time, the nation-building process turned nations into some of the strongest and most stable brands we know—much stronger and more lasting than any commercial brand.

While the case studies in the book give empirical evidence for this, they also point to a variety of new historical research agendas. The first conclusion in this regard must be that if nations are created as brands over a long time, then nation-branding analyses should generally have stronger historical integration, not only as part of an academic historical understanding of the evolution of nation states and nations as brand, but also in order to develop better and more efficient ways of nation branding and reputation management for nations today. In fact, it might be the case that the place- and nation-branding literature has more to learn from history than the other way around. If nations are some of the strongest brands or strongest brand images, then perhaps commercial brands ought to try to imitate the characteristics and features of nations.

This is not to say that historians have nothing to learn from the nation-branding paradigm. The diagnoses of globalization processes are in most aspects interesting and relevant. Nations and companies are entities that in several aspects share common features and can be analyzed as such. Nations not only work and act in the political and cultural sphere, they are also commercial actors, and this has to some extent been overlooked in history as well as in the field of nationalism studies. To consider nations historically through concepts and discourses from marketing and branding is thus a displacement in perspective that will shed new light on the historical construction of nations, and offer a broader and more interesting perspective on nations as phenomena. *Nation Branding in Modern History* should therefore not only be read as a collection of good cases, but also as a historical window to new research agendas in nation branding and nation studies.

Mads Mordhorst is associate professor in History at Copenhagen Business School, and director of the Centre for Business History. He has published several articles and books on nation branding. From 2017 to 2020, he is a visiting professor at Oslo University as a part of the research program "Nordic Branding." His current research focuses on present uses of national identity and national history, as commodities.

Notes

1. Rosemarijn Hoefte's "Suriname: Nation Building and Nation Branding in a Postcolonial State, 1945–2015," chapter 7 in this volume.
2. Svein Ivar Angell and Mads Mordhorst, "National Reputation Management and the Competition State," *Journal of Cultural Economy* 8, no. 2 (2015): 189.
3. See e.g., Angell and Mordhorst "National Reputation Management and the Competition State"; Sue Curry Jansen, "Designer Nations: Neo-liberal Nation Branding—Brand Estonia," *Social Identities: Journal for the Study of Race, Nation, and Culture* 14, no. 1 (January 2008): 121–42; Melissa Aronczyk, *Branding the Nation: The Global Business of National Identity* (Oxford: Oxford University Press, 2013).
4. Simon Anholt, "Nation-Brands of the Twenty-First Century," *Journal of Brand Management* 5, no. 6 (1998): 395–406.
5. Wally Olins, *Trading Identities* (London: The Foreign Policy Centre, 1999), 1.
6. Lee Hudson Teslik, "Nation Branding Explained," *Council on Foreign Relations*, 9 November, (2007).
7. Simon Anholt, *Competitive Identity: The New Brand Management for Nations, Cities and Regions* (Houndmills: Palgrave Macmillan, 2007), 1.
8. Michael L. Krenn, "The Art of Branding: Rethinking American Cultural Diplomacy during the Cold War," chapter 6 in this volume.
9. Philip G. Cerny, "Paradoxes of the Competition State: The Dynamics of Political Globalization," *Government and Opposition* 32, no. 1 (1997): 251–52.
10. Mads Mordhorst, "Public Diplomacy vs. Nation Branding: The Case of Denmark after the Cartoon Crises," in *Histories of Public Diplomacy and Nation Branding in the Nordic and Baltic Countries*, ed. Louise Clerc et al. (Boston: Brill, 2015): 237–56.
11. Simon Anholt, *Places: Identity, Image and Reputation* (Houndmills: Palgrave Macmillan, 2010), 2.
12. Ministry for Economic and Business Affairs, *Action Plan for the Global Marketing of Denmark* (Copenhagen: Ministry for Economic and Business Affairs, 2007).
13. Mordhorst, "Public Diplomacy vs. Nation Branding."
14. Steve Bell, "Denmark Seizing Refugees' Assets" (Guardian opinion cartoon), *The Guardian*, 28 January 2015; Lizzie Dearden, "Denmark Approves Controversial Refugee Bill Allowing Police to Seize Asylum Seekers' Cash and Valuables," *The Independent*, 28 January 2015.

Bibliography

Angell, Svein Ivar, and Mads Mordhorst. "National Reputation Management and the Competition State." *Journal of Cultural Economy* 8, no. 2 (2015): 184–201.

Anholt, Simon. "Nation-Brands of the Twenty-First Century." *Journal of Brand Management* 5, no. 6 (1998): 395–406.

———. *Competitive Identity: The New Brand Management for Nations, Cities and Regions*. Houndmills: Palgrave Macmillan, 2007.

————. *Places: Identity, Image and Reputation*. Houndmills: Palgrave Macmillan, 2010.

Aronczyk, Melissa. *Branding the Nation: The Global Business of National Identity*. Oxford: Oxford University Press, 2013.

Bell, Steve. "Denmark Seizing Refugees' Assets" (Guardian opinion cartoon). *The Guardian*. 28 January 2015.

Cerny, Philip G. "Paradoxes of the Competition State: The Dynamics of Political Globalization." *Government and Opposition* 32, no. 1 (1997): 251–65.

Dearden, Lizzie. "Denmark Approves Controversial Refugee Bill Allowing Police to Seize Asylum Seekers' Cash and Valuables." *The Independent*, 28 January 2015.

Denmark. Ministry for Economic and Business Affairs. *Action Plan for the Global Marketing of Denmark*. Copenhagen: Ministry for Economic and Business Affairs, 2007.

Dinnie, Keith. "Place Branding: Overview of an Emerging Literature." *Place Branding* 1, no. 1 (2004): 106–10.

————. *Nation Branding: Concepts, Issues, Practice*. Oxford: Butterworth-Heinemann, 2008.

Jansen, Sue Curry. "Designer Nations: Neo-Liberal Nation Branding—Brand Estonia." *Social Identities: Journal for the Study of Race, Nation, and Culture* 14, no. 1 (2008): 121–42.

Kotler, Philip, Donald H. Haider, and Irving J. Rein. *Marketing Places: Attracting Investment, Industry and Tourism to Cities, States, and Nations*. New York: The Free Press, 1993.

Kotler, Philip, Somkid Jatusripitak, and Suvit Maesincee. *The Marketing of Nations: A Strategic Approach to Building National Wealth*. New York: The Free Press, 1997.

Mordhorst, Mads. "Public Diplomacy vs. Nation Branding: The Case of Denmark after the Cartoon Crises." In *Histories of Public Diplomacy and Nation Branding in the Nordic and Baltic Countries*, edited by Louise Clerc et al., 237–57. Boston, MA: Brill, 2015.

Olins, Wally. *Trading Identities*. London: The Foreign Policy Centre, 1999.

Teslik, Lee Hudson. "Nation Branding Explained." *Council on Foreign Relations*, 9 November (2007).

PREFACE
The Diversity of Primary Sources and the
Concept of Nation Branding

The study of history means the study of sources. As we have seen in this volume, nation branding incorporates in its analyses a variety of actors and a wide range of primary sources beyond governmental records. Even more important, it provides us with new perspectives that may help us to understand the interplay of culture, presentation, and politics, and, thus, expand the scope of our interpretation.

The following chapters aim to present some sources that do exactly that—three authors describe and elaborate upon the analytical value of these sources in more detail than was possible within the framework of the case study chapters. All three provide us with perspectives on how governmental and semi-governmental actors implemented branding strategies in their everyday routines. They highlight the instruments actors used, and also examine reactions to their strategies. As the reader will see, the character of these sources varies greatly, both in regard to their format and their origins.

First, John Gripentrog explains how the Japanese Society for International Cultural Relations (Kokusai Bunka Shinkōkai, or KBS) pursued a strategy to promote its cultural heritage in the 1930s, publishing articles in a variety of journals and magazines. Titled "The Japanese People and Their Gardens" and composed by Baron Dan Inō, the present source was published in *NIPPON* in 1935, and emphasized the aesthetic and spiritual nature of the Japanese people. The goal of this reference to Japan's cultural heritage was to rebrand the image of Japan and its people as civilized, peaceful, and refined. As such, the source presents an example of how governmental and nongovernmental actors use cultural assets and apply nation branding techniques in order to improve the nation's reputation.

Next, Ilaria Scaglia offers four illustrations suggesting that nations can brand their cultural and national character in both an international and internationalist context. This is, she argues, precisely what the Republican Chinese government tried to accomplish during the Chinese Exhibition in London in 1935 and 1936. A number of pictures displaying moments of concrete interaction and cooperation among people from various nations illustrate Chinese attempts to simultaneously brand their own nation as an ancient civilization, yet be in tune with the idea of internationalism.

Finally, Michael Krenn illustrates domestic conflicts over identity and nation branding campaigns in the United States. Using the example of the *Advancing American Art* exhibit from 1946/47 and a memorandum from Assistant Secretary of State for Public Affairs William Benton, Krenn shows how the State Department countered media criticism and linked the Department's branding campaign to the emergence of the Cold War. Notably Benton's memo reveals how actors involved in the campaigning process tried to position themselves within the domestic power struggle over national identity in an effort to influence the agenda and frame individual projections.

In sum, the following chapters are meant to provide insight into the diverse range of sources available to historians interested in nation branding. In addition, they help to complete the intention of this volume to illustrate nation branding as both a concept and an object of historical investigation. Similar to the chapters in this book, they are meant to be illustrative but not exhaustive.

I

INTRODUCTION TO BARON DAN INŌ, "THE JAPANESE PEOPLE AND THEIR GARDENS" (1935)

John Gripentrog

The following primary source on Japanese gardens represents a poignant expression of Japanese efforts in the 1930s to brand Japan as a highly sophisticated and refined nation. In 1934, under the auspices of the Foreign Ministry, a diverse group of Japanese cosmopolitans established the Society for International Cultural Relations (Kokusai Bunka Shinkōkai, or KBS) to foreground the nation's traditional culture. Through the spectacle of its cultural treasures, KBS officials hoped to enhance Japan's status in the international community and thereby advance the foreign policy goals of the empire.

On the surface, Baron Dan Inō's[1] "The Japanese People and Their Gardens" stands on its own as a remarkably edifying—and timeless—insight into the principles, meaningfulness, and merits of the Japanese art of gardening. In the context of the era's international tensions, however, it reveals a carefully crafted example of how the KBS sought to market the "best information" about Japan. In addition to reinforcing the KBS message that Japan was aesthetically advanced, Dan conveyed the organization's desire to attach admirable values to Japanese society as a whole—suggesting a people who were naturally contemplative, temperate, and spiritual; in other words, traits and values in marked opposition to martial excess.

"The Japanese People and Their Gardens" appeared in a 1935 issue of *NIPPON*, a KBS-sponsored illustrated magazine.[2] Stylish and sophisticated, the Bauhaus-influenced *NIPPON* featured stunning

Notes for this section begin on page 264.

cover designs and alluring photomontages of Japanese arts and society. Consistent with KBS branding objectives, stories in the glossy quarterly celebrated the rich diversity of the nation's traditional arts, including pottery, textiles, painting, music, dance, masks, paper-making, literature, temples, and theater. Thus, in contrast to KBS art exhibitions and touring theatrical productions, *NIPPON* projected the nation brand as a vicarious experience. The KBS distributed *NIPPON* to targeted elites, including the diplomatic corps and members of Japan Societies abroad. America's ambassador to Japan, Joseph C. Grew, invariably received a copy, which he sometimes forwarded to Secretary of State Cordell Hull.

Among KBS officials, Baron Dan authored the most significant essays in *NIPPON* in terms of branding content—articles that reflected the pride of an increasingly nationalistic populace. In the larger context of the KBS's nation branding campaign, it is important to keep in mind that Baron Dan (1892–1973), like many KBS members, came of age during Japan's rapid rise to great power in the latter part of the Meiji Era. The exhilarating transformation exerted a strong psychological influence on an entire generation, many of whom would be in positions of political, economic, and intellectual authority during the fateful decade of the 1930s. A significant turning point in this transformation came in 1905 when Japan defeated tsarist Russia in a war over interests in northeast China. Dan was thirteen years old. The fruits of Japan's successful modernization precipitated among the Japanese a reexamination of Western cultural presumptions and the nation's place in a world dominated by the West.

Intellectuals like Nitobe Inazō (1862–1933) and Okakura Tenshin (1862–1913) shined a prideful light back toward Japan, hoping to awaken Westerners to the inherent value of Japanese civilization. Okakura, for example, assailed Westerners' seemingly smug unwillingness to learn from non-white cultures. In his *Book of Tea* (1906), Okakura calmly inquired, "When will the West understand or try to understand the East?" Using tea as a metaphor, Okakura invited Westerners to sip beyond the surface of Asian civilization and appreciate its profound undercurrents, asking, "Why not amuse yourselves at our expense?"[3] Okakura envisioned a genuinely cooperative pan-Asian community, with Japan as a vital contributor, as well as an evolving and ennobling fusion between Western and Asian cultures.

As a student of fine arts at Tokyo Imperial University in the 1910s, Dan Inō was deeply attuned to Okakura's philosophical renderings in the context of Japan's rising status in the world. Buoyed by his father Dan Takuma's influential social circles—in 1914, the elder Dan was named managing director of Mitsui, Japan's most powerful corporate conglomerate—the younger Dan studied abroad as a commissioner for the Imperial Household Ministry, spending time at the University of Lyon and Harvard University. At Harvard, Dan enjoyed close proximity to Harvard's Fogg Museum and the MFA, both of which possessed notable collections of Japanese art. In 1923, Dan carved out a budding career as an art historian, becoming a lecturer at Tokyo Imperial University; in 1928, he was appointed assistant professor.

In a paper submitted to a conference of the Institute of Pacific Relations in 1927, Dan drew upon the philosophical premises of Okakura and advocated Japan's continuing expression of its own artistic soul. The same year, Dan also reiterated Okakura's appeal for a respectful fusion of Asian and Western art forms. In "Art," written for an anthology edited by Nitobe, Dan recalled the "general reactionary movement against the prevalent Occidentalism" and the efforts of Ernest Fenollosa and Okakura to revive a "pure Japanese pictorial art." The problem going forward, Dan noted, was for artists all over the world "to establish a new world of art." Japanese artists, he assumed, would play an important role in the creative stage "about to be ushered in."[4]

At the heart of Dan's aesthetic worldview was a desire to edify Westerners on the guiding principles behind Japan's cultural achievements, and to explain why those achievements were exceptional. Embedded in these objectives were themes of identity, value, respect, and status. They were evolving themes, themes that would sharpen considerably in the aftermath of the Manchurian crisis (1931–33).

When Japanese officials established the Kokusai Bunka Shinkō-kai in 1934, the forty-two-year-old Dan was uniquely prepared to contribute to the task at hand. Dan was a respected authority on Japanese art who was well connected to Japan's business elite and had long extolled the merits of Japanese culture. The idea that Japan's cultural achievements represented a compelling national asset, one that might effectively serve the country during a time of crisis, clearly resonated with Dan. He subsequently became a leading figure in the KBS, a director who indefatigably put his energies into branding Japan to the outside world, especially the United States.

In 1935, the year his essay on Japanese gardens appeared in *NIPPON*, Baron Dan made an extensive trip to the United States in order to expand cultural networks and market Japanese refinement. Over a period of two months, Dan visited American academics, museum officials, journalists, businessmen, and politicians. In a subsequent report to fellow KBS officials, Dan said he found that "American people's interest in the affairs of the Orient, especially Japan, is becoming keener and more active."[5] Dan also became the KBS's point man for a pair of exhibitions in the United States—a display of Nō robes at the Metropolitan Museum of Art in New York, and a touring exhibition of women's ornamental hair accessories, which visited the Chicago Art Institute, the Museum of Fine Arts in Boston, the Metropolitan Museum of Art, the Brooklyn Museum, and the Cleveland Museum of Art. For both shows, Dan donated objects from his personal collection. He also played a key role in helping to stage the "Special Loan Exhibition of Japanese Art" at the MFA in Boston. For this event, Dan lent an exquisite fourteenth-century painting of a Buddhist monk, *Kōbō-Daishi as a Child*.

In "The Japanese People and Their Gardens" (*NIPPON* 3), Dan's nuanced insight into the traditional art simultaneously sought to educate foreign observers and induce admiration among them— and, most of all, to augment the KBS's branding of Japan as a highly refined nation. Dan stressed, for example, that the Japanese people cherished the "true quality" of nature, suggesting a people who placed a premium on authenticity and honesty. He similarly emphasized the close connections to Japanese spiritual life, thus ascribing the art of gardening with a transcendent set of values.

On a more personal level, what stands out is the frequency with which Dan invoked the phrase "for the Japanese" and "we Japanese" as if to assert that a pervasive, mass aestheticism coursed through the nation. Here, ostensibly, was an entire population with a deeply ingrained aesthetic sensibility, devoted to the gentle art of gardening. According to Dan, "For the Japanese people, gardens are never such things which allowed only for a few limited classes. . . . Even in the laborer's house the family . . . enjoy[s] sufficiently the charm of a garden." In this vein, Dan distilled fellow KBS scholar Anesaki Masaharu's idea of an "imbedded heritage," suggesting that the Japanese garden reflected the inherent taste of the nation—and a sophistication so deeply embedded as to be almost racially predisposed. Calling the garden "a necessary companion of life" to Japanese people, Dan conjured up the idyllic image of an advanced civilization that was, at heart, inordinately temperate and ruminative.[6] This was a nation, it seemed, more inclined toward artistic pursuits rather than imperial ambition.

In fact, for Japanese officials in the 1930s, these seemingly anti-thetical aspirations became interdependent. The curious result was that of a nation employing soft power to influence world opinion to accept foreign policy gains achieved by hard power. In one example, the power politics that played out on the vast Manchurian plains eventually became mediated in the pages of a glossy quarterly extolling Japanese aesthetics. In this way, an essay on Japanese gardening played a small but certain role in a nation branding strategy aimed at restoring Japan's reputation in the international community.

That KBS members like Baron Dan were not immersed inno-cently in cultural pursuits, oblivious to political concerns, becomes clear in a speech he gave to dedicate the Japanese pavilion at the 1939 world's fair in New York. At the time of the dedication, Japan's invasion of China and resultant damaging images reproduced by the US press had continued unabated for nearly two years. Dan avoided direct mention of hostilities in his speech, but nonetheless invoked an esoteric condensation of his nationalist-tinged pan-Asianism, one that echoed the government's "New East Asian Order." According to Dan, Japan was entering "a new era of creation" and preparing to establish "a new civilization based on harmonizing of the East and West with a renaissance of the East." He made clear that was how Japanese viewed "the shape of things to come in the world of tomorrow."[7]

Text

Baron Inō Dan, "The Japanese People and their Gardens," *NIPPON* 3 (1935): 41–43, 49.[8]

For the Japanese people, gardens are never such things which allowed only for a few limited classes. No doubt, the largest ones are seen in the residences of the daimyo in the feudal times, but they are not all. In our country almost all of the Buddhist temples have beau-tiful gardens, and the small houses of crowded cities also have little ones in their limited places, and even in a laborer's house the family put near their window a small box no bigger than a yard square, and placing in it some tiny unglazed earthenware bridges and farm houses of a few inches, and making a course of a stream and placing dwarf trees, they enjoy sufficiently the charm of a garden. Such taste of the nation stimulated the advance of various arts, especially in case of miniature gardens, those skills made much progress: the skill of a potted plants [*sic*] which shows in a plant of a few feet high an aspect of an old tree lived for several hundred years; or the skill of tray-landscape such as presenting on a lacquered tray an island in the sea by choosing stones of suitable forms and producing beaches and waves with white sands. There are even such things that make us feel as if we are in a large forest, only by planting little trees of several inches in small bowls, the smallest of which we can hold in our pocket.

We Japanese people, putting this tiny garden even on a corner of our work-tables, and when tired of writing refresh ourselves in nature. To the Japanese people, a garden is a necessary companion of life which from the noble to the laborers equally enjoy and love. It is a national comfort and pleasure.

For what reason the Japanese people formed such a habit? The oldest record in Japan about the gardens plainly dates back to the sixth century. We have an account that at that time a minister, Soga Umako by name, had a pond dug in his residence and an island built in it, and there he used to be absorbed in reading. Moreover, both in Manyo-shu, a collection of poems edited in the eighth century, and in Genji-monogatari, a novel written by lady Murasaki in the twelfth century, various descriptions of gardens are seen here and there. Perhaps, having such a long history, gardens might have become necessary things for the Japanese people. In the history of the Japanese civilization, many thoughts and arts which existed in the seventh or eighth centuries were mostly lost today. When we see the industrial products and the works of art preserved in the repository of Shosoin in Nara, which has the relics of the eighth century, we find that not only the arts were lost but also many utensils themselves were entirely gone out of use today. The gardens, however, have been improved and made progress together with the ages. Not merely thinking of the historically old origin of gardens, we must realize some close relation of them with the spiritual life of the Japanese people. . . .

One thing which we must consider here is that the notion of a garden of the Japanese people is as much different from that of the foreign people as it is entirely different in its shape. Anyone who has ever had a glance at the Japanese garden would have noticed [its] remarkably different appearance from those of Italy or France. He will find that, whilst the Italian gardens express a kind of melancholy and historical beauty in the contrast of the magnificent arts and the nature of the south country, and the large garden of Versailles built by Lenôtre shows a systematized and regularized beauty of nature in French characteristic style, the Japanese gardens abound in varieties and freedom and have still more true aspect of nature. Some critic says that foreign gardens are vista gardens which we must command as a whole, while the Japanese gardens are promenade gardens in which one strolls around appreciating their trees, stones, and streams, rather than to taste their synthetic arrangements. This is not, at least, a mistake. But that is not all the spirit of the Japanese gardens. As a reason of promoting the development of their special arrangements and techniques, we must advance to the philosophy of nature of the Japanese people.

In the proverbs of Confucious [*sic*], we find those words—"climbing high and look far." Just as this saying, it must be considered as one of the ways of observing nature to look down from the top of a high mountain and embrace a wide view of nature in our fields of vision as broad and far as possible. That is to say to recognize various kinds of nature and her rich quantity is one apprehension of nature. But at the same time we should not forget another way of recognition quite contrary to this. That is, to pick up a plain wild flower and perceive in it the most exquisite life of nature. We cannot deny that the cognition of nature in large quantity is one way to the comprehension of nature, however, we cannot but acknowledging that there is another proper way, namely, to taste true quality of nature in this simple flower.

The Japanese people's appreciation of nature always takes the latter of these two ways. The special art of Japanese flower arrangement proves it well. The Japanese, when they look at flowers, take, as a rule, a few little branches and arranging them in a flower vase feast their eyes on the few flowers of the branches. If it were big flowers of some grass, they take only one of them with two or three green leaves and placing it in the room with no other ornaments, look at it with the most concentrated attention. It is not only to see the flower but to appreciate all the poems and expressions of nature told by that flower. The Japanese pictures though often with simple Indian ink show mountains or trees very fragmentarily with only a few touches, they are enough to remind us of other great parts of nature by presenting us a small portion which represents the whole of her. This symbolic appreciation of nature is the basic idea of the Japanese gardens. Going straight to the point, a Japanese garden needs only a tree and a stone. That one stone indicates the eternal earth and the tree growing on it, leaning over the stone, and constantly changing, expresses the life of nature: now suffering from hard winds, or being exposed to rain; now rejoicing arrayed with blooming flowers, or mourning as they fade away in the chilly wind of autumn. Through those simple tree and stone, we see the variation of all things in nature.

The typical gardens made in this way are found at "Daitokuji" or Ninnaji" in Kyoto, the famous old temples of the fifteenth century. Their gardens are limited to such narrow grounds and so simply arranged with two or three stones and trees that they could hardly be called gardens; yet if one freely meditates in these gardens he would have deeper affection toward nature in that quiet atmosphere of the small gardens surrounded by the simple plain buildings, than in gorgeous large gardens of daimyo, which were made in the seventeenth and eighteenth centuries. The Japanese bronzes, for four or five hundred years, have been living in the communication of the larger self, the Universe, and the smaller self, the ego. The gardens, in Japan, served as agents connecting the human life and the spirit of nature. For the Japanese people, who could not live apart from nature, the gardens were the precious parts of their lives.

John Gripentrog is associate professor of History at Mars Hill University near Asheville, North Carolina. He received his Ph.D. from the University of Wisconsin-Madison. His work concerns relations between Japan and the United States in the 1930s. Articles and essays include "The Trans-National Pastime: Baseball and American Perceptions of Japan, 1931–1941" in *Diplomatic History* (April 2010); "Pearl Harbor: The Road to Irreconcilable Worldviews" for the *Society for Historians of Foreign Relations*; and a recent article on United States-Japan cultural relations in the *Pacific Historical Review* (November 2015). He is currently completing a book on the political and cultural relations of Japan and the United States in the interwar era.

Notes

1. Following the Asia-Pacific War, Dan Inō served in the House of Peers and then its reconstituted House of Councilors in the National Diet. He also became president of Fuji Precision Industries. When US Occupation officials sanctioned the return of the KBS, Dan reprised his involvement, eventually becoming the society's vice-president in 1955. He also became chairman of the Japan Art Association.
2. Baron Inō Dan, "The Japanese People and Their Gardens," *NIPPON* 3 (1935): 41–43, 49.
3. Okakura Kakuzo, *The Book of Tea* (New York and London: Putnam, 1906), 8.

4. Inō Dan, "Japanese Art and its Modernization," Box 458, "1927 Conference at Honolulu: Preliminary Papers (1)," Institute of Pacific Relations Records, Rare Book & Manuscript Library, Columbia University in the City of New York; Inō Dan, "Art," in *Western Influences in Modern Japan: A Series of Papers on Cultural Relations*, ed. Inazo Nitobe (Chicago: University of Chicago Press, 1931), 138–40.
5. Baron Inō Dan, "Broadening Cultural Contacts," *KBS Quarterly* 1 (Jan.–March 1936): 2–3.
6. Dan, "The Japanese People and Their Gardens," 41–42; Masaharu Anesaki, *Art, Life, and Nature in Japan* (Boston: Marshall Jones Company, 1933), 5, 178.
7. Dan quoted in Russell Porter, "Japan Dedicates Pavilion with 1,500-Year-Old 'Flame of Friendship,'" *New York Times*, 3 June 1939, 6.
8. The original text has not been edited and idiosyncrasies of language have been left intact.

Bibliography

Anesaki, Masaharu. *Art, Life, and Nature in Japan*. Boston: Marshall Jones Company, 1933.

Dan, Baron Inō. "Art." In *Western Influences in Modern Japan: A Series of Papers on Cultural Relations*, edited by Inazo Nitobe. Chicago, IL: University of Chicago Press, 1931.

———. "Broadening Cultural Contacts." *KBS Quarterly* 1, Jan.–March (1936): 2–3.

———. "The Japanese People and Their Gardens." *NIPPON* 3 (1935): 41–43, 49.

Kakuzo, Okakura. *The Book of Tea*. New York: Putnam, 1906.

II

IMAGES FROM THE 1935–36 INTERNATIONAL EXHIBITION OF CHINESE ART IN LONDON

Ilaria Scaglia

By analyzing a set of photographs from the 1935–36 International Exhibition of Chinese Art in London, the largest show of its kind and the first to be co-organized by both the British and the Chinese governments, this chapter explores how images served as important tools for nation branding in the interwar period. Thanks to technological innovations that allowed for the mass production and reproduction of visual material, photographs became a frequent feature in newspapers at this time. In the coverage of international cultural events such as the exhibition examined in this study, the images of individual objects and people came to be associated with their countries of origin, thereby affecting their reputations. Each artifact denoted the national tradition in which it was created; and people's bodies turned into instruments for nation branding, as their shape served as markers of national origin and their poses and expressions came to symbolize the character and intentions of the country they represented. The people creating, reproducing, and disseminating images of "authentic" and "real" events had now the power of framing them and providing them with meaning. They—arguably more than writers—came to play an essential role in the concrete practice of managing reputations (or nation branding), the process of instilling positive associations with certain products (in this case, the governments involved in staging this cultural event).

Notes for this section begin on page 273.

It is significant that many functional steps in the staging of the 1935–36 Chinese exhibition became public events and were captured in countless photographs and newsreels distributed on a mass scale. Analyzing how these images were produced and reproduced through a wide variety of media illuminates how the immortalizing of procedural tasks—accentuated by the use of specific camera angles and captions—reinforced the exhibition's internationalist message and branded the governments that had made it possible as engaged members of the international community.

It is relevant that the transportation of the artifacts that the Chinese government lent to the exhibition was thoroughly staged as a public spectacle and was widely publicized as such. We know from Foreign Office correspondence that this task had been carefully planned not only for its substantial but also for its performative aspects. As co-organizer of this event, the Chinese government had asked for demonstrable reassurances to assuage the many people in China who had opposed the exhibition on the grounds that the artifacts would be needlessly endangered during their journey from Shanghai to Portsmouth. When Secretary of State Sir John Simon contacted the Admiralty asking for a warship to accompany the Chinese objects, he mentioned this particular concern of the Chinese government. He acknowledged that a warship "does not add to the security of these treasures." Yet, he explained, a ship of war should make the Chinese public feel "considerably relieved" while also displaying "how greatly His Majesty's Government appreciate the carrying out of this proposal and how sincere is their wish to contribute in any way they can to carry the scheme through successfully and without untoward incident."[1] It is therefore clear that visibility and display were at the center of the process of organizing the transportation of these artifacts from China to the United Kingdom, and that the creation and dissemination of images to this effect played an important role.

Figure A.1, a photograph published in the *Evening News* of Portsmouth on 26 July 1935, represents a visible demonstration of how this scheme came to fruition. The main subject is the arrival of HMS *Suffolk* carrying the artifacts to be shown at the 1935–36 International Exhibition of Chinese Art. The term "Chinese Art Treasures" in the title communicated the priceless value of the objects approaching British shores. The sheer size of the ship— enlarged further by the depth and perspective of the photographic image—conveyed the strength of the escort awarded to the precious cargo. The crowd in the foreground, on the left-hand side, suggested

Figure A.1 Evening News (Portsmouth), Thursday 26 July 1935,
4. Top right: Chinese Art Treasures: HMS *Suffolk* arriving at
Portsmouth with the Chinese Art Treasures for the Burlington
House Exhibition. Bottom right: part of the treasures being loaded
for transport. Portsmouth Publishing and Printing Ltd. © Johnston
Press. Published with permission.

that the arrival of the artifacts had been met by much interest and
anticipation in Great Britain. Although the group was comprised
mostly of the wives of the sailors working on the ship who had been
at sea for more than two years, the impression given was that the
"Chinese Art Treasures" were eagerly awaited on the Portsmouth
docks.[2]

The unloading of the ship was a spectacle in itself, and was
widely covered by the media. On 29 July, *Universal News* released
footage depicting each phase of this complex endeavor. The original
images did not survive, but the accompanying commentary vividly
captures what the spectators were to see:

Probably never before has a warship carried such a valuable cargo as does HMS *Suffolk*. She arrives at Portsmouth with Chinese art treasures for the Royal Academy exhibition. A deputation from the Academy goes aboard, to watch the unloading of the precious cases. [. . . marks a pause] This is done under the watchful eyes of Tang *See*fen (T'ang Hsi-fen) and Chang Shang-yen (Chuang Shang-yen), secretaries to the Chinese Committee responsible for the Exhibition. With infinite care, British sailors carry the cases ashore, where Customs Officers affix their seals, prior to the dispatch of the treasures to London. There are ninety-five packing cases in all. [. . . pause] Some of the contents are more than three-thousand years old. [. . . pause] They are variously reported as being worth from three to ten million pounds. [. . . pause] I suppose the *real* [underlined in the original text to mark emphasis] truth of the matter is that they are priceless![3]

The emphasis on the value of the objects and on the "infinite care" in which they were handled effectively branded the United Kingdom as a caring host and as the ideal site for international cooperation.

A photographer from Topical Press Agency immortalized the moment when one of the cases carrying the Chinese artifacts was being unloaded (figure A.2). All eyes were on the British "bluejackets," who were stretching their arms to embrace each case as it was moved to safety. Another moment of the transfer was captured in a picture published on the *Portsmouth Evening News* (figure A.1, bottom right). The most publicized shot, however, was that of the British "bluejackets" parading the cases containing the artifacts from China in front of the many people who gathered to watch the scene. Figure A.3, published in the *Evening News* of Portsmouth on 25 July 1935, also appears in many of the clippings preserved at the archives of the London Royal Academy of Arts.

It is important to note that starting from 1934, the Royal Academy hired Alleyne Clarice Zander to act as a publicity agent. Zander began a press-cutting archive of all the exhibitions held at the Royal Academy.[4] In the case of the Chinese exhibition, press coverage came from newspapers published all over the world (particularly in English-language newspapers printed in the British colonies). This fact attests to the wide audience of such press coverage and the growing importance of publicity in this period. In this particular photograph, the black case itself occupied the center of the picture; on both sides were young British sailors enthusiastically parading the objects toward their final destination (one of the delivery vehicles rented to take the artifacts on the last leg of their long journey, from Portsmouth to London). The warning "Handle with

Figure A.2 Royal Academy of Arts (RAA), Photographic Archive, 05/3239. The International Exhibition of Chinese Art 1935–36. Hoisting a case from the deck of HMS *Suffolk*. Silver gelatin print, 236 × 182 mm. Photograph by an unknown photographer from Topical Press Agency. © Royal Academy of Arts, London. Published with permission.

Bluejackets carrying one of the treasure chests.

Figure A.3 Evening News (Portsmouth), Wednesday, 25 July 1935, 9—
Bluejackets carrying one of the treasure chests. Portsmouth Publishing
and Printing Ltd. © Johnston Press. Published with permission.

Care" prominently inscribed in large white capital letters placed at
the center of each case, served as a tagline for the event as a whole.
This image conveyed the message that both the Chinese and British
governments had carefully crafted: the Chinese artifacts were being
handled with the utmost care. This tagline branded the newly established Republic of China as the legitimate heir and owner of the
Chinese past, and by extension, of its present and future. It likewise
branded the British Empire as the rightful host of an unprecedented
event in the field of art and culture, one made possible by international cooperation among peoples and institutions from all over the
world.

International cooperation was showcased and celebrated in multiple forms of publicity. Figure A.4, showing a British and a Chinese
expert working together, branded the exhibition as an internationalist event by showing moments of concrete cooperation among
peoples from various nations. This shot was one of many taken by an
unknown photographer from Topical Press Agency throughout the
process of unwrapping and placing each object in its proper place of

Figure A.4 RAA, Photographic Archive, 05/3015. The International Exhibition of Chinese Art 1935–36. F. T. Cheng, Special Commissioner of the Chinese Government, and F. St. G. Spendlove, Assistant Secretary, Royal Academy, examining exhibits. Black and white silver gelatin print, 199 × 252 mm. Photograph by an unknown photographer from Topical Press Agency. © Royal Academy of Arts, London. Published with permission.

display in the galleries of the London Royal Academy at Burlington House. In this particular picture, the most prominent elements are not the artifacts but two persons, specifically two experts of Chinese art standing together, wearing similar, western-style outfits and engaged in the study and preservation of a cultural patrimony they both valued and appreciated. The message was that they belonged to the same community. In the post-1919 world, they could no longer ignore one another and rightfully embraced the opportunity to cooperate in the same endeavor.

As these images show, the nation branding process that accompanied the 1935–36 International Exhibition of Chinese Art in London shaped this cultural event well beyond the confines of the place where and the time when it was opened to its visitors (28 November 1935–7 March 1936). As each step of the organization was made public, choices in camera angles, cropping techniques, and captions helped to frame each moment as a solemn occasion of international cooperation. As these images reached viewers all over the world, the brand attached to their subjects accompanied them on every step of their journey. Their effect also proved enduring, as eighty years later these shots figured prominently in the commemoration of this landmark exhibition and continued to shape the brands and reputations of all the countries involved in its staging.[5]

Ilaria Scaglia is a lecturer in Modern History at Aston University in Birmingham, UK. She is the author of "The Aesthetics of Internationalism: Culture and Politics on Display at the 1935–1936 International Exhibition of Chinese Art," *Journal of World History* 26, no. 1 (March 2015), 105–37. She is also the recipient of the 2016–2017 Volkswagen-Mellon Postdoctoral Fellowship for Research in Germany.

Notes

1. The National Archives of the UK (TNA), FO 370/452, L 6779/308/405. Letter, dated 15 November 1934, from John Simon to Sir Bolton Eyres Monsell.
2. *Evening News and Southern Daily Mail* (Portsmouth, Hampshire), 25 July 1935, 9.
3. Universal News, "Warship's Art Cargo," issue no: 527, item 9/11, released on Monday 29 July 1935.
4. I thank the archivist of the London Royal Academy of Arts, Mr Mark Pomeroy, who kindly allowed me to access this archive while it was still in the process of being preserved and catalogued.
5. In 2005, the Royal Academy celebrated this landmark event with a commemorative exhibition entitled "From Peking to Piccadilly 70 Years Ago: A Display of Press Photographs Showing the Preparation of the Royal Academy's First Chinese Art Exhibition in 1935–36."

III

A MEMORANDUM ON THE *ADVANCING AMERICAN ART* FIASCO OF 1947

Michael L. Krenn

The following memorandum, written by Assistant Secretary of State for Public Affairs William Benton and sent to Deputy Assistant Secretary of State for Public Affairs Howland H. Sargeant (who is listed as "Howland S. Sargeant" in the note), was created right in the middle of the debacle surrounding the Department of State's *Advancing American Art* exhibit. The paintings and watercolors that made up the collection were mostly modern in nature, by some of the United States' most renowned artists such as Georgia O'Keeffe, John Marin, and others. The works were purchased by the Department of State in the spring and summer of 1946 as part of a new effort in cultural diplomacy in which the collection would be sent abroad to acquaint the foreign viewer with the latest trends in American art and, simultaneously, attempt to allay suspicions that the United States—despite all of its obvious power—was a cultural backwater, awash in materialism and artistic ignorance.

Successful showings in the United States prior to being shipped off to various locations in Europe and Latin America were followed by equally strong reviews from audiences in Paris, Prague, Havana, and Port-au-Prince. Despite this positive reception at home and abroad, trouble was brewing in the United States. More conservative art groups complained about the dominance of modern and abstract works in the collection. It was in February 1947 that the complaints turned into a crescendo of attacks. *Look* magazine fired the first salvo

Notes for this section begin on page 279.

with an article about the exhibit entitled, "Your Money Bought These Paintings." While not overly critical, the piece did ask why US tax dollars were being spent on such odd works of art, and the story was accompanied by pictures of several of the paintings. Other critics quickly joined in, including the famous radio commentator Fulton Lewis who fumed about the cost and concluded, "If that be American art, God save us." Perhaps most damning, however, were questions from Congressmen such as Representatives John Taber (R-NY) and Fred Busbey (R-IL) about not only the cost of the art work, but also about the background of the artists themselves, none-too-subtly suggesting that many of them might harbor "un-American" attitudes and beliefs.

This firestorm of controversy landed on the desk of William Benton. Prior to becoming Assistant Secretary of State for Public Affairs in 1945, Benton built an impressive record of accomplishment as a vice president of the University of Chicago and chairman of the board of Encyclopedia Britannica. He started his rise to fame and power, however, working in the mushrooming field of advertising in the 1920s and 1930s. It seemed like a perfect match, when in 1945 he was named the second Assistant Secretary for Public Affairs (the famous poet Archibald MacLeish was the first, serving from 1944 to 1945), a position that was designed, in many ways, to "advertise" the United States to the world. Just a year into his tenure, however, the *Advancing American Art* furor started to rise.

As seen in the document below, Benton tried to parry these early assaults—he specifically mentions the *Look* article and the recent request for information on the artists that had been received from Representative Taber. Benton and others in the Department of State were taken aback by the ferocity and variety of attacks on the exhibit. Many of them shared Benton's belief that American art could be an effective means to "advertise" the American way of life and convince other nations to follow the United States' lead in world affairs. Kenneth Holland, director of the Office of International Information and Cultural Affairs, claimed that "one of the popular misconceptions abroad about the United States is that ours is a purely mechanical civilization. The Nazis in their propaganda line emphasized this over and over again." Now, as the Cold War started to kick into high gear, "[t]he United States needs to be understood and respected in the world today so that our foreign policy will be supported and followed by the nations of the world." Like Benton, he understood *Advancing American Art* as an advertising campaign. Holland noted that "some of the biggest industries in the United

States believe art helps advertise their products and gain peoples support—in this case for products they sell." He then went on to name several large corporations that had "undertaken extensive activities in the field of art," such as IBM, Lucky Strike, Standard Oil, Pepsi, and Coke.[1]

Benton took this analogy even further, specifically referring to the foreign audience that would see the art exhibit as "customers." He saw the art as a kind of hook (the same "purpose that music serves on a radio program") that would grab the viewers' attention and make them more amenable to the sales pitch that would follow. Ironically, given what would happen in the months to come, he even tried to blunt the criticisms about cost by suggesting, "we would even sell the pictures!" As Benton, Holland, and others in the Department of State soon discovered, none of these arguments stemmed the tide of growing animosity toward *Advancing American Art*. The reports from Europe and Latin America indicating that foreign audiences actually liked the exhibit did nothing to dissuade artistic, public, and congressional criticisms that the exhibit was expensive, the art was most definitely *not* American, and—perhaps most damning in an increasingly paranoid Cold-War United States—that the artists themselves were un-American.

In short order, Congressional hearings were held during which the exhibit—as well as the entire idea of "cultural diplomacy"—was savaged. With no support from President Truman or Secretary of State George Marshall, Benton and others associated with the exhibit furiously backpedaled, fired the individual in the Department of State who was primarily responsible for assembling the artwork, halted the tour of the show, and then called *Advancing American Art* back home. Once back in the United States, the paintings and watercolors were auctioned off in 1948 for less than $6,000. By that time, Benton was already gone, having resigned under a cloud of blame and suspicion the year before.

Benton's memorandum and the entire *Advancing American Art* fiasco offer some interesting insights into how the theory of nation branding can help us better understand even these early examples of US cultural diplomacy. Indeed, we might well cite Benton as the "father of American nation branding." He and his associates in the Department of State quite consciously attempted to follow the example of business advertising, and even highlighted the use of art as an advertising tool by US corporations to bolster their case for the doomed exhibit. They saw the art as not simply a tool through which the United States might gain international respect for its cultural achievements, but as a very direct means of convincing the foreign audience to understand (and "follow") US leadership in world affairs.

Nation branding also helps us to understand the failure of *Advancing American Art* in different and important ways. Many of the scholars of nation branding theory, such as Melissa Aronczyk and Nadia Kaneva, emphasize the international and domestic contexts. To be truly effective, efforts at "branding" the United States must reflect some sort of national consensus on the nature of that brand. "Nation branding is successful," György Szondi argues, "when the brand is lived by the citizens."[2] While from our twenty-first century perspective it is easy to dismiss the critics of *Advancing American Art* as philistines or worse, these critics did, in fact, raise a crucial issue. The art in the exhibit quite consciously focused on one school of American art—modern art—to the exclusion of more traditional forms. And while it might have been true that the foreign audience appreciated this modern work, many of the critics back in the United States were essentially correct: the domestic audience for the most part actually preferred the works of Norman Rockwell over Milton Avery or Arthur Dove. In short, the "brand" that was being put on display in Latin America and Europe was not being "lived by the citizens" of the United States. In addition, if a central message of the exhibit was to demonstrate the cultural maturity and sophistication of the American nation, having President Truman famously declare that, "If that's art, I'm a hottentot," must have raised more than few eyebrows abroad.[3]

Finally, nation branding can also help us understand the direction of US cultural diplomacy after the ignoble end of the *Advancing American Art* exhibit. It is safe to say that the Department of State learned some hard lessons. From that point on, the Department of State adopted what Aronczyk refers to as a "'grassroots'-style approach to the creation of a new national identity." Instead of buying and organizing its own art exhibits, it increasingly turned to private groups such as the American Federation of Arts, museums, and—after the United States Information Agency took over most of the cultural diplomacy work—even the Smithsonian Institution to help in accomplishing the task of nation branding.

Text

Memorandum, William Benton to Mr. Howland S. Sargeant[4]
20 February 1947, Record Group 59, Records of the Assistant Secretary of State for Public Affairs, 1945–1950, Subject File, Box 7, ASNE folder, National Archives, College Park, Maryland

February 20, 1947
To: Mr. Howland S. Sargeant
From: William Benton
I do not know what further to do on the *Look* story. I think the suggested letter to John Taber from the Secretary is about all that can be done under the circumstances. My memorandum to the Secretary seems suitable. I am not too pleased with the memorandum giving background on the art program, but I think it is perhaps adequate.

Haven't we overlooked in these documents one of the biggest arguments of all? Isn't the art exhibit supposed to attract people into our institute in Latin America, thus helping to develop these institutes, and thus give us a better chance to talk sympathetically with such visitors? In other words, don't we need projects such as these art projects, to bring in to the institutes the kinds of people in whom we are interested? The so-called "customers" are then available for English language lessons, for round table and seminar discussions, et cetera.

This would mean that the art exhibits serve a double purpose, not only the purpose described in this memorandum, as seen by our own people under big-time billing—, but they also serve the kind of purpose that music serves on a radio program: to attract the customers who are then more numerous and more responsive to the sales story.

I am interested in the opinion expressed in this memorandum that the market value on this collection has gone up, and is now higher than the $49,000. If Congress doesn't approve of this project, should we suggest to Congress that it isn't yet out any money? On Congressional recommendation, we could even sell the pictures! (Perhaps the Encyclopaedia Britannica might buy some of them!!)[5]

Michael L. Krenn is a professor of history at Appalachian State University. He received his Ph.D. from Rutgers University in 1985 where he studied with Lloyd Gardner. He has published six books, including *The Color of Empire: Race and American Foreign Relations* (2006), *Fall-Out Shelters for the Human Spirit: American Art and the Cold War* (2005), and *The History of U.S. Cultural Diplomacy: From 1770 to the Present Day* (2017). Currently, he is serving as advisor for a documentary based on his 1999 book, *Black Diplomacy: African Americans and the State Department, 1945–69.*

Notes

1. Kenneth Holland to William T. Stone and William Benton, 10 March 1947, Record Group 59, Records of the Assistant Secretary of State for Public Affairs, 1945–1950, Subject File, Box 7, Art folder, National Archives, Washington, DC.
2. György Szondi, *Public Diplomacy and Nation Branding: Conceptual Similarities and Differences* (Hague, Netherlands: Clingendael Netherlands Institute of International Relations, 2008): 5.
3. Truman's remark was reported in Drew Pearson, "The Washington Merry-Go-Round," *Washington Post*, Feb. 1947, p. 9.
4. The correct name for the recipient of this memorandum is Howland H. Sargeant. Sargeant went on to become Assistant Secretary of State for Public Affairs in 1952.
5. This was an inside joke—Benton was the publisher of the world-renowned reference volumes. In the end, however, most of the paintings and watercolors were auctioned off to the University of Oklahoma and Auburn University. As an interesting side note, nearly all of the works from the original exhibit were organized for a new show called *Art Interrupted: Advancing American Art and the Politics of Cultural Diplomacy*, which toured the United States in 2012–14.

INDEX